The Red Sea

The Red Sea

IN SEARCH OF LOST SPACE

Alexis Wick

UNIVERSITY OF CALIFORNIA PRESS

University of California Press, one of the most distinguished university presses in the United States, enriches lives around the world by advancing scholarship in the humanities, social sciences, and natural sciences. Its activities are supported by the UC Press Foundation and by philanthropic contributions from individuals and institutions. For more information, visit www.ucpress.edu.

University of California Press
Oakland, California

Library of Congress Cataloging-in-Publication Data

Wick, Alexis, 1981–.
The Red Sea : in search of lost space / Alexis Wick.
p. cm.
Includes bibliographical references and index.
ISBN 978-0-520-28591-0 (cloth : alk. paper)
ISBN 978-0-520-28592-7 (pbk. : alk. paper)
ISBN 978-0-520-96126-5 (ebook)
1. Red Sea Region—History I. Title.
DT39.W53 2016
909′.096533—dc23
2015026502

Manufactured in the United States of America

25 24 23 22 21 20 19 18 17 16
10 9 8 7 6 5 4 3 2 1

In keeping with a commitment to support environmentally responsible and sustainable printing practices, UC Press has printed this book on Natures Natural, a fiber that contains 30% post-consumer waste and meets the minimum requirements of ANSI/NISO Z39.48-1992 (R 1997) (*Permanence of Paper*).

For my mother and father, who made it happen
And to the memory of my grandparents, who made it possible

If those arrangements were to disappear as they appeared, if some event of which we can at the moment do not more than sense the possibility—without knowing either what its form will be or what it promises—were to cause them to crumble, as the ground of Classical thought did, at the end of the eighteenth century, then one can certainly wager that man would be erased, like a face drawn in sand at the edge of the sea.

MICHEL FOUCAULT

The sea has no character, in the original sense of the word, which comes from the Greek *charassein,* meaning to engrave, to scratch, to imprint.

CARL SCHMITT

Isn't the sea what Algy calls it: a grey sweet mother? The snot-green sea. The scrotumtightening sea. Epi oinopa ponton. Ah, Dedalus, the Greeks. I must teach you. You must read them in the original. Thalatta! Thalatta! She is our great sweet mother. Come and look.

JAMES JOYCE

If there is anything that radically distinguishes the imagination of anti-imperialism, it is the primacy of the geographical element. Imperialism after all is an act of geographical violence through which virtually every space in the world is explored, charted, and finally brought under control. For the native, the history of colonial servitude is inaugurated by loss of the locality to the outside; its geographical identity must thereafter be searched for and somehow restored.

EDWARD SAID

CONTENTS

List of Illustrations ix
Acknowledgments xi
Note on Translation and Transliteration xv

Introduction. History at Sea: Space and the Other 1

1 · The Place in the Middle: A Geohistory of the Red Sea 18

2 · Thalassology *alla Turca*: Six Theses on the Philosophy of History 53

3 · Self-Portrait of the Ottoman Red Sea, June 21, 1777 88

4 · The Scientific Invention of the Red Sea 121

5 · Thalassomania: Modernity and the Sea 155

Conclusion. Rigging the Historian's Craft: For an Epistemology of Composition 186

Notes 197
Bibliography 235
Index 253

ILLUSTRATIONS

MAPS

1. A Most Aquatic Empire *3*
2. Red Sea Topography *23*

FIGURES

1. Mühimme-i Mısır *97*
2. Document 227, Part 1 *98*
3. Document 227, Part 2 *99*
4. *Baḥr-ı Aḥmer,* North and South *150–51*

ACKNOWLEDGMENTS

This book has been long in the making, and it is with great pleasure, but also some trepidation, that I seize this opportunity finally to show my profound gratitude for the many debts accrued along the way.

For as long as I can remember, things maritime have been an integral part of my life. This, like much else, has a lot to do with my mother and father. Great lovers of the sea, they made a home in Palestine, a land nestled between the eastern Mediterranean and the northern Red Sea, the destination of many of our family trips. I loved the Mediterranean—and indeed, now with a family of my own, we have settled on its coast, drawing from it daily inspiration—but I was spellbound by the Red Sea and its breathtaking wonders. If the Mediterranean embraces like a gentle parent, the Red Sea stuns like a wild lover. There was, then, a clear if subliminal element of predestination to this study, though I think it only now, and it bears in its very subject matter the obvious imprint of my own deep past.

As an academic venture, the project began in earnest with a doctoral dissertation at Columbia University, where I had the luxury of learning amid an embarrassment of scholarly riches. The university as a whole—faculty and staff, students and visitors, buildings and lawns, squirrels and pigeons—and the history department in particular deserve my heartfelt thanks for their collective instruction. The Richard Hofstadter fellowship, the Foreign Language and Area Studies fellowship, and the Fulbright-Hayes fellowship funded me throughout this period.

Richard Bulliet was crucial to the formulation and composition of the dissertation from the start by his encouragement to view the past from the perspective of its many edges. Rashid Khalidi helped me to think about the effects of nationalism on the writing of Ottoman history. Gil Anidjar was key in pushing me to reflect seriously about space and time, knowing and writing. He engaged my earliest ideas and drafts with great generosity and insight. And Timothy Mitchell read the thesis with acumen.

Studying with Joseph Massad was formative. Though he was not formally involved in the dissertation process, his impact on it was significant, especially in thinking through the intricate relationship between history and power. Beyond being a munificent exemplar, he has provided much-needed sustenance (culinary, emotional, and intellectual) over the years, particularly during the writing stints in Cairo and in the first (and last) steps of the publication process. I am humbled by his care.

Graduate studies could never have been so satisfying without the many fellow-travellers on Morningside Heights. I would like to thank Ramzi Rouighi, Nada Moumtaz, Joshua Georgy, Elizabeth Johnston, Beth Holt, and Jason Frydman for the stimulation, merriment, and comradeship, which have helped shape the following pages in more ways than they know. Ramzi and Nada know all too well how many they have read and improved.

The American University of Beirut has become my new nest, professional and personal. The members of the history and archaeology department welcomed me into its tight-knit fold with amazing grace. There could not have been a more seamless and pleasant transition to the postgraduate condition. For their quotidian collegiality, I thank them all, especially Abdulrahim Abu Husayn, whose wit and knowledge are matched by his generosity and hospitality. He and John Meloy read parts of the manuscript with attention and encouragement. I am much obliged also to Tarif Khalidi, Samir Seikaly, Nadia el Cheikh, and Bilal Orfali for the many conversations, and to Provost Ahmad Dallal for his stalwart support.

Vijay Prashad, Lisa Armstrong, Alex Lubin, Mona Fawaz, and Ray Brassier read the whole manuscript out of the goodness of their heart; I thank them for their generosity and critical feedback. In addition to being a magnificent friend and reader, Vijay was instrumental in guiding me through the process of academic publishing.

Outside of my comfort zone, Ian Baucom was the first to read an initial version of this book, and his comments managed to interpret the kernel of my arguments better than I had, convincing me of the larger value of my endeavors. I cannot thank him enough for his inestimable contribution. I am similarly grateful to Isa Blumi and the other two anonymous reviewers, who did the same with a later iteration of the manuscript.

Parts of the following chapters were presented at conferences and workshops in Florence, Beirut, Lamu, and twice Istanbul. I thank the organizers and participants for the opportunity to share this work, especially Anne Bang and Dejanirah Couto, who engineered my participation in important meetings in Lamu and Istanbul respectively. An earlier version of chapter 3 was published in *Osmanlı Araştırmaları/ Journal of Ottoman Studies* 40 (2012): 399–434. I am grateful to the editors, Baki Tezcan and Gottfried Hagen, for their helpful comments.

At the University of California Press, Niels Hooper immediately showed interest in the project and steered it steadily. I remain appreciative of his efforts, as well as those of the always dependable and efficient Bradley Depew, and of Elisabeth Magnus, whose expert copyediting managed to be both light and consequential.

Finally, I am immensely indebted to Nasser Soumi for allowing me to use as cover his extraordinary piece and to my brother-in-law Samer Jabbour for guiding me to it. The power of Nasser's art is inspiring, and I could not dream of a more beautiful jacket.

Together, all of these contributions have improved the final product beyond recognition. By a stroke of cosmic good fortune, it was above all those closest to me who have been the greatest companions, most insightful interlocutors, and strongest critics: my wife Dahlia Gubara, my sister Livia Wick, and my parents, Laura Wick and Roger Heacock. This book would never have seen the light of day without their dedicated encouragement and input, from the superficial edits to the wider arguments. More profoundly, their own writing, thinking, and being have influenced me in more ways probably than I can acknowledge. My first exposure to Mediterranean history came from my father, and much of the following results from exchanges with him. My mother's work has taught me to approach even the most scientific disciplines critically, with an eye to their social and institutional conditions. My sister's uncanny sensitivity to her material always reminded me that people and concepts matter. My wife and I share our training as well as our everyday life: her impact is palpable everywhere. Further, she has imparted to me an immeasurable gift: a basic recognition of the value of other ways of being and thinking.

My brother Jamal Wick too has affected this book deeply, despite being in a totally different line of work: I can only hope that a glimmer of his vivacity of soul and generosity of spirit has rubbed off on my writing. One full chapter was composed in his apartment, at a critical moment of the manuscript's trajectory.

Of course, none of any of this is imaginable without the life-giving nurture of family and friends. In addition to some already mentioned above, I would like to express my gratitude to Alan Audi, Tareq Abboushi, Myriam Abousamra, Raphaël Botiveau, and Olivier Pironet for their enduring and sustaining friendship. Natalia Lopez-Castro's warm hospitality is also very much appreciated.

Munira Khayyat has been an integral part of my life for almost two decades now: I thank her especially for her remarkable ability to make any city feel like home, and any conversation fun and rewarding.

Rajaa Hilu, Siham Siyala, Filippo Del Lucchese, Sari Kassis, Zeina Osman, Issam Srour, Paolo Orlandi, Alex Lubin, Yemi Tessema, Heinrich zu Dohna, and Nada and Marwan Tarraf have been decisive in keeping me sane in Beirut, no small feat, and one deserving my grateful recognition.

Ron Suny and Jean-Jacques Poucel acted as a surrogate kinship network in academia, to complement the constant care of my dear aunts: Marion, Tina, Wendy, Sandy. With the help of their houses and families, and of course their warm hearts, they all succeeded in making the United States feel like a genuine part of me.

My family makes the world go around. Dahlia and our two daughters, Amalia and Shams, make life possible; my siblings Jamal and Livia, along with her husband Samer and their children Ramla, Naji, and Yamen, make life livable, indeed alive; my in-laws—Khala Su'ad, Waleed and Mona, Khaled and Iman, Rabha and Eid, and Rabab and Aziz, along with all their delightful children—make life's horizons expand. There would be little without all their constant devotion.

My parents, Laura and Roger, are the bedrock of life itself. They reared me with a love that knows no bounds; seeing this work through is only their latest contribution. They have been essential to every step of the way. This book is, naturally, for them, and in memory of my grandparents, Paul and Christine Wick and Marieluise Heacock.

NOTE ON TRANSLATION AND TRANSLITERATION

All translations throughout this volume are my own unless otherwise indicated. The standard English translations of the published works cited in the text have been used whenever these are available.

For the transliteration of Ottoman Turkish and Arabic words, the system set by the *International Journal of Middle East Studies* has been employed, following the language of the original source. The same word may thus appear in two different forms (e.g. *ḥajj* and *ḥacc*). Diacritical marks have been included for names of individuals but have been omitted from place-names and words that have become common in English (except in direct quotations).

INTRODUCTION

History at Sea

SPACE AND THE OTHER

IN THE BEGINNING WAS WATER.

This dictum evokes a famous verse in the Quran, which affirms that "every living thing is made of water" (*wa jaʿalnā min al-māʾi kulla shayʾin ḥayyin,* 21:30); it is implicit in Genesis 1, where the earth and the heavens are created by a division of the waters; it forms a basic truth claim in modern astronomical science, so that the mere presence of water on a planet may be a sign of life; it is found in many creation myths and much common sense. Thales, who launched the great adventure of Greek philosophy, also affirmed as much. There is something vital about water, then, clearly, but which waters exactly? The key lies in the sea, both as the largest expanse of water and, by way of evaporation and rain, as a source replenishing the sweet water reserves of the land.

WATER, WATER EVERYWHERE

From its ancient mythological origins, one may affirm with scant irony that the concept of the sea has itself been "at sea." Thalassa, daughter of Hemera (terrestrial light) and Aether (celestial light), is a primordial Greek goddess, associated with the sea in general and the Mediterranean in particular. She may also personify a riverbed. In the Quran, the world's waters are divided in two, often appearing in the dual form (*baḥrayn,* the two seas) to mark the difference between the bitter brine and the thirst-quenching sweet. The separation between the two types of water was in itself deemed evidence of the miracle of divine power (25:53; 27:61). The entry for "Mer" in the *Encyclopédie* of Diderot and D'Alembert opens by presenting two contradictory meanings: the sea is both "that great mass of water which surrounds the entire earth, & is more properly called Ocean," and "a particular division or portion of the Ocean, which takes the name from the countries that it borders, or other circumstances."[1] Faithful to its roots, "the sea" remains a slippery concept.

Like *water* and *sea*, the signifier *Ottoman* has a similarly floating quality, connoting multiple meanings. The name of a dynasty ruling continuously from the turn of the fourteenth to the twentieth century, it may also invoke a space, a language, a culture, a political-economic system, a mode of governance, and much else. One thing is certain: a simple glance at the map shows that the sea thoroughly pervades Ottoman geography (map 1). The empire included, at one point or another, all the Black Sea coast, the longest stretch on the Mediterranean, the Red Sea in its entirety, significant parts of the Persian Gulf, even a portion of the Caspian (not to mention the multiple excursions across the Indian Ocean and down the Swahili coast). Its capital city, Constantinople/Istanbul, was eminently maritime, dominating the crucial waterway connecting the empire's many seas. So was the imperial court itself, for the Topkapı palace, as if positioned by a master planner's *mise en abyme,* is set on top of the promontory formed where the Golden Horn flows into the Bosporus, with a clear view northwards along the straits and south to the Sea of Marmara. The empire also cohered around many of the great rivers of the Afro-Eurasian landmass, which were like main arteries of a massive body. Two of the four rivers of Bernini's *Fontana dei quattri fiumi* in Rome traversed mainly Ottoman lands (the Danube and the Nile); they could have been three, had the baroque sculptor chosen the Euphrates or the Tigris to represent Asia instead of the Ganges.

Some Ottomans at least were quite conscious of such a predominance of the aquatic element. For example, the famed seventeenth-century polymath Kātib Çelebī had this to say about the Ottoman space: "It is no secret that maritime conditions constitute the greatest pillar in this exalted state, to which affairs the utmost attention and care must be given, inasmuch as the splendor and title of an ever-increasing state is to be with dominion over the two lands and the two seas. Apart from this, there is absolutely no doubt that most of the well-protected domains are composed of islands and seacoasts, and particularly that the benefaction of the seat of the exalted sultanate, that is, the city of Constantinople, lies in the two seas."[2]

And yet, as far as the modern historical imagination is concerned, "Ottoman" does not tend to rhyme much with "water." There has long been

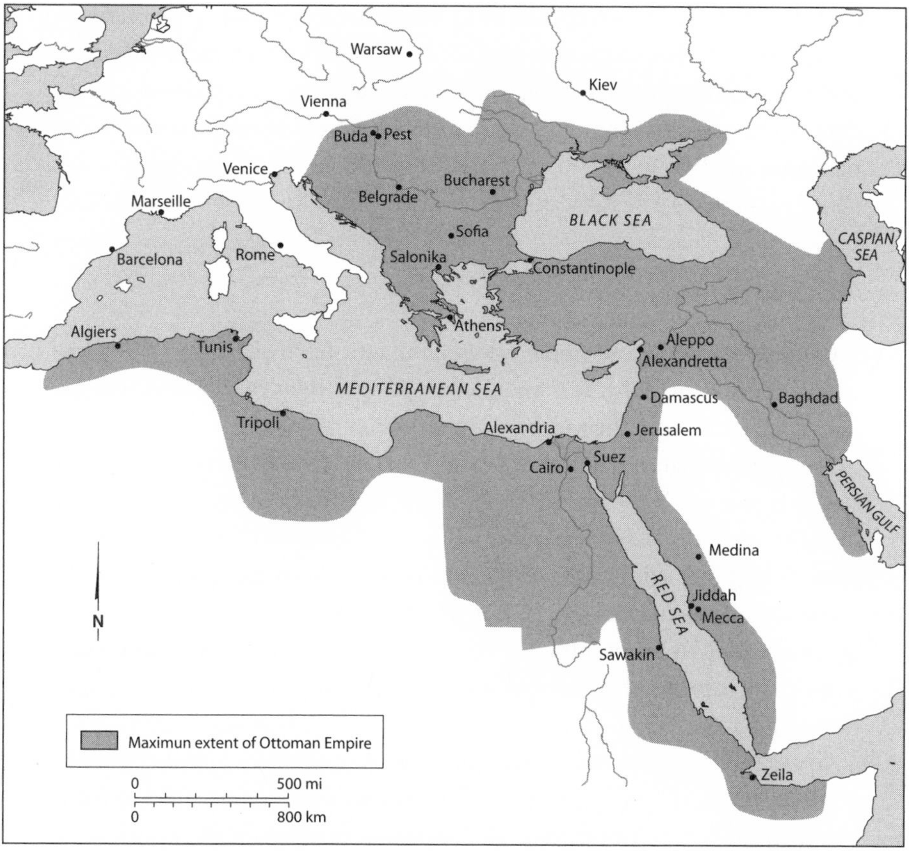

MAP 1. A Most Aquatic Empire. © Bill Nelson.

a terrestrial bias in the conception of the Ottoman past, which has always evoked more of a land-bound Behemoth than a water-soaked Leviathan. Despite a few scholars' repeated efforts to contest the land-oriented historiographical bias, much of the literature concerned with the Ottoman state (and its relationship with its subjects and neighbors) relies on the assumption that commercial and naval matters were tangential to an administration focused on agricultural and military affairs.[3] Tracing the long-standing genealogy of this discourse well into the heart of the European modern, this book explains why.

The short answer, which the following chapters explore in depth, is simply that the idea of maritimity itself is embedded in the narrative birth of modernity, so that the concepts of Europe and the sea are mutually constitutive, both evoking freedom and progress. Ottomanity, by contrast, is projected in its very idea as a theocratic Islamic space dominated by an imperial elite seeking to draw profit primarily from agricultural revenue. Thus layers of historiography have created the appearance of tension from the start between the maritime/the European and its Others, notably the Ottoman, but also the Muslim, the Arab, the African—all germane to the history of the Red Sea.

. . .

This is a story of seas and empires, water and writing, texts and archives, history and historiography. It is about concepts and their discursive function, about disciplines and their generic production.

It is a book that may be viewed as a historian's echo to Johannes Fabian's classic account of "how anthropology makes its object": in conversation with his *Time and the Other,* it presents a reflection on *space* and the Other.[4] By evoking the very conditions of possibility of modern historical discourse ("how history makes its object"), it dwells most notably on the enduring weight of modern Eurocentric notions of both space and time. Furthermore, it seeks to display what writing outside this Eurocentric analytic might look like.

Space and time are not unitary and neutral categories, nor can they be naturalized points of departure. Rather, they should enter the field of interrogation, for they are not, to extend Maurice Merleau-Ponty's words concerning space, "the setting (real or imagined) in which things are arranged, but the means whereby the positing of things becomes possible."[5] Even further, as Michel Foucault has shown, the assumption by space and time of objective, universal features was a fundamental mechanism by which a new sort of power both established and concealed itself. More efficient because better hidden, the disciplinary power of modernity exercised its authority by focusing on the biopolitical realm. This was realized by codifying time and space into regular units, and by asserting that this order was external to, indeed preceded, the institutionalized practices of control.[6]

On the question of space and time and their plural constitution, Edward Said makes the point succinctly, drawing on Gaston Bachelard's notion of the poetics of space (in his book by that title): "The objective space of a house—its corners, corridors, cellar, rooms—is far less important than what poetically it is endowed with, which is usually a quality with an imaginative or figurative value we can name and feel: thus a house may be haunted, or homelike, or prisonlike, or magical. So space acquires emotional and even rational sense by a kind of poetic process, whereby the vacant or anonymous reaches of distance are converted into meaning for us here. The same process occurs when we deal with time."[7]

The project of this book emerged from a startling realization: there had been no historical account of the Red Sea even remotely comparable to Fernand Braudel's Mediterranean. Many maritime basins had inspired attempts at Braudellian projects of all kinds: the Atlantic Ocean had its historians, steered by the pioneering efforts of Bernard Bailyn,[8] and so did the Indian Ocean, with the great K.N. Chaudhuri, an avowed disciple of the French master, in the vanguard.[9] Even the massive Pacific, the elusive Baltic, and the dark Black Sea were elected to the noble academy of historical subjects.[10] But nobody had raised properly the idea of the history of the Red Sea.[11] Even the efforts pointing in that direction were not convincing in the way that accounts of the Red Sea's White counterpart (as the Mediterranean is also known) had been, well before Braudel's summation.[12]

Yet the Red Sea offered itself as the ideal unitary space, in terms of geographical, climatic, religious, linguistic, social, commercial, human, even political and juridical integration of a sort Mediterraneanists could only dream about. Not only were the natural and cultural commonalities of the various shores evident, but it had been, essentially, an Ottoman lake for about four centuries. This ought to justify its treatment as a historical actor à la Braudel, especially considering the current mood of the discipline at large in its oceanic turn.[13]

This book thus reveals a dynamic Ottoman Red Sea world even as it traces the genealogy of its scholarly marginalization as a historical subject. But it does much more, as it reflects on the organizing category itself. What is shown is that the sea does not have a natural and eternal purchase on an objective reality. It is rather a heavily laden concept.

To take the example that forms the discovery at the core of this book: lengthy research in the extensive Ottoman records of the Prime Minister's Archives in Istanbul revealed an absence of the category "Red Sea" prior to the nineteenth century. There are, of course, innumerable sources that *a modern historian* can project backwards onto her idea of the Red Sea (accounts that mention a certain port of the region, a specific commodity that belonged to it, ships that sailed it, fluxes and exchanges that traversed it). But nowhere was there any evidence of the historical presence of the Red Sea, that internal Ottoman lake, as a unified subject. In none of the documents examined in search of remnants that could be used as evidence in the reconstitution of its past existence, did the category "Red Sea" make an appearance. None, that is, until the age of European hegemony.

The most common designation to appear in Ottoman documents for (portions of) the maritime domains that are now identified as the Red Sea was *Baḥr-ı Süveys,* named after the port city Suez, through which Ottoman power in the region was projected. Starting at a certain point in the mid-nineteenth century, the term *Baḥr-ı Süveys* suddenly disappears from the Ottoman record in favor of the now familiar *Baḥr-ı Aḥmer* (the *red* sea).

Such a simple observation may not at first glance seem to be of great importance. The following argument demonstrates that it is, and that the semantic shift incites a reassessment of basic assumptions regarding philosophy, political economy, cartography, geography, and of course history. By homing in on the presence/absence of the Red Sea from the scholarly arena, the argument poses a set of fundamental questions concerning historical practice in general: What discursive procedures enable an object to become a viable subject for history? How do particular subjects qualify as historical? How did the sea, its past and its present, become a subject of historical analysis in and of itself? And most importantly, for whom and by whom does the becoming-historical of the sea materialize? Should there be, *can* there be, a universal history of the sea? Or are there rather a series of deep-rooted though well-hidden predispositions in the modern discipline of history that explain the absence of an integrated history of the Red Sea and that reveal how Europe produced the hegemonic history and geography of the universal present?

The Red Sea had to be *produced* as a scientific object, and this process took place under particular historical circumstances: the extension of European colonial hegemony over the region (and the globe). There simply was no Ottoman production of the idea of a sovereign sea before the mid-nineteenth century, and the Ottomans did not give the entirety of the Red Sea a singular name before that time either. Having explained why the Red Sea has not previously become a proper subject of history, the book also explores the potentiality of a history written *without* the weight of Eurocentric geohistoricism, opening the path onto a more evocative genealogical history, one composed of fissures and breaks, in which time is not chronometric but heterosynchronous, and space not homogeneous but fractal.[14]

Instead of a limited move that would seek inclusion of the Red Sea in the realm of the discipline, the challenge is to push the critique of Eurocentrism further, arguing that the organizing categories of modern geography (the sea, the ocean, the region, etc.) are neither objective nor neutral. Instead, they belong to a specific discursive formation that takes shape with the birth of the human sciences in early nineteenth-century Europe, in which history and geography emerged as autonomous disciplines. Historicism was always a geohistoricism, and the sea featured prominently in it from the very start. In a striking reenactment of the myth of Narcissus, it was in the waters of the sea that Europe came to recognize and admire itself in its past and present.[15]

This book thus engages the practice of history writing through a sustained interrogation of the concept of the sea. What is shown, in sum, is that the question of the maritime is far more than a subfield of historical writing. It is, indeed, a central and vital category of philosophy of history.

• • •

Historical studies focused on bodies of water have proliferated in recent years, usually under the broad label of "the new thalassology," an appealing combination of classical, Hellenic authority and radical novelty.

An etymological explanation is required. The now common neologism *thalassology* is usually traced back to the recent review essay by Edward Peters, which hailed Peregrine Horden and Nicholas Purcell's *The Corrupting Sea* (2000) as one of the two books constituting "the hypertext of the new thalassology."[16] It should be noted that Claudio Magris uses the term *thalassologist* to describe the intellectual project of Pedrag Matvejević in the introduction to his book on the Mediterranean.[17] In fact, it also has a much older incarnation.

In the late nineteenth century, the term *thalassology* referred to the holistic study of oceans and seas combining elements from a multitude of disciplines (most notably biology, meteorology, and geography), akin to today's oceanography. Although the use of the term seems to have been rather uncommon, it was recurrently advocated in prominent arenas by the Italian scientist Ludovico Marini.[18] There is no indication that this meaning bears any relation to contemporary usage.

Neither Peters's review nor any work subsequently iterating the term explains how its approach is a "new" articulation of an older form of discourse. The approach is simply declared to be "genuinely new" in being a "microregional history of the Mediterranean with the enigmatic sea (or several seas) as its flexible center."[19] Nor indeed is it made clear what constitutes the *old* thalassology, although the short discussion of Fernand Braudel (who, we are told, "if he did not invent thalassology in 1949 . . . certainly put it spectacularly on the historian's map) perhaps places Braudel at the opening as the embodiment of the old.[20] In any case, the resuscitation of the old-new term has snowballed and has become the standard appellation for the recent crop of studies focusing on water basins (although how recent is obviously a contentious issue: Marcus Vink speaks of a "new thalassology" of the Indian Ocean that emerged in the 1980s).[21]

After the end of the Cold War came a proliferation of innovative studies of seas and oceans, as well as special chairs at prestigious universities, series in major publishing houses, and well-endowed, multiannual academic programs and conferences. History departments everywhere indulged the fashion. Here, finally, was a providential way out of the historians' existential dilemma after the generalized and devastating critiques of modernization theory and its attendant spatial paradigms, the nation-state and area studies. These were increasingly seen as nefarious residues of Cold War or, even worse, colonial politics—and therefore inimical to proper historical inquiry. This oceanic turn in the disciplines appeared to lead its practitioners to the promised land of scholarly renewal, liberated from the constraints of the past. There was, however, something uncanny about it all. The celebrations of the sea as a zone of historical inquiry free from political and discursive weight were trumpeted too loudly and quickly. Notably absent was an explanation of genealogies and implications. The sea was a self-evident category, and thalassology—the assumption by the sea of a subject-position in historical accounts—was a recent critical project. If it had antecedents, the precursor was Fernand Braudel.

In the summer of 2006, the subfield was consecrated by one of the profession's established institutional organs when the *American Historical Review* devoted its featured forum to the theme "Oceans of History." In her introduction to the collection the historian Kären Wigen celebrated the importance of the new trend: "Chances are, readers of the *AHR* have found the ocean catching their eye of late. Maritime scholarship seems to have burst its bounds; across the discipline, the sea is swinging into view. . . . No longer outside time, the sea is being given a history, even as the history of the world is being retold from the perspective of the sea."[22]

This recent sea-centered literature begins with a dual proposition: it is original and it is uncommon. Thus Peregrine Horden and Nicholas Purcell, leading latter-day proponents of Mediterranean history, introduce their review of the field with that very postulate: "Sea and ocean history is more novel than it sounds. It admirably exemplifies a new historiography of large areas.... Both its scope and its methods are so distinctive as to make it an exciting—and quite unpredictable—area of reflection and research."[23]

The crucial justification for a focus on bodies of water is, then, that such spatial units "tend to be politically neutral."[24] The history of the sea, it is argued in near unanimity, subverts the constraints of both national and imperial discourse. As an example of how, thanks to a focus on seas and oceans, conventional politics are set aside, Horden and Purcell mention "the 'new' Atlantic historiography, [in which] a 'white,' a 'black,' a 'green' (Irish), and even a 'red' (Marxist) Atlantic may coexist in equilibrium."[25]

In some sense, this is obviously true. The focus on nonterritorial spatialities runs against a well-established historiographical tradition that has reinforced forms of nationalist politics by assuming and therefore naturalizing conventional geographies. This does not make maritime history politically neutral. Can historical discourse ever be? As Hayden White has argued: "The politicalization of historical thinking was a virtual precondition of its own professionalization, the basis of its promotion to the status of a discipline worthy of being taught in the universities, and a prerequisite of whatever 'constructive' social function historical knowledge was thought to serve."[26]

It also remains unclear why polychromatic perspectives are specific to nonconventional geographies: Why there could not be, say, a blue, white, and red France, or even a brown, black, or rainbow France? The spatial units that frame historical narratives are all always already full of meaning; they derive from particular historical conditions, they come with their own discursive baggage, they have distinct conceptual implications, and they are all essentially and equally political.

Moreover, histories that take as their subject nonconventional geographic units still assume the very conceptual and cognitive framework that structures the mode of historical writing inherited from the nineteenth century with the professionalization of the discipline. This discursive arrangement rests on specific parameters: time and space are reduced to universal, homogeneous, and neutral—in a word, *objective*—categories, combining in what Heidegger describes as "the conquest of the world as picture,"[27] where time is unitary, linear, and teleological, and space is made up of coherent, bounded units with inherent characteristics that can be defined according to a set of scientific criteria—geographical, cartographic, ecological, but also ethnological, philological, and cultural. Thus was the subject of disciplined history produced: a cogent and representational, indeed anthropomorphic, central actor (appearing in the title, usually in the format "History of X") whose regular progress along a stable chronology was rendered in the form of a narrative.[28]

In this perspective, histories of nonconventional geographical units in fact partake of precisely the same politics as their more conventional counterparts—a politics of realism and the status quo that Hayden White has extensively critiqued.[29] Thalassology is thus saddled with an ambiguous paradox: subversive of the dominant state-centric approach to history, it tends nonetheless to reproduce the pillars upon which this discourse is founded. For this very reason, thalassology is a particularly fruitful site of interrogation about the nature of history, if it is executed according to a critical and genealogical method. What better locus to think about history, about the problematic of space, time, and the historical object, than the sea, a place that can host neither archive nor seminar, the two foundational features of the professionalized historical discipline?[30]

• • •

The making of the modern discipline of history is often narrated as a dramatized struggle between two opposite poles, neatly represented by two prominent individuals: G. W. F. Hegel and Leopold von Ranke. Both figures loom particularly large over Western historical discourse, and both played a crucial part in the formulation of the professionalized discipline. While the former dominates philosophical reflection about the nature, orientations, and meanings of history and is an unavoidable reference for any theoretical discussion of the discipline, the latter almost single-handedly created its methods and scope, forging the historian's self-identity and practice through his legendary seminars and archival heroics.

They were, of course, very much writing against one another, and these two approaches to history have maintained a rather tense relationship to this day, where, grossly, a theorizing impulse clashes with an empiricist one. History *à la* Ranke, Hegel surmised, was incapable of assigning any meaning or larger structure to the legacy of the past, and those who practice it gather their materials "from every conceivable source (Ranke). A motley assortment of details, petty interests, actions of soldiers, private affairs, which have no influence on political interests,—they are incapable [of recognizing] a whole, a general design."[31] Ranke, for his part, could not accept the intimation that the historian would superimpose preordained ideas onto the past; on the contrary, he ought to let reality speak for itself directly, by way of the historical record (*wie es eigentlich gewesen*—"what actually happened," or "the way it actually was"). Ranke makes clear his yearning for an autonomous discipline of history, separated especially from philosophy.[32] The philosopher, Ranke complained, "view[s] history from his vantage point, seeks infinity merely in progression, development, and totality."[33] Proper history, by contrast, "recognizes something infinite in every existence: in every condition, in every being, something eternal, coming from God; and this is its vital principle."[34]

Their important differences notwithstanding, the two writers had much in common in terms of the spatial and temporal configurations that for them framed history. Three of these shared characteristics are particularly relevant to the arguments of this book.

First, they both explicitly repudiated the model of exemplar history of previous epochs.[35] Second, history, for both Hegel and Ranke, needed a primary actor, and in both cases the nation-state took center stage, as the incarnation of homogeneous space-time. Ranke disagreed with Hegel as to whether history ought to be interpreted as the unfolding of a universal story along hierarchical stages that could be defined by a singular idea (or rather, Idea); but he, like his opponent, saw the world (and Europe in particular) as divided into a certain number of nation-states that had to be allotted a particular moral character, the ideal fulfillment of which formed the essence of history.[36] Moreover, both assumed and affirmed the uniqueness of the European continent and its civilization, encapsulated precisely by the special place of history within it. There was something distinctly European about universal history, and something distinctly historical about Europe. And that distinction was connected to the progressive constitution of the nation-state.[37] In other words, history, from its very beginning as a professionalized discipline, was thoroughly territorial, with both its practical-empiricist and its philosophizing bent bound by the unit of the nation-state. Transcending the state, moreover, both Ranke and Hegel also saw a European self that combined the various trajectories of individual nations into a higher whole, the culmination of world civilization.

Finally, both Hegel and Ranke conceived of the Mediterranean as having a sovereign coherence, and as playing a central role in the movement of world history. Indeed, Ranke had published a text entitled *The Ottoman and Spanish Empires in the Sixteenth and Seventeenth Centuries,* as the opening volume of the four-volume series *Sovereigns and Peoples of Southern Europe.*

At the very outset, Ranke describes the sequence of grandeur and decline of the states of southern Europe, strikingly putting within the same frame of historical analysis the Spaniards, the Italians, and the Ottomans.[38] He goes on to chastise existing narratives for being "engrossed . . . with the event of political and religious strife" and therefore incapable of delivering the "internal developments" that explain the shift of the center of gravity of world history from southern to northern Europe.[39] These, he then suggests, had something to do with the locale, and here the Mediterranean makes an appearance as the defining feature that gives coherence to the analytical frame: "Whilst these three nations made themselves formidable or conspicuous among the rest, they encountered each other directly in the Mediterranean; they filled all its coasts and waters with life and motion, and formed there a peculiar circle of their own."[40]

Always more vigorous in his theorizations, Hegel turns the Mediterranean into an abstract, coherent system. Having postulated the idea of the "Geographical Basis of History," he goes on to delineate its various incarnations; and this is where the sea comes to the fore: "The Old World . . . has its continuity interrupted by a deep inlet—the Mediterranean Sea. The three Continents that compose it have an essential relation to each other, and constitute a totality. Their peculiar feature is that they lie round this Sea, and therefore have an easy means of communication; for rivers and seas are not to be regarded as disjoining, but as uniting. . . . For the three quarters of the globe the Mediterranean Sea is similarly the uniting element, and the centre of World-History."[41]

Hegel proposes as a "fundamental principle that nothing *unites* so much as water" against the customary tendency to view it as the "separating element."[42] Recent times, he complains, have seen a particular insistence on finding natural borders to states, and thus has the sea often been wrongly viewed as forming a barrier. Much to the contrary, it is, he recurrently opines, a coherent and dynamic unit that generates interaction and connectivity. And as such, it is the fundamental feature, indeed the motor, of historical progress. Water acts as a connector, and this is evidenced, for Hegel, by the fact that Europeans maintained regular contact with America but not with the interiors of Africa and Asia and by the tendency of coastal regions to separate from the interior.[43] The sea, therefore, and the Mediterranean Sea in particular, lies at the very heart of Hegel's geohistorical and philosophical complex: "The sea gives us the idea of the indefinite, the unlimited, and infinite; and in *feeling his own infinite* in that Infinite, man is stimulated and emboldened to stretch beyond the limited: the sea invites man to conquest, and to piratical plunder, but also to honest gain and to commerce. The land . . . attaches him to the soil; it involves him in an infinite multitude of dependencies, but the sea carries him out beyond the limited circles of thought and action."[44] This is quite a momentous argument, especially in light of the text's insistence on the place of the territorial state in the constitution of history, and Hegel can be considered to have been among the first advocates of Mediterranean unity, as well as the prophet of thalassology.

These two positions are related, as the new thalassologists repeatedly assert by hailing the Mediterranean as the "*ur*-sea" or the "great original of seas."[45] This relation does not emerge, however, from some particular Mediterranean primeval unity or propensity for connectivity. Nor does it derive, as Braudel has it, from the "fact" that the Mediterranean is "the oldest stretch of sea ever dominated [*saisi*] by Man," unlike the Atlantic, which has "nothing but a borrowed and hastily constructed past."[46] Indeed, as will be discussed below, in the case of Bory de Saint-Vincent, who theorized the unity of water basins, the Atlantic Ocean featured just as prominently as the Mediterranean in relation to the idea of coherent bodies of water. Besides, the Red Sea probably has a much better claim to being "the oldest stretch of sea ever dominated by Man." The connection, rather, is due to the simple fact that the invention of the Mediterranean and of thalassology are coeval, to each other and to the constitution of a particular self-identity of imperial Europe, rendering one the yardstick for the other.

• • •

A concept, says Louis Althusser, writing about capitalist time, "is never immediately 'given,' never *legible* in visible reality: like every concept this concept must be *produced, constructed*."[47] This book is devoted to the production of the sea as concept. It explores the trajectories that have opened the discursive space for making the sea an object of historical analysis. It follows various twists and turns that have led to the constitution of the sea as a viable subject of history by evoking a number of steps of its historiographical becoming.

In recent years, the posited European monopoly on maritimity has been subjected to critique, often with the aim of demonstrating instead that the sea was important to non-European states and peoples too, and in some cases well before the rise of Europe. These studies are important and have helped to reshape historical practice and method as a whole. Particularly inspiring for the arguments of this book are a series of interventions that have fundamentally transformed the way the Pacific and its islands are conceived and written about. The opening salvo in this adventure was Epeli Hau'ofa's evocative essay "Our Sea of Islands," in which the Tongan scholar sought to counter the dominant production of knowledge that defined the Pacific islands as "too small, too poor, and too isolated to develop any meaningful degree of autonomy."[48] Hau'ofa contrasts this external and expert-induced *belittlement* to alternative, indigenous notions of space: "But if we look at the myths, legends, and oral traditions, indeed the cosmologies of the peoples of Oceania, it becomes evident that they did not conceive of their world in such microscopic proportions. Their universe comprised not only land surfaces but the surrounding ocean as far as they could traverse and exploit it, the underworld with its fire-controlling and earth-shaking denizens, and the heavens above with their hierarchies of powerful gods and named stars and constellations that people could count on to guide their ways across the seas. Their world was anything but tiny."[49]

This long-standing sense of place and identity of the Oceanian Islanders enables a radical reconfiguration of geographical typology, from "islands in a far sea" to "a sea of islands." Here too, a simple semantic shift leads to a dramatic conceptual rearticulation. The first expression, Hau'ofa explains, "emphasises dry surfaces in a vast ocean far from the centres of power," whereas the second "is a more holistic perspective in which things are seen in the totality of their relationship."[50] Thus the very basis of the modern conception of what "land" and "sea" mean, and how they relate to each other, is transformed—an epistemological break that has inspired a whole series of contributions on Oceania's many lands and seas that go well beyond the colonial categories of and in the Pacific. It has bred a different style of scholarship, but also art and activism—indeed, a whole way of life and thought.[51]

The danger, therefore, as Hau'ofa and others suggest, is the tendency to reproduce uncritically the geographical categories of the European modern. What remains rather underexplored in the case of many maritime histories, even in many works that propose alternative historical narratives, is the set of deeper theoretical underpinnings of history writing and history making outside Europe, as well as the divergent manner in which the Ottomans themselves, or any others, conceived space, time, and identity before European hegemony and their potential implications for today.

In addition to sketching a history of the Red Sea akin to Braudel's Mediterranean, this book uncovers the genealogy of maritimity as a central element in the cosmos of modernity and the birth of the idea of the sovereign sea along with the human sciences in Europe in the early nineteenth century. Any historical study that takes the sovereign sea as a neutral historical concept and an innocent geographical space will inevitably reproduce components of Eurocentric thought. In avoiding this pitfall, one chapter seeks to conjure alternative notions of spatiality, inspired by the Ottoman archival record concerning the Red Sea. The objective is to reflect upon the historian's craft in general and to produce a historical account of the Ottoman Red Sea but also to evoke the possibilities for imagining today a different relationship to landscape and ecology (whether maritime or terrestrial) as an inhabited and meaningful place, based on a relational rather than a managerial understanding of space. What is suggested, quite simply, is that Ottoman history may contain perspectives, even within a seemingly trivial archival document, that allow for an alternative way of thinking and being in this world.

BOOK OUTLINE

The five chapters that follow are intended to illustrate and provide depth to the ideas sketched above. Each one engages particular clusters of questions related to the general theme and builds on existing scholarship, both theoretical and empirical, while tracing original research perspectives. These are elaborated in the Conclusion, which presents the horizons that are opened by the book's various arguments considered as a whole.

Chapter 1, "The Place in the Middle: A Geohistory of the Red Sea," provides the basic setting of the Red Sea in the long term, as it has come to be imagined today. Consciously written in the Braudellian mode, it puts forward the foundational long-term features of the spacetime signified by the name "the Red Sea." Beginning with the geological and the climatic domains (Braudel's *longue durée*), it then broaches the central features of the social and economic dimensions of the sea (*conjonctures*) before presenting a narrative emplotment of the place (*évènements*). An additional segment follows, complementing the three-tiered schema with a perspective of world history from the angle of a nonhuman actor that was particularly tied to the Ottoman Red Sea world: coffee.

Chapter 2, "Thalassology *alla Turca:* Six Theses on the Philosophy of History," seeks to produce a philosophy of history from the outside (of Europe). It follows on previous scholarship dealing with the Ottoman past in theoretical terms.[52] Over the past few decades, Ottomanist historians have been coming out of their parochial niche and posing questions of global import. There is no longer any reason to assume that Ottoman history should not provide for a rich reflection of universal value on the practice of history itself, on potential alternative worldviews, or on transregional processes, for example. In six basic theses, ranging from the world-historical to the micro-historical, the chapter reveals what the philosophy of history looks like from the Bosporus and why the history of the Ottoman Red Sea does not, perhaps could not, or even *should* not exist.

Chapter 3, "Self-Portrait of the Ottoman Red Sea, June 21, 1777," narrates the history of the region through the prism of the sources themselves, rather than the objectivist analytic of Braudellian-inspired thalassology. With the aim of exploring how some Ottomans themselves saw the Red Sea and its world in the late eighteenth century, a close exegesis of an official document is undertaken, though which is revealed the special nature of that world as lived and imagined by its administrators and practitioners. An investigation of the various spatialities and temporalities embedded in the content and form of that document unveils a complex universe, involving local and global politics, the movement of tides and winds, the difficulties of shipbuilding and seafaring, the relationships within and between Ottoman state and society, various cycles of exchange and mobility, and other factors.

Chapter 4, "The Scientific Invention of the Red Sea," focuses the analysis directly on the creation of the Red Sea as an object of knowledge and power. The story here follows the dramatic expansion of European (and mainly British) military power over the region, and the actual production of the Red Sea as a scientific object, culminating in its thorough charting in the second quarter of the nineteenth century. Only then does it become a sovereign, organic space, about which particular truth claims can be made. And this becoming-scientific of the Red Sea went hand in hand with British imperial expansion in the region (and the world). The chapter then evokes the eventual rise to hegemony of these spatial and temporal notions, and their internalization by the Ottomans and Egyptians themselves, who adopt the category "Red Sea" in the 1850s and beyond.

Chapter 5, "Thalassomania: Modernity and the Sea," examines the emergence of the sea as an operative concept at the center of the discursive formation of modernity and reveals the surprisingly important place of the sea in the writings of major figures of modern thought. The assumption of the sea as an analytical unit was not the outcome of a natural teleological process. Seas and oceans, just like the stories told about them, are not discovered as such in nature. The chapter shows that the idea of the sea forming a unitary and coherent space can be traced back to the early nineteenth century and the foundations of the modern disciplines (of history, geography, botany, and oceanography most importantly).

The analysis here exposes the common parameters, anchored in organic realism, of the modern disciplines, through its concentration on the genealogy of a single object (the sea). The chapter also explores the ontological implications that accompanied the new epistemic setting. What is shown in this regard is that most significant in the differentiation between the haves and have-nots of History in modern philosophy of history is a certain idea of the sea.

One important caveat must be kept in mind before embarking on this journey. What is envisioned today as "the Red Sea" was, from time immemorial and certainly in the Ottoman period, an eminently cosmopolitan space, replete with mobility and exchange of all kinds.[53] This book does not concern itself primarily with these important historical flows, nor does it seek to reveal an authentic experience of the sea by people, locals and others, who encountered it. Obviously, the scholars, pilgrims, traders, administrators, coastal communities, and the rest, who lived "the Red Sea," conceived of the maritime spaces in multiple ways that do not necessarily conform to imperial norms, whether European or Ottoman (though they were certainly affected by them). These various experiences of the sea are fascinating in their own right, and they can never be subjected fully to the objectifying ambitions of elites—but they do not fit, for reasons both practical and methodological, into the subject of this book.

ONE

The Place in the Middle

A GEOHISTORY OF THE RED SEA

THOUGH IT WAS ONCE AN object of great scholarly debate, few people ask any more what is meant by "the Red Sea" or why it is so called. There is scant curiosity regarding the potentialities attached to the name, even though long ago already Marcel Proust most evocatively demonstrated that the name of a place is a convoluted and significant matter.[1]

WHAT'S IN A NAME?

The now seemingly established explanation for the origin of the name "Red" (that it derives from the common ancient practice of assigning particular colors to the different cardinal points) is charming in its simplicity,[2] but it fails to take into account the fact that from ancient times, almost from the very first still extant writings on the sea, authors have been debating the roots of the name that has become hegemonic in reference to the maritime space running from Suez and Aqaba in the north to Bab al-Mandab in the south, separating the Arabian Peninsula to the east from the African landmass to the west. Nor does it recognize the problem of those waters having been named *green* in many instances. None other than the giants Ptolemy and Ibn Khaldūn called portions of the Indian Ocean green: the further, southern part in the case of the former, as in *πρασώδης θάλασσα* (usually translated as "leek-green sea"), and what is today called the Persian Gulf for the latter, as in *al-khalīj al-akhḍar*.[3] And finally, it simply does not acknowledge the basic fact that until very recently the people most invested in the sea (whether those living around it or those officially governing it) did not call it red or even necessarily conceive of it as a coherent unit.

In any case, the appellation "Red Sea" is commonly traced back to ancient Greek, occurring in numerous texts from Herodotus onwards. It must be recalled, however, that the area described as the Erythraean Sea, in all ancient accounts, was much larger than the present-day Red Sea (which was then commonly called the Arabian Gulf), approximating what would today be imagined by the category "Indian Ocean," especially its northwestern part (including attendant gulfs, bays, and seas).[4] In fact, Herodotus himself explicitly differentiated the Arabian Gulf from the Erythraean Sea.[5]

As early as the second century BCE, however, the origin of the name came under critical scrutiny. Indeed, Agatharchides of Cnidus in the first book of his *On the Erythraean Sea* refers to a series of established explanations for the appellation before refuting them.[6] From the outset (the second and third entries of the text), he notably dismisses the ascription of the name to the color of the water. He himself attributes the origin of the designation to a Persian source by the name of Boxos, who affirmed that it was derived from a king of legendary reputation who ruled on its shores. "There was a Persian," writes Agatharchides, "the son of Muozaios, named Eruthras, well known for his courage and wealth, who lived not far from the sea opposite two islands which are now inhabited but were deserted in the time of the Median empire when Eruthras knew them."[7] There follows a tale of unexpected discovery, early colonization, and original civilization: "Much taken with the island, he built there a port in a suitable place, and brought over from the mainland people who were living in poor circumstances; after this he established other settlers in the remaining uninhabited island."[8] The sea thus ought to be referred to, Agatharchides continues, as the sea of the man Erythras, rather than the common deformation of the name that leads to the adjectival form of *red*.

As Strabo subsequently summarized in his foundational *Geography:*

> [Artemidorus] says that some writers call the sea "Erythra" from the colour it presents as the result of reflection, whether from the rays of the sun when it is in the zenith, or from the mountains, which have been reddened by the scorching heat; . . . but Ctesias the Cnidian reports a spring, consisting of red and ochre-coloured water, as emptying into the sea; and Agatharcides, a fellow-citizen of Ctesias, reports from a certain Boxus, of Persian descent, that when a herd of horses had been driven out of the country by a passion-frenzied lioness as far as the sea and from there the herd had crossed over to a certain island, a certain Persian, Erythras by name, built a raft and was the first man to cross to the island; and that when he saw that it was beautifully adapted to habitation, he drove the herd back to Persis, sent forth colonists to that island and to the others and to the coast, and caused the sea to be named after himself.[9]

The conversation on the origin of the term *Red Sea* would continue unabated throughout the centuries. Carsten Niebuhr, a member of the expedition sent out in the 1760s by the king of Denmark to explore Egypt, Arabia, and Syria, hearkens back to the ancient authors and ultimately casts his lot with the Semitic etymology linking the origin name to the kingdom of Edom (also meaning red in Hebrew) of biblical fame:

> Europeans usually call the Arabian Gulf the Red Sea. As for me, I didn't find it redder than the black sea, or the archipelago that the Turks call the White Sea, or any other sea in the world. If one were really to find at the bottom of this sea reddish grasses, as some scholars believe, then it is very rare. So it is improbable that it was named from that, or that it got its name from a few specks of red sand, or from the bright red little corals called organ pipes, or from the few mountains which in the distance appear somewhat reddish, and so on. Others have thought the Greeks named the Arabian Gulf *Mare Erythraeum* after King Erythroeus. But as already noted on p. 309, the name had in ancient times been given to the Persian Gulf. As for me, I find very well founded the view of those who suppose that the gulf was named after the kingdom of Edom, Mare Idumaeum, and finally the Red Sea, because the kingdom of Edom abutted the northernmost part of that gulf.[10]

The question of the scriptures raises another unavoidable dimension in the issue of the name: that of the long-standing tradition whereby Moses led the children of Israel to safety when the Red Sea parted for them, then closed on the pursuing Egyptian armies (Exodus 14). In fact, there is no qualifier *red* to the sea in the text at all, though the epithet used in Hebrew may have implied reeds, or even simply a poetic space involving purifying waters.[11] Later, following Herodotus's naming of the Red Sea, which seemingly echoed common usage by sailors of the time, Greek translations of the Bible added the adjective *red*.[12] The attractions of this long-standing multilingual philological swamp notwithstanding, what is important to remember is that the designation of the sea as "red" is not in any way primordial but is historically bounded and discursively constituted. In other words, as Proust advocated, it is crucial always to keep in mind the basic analytical distinction between names and places.

. . .

To be treated historically, a particular object needs to be transformed into a coherent *subject*. This occurs through a variety of maneuvers, an essential one being the act of naming. The Mediterranean, for example, has long been conceptualized in its plenitude, holding a conspicuous and coherent place at the center of the world, as implied by its very name. The T-O (orbis terrarum) maps of the medieval imagination are perfect examples of its special character: the world is represented as a circle with the Inner Sea at its center, while the surrounding lands are peripheral appendages to the maritime space. Such cumulative visual imagining made it easy to transform the Mediterranean into a commonsensical notion and from there into a historical personage.

By contrast, the Red Sea has over the centuries had a great variety of names. Adding to the obstacles that faced any formulation of the Red Sea as subject of history has been its longtime identification as a simple corridor. Small, narrow, elongated, it is often described as a tract connecting one uniform world (the Mediterranean, Europe, the West) to another (that of the Indian Ocean, of India, of the Orient). As William Facey writes, in the opening line of the first chapter of the series of publications connected to the important "Red Sea Project," jointly coordinated by the Society for Arabian Studies and the British Museum, which have come to serve as the benchmark in this nascent field: "As a sweeping historical generalisation, one might say that the Red Sea is an extreme example of a sea on the way to somewhere else."[13]

Here one can only agree with Braudel, responding to the description of the Mediterranean as a lake: the historian must detach himself at all costs from such a conception of the sea. The "Red Sea" of Selīm I, of Meḥmed ʿAlī, or of Sharif Surūr was relatively speaking, in terms of modes and times of transportation, one hundred, one thousand times its dimensions as conceived today. It too once was, in itself, a universe.[14] Though a much larger space than it is today, the Red Sea was also, in many ways, a smaller and more coherent one before the age of nation-states and their boundaries, and the world economy and its gravity. The connotations of the word *universe* are revealing here: both infinitely boundless and intimately interconnected.

But what kind of universe? Can one imagine the Red Sea as a cogent historical actor? For this, it would need to possess coherence both in the long term, giving a potential narrative consistency and depth, and in the short term, extracting that narrative from mere geographic description. Before it merits a history of its own, the subject needs to go native, as it were, and assume anthropomorphic features. It has now a commonly ascribed name, that is a start, but it requires a firmer body and fuller mind. Only then can it become a story.

THE GEOLOGICAL STRUCTURE: A SPACE ON THE RIDGE

The Red Sea, as it is known today, is a long and narrow body of water oriented northwest-southeast that separates northeastern Africa from the Arabian Peninsula and connects the eastern Mediterranean to the western Indian Ocean. Almost completely enclosed, it is located between 30°N and 12°30′N and is about 2,000 kilometers long, while averaging 280 kilometers in width. Its only natural exit point (other than the numerous manmade canals that were pierced in various ages in order to connect it to the Nile or the Mediterranean) is in the south, at the very tight and shallow "Gate of Lamentation" (Bab al-Mandab), whose barely thirty kilometers are further constricted by the presence of islands. Though widely connected to its surrounding regions and beyond, the Red Sea is a unique and quite coherent environment.[15]

"For the geologist the Red Sea is an ocean," writes Colin Braithwaite, beginning his compact introduction to the paleogeography of the region with a startling counterintuitive assertion.[16] He is relating the category "ocean" to its underlying geological substratum, as opposed to its size, as the commonsensical meaning would have it. The Red Sea was born millions of years ago, created by tectonic forces. It probably began in the mid-Eocene epoch, just as the Arabian plate divorced from its African consort, and then grew and took form as the two plates drifted further and further apart with a dramatic separation in the Oligocene. Indeed, if the current tectonic effects persist, it appears that the Red Sea could become as wide as the Atlantic (in about 150 million years).[17]

Lying along a major rift complex beginning in the western Indian Ocean (the Carlsberg Ridge and the Owen Fracture Zone), the Red Sea Rift is extended in the north by the Dead Sea transform fault system—also a by-product of the same plate divergence. In the south, it feeds into the Afar Triple Junction, where it meets the Aden Ridge and the East African Rift.

This geological history conditions the basic formal topography of the Red Sea world, characterized by the striking deep trough along its central axis, which is flanked by a shallow coastal shelf. This shelf, extensive in the south, facing Yemen and Eritrea, but increasingly narrow going north and into the Gulf of Aqaba, is perhaps the most distinctive feature of the waters, for it is brimming with coral reefs along most of its range.

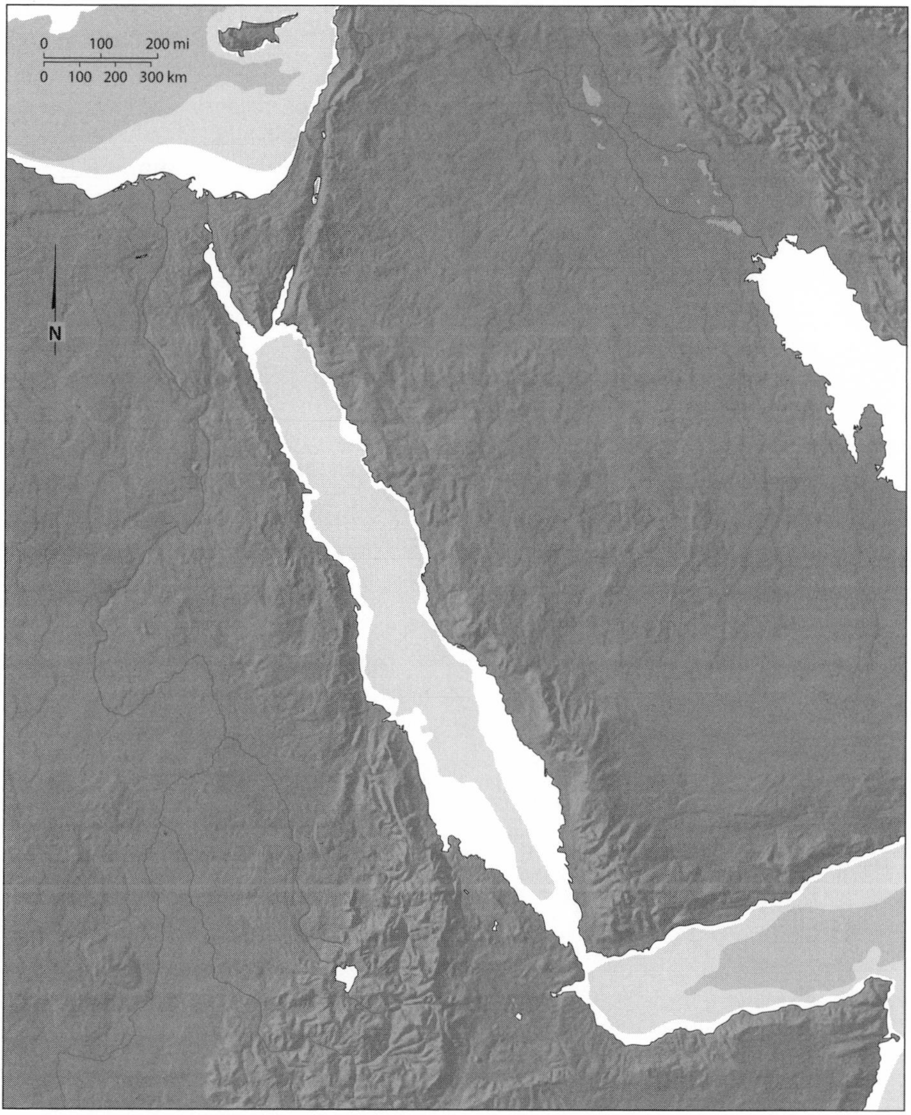

MAP 2. Red Sea Topography. © Bill Nelson.

The shallow underwater shelf is followed on land by a thin plain skirted by the dramatic uplift of the mountain ranges that dominate the length of the Red Sea (map 2).[18] On all sides, the coastal plain suddenly ascends along steep rocky mountains, separating that world from the lands further afield. Agatharchides of Cnidus, who wrote the first extant description of the Red

Sea, noted this striking feature at the very beginning of his book: "The navigable passage is narrow, with peaks and mounds overhanging it on each side of the gulf."[19]

The Sinai Peninsula almost in its entirety is formed by rugged mountains reaching an altitude of over 2,600 meters at the top of the twin summits of Mount Zebir and Mount Catherine. Along the eastern shore, the coast abuts the Sarawat mountain range that runs from Jordan in the north to the Gulf of Aden in the south, cutting off the Red Sea from the oasis-spotted desert and the lush plateaus. The altitudes vary considerably, reaching over 2,500 meters in the very north and over 3,600 further south near the Yemeni capital of Sanaa, but everywhere the range falls abruptly onto the coastal plains. Indeed, the very word *Ḥijāz* evokes this topographic aspect: a mountainous *barrier* separating the coast in the west from the interior. In striking symmetry to the eastern coast, the Red Sea Hills of Egypt, Sudan, and Eritrea run almost continuously along the western shore, southwards leading up to the beginnings of the highlands of Ethiopia, where altitudes rise highest in the region (at over 4,500 meters).

The geological substratum also determines another dominant characteristic of the Red Sea: its arid climate. The name *Tihāma* itself, the Arabic term for the length of the western seaboard, comes from a root word meaning intensity of heat and stillness of air, according to the classical lexicographers, though later European philologists have attributed to it a possible earlier etymon with meanings relating to "the sea."[20] It is remarkable that, despite the significant latitudinal range of the area, the climate should be so regular and similar throughout (allowing, of course, for minor differences, especially between the southern and northern edges), characterized by intense heat and barrenness.[21] In the words of Frederick Edwards: "The salient feature of the weather is monotony."[22]

Its surrounding shores are unreceptive to agricultural production of any sort because of high aridity and elevated temperatures. Rainfall is sparse, varied, and irregular, and there are no significant coastal rivers, no sizable permanent sweet-water inflow toward the sea. The Red Sea world is thus also defined by its natural inhospitability to human settlement, a common trope concerning the region, from the classical accounts of the Roman general Aelius Gallus's disastrous campaign in Arabia to Romain Gary's *Les trésors de la mer Rouge.*[23]

This distinctive climactic factor concerns not only the land but also the very waters, which are unique. Indeed, the natural conditions of the area have also caused the Red Sea to be unusually warm and saline, especially considering its depth: "Very high surface temperatures, coupled with extreme salinities make this one of the hottest and saltiest bodies of seawater anywhere. . . . Unlike all of the open oceans of the world where the water at depth is close to freezing point, the waters of the Red Sea are warm throughout."[24]

This is a direct consequence of the Red Sea's geographic and geological situation, as it is located at the center of a vast desertic stretch running from the Atlantic shores to the Mongolian interior. The northern edges of the Red Sea world, abutting the Mediterranean, are also rather arid, with only the occasional winter rains. The southern extensions, both to the east and to the west, are much better watered, though neither the rains of the Ethiopian highlands nor the showers associated with the Indian Ocean monsoon quite reach the Red Sea, breaking instead along the mountains encircling its fringes. Furthermore, the tectonic dynamics of the major rift mentioned above, which created the deep axial trough and the sharp uplift along the coasts, also lead to the recurrent introduction of new crust and lava into the marine depths, which thus feature distinctive pools of hot brine.[25] The high evaporation rate and lack of sweet-water inflow compound the high temperature of the waters with high salinity.

These constitutive features have in turn significant consequences for the order of life in and on the sea, with its exceptionally rich palette of bio-ecological features and fierce unpredictable currents, resulting in serious navigational challenges. The Bible itself speaks to this theme when it evokes the wreckage of Jehoshaphat's fleet at Ezion-geber, associating those waters with the hazards of navigation (1 Kings 22).

The abundance of corals and shoals caused incessant worries to pilots and provides another important geohistorical feature of the Red Sea. The concentration of such treacherous underwater protruding formations made it singular, with perhaps the greatest concentration of reefs in the world.

In fact, the coral of the Red Sea has always been one of its distinguishing characteristics, an essential element to any portrait. Today, it is mainly the object of enjoyment for lovers of its underwater world and amateurs of jewelry, but it was once a crucial feature of the local urban architecture, from the structures of the ancient port city of Berenike to the Ottoman-era buildings of Sawakin, Jiddah, Massawa, Hudayda, Luhayya, and other coastal towns.

The corals of the Red Sea served its coastal communities as sources of material for construction but also as a significant source of income, through trade over enormous distances, and even apparently as a source of food. It should not come as a surprise, then, that its coral reefs have been associated with the origin of the sea's name (although a reader of the *Journal of the Royal Asiatic Society of Great Britain and Ireland,* in his correspondence to the journal, squarely dismissed such onomastic meanderings with a flat "There is no red coral found in the Red Sea").[26] Still, the standard modern dictionaries of the Ottoman language list *Şab deñizi,* the Coral Sea, as a common name for the Red Sea.[27] Such Ottomanist corals, admittedly, need not be red, but it cannot be denied that corals hold a unique place in the portrait of the sea, and in its very definition as a historical object.

Besides reefs and shoals, there was the problem of fierce and capricious currents and tides. The perniciousness of the currents and the abundance of corals are intimately connected, and not only because they feature together as prime tormentors of navigators and their passengers. They also have a common origin, since both result from the particular climatic and geological conditions of the region: the high temperature and salinity of the waters provide an ideal setting for the nurture of various species of corals, just as they provoke differentials of density that lead to erratic underwater flux. The currents had another source, determining both their strength and unreliability: the vicious wind factor.

The most spectacular threat to ships sailing the Red Sea was thus the often violent and impulsive winds that would frequently, although unpredictably, sweep through the narrow waterways that had to be navigated between the many reefs, islands, and coasts. The general wind patterns were well known for millennia—and they modeled the navigation of the sea in the first place, determining sailing seasons, paces, and even the disposition of ports. But there were also the more variable and intense winds that could not be mapped in either time or space, for they did not follow any sensible, uniform configuration at all. These were particularly insidious in the north, where depressions moving along the Mediterranean coast engender "cold frontal troughs" that "swing from north-west to south-east across the northern part of the Red Sea as the parent depressions move eastwards. Ahead of such fronts the winds back (i.e. change direction in an anticlockwise sense) from north through west, to south-west or south and may become quite strong, even gale force for a time."[28]

There is one fundamental feature of the region's general wind regime, splitting the sea into two roughly equal climatic and therefore navigational zones:

> In the south the dominating factor is the Asian anticyclone, on the south side of which, the very extensive North-East Monsoon covers the whole of

> southern Asia and the north Indian Ocean. Part of this enters the Gulf of Aden from the east as a mainly easterly wind and takes the path of least resistance out at the western end through the Straits of Bab al Mandab and flows towards the low pressure trough over the Red Sea. The southern part of the Red Sea is thus covered by winds from between south and south-east which are, in effect, part of the North-East Monsoon. Over the northern part of the Sea, the main influence is the North African anticyclone which produces, on its eastern flank, a mainly northerly airflow again directed towards the Red Sea low pressure trough, as a result of which the northern part of the Red Sea is covered with predominantly north-west to north winds. These two wind systems meet in an area somewhat to the south of the middle latitude of the Sea, that is at about 18–20°N in January but a little farther south in late autumn and early spring. In this area of convergence there is a belt of light and variable winds with a high frequency of calms.[29]

Above the waves, then, the partition was defined, first, by varying wind patterns. The northern portion was governed by a unique wind regime that arranged the naval shuttle service between Suez and Jiddah on a cyclical basis (roughly from December to May the winds favored the navigation to Suez from Jiddah, while the rest of the year it was the other way around). The southern parts of the sea, by contrast, were subject to wind patterns resulting from the monsoon seasons. Ships from beyond Bab al-Mandab were therefore unlikely to pursue their travels north of Jiddah for fear of missing the return winds.

The underwater worlds too differ significantly, with the characteristic diversity of corals dominating in the north, and seagrasses in the south. Salinity decreases the closer one gets to Bab al-Mandab, from which the Red Sea exchanges with the less salty waters of the Gulf of Aden. This all leads to variations in ecosystems more largely, and notably in the assemblages of fish species (of which the Red Sea carries probably the highest diversity overall).

The division of the Red Sea into two was formalized with oceanographic explorations almost always divided into two separate missions, one for each half. Thus the very first expedition sent to survey the sea in systematic fashion (in 1829, by the British authorities) consisted of two ships with different commanders and crews, one for the area north of Jiddah, the other for the area south. Over one hundred years later, the Egyptian government sent out the *Mabāḥith* research ship to examine the northern part of the sea, partially to offset the focus of immediately preceding oceanographic expeditions on the southern half.[30] In between these two dates, an Austrian expedition of reconnaissance was sent, and although it was executed by a single ship (the *Pola*) its work was divided into two segments separated by a yearlong hiatus, and its preliminary conclusions were entirely devoted to outlining the differences between the northern and southern parts of the sea split along the latitude of Jiddah.[31] As chapter 4 will show, however, in time the north-south division became less relevant and gradually disappeared from accounts, even as "the Red Sea" was being scientifically produced and as steam was increasingly becoming the dominant mode of transport.

THE HUMAN FACTOR: A SEA OF PARADOX

From its earliest appearances in the documentary record, the Red Sea has featured as a liminal zone, a place in-between, on the global scale as much as the local one. Indeed, the very same conditions described above that made life and movement on the sea difficult also dictated the need for incessant navigation in the first place. As Head explains: "The dearth of rain and vegetation has been the principal reason for the low human population levels anywhere along the Red Sea coast, which even now [1987] do not exceed about 20 to the square kilometer *except in the vicinity of major towns.*"[32]

And this is, precisely, another feature of the Red Sea in the *longue durée:* despite the inhospitable natural conditions, there have been, all around the coast and throughout the ages, important cities, whose significance was based on various factors: commercial, first and foremost, but also political and theological, with the twin holy cities of Mecca and Medina not too far from the coast, as well as strategic and symbolic—perhaps the most crucial in an age of global struggle for hegemony. None of these cities could survive in autarky, and most were unsustainable in isolation from the sea itself, whence came the goods essential to their physical sustenance. The major purveyors of these primary necessities were the agricultural lands along the Nile, and the traffic in foodstuffs across the Red Sea was heavily oriented in the direction of the Arabian shore.[33] Indeed, the entire Hijaz was reliant on grains coming from the opposite side, and originating for the most part in the Egyptian delta. This geo-bio-social feature of the region was given divine consecration in the Quran, when the prophet Abraham implores: "O our Lord! I have made some of my offspring to dwell in a valley without cultivation, by Thy Sacred House; in order, O our Lord, that they may establish regular Prayer: so fill the hearts of some among men with love towards them, and feed them with fruits: so that they may give thanks."[34]

This state of dependence was not limited to the Hijaz: descriptions of the market of the Yemeni city of Mocha, for example, often note the ubiquitous presence of goods from the opposite shore, especially of the edible kind (and usually described as "Abyssinian" in origin by Western writers). Eyles Irwin noticed this when passing through the area in the late 1770s, describing the predicament of the Red Sea world well:

> To survey the desart on which it stands, a stranger must be surprized at the plenty which reigns in the markets. There is not a tree within ken, that produces any fruit, but the date, or herbage of any kind, to support the cattle which are daily exposed for sale.... And indeed, when we are informed that the sheep which are sold here, are all brought from the opposite coast of Abyssinia, and the simplest vegetable, at no less a distance than fifteen miles from Mocha, conjecture would lose itself in accounting for such plenty, were a clue not given to unravel the mystery.[35]

There is clear evidence that this had been the case already in antiquity: the *Periplus of the Erythraean Sea* mentions the export of grain from the ancient emporium of Berenike, seemingly close to the border between modern Egypt and Sudan, to ports on all sides of the Red Sea, notably its southeastern coast.[36]

In the opposite direction, the most important movement of agriculture in the Ottoman period concerned the trade in coffee. For the first two centuries of its consumption, this was an exclusively Red Sea commodity. Grown in the elevated hills of the Yemen, it was, for the most part, shipped off from any one of the port cities of the Tihama coast, mainly Hudayda, Luhayya, and Mocha.[37]

But perhaps the most conspicuous material dearth in this nautical environment was the absence anywhere nearby of a source of adequate timber for the construction of boats. An elaborate network of transmaritime and transcontinental exchanges thus existed from the earliest times to make possible the crossing of the sea.[38] Indeed, what Lionel Casson describes as "the world's first articulate record of large-scale overseas commerce" concerned the importation of timber for shipbuilding from Mount Lebanon to Egypt, as recorded by a scribe celebrating one of the great accomplishments of Pharaoh Snefru: "Bringing of forty ships filled with cedar logs."[39] Certainly, the remains at the ancient port of Berenike show that the Romans imported wood into the Red Sea area through extensive routes of global exchange.[40] Moreover, even before this historic record, the waters of the Red Sea were, in all probability, some of the first to be navigated.[41] At the core of the Red Sea as a historical actor thus lay a tense paradox: because of its strategic, commercial, and cultural importance, it had to have a certain population at various points, yet it is thoroughly inhospitable; it absolutely had to be navigated, if only to sustain the population and foster commercial exchange, yet for the very same geological reasons navigation of its waters was full of dangers; and given the absence of trees locally, it could not produce ships in sufficient quantities and at an adequate speed. This essential peculiarity of the Red Sea was captured well by the great late fifteenth-century navigator Aḥmad ibn Mājid:

> The Sea of Qulzum al-ʿArab is the most dangerous of all the seas of the world and yet people use it more than all the seas of the world because of the "Ancient House" and the pilgrimage of the Prophet and because of the means of subsistence and the going and coming of food. The Ḥijāz is barren with little food. And on one side of it is the Green Yemen which is not cut off from it by road all the year round. In the autumn the Abyssinian and Indian Kharīf comes and in the winter the rain of the Arab coast reaches it (the Yemen) and so it remains fertile all the time. But the Ḥijāz remains barren because the winter rains never reach it except a little and the rains of Abyssinia in the Dabūr wind do not reach it from the Abyssian [*sic*] highlands.[42]

This translates, at the level of human settlement, into a remarkable vagary of the fate of the port cities along the shore. Since their very existence depended on dynamics outside of their direct control, their destiny was always uncertain. As John Meloy poetically writes, "The landscape of the Red Sea is littered with ghost towns."[43] Indeed, though the flow of traffic through the Red Sea, however variable across the years and centuries, never stopped, the specific routes and ports along the way display a striking variability: Aden, Mocha, Hudayda, Luhayya, Jiddah, Ayla, Tor, Qulzum, Suez, Qusayr, Aydhab, Sawakin, Dahlak, Mussawa—all of these, and there are many more running from antiquity to the present, were at some point or another major centers of regional and interregional trade; some of them are now mere ruins, revealing their past glories only through archaeological excavations, while others have seen their fortunes rise and fall, and sometimes even rise again (as in the special case of Aden, which, though outside the Red Sea proper, was always integrally connected to its maritime networks). Of these, only Jiddah demonstrates an unusual longevity, due no doubt to its special location at the center of the concordance zone between the disparate wind regimes of the northern and southern Red Sea, and as the gateway to the noble sanctuaries of the Hijaz.

At any rate, strong data point toward the Red Sea being the site of some of the earliest human coastal colonization and maritime activity: "Recent discoveries confirm that in the Middle Stone Age, some 125,000 years ago, early modern humans (*Homo Sapiens*) settled a coastal strip on the Buri Peninsula, in what is now modern Eritrea."[44] In fact, the earliest hominid remains anywhere were found not too far from the coast, in the Afar Depression, a part of the larger rift complex of which the Red Sea is also the product. The most famous of these *Australopithecus afarensis,* Lucy (dated to approximately 3.2 million years ago), died about 320 kilometers from the sea.

It is typical of this peculiar place that, in the words of another archaeologist, "despite its importance, the Red Sea never spawned a civilization of its own," and, even more revealing, that the evidence itself of the maritime activities over the Red Sea is not indigenous but rather derives from regions further afield, notably the Nile valley.[45] The region's difficult natural conditions have made the actual shores of the Red Sea inhospitable to permanent settlement, needed for the development of a centralized authority likely to foster autonomous and enduring material or documentary production. Not too far inland, by contrast, are habitats ideal for the establishment of large and enduring urban societies (the Nile valley, the Ethiopian and Yemeni highlands, and oases of various sorts and sizes), all of which invested and competed in maintaining a presence on, and some control over, the coasts. The links between the well-watered and populated zones inland and the coast were facilitated by a broad network of natural draining channels that cut through the mountain escarpments that surround the sea at a right angle. "These wadis," explains Meloy, speaking of the Hijaz, though his words would apply to the entire Red Sea region, "serve as transportation routes through the mountains and occasionally yield springs, fed by groundwater that in places could be reached with minimal digging."[46] This helps explain the "surprisingly dense road system [that] was developed in the Eastern Desert of Egypt" already by the Romans.[47]

Like many other details, these special features had already been captured by Agatharchides. To the south of Egypt, he writes, there are four races of mankind: riverain peoples, marsh dwellers, nomads, and those who live by the sea. The latter race, he explains, "has neither towns nor districts, nor even the most rudimentary civilization. . . . The places nearest to the sea are devoid of all that might sustain life, as are also those adjacent to the great coasts. But the country inland offers good hunting; and the people are averse neither to fish nor to any kind of game."[48]

Humans have thus been interacting with the sea and its coast from time immemorial. The "Neolithic revolution" occurred (independently) to the north, east, and southeast, where agriculture was adopted and with it centralized political and social organizations. Two key transformative developments for human interactions around the Red Sea world were the domestication of the camel, which facilitated mobility and exchange along its arid shores, and the exponential rise in the so-called spice trade, primarily incense from the southern borders of the region and spices from further afield.[49] Both features probably began sometime in the second millennium BC and would continue to be characteristic of the area until well into the twentieth century. Indeed, from prehistoric up to postmodern times, the Red Sea has been one of the most important and navigated sea-lanes in the world. There are local and transregional reasons for this. One is the production of unique commodities along its shores, most famously incense and myrrh in antiquity and coffee under the Ottomans, but also a significant presence of mineral wealth of various kinds. Another is its role as a hyphen between the world of the Mediterranean and that of the Indian Ocean, and of course the world beyond them both as well: northern Europe, West Africa, and eventually the Americas to the west; and China and other parts of East Asia to the east. Finally, there is the location near the coast of the two holiest cities in Islam, pilgrimage to which is incumbent as a spiritual duty on every capable Muslim.

The rhythm of mobility and exchange in the Red Sea world was thus subjected to a triple cosmic metronome, as Michel Tuchscherer has noted: one followed the sun and the agricultural cycles of the harvesting and processing of the various crops (grains, spices, cotton, coffee, etc.), each of course having its appropriate timing; another abided by the major wind patterns evoked above; and yet another obeyed the moon, which determined the correct time for the pilgrimage.[50]

Though the specific peoples and goods concerned evolved over time, as did the particular ports and markets, the basic structures of trade and transportation followed a strikingly similar pattern throughout, from ancient Egyptian travels to the land of Punt for frankincense and myrrh, to the Mamluk retail in pepper, and on to the Ottoman commerce in Yemeni coffee and Indian goods, to mention only some of the most famous examples from across the ages. Braudel put it thus in his inimitable prose: "If pepper became commonplace and declined in value, tea, coffee, or calicoes were waiting in the wings to take the place of the former prima donna."[51]

In fact, a great variety of commodities, from the most habitual to the most rare, were traded in and through the region; and undoubtedly the greatest revenues derived from the more mundane items, such as cloth or grain. Perhaps the best lesson in this regard can be derived from the excavations at Qusayr al-Qadim: against all expectations, this port on the Egyptian coast that had been a nodal point of regional commercial networks showed little evidence of the so-called spice trade, containing instead remains of rather less lavish products.[52]

Moreover, it is important not to see such trade as a mere bipolar exchange between one end (western Indian Ocean) and the other (the Mediterranean/Europe)—many of the spices in question furnished a variety of locales, with Indian and Chinese markets probably consuming the most. This basic point was made long ago already by Marshall Hodgson; yet it seems in need of repetition given the power of attraction of the "spice trade" master-narrative.[53] Thus John Meloy, in his important study of Mecca, had to reaffirm Hodgson's insight, since the existing scholarship "tended to ignore that the economic benefit of this trade did not simply accrue to the terminal points of this commerce, whether in India or Italy, or to the major metropolitan centers along the way, such as Cairo, but also to all points in between."[54]

Even more fundamentally, in fact, the very abstract concept of spices, as it is conceived today, did not have a stable or coherent place in the conceptual grammar of earlier epochs. As Albert Dietrich shows, for example, there is no single Arabic word for "spices," and Arabic historical texts do not strictly differentiate between spices, condiments (*afāwīh, tawābil*), aromatic products (*ʿitr, ṭīb*), and medical drugs (*ʿakkār*), the various categories blending into each other depending on author, time, and place. In the tenth century, the famous scholar al-Masʿūdī classified twenty-five principal spices, yet this list does not include pepper, the most common and important spice as far as global trade is concerned; al-Dimashqī (twelfth century), by contrast, enumerates only thirteen important spices, and this time pepper (*fulful*) features, along with indigo (*nīl*), brazilwood (*baqqām*), incense (*lubān*), mastic (*mastaka*), and ginger (*zanjabīl*).[55] The standard term in Arabic today for spices (*bahār*) was also used historically, though it definitely did not have the currency and all-inclusiveness that it projects now.[56]

Similarly, though much has been written about "spice merchants," the contemporary sources do not give any indication that there was a separate commerce specializing in these products. The case of the famous, and still rather mysterious, *kārimī* merchants, who are often identified as "spice merchants," is indicative. Categories like *al-kārim* and *tujjār al-kārim* certainly do appear in the texts of the period, in reference to a number of major merchants and merchant fleets operating in the Red Sea region (mainly along the Cairo-Aden axis) between the eleventh and the fifteenth centuries, but these networks readily traded in numerous products in addition to "spices."[57]

Still, a constant feature of the Red Sea world in the very long term was its role as a hub for the exchange of commodities that were small and light but of great value at terminus (and all along the way, it goes without saying). And it is this spectacular trade, combining glamour and riches with the exotic and the mysterious, that has captured the imagination of visitors, administrators, and rulers (virtual, potential, or actual) from the earliest sources onwards. The first-century text *Anabasis of Alexander* by Arrian, which recounts the great conquests of the youthful Macedonian, speaks of a project that he entertained of conquering the land of the Arabs, attracted by what he had heard of the natural wealth of this country where "people obtained cassia from the lakes, and myrrh and frankincense from the trees," "cinnamon was cut from the shrubs," and "meadows produce spikenard without any cultivation."[58]

The mortuary temple of Hatshepsut, across the river from Luxor, clearly depicts a maritime expedition on the waters of the Red Sea reaching for the Land of Punt, from which Egypt had been importing numerous goods, notably myrrh and incense, for centuries already. A number of reliefs portray myrrh and incense trees, and the attendant texts refer explicitly to the trade in these highly aromatic products that were central to rituals of life and death in the ancient Egyptian tradition (as in many others).

In the Bible, too, the southern end of the Red Sea (under the name of the kingdom of Sheba) is repeatedly associated with myrrh and frankincense, and exchanges in these commodities between the various regions involved are mentioned quite often—again, in connection with ritual practices. A celebration of royal expeditions in the Red Sea, remarkably resonant with Hatshepsut's, is consecrated in the Book of Kings: "Now three times a year Solomon offered burnt offerings and peace offerings on the altar which he built to the Lord, burning incense with them on the altar which was before the Lord. So he finished the house. / King Solomon also built a fleet of ships in Ezion-geber, which is near Eloth on the shore of the Red Sea, in the land of Edom" (1 Kings 9:25–26). In this case, however, the navy sails to the (nowadays equally mysterious) Land of Ophir, and the only mentioned merchandise they bring back is gold. In the New Testament, frankincense and myrrh appear perhaps most famously as two out of the three gifts offered to the newborn Jesus by the Three Magi (Matt. 2:11).

The centrality of this trade to the constitution of the historical character of the Red Sea as a narrativized space cannot be overstated. Indeed, as Steven Sidebotham writes, "Frankincense and myrrh were consumed in prodigious amounts for funerary, religious, and medicinal purposes in the Mediterranean world [and presumably elsewhere too, especially around the Red Sea] throughout antiquity, and in ever-increasing amounts in Roman times, as numerous contemporary authors tell us."[59] As in the case of coffee in Ottoman times, the southern Red Sea world, which retained a quasi-monopoly over the culture of the delectable plants in question, was apparently never able to produce sufficient quantities to satisfy demand.

Commercially even more important than myrrh and incense, perhaps, was the transoceanic trade in condiments, especially but not exclusively pepper, which derived primarily from age-old zones of production in the eastern parts of the Indian Ocean. In this case as well, the Red Sea features prominently throughout the ages. Archaeological evidence indicates that pepper was reaching Mediterranean ports from at least the second millennium BC.[60] The Red Sea was not the only route available for the peppers and spice to reach the Mediterranean (the main alternative was the Persian Gulf and overland through the Syrian desert), but it was certainly a constant one, "one whose activity was rarely interrupted since antiquity," to quote the great social historian of the region André Raymond.[61] The particular centrality of the Red Sea derives in part from its location: the entire southern half is an inherent part of the major global highway constituted by the monsoon, which permitted an enormous span of the world's inhabited spaces to be integrally connected, so that from very early on one could go back and forth across the Indian Ocean within a single calendar year.

But the most common and cumulatively high-value merchandise consisted of the more banal items of everyday necessity: cloth (linen, cotton, wool, silk), ceramics, grain, and the like. Cotton especially, primarily produced in India but also in Egypt, and consumed avidly throughout the Red Sea and Mediterranean regions and beyond, from antiquity to the modern period, features prominently in any discussion of Red Sea trade networks, as do foodstuffs, for all the geographical, climatic, and ideological reasons evoked above.

A further remark needs to be made concerning the commercial flows in and through the Red Sea: as mentioned above, various commodities traveled in a multiplicity of directions, and, considering the nature of the evidence, the trade is difficult to quantify properly.[62] One unmistakable feature of the structure of the transit trade over the *longue durée*, however, is the flow of bullion eastwards. This "does not necessarily indicate a balance-of-trade deficit" on the part of the Mediterranean economies, as Sidebotham rightly cautions in relation to the Roman period, for this bullion may have had multiple uses and was itself differentially commoditized.[63] Still, one cannot fail to note this characteristic of interregional exchanges over the centuries, a feature so startling that one authoritative commentator, specializing this time in the Ottoman period though referring to a long-term phenomenon, speaks of a "constant hemorrhage of cash [*numéraire*] from the Mediterranean in the direction of India and the Far East."[64]

The merchants operating this trade, both short and long distance, were remarkably diverse in cultural, religious, linguistic, and social background, and varied over the ages. The ships used were also of numerous types; and though it is clear that most, if not all, of the material necessary for shipbuilding was imported into the Red Sea region from more fertile lands beyond (mainly India and neighboring islands), it is equally incontestable that ships were nevertheless constructed in local shipyards.[65] Indeed, Margariti has demonstrated that shipbuilding in Aden was sufficiently profitable and reliable to warrant investments by intercontinental merchant alliances. The port of Aden (at least in the Fatimid, Ayyubid, and Rasulid periods) included all the institutions and resources necessary for naval construction, with the material often imported by way of associates on the western coast of India.[66]

Teak (*sāj*), abundant in Southeast Asia, was unanimously appreciated as, quite simply, the best timber for ocean-bound ships. Perhaps the most distinctive feature of the boats of the Red Sea in particular and the Indian Ocean more largely was that they were sewn together by cords and fibers, with no use of metal whatsoever, whether frames or nails. Although one archaeological find may indicate the use of iron nails in the northern Red Sea before the arrival of the Portuguese in the Indian Ocean, the overwhelming evidence (mainly textual, but also pictorial, material, and even ethnographic) points to the ubiquitous construction of metal-free crafts stitched with natural cords. The *Periplus of the Erythraean Sea* already refers to this characteristic of the local boats—indeed, so remarkable a feature that it explicitly bequeathed its name to the attendant port.[67] The Andalusian Ibn Jubayr (d. 1217 CE) offers a vivid portrait of vessels built in the Egyptian port of Aydhab in his famous travel narrative, though his view is somewhat tinged by a bad experience at sea and warped by a typical sense of the superiority of (Mediterranean and Atlantic) ships fastened by metal nails.[68]

NARRATIVE EMPLOTMENT

As mentioned above, the Red Sea was probably one of the earliest seas to be navigated, and by the time the *Periplus of the Erythraean Sea* was written by an unnamed, but practiced, traveler the area was fairly integrated into well-trodden networks of exchange, so that in the period of late antiquity (2nd-6th c.), not only would regional powers increasingly seek to appropriate the wealth and strategic assets associated with the sea (including, for example, the state of Aksum, which would expand *across* the sea into southern Arabia), but also a more amorphous cultural diffusion paralleling commercial interaction is clearly evident. Indeed, it has been suggested that the remarkable expansion of both Judaism and Christianity in the region at this time must be understood as operating as a part of these larger dynamics. The increased commercial exchanges throughout the shores in the fourth century and beyond led to unprecedented integration of the zone and to the "emergence of a 'globalizing' Hellenic and Judeo-Christian *koine* culture throughout the Red Sea basin, naturally to varying degrees of adoption and assimilation, but nonetheless universal in breadth."[69]

Contacts were intensifying both within the region and without, all along the eastern Mediterranean and the Indian Ocean, following the monsoon winds, from its east African to its east Asian coasts. There seems to be a wider dynamic at play here, since navigation was intensifying in the western Indian Ocean and the Pacific Ocean too.[70] At the very heart of it all, Sri Lanka can be seen as the prototypical emblem of this globalizing thrust of the late antique world system, as described by the famous sixth-century Alexandrine traveler and monk Cosmas Indicopleustes:

> The island [of Sri Lanka] being, as it is, in a central position, is much frequented by ships from all parts of India and from Persia and Ethiopia, and it likewise sends out many of its own. And from the remotest countries, I mean Tzinista [China] and other trading places, it receives silk, aloes, cloves, sandalwood and other products, and these again are passed on to marts on this side, such as Male [Malabar coast], where pepper grows, and to Calliana [Kaliana, near Bombay] which exports copper and sesame-logs, and cloth for making dresses, for it also is a great place of business. And to Sind also where

> musk and castor is procured and spikenard, and to Persia and the Himyarite country, and to Adulis. And the island receives imports from all these marts which we have mentioned and passes them on to the remoter ports, while, at the same time, exporting its own produce in both directions.[71]

It was within this gravitational field of a nascent world system, an "archipelago of world cities" in the felicitous expression of Janet Abu-Lughod (who is speaking of a later period), that Muḥammad ibn ʿAbd Allah would soon be born and would eventually oversee the launching of "the venture of Islam," to borrow another famous formulation. The pre-Islamic and early Islamic history of the Hijaz is quite simply unintelligible if abstracted from the Red Sea world of which it formed an integral part, as are the strikingly rapid conquests that followed the consolidation of the Islamic polity in the peninsula if one ignores the various networks of mobility and exchange of which the Red Sea was a crucial hub. Its geostrategic location as well as its own resources and the long-standing mutual interdependence of its various shores are key factors in the constitution and rapid spread of the new faith.

As for the importance of the broader environment, suffice it to mention that there are numerous loan words in the Quran itself from a variety of different languages present in the wider Red Sea world;[72] that the Kaʿba was rebuilt not long before the beginning of Muḥammad's revelation by a Greek, Coptic, or Ethiopian carpenter, who used, in this land with so little native timber, the remains of a shipwreck;[73] and that, to escape the persecution of the Meccan authorities, a significant number of the Prophet's companions took refuge across the sea in Abyssinia, in repeated waves of migration.

The importance of wider networks and flows in the rapid expansion of the new Islamic polity is attested by massive evidence, from narratives of travels far and wide of some early Muslims, to the speedy foundation of a number of new ports around the Red Sea. The ancient canal linking the Red Sea to the Nile was reopened by the new Muslim governor of Egypt, ʿAmr ibn al-ʿĀṣ, in the effort to alleviate the food penuries in the Hijaz, and more largely, to further integrate the Red Sea, which would soon be dominated in its entirety by the Caliphate. Known earlier as Trajan's Canal in honor of the famous Roman emperor, it was now renamed *Khalīj amīr al-muʾminīn*, after the new ruler, and it connected Fustat, a newly founded garrison town on the Nile, to the port of al-Qulzum (the previous incarnation of Suez, established in a later century not far away) at the head of the Gulf, where the river reaches closest to the sea. The great Cairene scholar al-Maqrīzī (d. 1442 CE) describes this canal as well as its predecessors going back to antiquity and connects it explicitly to the sustenance of the Hijaz. The first to dig the canal, explained al-Maqrīzī, was Ṭūṭīs ibn Mālīā, one of the rulers of Egypt who lived in the town of Memphis and was a contemporary of the Prophet Abraham. When Abraham took his wife Sarah's Egyptian handmaiden Hagar and her young son and installed them in the Hijaz, Hagar wrote to the Egyptian king, telling him about the arid desolation around her and asking for relief. Ṭūṭīs then ordered the digging of the canal, ships were sent with foodstuffs to Jiddah, and the Hijaz was thus vitalized.[74]

In the following periods, under the Umayyad and the Abbasid dynasties, the Red Sea world witnessed further integration, especially as the new order maintained great symbolic investment in the Hijaz, the destination of a growing yearly pilgrimage traffic, often maritime. There is also evidence of an intensification of mining exploration and exploitation on the surrounding shores, rich in a variety of mineral products, and of the maintenance of the transmaritime eastern trade from the Mediterranean to the Yellow Sea.

The last third of the tenth century constitutes a significant watershed for the region, as the Fatimid dynasty, installed in Tunisia since the beginning of the century, conquered Egypt from the Abbasids. Already before them the Ikhshidid dynasty, though nominal vassals to the caliph in Baghdad, and even the Tulunids before that, had ruled the northern Red Sea (and eastern Mediterranean) coasts as an autonomous entity. This configuration, with the Red Sea increasingly at the heart of a broad administrative unit, was consolidated by the Fatimids and was bequeathed to all subsequent rulers, culminating in the emergence in the thirteenth century of the Mamluk sultanate based in Cairo and of the Rasulid dynasty on the other side of the sea in Aden (both taking over from the Ayyubids, who had replaced the Fatimids and had returned the region to the nominal suzerainty of the Abbasid caliph in Baghdad). Throughout, the implication of the social and political elites in regional trade emerges clearly in the historical sources, and it is incontestable that the sea played a crucial role in the economic, diplomatic, and symbolic structures of the various surrounding states. Perhaps most famous in this regard are the various attempts in the years 1420–30 on the part of the Mamluk sultan al-Ashraf Barsbāy to formalize more strictly the relationship between trade and state. Too much has been said about his so-called politics of monopoly over the spice trade; these were instead, as John Meloy clearly shows, a series of precise, almost pointillistic, though also coherent, interventions that targeted specific products (sugar, pepper) with the goal of augmenting the revenues of the central treasury, part of a broader logic of imperial expansion (for example, by adopting Jiddah instead of Aden as the principal entrepôt of the transoceanic trade). The policy was also a response to certain local political constraints (such as the sharing of power over the Hijaz with the Meccan sharifs).[75] Though perennially difficult to quantify, the available evidence has led to a scholarly consensus that the dynamism of the Red Sea region was ever-increasing in these centuries because of the heightened integration of mobility and exchange throughout the Indian Ocean, the further spread of Islam along many of its coasts, and the added importance given to the pilgrimage to Mecca.

Another enduring legacy from the period on the constitution of the Red Sea was the establishment of numerous and sizable pious foundations (Arabic *awqāf,* sing. *waqf*), the products and revenues of which were earmarked explicitly for the sustenance of the Hijaz. This was especially, though by no means exclusively, the case in Egypt under the Mamluks (there were similar *awqāf* in Yemen, for example, and there is clear evidence of similar practices in previous administrations too).[76] Still, the Mamluk regime of Cairo put great effort into consolidating a steady trend of provisioning the Hijaz from its fertile lands—a tradition that would endure the subsequent profound transformation of the political organization of the Red Sea. It is well known that the inhabitants of the Hijaz were provided for, under the aegis of the Ottoman state, almost entirely through the establishment of such foundations, a practice it inherited directly from the former rulers. Thus "[Mamluk] sultan Djaḳmaḳ and Ḳaʾitbāy's endowments for the Holy Cities (*dashīsha kubrā*) were enlarged by [Ottoman sultans] Selīm I and Süleymān the Magnificent; Murād III made a new endowment called the *dashīsha ṣughrā,* and Meḥemmed IV's wife also alienated agricultural land in Egypt for the Holy Cities. The Ottomans thus supported the *Ḥaramayn* mainly with the *waḳf* revenue of Egyptian land. Following Ḳaʾitbāy's example, Süleymān and Murād III endowed ships for the transportation of wheat from Egypt to Mecca and Medina."[77]

Following in the footsteps of their Mamluk predecessors, the armies of Sultan Selīm the First (also known by the sobriquet *Yavuz,* implying a mixture of stern, ferocious, inexorable, and good) conquered the lands surrounding the entire Red Sea in a highly deliberate, strategic move. The Mamluks had already been consolidating their control over the area for the preceding century or so. As mentioned above, the Red Sea region had been the prime area of operations of Mamluk economic policy and expansionism at least since Sultan Barsbāy (1422–37), who sought to redirect trade and traffic within it by favoring Jiddah as main emporium. The focus on the region only gained pace as the Portuguese suddenly erupted into the Indian Ocean world and sought to become direct rivals.

The Ottomans invaded the northern flanks of the Mamluk sultanate just as the Mamluks were seeking to extend their hegemony over all the contours of the Red Sea and beyond. It is quite ironic, as Albert Kammerer noted long ago, that the spring of 1517 saw the execution, two thousand kilometers apart but within a month of each other, of the last Tahirid sultan in Yemen by a Mamluk force and of the last Mamluk sultan in Egypt by order of the Ottoman sultan.[78] Since he was left at the helm of the home front, al-Ashraf Ṭūmān Bāy did not suffer the terrible defeat of Marj Dabiq (August 1516) where his predecessor al-Ashraf Qānsūh al-Ghūrī was killed, and he even survived Yavuz Selīm's triumphant entry into Cairo as he escaped toward Giza across the Nile. From there, Ṭūmān Bāy headed a series of encounters, both military and diplomatic, with the new rulers of Cairo, but he was eventually captured, killed, and left hanging for three days at the entrance of the city at Bāb Zuwayla. This happened, according to the chronicler of the Ottoman conquest of Egypt Ibn Iyās, on the 22nd of *Rabīʿ al-awwal* 923 AH (April 15, 1517 CE).[79]

Over approximately the same period, forces under the leadership of Ḥusayn al-Kurdī sent originally by Qānsūh al-Ghūrī in the direction of the Indian Ocean were taking over Yemen from its Banū Ṭāhir rulers, who had succeeded the Banū Rasūl as the main sovereigns of the strategically and commercially crucial hub that dominated the Gulf of Aden and the entrance to the Red Sea. Though an erstwhile ally of Qānsūh al-Ghūrī, from whom he had requested military aid, the Tahirid sultan ʿĀmir ibn ʿAbd al-Wahhāb became estranged from the Mamluk forces once they approached his lands too closely. Installed on the barren Kamaran Island, Ḥusayn al-Kurdī had requested provisions from the Yemeni ruler, who refused; thus began the Mamluk conquest of Yemen, supported by new local allies. And though Sultan ʿĀmir survived the taking of the cities of Zabid, Taiz, and others, he was eventually overwhelmed and died in battle. It was, according to the chronicler of the Ottoman conquest of Yemen al-Nahrawālī, the 23rd of *Rabīʿ al-ākhir* 923 AH (May 14, 1517 CE), that is, just about thirty days after the death of Ṭumān Bāy.[80]

This chronological concordance was in no way a coincidence. The ships of the Portuguese crown had attempted to close off maritime access to the Red Sea in 1507, had roundly defeated an allied Mamluk-Gujarati fleet off the coast of Diu in 1509, had laid siege to Aden and occupied the island of Kamaran in 1513, and had set their sights on Egypt and Palestine even as they attempted to divert the so-called spice trade from its traditional amphibian ways (via the Persian Gulf and, more commonly, the Red Sea) to the maritime route around the Cape of Good Hope. The commercial, political, and religious system of the entire region, with the Red Sea and eastern Mediterranean as its hub, was at risk.[81]

Ottoman naval and military men (to say nothing of traders, pilgrims, and others) had been present in the Red Sea ports well before the formal annexation of the region. Even further afield, there had been an extensive network of Ottoman émigrés, as Giancarlo Casale calls them, across the ocean on the Indian coast. In fact, the fleet that the Mamluk sultan Qānṣūh al-Ghūrī was building in Suez following the defeat of Diu to confront the Portuguese in the Indian Ocean once again was largely financed by Ottoman benefaction and manned by Ottoman subjects. The commander of the fleet that departed Suez in 1515 was none other than Selmān Reʾīs, who would subsequently play a major part in Ottoman policy around the Indian Ocean.[82] Selmān Reʾīs's fleet was at sea when news arrived of the Ottoman routing of the Mamluks at the battle of Marj Dābiq and of the possible change of sovereignty over the entire area. He thus returned with his fleet to Jiddah, where he declared allegiance to Yavuz Selīm, and successfully defended the city from a Portuguese attack in the spring of 1517, just as Ṭumān Bāy and ʿĀmir ibn ʿAbd al-Wahhāb were facing their terminal fate.[83]

For the Ottomans, then, controlling that area was a first step in the assumption of their new position in a changed *nomos* of the earth, which resulted from the beginning of the conquest of the Americas by the Iberians and the penetration of the Portuguese into the world of the Indian Ocean, along with the rise of the Safavid and Mughal powers.[84] The Ottoman expansion over the region did not happen overnight but was a long-drawn-out affair, with many setbacks, that took much of the rest of the century.

Thereafter, almost all of the lands surrounding the Red Sea were in effect to remain within the Ottoman fold for four centuries, after which the region, along with the rest of the empire, transmuted into the nation-states recognizable today. The sole (and only partial) exception is the case of Yemen: there, the imam of Sana'a succeeded, by the second quarter of the seventeenth century, in extending his authority all the way down most of the coast until the second quarter of the nineteenth century, when the Ottoman state (by way of its local strongman, the governor of Egypt Meḥmed ʿAlī) again gradually took control over all of southern Arabia. The firmness of Ottoman control obviously varied, depending on period and area. In some zones, it did not reach as far inland away from the shores as elsewhere. But the Red Sea was clearly an Ottoman lake (as much as such a turn of phrase can be taken to mean anything for this period at all).

Concerning this historic moment, a well-known document remains in the archive of the Topkapı palace in Istanbul.[85] It is a remarkably suggestive report from 1525 CE on the Ottoman garrison in Jiddah and on the new global situation resulting from the presence of the Portuguese in the Indian Ocean. Though it is unsigned, its author is generally acknowledged as being Selmān Reʾīs, the Ottoman admiral and corsair mentioned above. He was clearly devoted to convincing the powerful grand vizier, who had just arrived in Egypt to subdue a revolt and consolidate Ottoman control, of the virtues of sending another naval expedition, so some of his conclusions were evidently exaggerated (for example, he suggested that the Ottomans could expel the Portuguese from the totality of their Indian Ocean possessions if only they rearmed the fleet present at Jiddah). Of special relevance to the present argument is the fact that the author envisioned the area of the Red Sea, extended into the Gulf of Aden, as a coherent geostrategic entity that should be treated as such by Ottoman policy. Following an exposition of the conditions of the squadron in the port of Jiddah, and the holdings of the Portuguese around the Indian Ocean, the report follows the coasts of the Red Sea and Gulf of Aden (mainly focusing on the provinces of Yemen and Abyssinia and their surroundings), decrying the state of generalized oppression because of tyrannical rulers, both Muslim and non-Muslim, or anarchy, and urging the intervention of the Sublime Porte. The report is also highly explicit regarding potential financial returns: not only does it describe a number of resources of the various lands, especially Yemen, whose "resources are unlimited" (*ḥaṣılının ḥaddi va ḥasrı olmayup*), but also it complains of the Portuguese monopolization of the spice trade, which in the past accrued to the province of Egypt.[86] The Ottomans did send a number of naval expeditions into the Indian Ocean, which became for the subsequent few decades the site of a drawn-out maritime world war. They never succeeded in forcing the Portuguese out of the Indian Ocean arena, but neither did the Portuguese manage to roll the Ottomans back in the Red Sea, so that in the end a certain implicit modus vivendi imposed itself upon all parties.

It is important to repeat, here, the well-established fact (analyzed by Braudel himself) that the arrival of the Europeans in the Indian Ocean did not fundamentally disrupt the age-old dynamism of the Red Sea as an integrated space of exchange.[87] Indeed, the Portuguese did not even have much of an enduring impact on the "spice trade," except perhaps sporadically, and they certainly never succeeded in blockading the commercial routes that went through Ottoman domains. Only with the installation in the Indian Ocean, in subsequent centuries, of the Dutch and the English and their successful attempt to control the zones of production of the spices themselves were the patterns of trade affected significantly, and the all-maritime route around the Cape began to take an increasing share of the imports of spices into Europe (indeed, it led, eventually, to the arrival of these spices in Ottoman markets). Still, as André Raymond has demonstrated, though the exports to Europe by way of the Red Sea certainly decreased, these formed only a small part of the commercial dynamics of this region—and the continuation of the trade by way of the Red Sea had much to do with the opening of the vast internal market of the Ottoman space, the new administrative framework that extended across enormous terrains. Moreover, the trade in coffee, grown in Yemen, had witnessed a tremendous boom in the sixteenth and seventeenth centuries and contributed significantly to the continuing wealth of the Red Sea structure of trade. Over the course of the eighteenth century these tendencies remain in evidence, even though coffee, as in the case of the spices before, would penetrate the Ottoman market from Europe and its colonies too. Not until the nineteenth century, concludes Raymond, did "the reversal of trade patterns produce a veritable revolution in the great commerce of Egypt, by including Egypt in the world market of which Europe had become the center."[88]

It is in this context then, and in light of the long-term destiny of the Red Sea, that the regional policies of the Ottoman governor of Egypt, Meḥmed ʿAlī Paşa, must be read. Like many before him, he sought to project his power over the contours of the Red Sea as a geostrategic whole, extending inland into the Arabian and African interiors.[89] Indeed, Fred Lawson, inspired notably by the pioneering work of Peter Gran, has argued that much of "Egyptian expansionism" during this period can be explained by the state's consolidated alliance with the Red Sea merchants in Cairo and their shared interest in facilitating commercial interaction throughout the sea.[90] From this angle, even the conquest of the province of Syria by the paşa should be read as conducted "partly to dislodge outsiders from the Red Sea trade."[91] Whatever the possible reductionism of this thesis, as Khaled Fahmy avers in his critique, it is incontestable that the paşa of Cairo, in invading the lands surrounding the Red Sea as a whole, was simply pursuing, as Fernand Braudel would have put it, the "geographical mission" of that particular space, which he ruled.[92] Already in early 1811 al-Jabartī describes well the strategic ambitions over the sea as a whole: "On arriving in Suez, [Meḥmed ʿAlī Paşa] confiscated the boats which had arrived with the *maḥmal.* He sent out some of the ships he had built to seize the boats and ships that were in the ports. He took possession of the coffee he found in Suez belonging to the merchants. . . . [It was reported that he] had sent five of the ships he had built from Suez to the Yemen in order to commandeer any ships they found."[93]

These circumstances, and their accompanying events, led to what Isa Blumi calls a "local scramble for ascendancy" in the Red Sea arena, involving a multiplicity of actors, from small-scale indigenous leaders to the well-established East India Company and newly globalized traders from North America. Building upon other treaties imposed in various locations around the Indian Ocean (notably in and around the Persian Gulf, beginning with the 1798 friendship agreement with Sulṭān ibn Aḥmad Āl Bū Saʿīd of Muscat, and the famous "General Treaty" of 1820, which changed the Pirate Coast into the Trucial Coast), Bombay took advantage of anxieties concerning Egyptian expansionism to take control of the strategic port of Aden, which dominated the entrance to the Red Sea and would operate as a crucial coaling station for steamers on the route to India.[94] This was the prelude to the swan song of the Red Sea as an autonomous and coherent space, as far as world history is concerned. Though, of course many of the dynamics described in this chapter continued, in one way or another, well beyond that date, and indeed continue to this very day, the British settlement of Aden, followed by the increasing mechanization of sea travel, the opening of the Suez Canal, and eventually the occupation of Egypt in 1882 would radically transform the structures and flows in and around the Red Sea, making it increasingly appear like the figure of Facey's "sea on the way to somewhere else." This image, in turn, has resulted in the great difficulty that the historiography has had in formulating the Red Sea as a coherent actor in the long-term historical drama, meaningful in and of itself, rather than simply as an empty corridor connecting other times and places.

TRACING A RED SEA COMMODITY

Perhaps no single thing conjures up, just in itself, the Ottoman Red Sea and its world better than coffee, a bean with an aroma so potent and delicious, it had to be either divine or diabolical. To those who professed that "he who dies with some coffee in his body enters not into hell-fire," others warned that those who consumed coffee would appear on the Day of Judgment with faces darker than the drink.[95] It was a concoction so distinctly Ottoman that most post-Ottoman states have sought to claim it as part of their specific national tradition (Greek coffee, Cyprus coffee, Turkish coffee, etc.) and a drug so special it seemed both luxurious and popular at the same time. The early nineteenth-century Cairene scholar ʿAbd al-Raḥmān al-Jabartī's chronicle shows this well: on two successive pages, coffee is listed as part of a "splendid gift" that is offered to the Ottoman governor by the erstwhile strongman in Egypt Ismāʿīl Bey, yet is also referred to as an "everyday need."[96] Though the drink was famously much appreciated by the highest echelons of the Ottoman elite (the emperor Sulaymān the Magnificent himself was said to be an early aficionado), coffee's association with "the rabble" is just as much a leitmotif of its history.[97]

In his magisterial exploration of "the structures of everyday life" in the early modern world, Braudel writes that the history of coffee is dangerous because so prone to the legendary, that supposedly antihistorical genre par excellence: "There is a danger that the history of coffee may lead us astray. The anecdotal, the picturesque, and the unreliable play an enormous part in it."[98] Perhaps exemplary of Braudel's misgivings about such a venture is the now common myth of origin of the human consumption of coffee. Like all good legends, this one is highly realistic, and rather plausible, even though it is quite improbable. It recounts the story of a shepherd (in either the Ethiopian or the Yemeni highlands) who eventually joined his goats in chewing the berries of an unfamiliar bush that produced excitement.[99]

Counterintuitively, and despite the undoubted mystique of the fabulous beverage, the problem with the conjugation of coffee and history is almost the very opposite of Braudel's concern: the danger of the history of coffee is its tendency to lead us astray into the standard Eurocentric master-narrative of modernity and colonial globalization. Indeed, Braudel at least is refreshingly candid about his perspective on world history and the place of coffee within it, for example when he confidently asserts that "Europe, at the centre of the innovations of the world, discovered three new drinks, stimulants and tonics: coffee, tea and chocolate."[100] This statement contains all of the problems related to the history of coffee in concentrate. "Europe" in this view is a self-evident, straightforward, natural entity. Not only that, it is in fact the *central* entity in world history. It is, indeed, at the center of *the innovations of the world.* Finally, Braudel's use of the term *discovery* reveals his point of departure: as with the Americas and their discovery, before the White Man appears there is nothing of significance. The drinks supposedly "discovered" by Europe in the seventeenth century were all, of course, a major part of the diet of innumerable peoples before that, and had been for a while. But obviously it is of little importance, since the critical juncture is when these drinks, or these continents, or whatever else, were *discovered by Europe.* The story, as it is told in most accounts of the history of coffee, thus begins with the birth of the product in some foreign land, namely Ethiopia, but only as a manner of demonstrating subsequently the domination and domestication of the non-European by Europe. Most histories of coffee begin with the propagation of the coffee plant—that is, its appropriation by the colonial powers, with quite a few heroic vignettes of the great men involved. Thus the recent book *Histoire du café* by Frédéric Mauro, the major French historian of Portugal, Brazil, and the Atlantic world, as well as William Ukers's earlier classic *All about Coffee* (first published in 1922), upon which it is based, both open their accounts with the domestication of the product by the Europeans.[101] This is because the history of coffee fits into a larger model whereby the history of the rest of the world becomes folded into the grand narrative of the making of the modern West.

Without a doubt, much of the subsequent history of Europe and its global extensions is unthinkable without such staple colonial crops as coffee (and many others, such as sugar, cotton, and tobacco). But the obvious problem with such a formula is that it fetishizes the West and relegates the rest to the simple role of being a nursery, producing primary goods for consumption elsewhere. And it invites the reader to ignore the simple fact that, as Tuchscherer notes in his introduction to the important collection of articles on the coffee trade *before* that great expansion of the colonial plantations: "The first of coffee's adventures spans a lengthy period of about four centuries, which remains poorly known. For the most part, that history lies outside of Europe, first around the Red Sea, and then on the Muslim shore of the Mediterranean, and around the Indian Ocean."[102]

Indeed, the coffee plant is native to the region of the southern Red Sea. It is thought to have originated first in Ethiopia, and there is some evidence that the wild berry was consumed and even traded there.[103] But the bean truly became commoditized only after it crossed the sea to Yemen, where it was cultivated and commercialized over the course of the fifteenth century. An evergreen shrub classified within the large family of the Rubiaceae, it grows best at some altitude with climatic conditions combining high humidity with consistent warm temperatures along with significant rainfall. In other words, it was perfectly designed to flourish in the peculiar geographical area of the southern Red Sea world, which, as described at the beginning of this chapter, contained all the necessary characteristics: warm and humid all year round, like the rest of the zone, it had the added particularity of featuring high mountains on either side of the sea that captured the only significant water downpour that reaches the area. Sophisticated irrigation systems were developed early on to maintain regular moisture, and other, taller and leafier, trees were planted alongside the bushes if shade was needed from excessive sunlight.[104]

The earliest attested reference to coffee goes back to 1497, an invoice found at Tor in Sinai, with the husks of the bean (from which one type of coffee was made) mentioned alongside indigo, frankincense, and turmeric.[105] Thus, at the turn of the sixteenth century, not long before the Ottoman conquests in the region, coffee had already traversed the whole length of the Red Sea for purposes of commerce. The earliest narrative sources concerning coffee date from later in the century—a series of well-known works repeatedly discussed in the literature.[106] The most significant and probably the oldest such narrative source is the treatise entitled *ʿUmdat al-ṣafwa fī ḥall al-qahwa* by a certain ʿAbd al-Qādir al-Jazīrī, written in the late sixteenth century. It is a well-known text, canonized into the very structures of Orientalist pedagogy by its appearance in Silvestre de Sacy's foundational textbook for studying Arabic, *Chrestomathie arabe*.[107]

The various authors differ on the identity of the person who introduced the beverage to Yemen, but all accounts seem to corroborate two principal elements: as far as the actual plant is concerned, its origin is associated with Ethiopia; as for the spread of its consumption, it is in all references connected to the activities of Sufi brotherhoods. One *ṭariqa* in particular is intimately linked to coffee: the Shādhiliyya, one of whose *shaykhs* by the name of ʿAlī ibn ʿUmar al-Shādhilī is, in one version, associated with the introduction of the drink in Yemen; he is also deemed to have founded the port city of Mocha on the Yemeni Tihama—a town that would become so closely associated with coffee in the European imagination that it would bequeath its name to a version of the drink—and is often identified as the "patron saint of coffee-growers, coffee-house keepers and coffee-drinkers."[108] The association with Sufi congregations, and the Shādhiliyya order in particular, would follow the spread of coffee: the great Damascene scholar Ibn Ṭūlūn recounted the introduction of coffee into his native city as being due to the celebration of a *mawlid* by a Shādhilī shaykh.[109]

The migration of the plant and the drinking habit across the sea is not surprising: as mentioned above, relations between its many shores were endemic throughout the ages, and, more specifically, the connections between Ethiopia and Yemen were common, and probably increasing in this age of intensifying trade in the region. There is some evidence that the Rasulid rulers of Yemen, for example, sometimes claimed some form of suzerainty over the African coast as well. This would become incontestable with the Ottoman conquests along all the shores. The intimate interaction between the shores is in fact substantiated in the very story of the introduction of coffee, especially in the version put forward by Kātib Çelebī, where the narrative goes back and forth repeatedly between Sawakin on the western coast and Mocha on the eastern coast.[110] Further evidence of this intense cross-maritime interaction is the fact that the port city of Zeila, one the most important maritime outlets of southern Ethiopia and the Horn of Africa, came in the late seventeenth century under the control of the Qasimi imams, who had already managed to wrest control of most of Yemen from the Ottomans in the 1630s.[111]

It is absolutely crucial, in order to understand the remarkable story of the beginnings of coffee consumption, to keep in mind the thorough and long-standing internal integration of the Red Sea world, which was crisscrossed by multiple networks of mobility and exchange. Most significantly, these various connections across the sea transcended, in their general structure at least, the recurrent political upheavals in the region.[112]

Appreciation for the concoction spread quickly and extensively: following Ethiopia and Yemen, the habit took on in the Hijaz and in Egypt (as evidenced by the invoice found at Tor). Al-Jazīrī narrates the introduction of coffee in Cairo by way of the presence of Yemeni and Hijazi students in the famed al-Azhar mosque complex (where, indeed they had a special lodge [*riwāq*] dedicated to them) and dates it to the turn of the sixteenth century CE (actually, "the first decade of this [the tenth] century [AH]").[113] In Egypt too, its original spread is explicitly associated with the devotional practices of mystics (*fuqarāʾ*), who, the texts says, would drink it every Monday and Friday night to accompany their prayers and chants.[114] The lay audience too would partake in the drink, as the stimulant would allow them to stay awake and join in the nightly rituals. It thus circulated in the environs of the mosque and eventually beyond as well.[115]

Michel Tuchscherer suggests that coffee was being consumed in the Holy Cities of the Hijaz around 1475.[116] Further indication of the coherence of the Red Sea as an integrated zone of intense intermingling of the inhabitants of its various shores is the assertion by al-Jazīrī that the Hijazis knew of coffee as a natural product well before they had encountered the drink itself, since Abyssinians (*al-ḥabasha*) had the habit of chewing the beans in their country. About Mecca in particular, al-Jazīrī asserts that no *dhikr* or *mawlid* (popular religious events associated particularly with Sufism) would take place without the drink.[117] Beyond doubt is that in 1511 a Mamluk high official in Mecca Khāʾir Bey held a tribunal for the suspicious bean, where it was adjudged to be harmful (for mind, body, and society) and therefore illegal. The ensuing decree from the sultan in Cairo, however, did not confirm the negative ruling, and the consumption of coffee, having never stopped in secret, reverted to being licit and public.[118]

This was only the first of a series of disputes over the status of the drug and attempts at its prohibition.[119] The efforts to make coffee illegal always ended in failure, however: by the time it became a concern for the authorities, coffee had become a wildly popular drink, and it was too easily available around the Red Sea to make the recurrent bans succeed. In fact, the very inverse came to be true, as access to coffee developed into something of an entitlement—a right of the populace vis-à-vis the government, but even, seemingly, of a dependent vis-à-vis the head of a household.

By 1516–17, coffee was thus well entrenched in the mores of the peoples around the Red Sea (at least in the urban centers where cosmopolitan inhabitants would have been exposed to the practice). The Ottoman conquests in those years opened an enormous market for coffee consumption, and the new commodity exploited this windfall with massive success: within a few decades, coffee is well attested in the capital city itself, as well as in all the major cities along the way from the Hijaz or Cairo, whence it diffused, and beyond.[120] By the end of the century, the drug was increasingly present in smaller towns and even in some rural areas of the empire.[121] The expansion proceeded with lightning speed, leading to profound social and intellectual transformations, as the urban landscape as well as the mores, customs, tastes, and styles, indeed, the very "structures of everyday life," changed.

Certainly the "economic" organization was reformatted, as coffee came to constitute a major portion of trade but also a reliable standard in the economy of debt.[122] This was particularly the case in Yemen, where coffee was produced, and Jiddah, where the customs officials and transit merchants depended significantly on coffee, and even more so in Cairo, where coffee dominated big commerce, but also throughout the rest of the Ottoman space, where it was an essential item of exchange, from shipping lanes to coffeehouse queues.

One particular novelty that accompanied the increasing consumption of coffee reoriented Ottoman social space in a striking manner: the coffee shop, which began to spring up everywhere, often to the displeasure and anxiety of the authorities. Attending to the variability in the possible customers, coffeehouses ranged from the great and the sublime to the seedy and lowly. Some operated as religious or political rallying points, others served basically as brothels.[123] They were, in any case, tremendously popular. Within a few decades of the introduction of coffee in Istanbul, there were, according to Mouradgea d'Ohsson's famous account of the Ottoman Empire, over six hundred cafés in town.[124]

The changes ran in fact much deeper: not only did cafés emerge everywhere, ever more popular, because the product was affordable, and they were not necessarily improper (although they certainly could be), but, further, the very existence of such a new communal institution led to a transformation of the modes of sociability and civility, whereby basic notions such as public versus private were reoriented.[125] Along with the new practice and institution, there developed a new vocabulary and new tastes, indeed, a different way of living, as Cemal Kafadar has recently shown, involving the conquest of the night as a time of entertainment, socializing, work, and ritual, and changing norms of leisure, of literary and artistic form, of everyday life, and even of morality.[126]

As in the case of spices before it, the major world-historical shift was neither the arrival of the Europeans in the Mocha marketplace to buy coffee (especially given that they were always secondary customers and obtained lower-quality beans than those destined for the Ottoman market) nor the adoption of the drink in Europe, but rather the slow encroachment over the production process itself. In the case of spices, as mentioned above, this would begin with the installation of the Dutch in the spice-producing areas of the eastern Indian Ocean in the early seventeenth century; as for coffee, it occurred with the successful adoption of the crop in the early eighteenth century in both the East and West Indies. By the third decade of the eighteenth century, coffee from European colonial plantations was sold in Ottoman markets;

this was in some cases to the delight of the authorities in need of satisfying an ever-eager demand (especially in Istanbul), in others, to their chagrin, as it threatened powerful merchants' interests (as in Cairo, most prominently).[127] That said, the age-old structure of production and exchange of coffee in the Red Sea world did not disappear, with imported beans complementing rather than replacing the regional variety. To begin with, Yemeni coffee maintained an aura of superior quality, so that those Ottoman buyers who could afford it remained faithful.[128] Coffee merchants thus had to differentiate strictly between beans from the Red Sea and from elsewhere.[129]

Moreover, coffee culture on the African side of the southern Red Sea world increased significantly over the course of this period as well, much of its production also making its way into Ottoman lands. In any case, in the early nineteenth century coffee was clearly still a predominant item of trade in the region, notably at Suez and Jiddah, and all around the sea more largely.[130] Clear evidence of this is the simple fact that coffee prices in Cairo would skyrocket whenever the regular shuttle between the Hijaz and Egypt was disrupted.[131]

It was not until the turn of the twentieth century that the dynamics of coffee as a distinct feature of the Red Sea world shifted unrecognizably, as the enforced integration into the world economy compromised the integrity and coherence of that place in the middle.

TWO

Thalassology alla Turca

SIX THESES ON THE PHILOSOPHY OF HISTORY

AS A MODERN FIELD OF study, Ottoman historiography is unusual, primarily because of its ambivalent relation to that hegemon of hyper-reality, Europe—finding and placing itself both within and without. For much of its existence, the Ottoman Empire was dominated (demographically, economically, politically, ideologically) by its provinces in regions considered now geographically as part of Europe. This is something Ottoman authors often remarked upon when discussing the divisions of European geography, which the Well-Protected Domains straddled.

THE PROBLEM OF OTTOMAN STUDIES

Indeed, as mentioned above, the fountainhead of disciplined history, Leopold von Ranke himself, who was explicit in associating history with European identity, included a treatment of the Ottomans in the first volume of his history of southern Europe, alongside the Spaniards and the Italians. Ranke's contemporary (whom he cites, though sparingly), the Viennese diplomat and first president of the Austrian Academy of Sciences Joseph von Hammer-Purgstall, is often identified as the founding father of Ottoman historiography in the West, with the publication beginning in 1827 of his monumental ten-volume *Geschichte des osmanischen Reiches*. The Ottomans, unlike many others, thus had a place, however awkward, at the table of proper history. This was not always the case, however: Hegel, for example, had a much more dismissive attitude toward the world-historical role of those "Turks . . . who have proven themselves incapable of any culture."[1]

Neither completely Asiatic, nor simply European: this was the conundrum that the Western analysts of Ottoman history had to contend with, especially in the twentieth century as the elite of the nascent Turkish republic sought to exorcise its Oriental connections and assert a Western affiliation. The pioneering work by Herbert Gibbons speaks to this problem. He resolved the dilemma, in accordance with the increasingly racialized language of the late nineteenth century and beyond, by suggesting that the inherent spirit of the Ottoman venture must be accounted for by the dominance of a European factor over an Asiatic one, so that the Osmanlis were to be counted a new race altogether.[2]

As a result, the study of the Ottoman past was, perhaps uniquely, split from the start between the two institutionalized disciplines of Orientalism and history. This is evidenced by the common remark concerning Ottomanists that it is difficult to decide whether they are Orientalists who write history or historians who know Oriental languages.[3] The trajectory of Paul Wittek, one of the leading figures of Ottoman studies in twentieth-century western Europe (and, like Hammer-Purgstall, also an Austrian) is indicative: having learned Ottoman by a twist of fate (he was stationed in Ottoman lands during the Great War), he then trained as a historian of antiquity (with a dissertation on Roman social and constitutional history), before returning to the study of Ottoman paleography and eventually becoming the holder of the chair of Turkish at the School of Oriental and African Studies in London.

The disciplines of history and Orientalism have shared from the outset a distrust of theory and philosophy, a legacy that Ottoman studies, perhaps more than any other field, has inherited. Such resistance to theory was constitutive of the very professionalization and institutionalization of the disciplines, as shown by Hayden White and Carlo Ginzburg in the case of history and Edward Said and Talal Asad for Orientalism and its successors. Furthermore, the reticence on the part of Ottomanists to engage in theoretical reflection about their field as a scholarly venture was compounded, and (for them) justified, by the immense treasure trove that are the Ottoman archives, containing a wealth of continuous documentary remains across time and space probably unequaled in the world.

The field has changed greatly since the first decades of the twentieth century and, especially in the US academy, has expanded in an unprecedented manner in the past few years, to the point that one commentator speaks of a "golden age" for Ottoman history.[4] Yet sustained interrogations of the conceptual, theoretical, and narratological bases of the craft of Ottoman historiography remain rather rare, something to which the few exceptions that prove the rule all allude. Cemal Kafadar, primary inspiration for any critically reflexive Ottoman historiography, notes this in the preface to his brilliant *Between Two Worlds:* "The field of Ottoman studies did not and still is often reluctant to directly engage in a theoretical discourse."[5] His follower Gabriel Piterberg also bemoans such a dearth of attention to theory, as "the field of Ottoman history has been overwhelmed for a long period by, metaphorically speaking, the fetish of the *defter,* literally the register, figuratively the ultimate document."[6] More recently, Virginia Aksan, in her review article of Piterberg's *An Ottoman Tragedy,* significantly titled "Theoretical Ottomans," also notes that, though "Ottoman history could be said to be experiencing a golden age," the "critique of the craft . . . remains underdeveloped."[7] As for Murat Dağlı, in his important critique of the overused concept of "Ottoman pragmatism," he too decries "the fact that political theory is still at best tangential to the field of Ottoman history."[8] Finally, the most comprehensive reflection on the theoretical potential of Ottoman history is found in Isa Blumi's work. He criticizes the existing literature for failing adequately to address the problem of the coherence (or lack thereof) of the very idea of "the Ottoman Empire," a generic unit that serves to fold a multiplicity of moments and places into a singular trajectory pegged ultimately to the master-narrative of Modernity.[9]

This chapter contributes to these recent debates in the field by way of an in-depth examination of the particular temporality and spatiality of "the Ottoman Red Sea." With the surprising absence of a proper history of the Ottoman Red Sea as its point of departure, it excavates the genealogical layers that explain this historiographical lacuna and thereby offers six nodes of reflection on the fundamental question of what frames Ottoman history.

THE IDEA OF A HISTORY OF THE OTTOMAN RED SEA

The Ottoman Red Sea does not exist. And yet all appearances suggest that it should.

This is not to say that affairs and events relating to the Red Sea in Ottoman times do not appear in historical accounts. Of course they do. Rather, the concern here is with the formulation of the Red Sea as a coherent subject of Ottoman history, an effort not previously undertaken. In other words, though there is a pervasive incitement in the field to adopt thalassocentric approaches in the writing of history, and though the "Red Sea" has become hegemonic in reference to that body of water, there is no history of the Ottoman Red Sea.

This chapter thus seeks to disentangle the paradox of the evasive presence-absence of the Ottoman Red Sea by exploring simultaneously the three domains that lie at the basis of historical writing: the conceptual, the archival, and the empirical. Effaced behind naturalized categories and buried in footnotes, these planes blend together into the narrative that is presented as the final outcome of the historian's craft. The premise here is that facts are not out there waiting to be exposed by some rigorous method and that these facts, even once established, do not present themselves in any special form (of, say, a narrative story). A critical approach should thus engage all historiographical levels by recovering the genealogical plots underpinning the concepts and categories through which one reads sources and writes histories. Empirical data are themselves likewise produced by particular modes of recording, and only then interpreted and translated according to specific structures of emplotment. All of these operations, different but connected, require attention. This chapter will therefore proceed by moving freely between different domains (narratives, concepts, sources) in an effort to explore the idea of a history of the Ottoman Red Sea, why it has not yet ever been produced, and what potentialities it affords for alternative accounts.

It proceeds from the capital axiom that, for a history to be written, the possibility of its very idea must first be produced. In other words, before empirical data about a place can accumulate, that place has to be a part of the imagination, and before events can become historical, hierarchies must be established. It is the absence of such an idea that has prevented the Red Sea from joining the ranks of the basins graced by thalassological attention. This particular impossibility, based on a number of factors (discursive, conceptual, historiographical, archival, and linguistic), is suggestive for historical inquiry in general and the history of the region in Ottoman times in particular. Through its analysis of a specific facet, the chapter poses the central question of the problem of Ottoman history, in the sense of the *histoire-problème* in the *Annales* mode. In other words, if the Ottoman Empire, or Ottomanity, constitutes a subject, or a problem, of history, then it must have had a formulated idea, and that idea ought to have some parameters that are clearly identifiable. They shall not be rehearsed here, but it can be noted, for a particularly revealing example, that the possibility of an "Ottoman Africa" has not been properly envisaged in historical scholarship, whereas the categories of an "Ottoman Arab world" and of the "Ottoman Balkans" are ubiquitous to the field and require no explanation whatsoever (though the concepts of "the Arab world" and "the Balkans" are no more objective and no less anachronistic than that of "Africa"). More generally, the chapter engages the confrontation between the hegemonic knowledge of the commonsensical existence of the Red Sea and its complete absence from the Ottoman historical record, and what that rift may teach about history, its objects, and its writing.

ONE

The Ottoman Red Sea does not exist because of a long-standing identification of maritimity with Europe, and the collateral affirmation of the incompatibility of Islam and the sea.

The thalassological tradition, in which bodies of water are taken as coherent historical actors, was paralleled by an intellectual trajectory that identified the very essence of Europe with its special connection to the sea. By symmetry, it was established that the non-European was characterized by a lack of what defined the European as such: the non-European was detached from the sea. Thus Africa, Islam, the Orient were defined by an essential *landedness*, which dictated their historical trajectory (and in particular, their incapacity to espouse the concepts of freedom, universality, and openness to the Other that are said to mark European history so strikingly).

As explored in chapter 5, from Adam Smith, Carl Ritter, and especially Hegel onwards, the essential determinant in the constitution of the civilizations and cultures was connected to the place of the sea in their geohistorical essence. Of course, the sea exists in Asia, but, Hegel explains, it "is without significance, and the Asiatic nations have in fact shut themselves off from it." His empirical example (India) is without appeal: "Going to sea is positively forbidden by religion." This is to be contrasted with the aquatic constitution of Europe, where "this maritime relationship is of vital importance, and it creates an enduring difference between the two continents." Hegel then formulates a definition of Europeanness that is as simple in its directness as it is revealing of his larger system: "The European state is truly European only in so far as it has links with the sea." For it is the sea, again and again, that allows for the outward turn, that "outlet which enables life to step beyond itself." And this is what leads directly to that most European of features, where the "principle of individual freedom" defines life.[10]

Geographical determinism is thus both extensive and relative in Hegel's thought. There is, clearly, a geographical basis to history, but this or that geographical feature is not enough. He explained this in the *Philosophy of Mind* with the same example. "Proximity to the sea," he writes of what was clearly one of his favorite subjects, "cannot, however, of itself alone make mind or spirit free." How does one know this? Because of the case of "the natives of India who have slavishly submitted to a law existing among them from the earliest times which forbids them to cross the sea which Nature has opened to them."[11] Hegel then formulates what is perhaps his clearest pronouncement on the maritime theme: "In this despotic separation of them from this wide, free element, from this natural existence of universality, they show no sign of being able to free themselves from the freedom-destroying ossification of the class divisions of the caste system which would be intolerable to a nation navigating the oceans of its own free will."[12] Since the sea is that "wide, free element" and that "natural existence of universality," the Indians' law, to which they "slavishly submit," is "despotic," indeed "freedom-destroying," as in the "caste system," which would be "intolerable" to seagoing people.

The identification of the sea as the most important geographical element in the articulation of history and the key to the essence of the European self constitutes one of Hegel's important legacies to Western historical discourse. This initial presentation of concepts and ideas paved the way for the subsequent amassing of a great deal of empirical data affirming the identity of Europe and the sea and the contradiction between maritimity and the non-European. Hegel theorized the concept of the sea and interlaced it with the concepts of Europe and its Other.

The grammar of these concepts could then be declined by adduction to whatever signifier necessary: Africa, but also Asia more generally (India, China, Egypt), for Hegel; the Arabs, for many; the premoderns (not to be confused with the ancients), for most. All of these cultures are said to have had problems with the sea, and all of these arguments are directed at confirming (modern) Europe's exceptional intimacy with the sea.

For Hegel, the nonmaritime category par excellence was Africa, the nadir of barbarity and darkness. In addition, at various points throughout his work, the unhistorical character of other entities is also explained by their repulsion toward the sea. China, India, Egypt, all fail the thalassological test. And Islam does too, although this is never stated explicitly. The incompatibility of Islam and the sea would, however, become a staple of Orientalist discourse over time.[13]

Islam holds a particular place in Hegel's thought: non-European and non-Christian, it is nevertheless included in the (otherwise European and Christian) domain of self-realized Spirit. It gave birth to a great civilization, grand art, noble literature; it affirmed absolute equality; it conceived of the Universal. It was, indeed, the "*Revolution of the East.*"[14] Still, it clearly did not have within it the germ of true historical progress: it is, after all, not Europe, and in fact its contribution to world history, the submission of all to the Universal (to the One God), emerges as the necessary antithesis to developments in the West, where "nations [were] taking firm root," creating "a world of free reality expanded and developed in every direction" and "bringing all social relations under the form of *particularity.*"[15] Islam's incapacity to embrace particularity along with universality is not fully explored, but it is, if one is to follow Hegel's own theorization, linked to its geographical origin. "The Mohametan religion," he says, "originated among the Arabs."[16] And the Arabs, it is well known, inhabit that most terrestrial and unaquatic of landscapes, the desert. The association of the Arabs and Islam with the desert is of course commonplace in Western accounts, and not exclusively in the ubiquitous camel drivers and towel-heads of popular culture. André Servier puts it most bluntly: "In order to understand the *Muslim,* one must study *Islam.* In order to know and understand the *Bedouin,* one must study the *Desert.* The *Desert* environment explains the special mentality of the Bedouin, his conception of existence, his qualities and his faults."[17] Fernand Braudel himself echoes the familiar refrain, calling Islam a "child of the desert" and going on to quote an even more categorical statement by the colorful writer Essad Bey: "Islam is the desert." It is "the emptiness, the ascetic rigour, the inherent mysticism, the devotion to the implacable sun, unifying principle on which myths are founded, and the thousand consequences of this human vacuum."[18] For the Sorbonne historical geographer Xavier de Planhol, whose views on Islam and the sea will be encountered in more detail below, the association between the Muslim and the desert is such that the spread of Islam brought with it the desertification and Bedouinization of the conquered lands.[19]

To return to Hegel, "Here," he continues, providing the only actual determinants of Islam's historical essence, "Spirit exists in its simplest form, and the sense of the Formless has its especial abode; for in their [the Arabs'] deserts nothing can be brought into a firm consistent shape."[20] Thus Islam, the reader is left to surmise, cannot conceive of an opposite to the Universal and holds no progressive impulse within itself because its original nature contains no disposition toward maritimity.

In fact, well before Hegel, the famous diplomat-cum-chronicler Paul Rycaut reported that the Ottomans despised control of the sea and left it to the infidels for unclear, but somehow distinctly Islamic, reasons. His *Present State of the Ottoman Empire,* first published in 1665 and reedited innumerable times thereafter, remains even today a foundational source for Ottoman historians. In the twelfth and final chapter of the third and final book, concerning "Of the Turks Naval Force, and Strength at Sea," Rycaut begins by arguing that "certainly a Prince can never be said to be truly puissant, who is not master in both Elements"—land and sea, that is.[21] Then he goes on to fault the Ottomans for not exploiting their significant resources to gain a strategic advantage upon the waves. Unlike the Christian powers generally, and Venice, mentioned repeatedly, in particular, "the Turks . . . unwillingly apply their minds to Maritime affairs."[22] They are said themselves to acknowledge "their inabilities in Sea affairs, and say: *That God hath given the Sea to the Christians, but the land to them.*"[23] It is, then, by divine covenant that the Turkish (read Islamic) mind goes awry when it comes to matters of the sea. And Rycaut concludes, celebrating the special Christian intimacy with the sea, that it must be "the large possessions and riches [the Turks] enjoy on the stable Element of the Earth" that render them aloof from "matters of the Sea, which is almost solely managed by Renegadoes amongst them, who have abandoned their Faith and their Country."[24]

Giancarlo Casale contrasts this phrase with the words of the Ottoman scholar Taʿlīḳīzāde, who, at the turn of the seventeenth century, composed a list of twenty characteristics of Ottoman governance, of which the fourth was, precisely, the fact that the empire "ruled over both the land and the sea."[25] Proudly boasting about this, the Ottoman sultan Süleymān, son of Selīm, known in the West as the Magnificent, ordered his imperial signet ring to be inscribed with the words "Sultan of the Land and of the Sea" (*Sulṭān-ı berr-ü-baḥr*).[26] As mentioned in the Introduction, Kātib Çelebī noted this explicitly in his classic naval annals *Tuḥfat al-kibār,* where he argued that sea power was of extreme importance to the Ottoman state, first because one of its titles asserts governance over the two lands and the two seas.[27]

The explicit affirmation of sovereignty over the sea as well as the land in Ottoman imperial discourse and practice had been common practice throughout. Moreover, such a claim to sovereignty was usually recognized and confirmed by other rulers. In the late eighteenth century, the Ottoman ruler ʿAbdülḥamīd I was addressed, in an official diplomatic letter and amid a much longer list of titles, as "*sulṭān ül-berreyn ḫāḳān ül-baḥreyn ḫādim ül-ḥarameyn ül-şerīfeyn el-sulṭān ibn el-sulṭān el-sulṭān 'Abdülḥamīd*"—that is, roughly, "Sultan of the Two Lands, Emperor of the Two Seas, Servant of the Two Sanctuaries, the Sultan, Son of the Sultan."[28] Similarly, when Selīm entered Cairo at the end of January 1517, the Friday *khutba* was read in his name, as "the Sultan, son of the Sultan, the Possessor of the Two Lands and the Two Seas" (*al-sulṭān ibn al-sulṭān, mālik al-barrayn wa al-baḥrayn*).[29] Fātih Meḥmed II himself had adopted the title "Sultan of the Two Lands and the Two Seas" after taking Constantinople.[30]

In fact, this custom of claiming sovereignty over land and sea well predated the Ottomans in the region, both in Anatolia and in Egypt. It had been standard Mamluk practice, and already the thirteenth-century Ayyubid ruler al-Malik al-Ṣāliḥ in Cairo styled himself (among other titles) "*malik al-barrayn wa al-baḥrayn,*"[31] as did his contemporaries, the Rum Seljuk rulers Kaykāwus and Kayqubād—sovereign of the two lands and the two seas.[32] Sultanic claim over both land and sea was established custom.

Of course, this does not imply that the authorities intimately controlled these areas, whether maritime or terrestrial; indeed, sovereignty is a complex discursive realm, not a precise actual one, a convoluted network of places, not a homogeneous space.[33] It does, however, demonstrate clearly that Rycaut was wrong concerning an Ottoman-Islamic relinquishing of claims on the sea.

The dual-helixed thalassocentric framework for understanding world history, where Europe ranges the sea and the non-European is bound by land, was obviously not an invention of Hegel's. But through him, it bequeathed to the historical discipline a particular conceptual disposition that persists in many forms. This tradition found its present-day consecration with the publication of two echoing texts by eminent French scholars, Michel Mollat du Jourdin's *L'Europe et la mer* (1993) and Xavier de Planhol's *L'Islam et la mer* (2000), both of which underscore the inherent *maritimity* of European civilization.[34] The former does so by positively affirming the intimacy of Europe and the sea, and the latter, in negative mode, uncovers the incompatibility of Islam and the sea. These texts confirm the familiar contours of the thalassological genealogy of the Western tradition: the sea is freedom, the defining characteristic of European civilization; the sea is above all the Mediterranean Sea, the cradle of European civilization; the sea is the matrix of the Discoveries, the acme of European civilization's rebirth into modernity.

It is striking how fraught the scholarly investigation is into the maritime dimensions of the history of the Islamic world—even though, if one were to admit the category "Islamic world" in history, the sea would be, arguably, its most evident geographical characteristic. But that would be mobilizing factual elements according to different conceptual grids, and these books are good examples of the way theoretical predispositions produce their empirical data, just as much as the reverse. The concepts that serve as points of departure in these studies, and that therefore remain largely unquestioned, are the very ones purported to be the objects of inquiry. Most importantly, Europe, Islam, and the sea are assumed to be fixed, stable, and objective determinants, to which data of all sorts (facts, events, even ideas and morals) can be attributed. The confusion is only increased by the polyvalence of the signifiers *Europe* and *Islam*, which claim relevance on multiple scientific planes at once: geographical, historical, political, ideological, racial, religious.

Mollat's attempt to prove Europe's "intimacy with the sea" is instructive. Oscillating between antiquity and the present, he ascribes primordial links between Europe and the sea, since the heroine from whom the name derived was abducted by Zeus as she picked flowers on the seashore. "Myth and legend do not necessarily conflict with geography and history," he adds.[35] Having thus received the blessing of the myth of origin, Mollat moves to common sense: "Regardless of the way the Earth is represented . . ., Europe's silhouette conveys its intimacy with the marine element: it is a small, very small, peninsula surrounded by the seas which assail it."[36]

Seeking an answer to the question of where Asia ends and Europe begins, he then returns to antiquity and past representations, for "when geography hesitates, history offers its hypotheses."[37] Throughout time, he says, from Herodotus to de Gaulle, and through the Middle Ages, the limit differed; at one time it was placed at the banks of the river Don, at another, at the Volga, yet another along the Ural mountain chain. But the variability of the possible borders only serves to reinforce the fundamental stability and endurance of what they enclose, namely Europe. Indeed, the category "Europe" remains the fixed referent concerning which Mollat seeks information in history; never is it conceived that Herodotus and de Gaulle meant something different by borders and by what these contained. The category "Europe" is not here a product of specific processes—variable, unstable, even incoherent. It is rather the timeless, objective reality by which Herodotus and de Gaulle are folded into one singular trajectory, and according to which their judgments ought to be evaluated. Hence the sudden reappearance in midparagraph of geography, which had earlier been abandoned for lack of decisiveness: "Geography remains both less precise and more concrete. For geography, the contrast between Asia and Europe runs though continentality."[38] And it is a hyperquantitative geography at that:

> The contrast is clear. To go swimming in the sea no Western European travels more than 350 kilometers; the distance is doubled for an inhabitant of Central Europe; it reaches 11,000 kilometers for a kulak of the Russian plains; and as for the nomads of Central Asia, their endless travels over the steppes and deserts do not lead them to marine water, which they never see. There is nothing surprising in this, given the ratio of the length of the coasts to the continental area in Europe and in Asia: 4km per 1000 square km for the former, 1.7 for the latter.[39]

So much for geography being too imprecise or too hesitating. The strictly geographical "opposition" between Asia and Europe is now "clear";[40] indeed, it is reducible to basic numbers. Maritimity then was a distinctly European affair. Historiographically speaking, this has led to the state of maritime history being dominated by matters connected to Europe (including when the geographical setting is elsewhere). Mollat's spatial categories, through which he establishes his figures for maritimity via geographical measurements, are continental and therefore objective. But Europe is (like all geographical categories) an explicitly *political* concept, something to which the active verb in *Faire l'Europe,* the name of the collection within which Mollat's book was published, attests. Moreover, this is confirmed by his use of "western" and "central" Europe as coherent, self-evident entities (the third element—"eastern"—is signified here by the reference to the "Russian plains"). In order to characterize Europe, he is reduced to resorting to a full tautology: defined by a special relationship to the sea, it is particularly maritime. If we take the Ottoman Empire as a unit of analysis, it is ironic to note that the place from which an Ottoman would have had to travel the furthest to go swimming would have been in Europe, somewhere in today's Hungary. Another good contrast would be the Arabian Peninsula, the "cradle of Islam," which is remarkably adjacent to the sea from all points within and in all directions.

Xavier de Planhol thus has to adopt a different strategy in divorcing Islam from the sea. There is no attempt at geographical predestination in the book, which is surprising, since he is best known for mobilizing precisely such geographicist analyses, for example in a foundational text of Orientalist historical geography found in *The Cambridge History of Islam* and entitled "The Geographical Setting." In that text, he argues for the singularity of Islam as a religion, for "There is a closer relationship between Islam and its geographical setting, than that of any other of the great monotheistic religions."[41] Yet again, the reader is requested to use common sense: "Glance at a general map of the distribution of Muslims throughout the world, and a pattern is revealed which coincides extensively, at least in its principal features, with the arid zone of the Old World. From the Atlantic to Central Asia, Islam found its primary field of expansion in and around the great desert."[42]

The American popular meteorologist Ralph Abercromby had already in his 1888 book, *Seas and Skies in Many Latitudes,* expressed an almost identical argument by showing "how the extension of Islam is almost coterminous with certain very dry regions of the earth."[43] The idea fits into a long tradition, stretching back not least to Hegel (as evidenced above), but also to Renan's classic formulation: "In the Arab or Semitic conception nature does not live. The desert is monotheistic. Sublime in its immense uniformity, it revealed from the first day the idea of the infinite, but not that feeling of fecund activity with which an incessantly creative nature has inspired the Indo-European. This is why Arabia has always been the highway of monotheism."[44]

As for *L'Islam et la mer,* the analysis remains here connected to the civilizational plane, defined by an ethnic (Arab) and religious (Muslim) essence that is to be accessed through the exegesis of its textual heritage. It is "the confrontation of *homo islamicus* with the sea" that de Planhol seeks to investigate, and the conclusion, quick to appear, is staggering in its confident absoluteness: "The reality, it will soon be understood, is that of a long series of rejections, of failures and of missed opportunities."[45] The intended comparison does not lie hidden for long: "Christianity triumphed over the sea, Islam could not adapt to it" (10). By *Christianity,* Planhol obviously means Europe—and this is, ultimately, the contrast he seeks to highlight.

Homo Islamicus, fundamentally linked to his sibling *Homo Arabicus,* was thus singular throughout the ages, encapsulated by certain essential characteristics. With regard to the sea, Arab-Islamic civilization was originally and enduringly antagonistic toward it. Any empirical evidence running contrary, of which de Planhol ironically amasses quite a significant amount, is the result of factors external to the core essence of *Homo Islamicus.* In pre-Islamic times already, the Arabs rejected the sea. Only on the eastern shore of the peninsula could one "meet Arab sailors." But of course, these weren't even real Arabs, and navigation was "originally just a foreign cultural imprint" from Iran (15). Similarly, everything concords to show, he claims, that it was Christians who controlled maritime traffic in the Red Sea around the time of the Prophet Muḥammad (18). It was the "pure bellicose zeal," the "fanaticism of the warriors of the faith," that gave the Arabs their first victories on the sea (30). Nonempirical deductions are also permitted in de Planhol's argument: speaking of the lateen sail commonly attributed to "the Arabs," he writes that "it seems rather illogical to attribute such a significant discovery, so rich in consequences, to a people far removed from the things of the sea" (35). Mobilizing another common leitmotif signifying the supremacy of Europe in maritime affairs, he writes that the navies of *Dār al-Islām* were manned by Christians, renegades, and new converts, "to whom they systematically resorted" (51). Yet the only serious analysis of the composition of Ottoman crews shows that "black slaves from East Africa were probably on the whole much more numerous than any contingent of 'Frankish' rowers from Western Europe."[46] Perhaps the best part of this irony is that black Africans were Hegel's paradigmatic nonmaritime people.

In any case, de Planhol constantly needs to find a non-Arab/Islamic origin to his recurrent exceptions regarding maritimity: they are due to pre-Islamic Persian influence, to "Berber and Turkish newcomers," or to conniving British imperialists (89, 92–115, 403). The list goes on. The most revealing point, surely, is the typical, and necessary, Andalusian exception: it was of course "an indigenous resurgence," where new converts and Christians maintained the "exceptional intensity of maritime life in Andalusia" (67). Indeed, de Planhol explains, this was precisely "one of the many cultural characteristics which made it, even during the centuries of Muslim domination, a 'Europe' before its time" (67). Of course, because Europe is the sea.

TWO

The Ottoman Red Sea does not exist because of the dominant paradigm of provisionism used to explain the behavior of the Ottoman state and the operations of the Ottoman economic ideology. Although this paradigm has many critics, it is still pervasive, nurturing a number of widely held assumptions about the Ottoman character, just as it has slanted the scholarly production on Ottoman history in particular directions.[47] It may have older forebears (Rycaut attributed the Turks' lack of "attention to matters of the Sea" to the "large possessions and riches they enjoy on the stable Element of the Earth"), but the general model is grounded in theories of the European miracle (and its Oriental antithesis), whether idealist or materialist, liberal or Marxist, which became hegemonic in the course of the nineteenth century. From the industrial revolution onwards, discovering "the genesis of the superiority of Europe" (Braudel) was the fundamental question that the discipline of history and its philosophy sought to explain, whether in the mold of Smith, Hegel, Marx, Weber, or any other. It was, Braudel declared, the "Gordian knot of the history of the world," the "essential problem of the history of the modern world."[48]

In the specific case of Ottoman historiography, the model found a compact formulation in Halil İnalcık's influential 1970 article "The Ottoman Economic Mind and Aspects of the Ottoman Economy."[49] Since then, Mehmet Genç has repeatedly expanded the scope and details of the theory, on the basis of his profound archival investigations of Ottoman economic sources, culminating in the publication in 2000 of *Osmanlı İmparatorluğu'nda Devlet ve Ekonomi*.[50] Notably, Genç coined the three-headed formula of traditionalism, provisionism, and fiscalism, which has come to dominate the discussions of Ottoman economic policy. These efforts are important in the attempt to think Ottoman history in its own terms and to view the world from the perspective of the Ottoman state bureaucracy. Indeed, few scholars have been so successful as İnalcık and Genç in gearing the field toward archivally grounded reflection of Ottoman realities from the point of view of the Ottomans themselves. Still, the model has a number of biases that justify elucidation and reassessment.

Simply put, the argument runs as follows: the guiding economic philosophy of the Ottoman Empire, from its inception to the Western-inspired reforms of the mid-nineteenth century, was concerned above all else with the provisioning of the imperial capital, the army, and the state bureaucracy. The assurance of a steady supply of goods to the urban economy was the government's first, almost obsessive priority. The result was a dislike of exports considered a drain of resources (at least until the internal market was fully served) and a tendency toward state intervention. Provisionism therefore explains the special flavor of the Ottoman command economy: all elements of the economic, commercial, and financial domain were contingent upon, and subservient to, the maintenance of a continuous, abundant, and cheap influx of commodities to the imperial center. Devoted to the maximization of revenues and goods available for immediate public consumption, the Ottoman state would not accord measures to support its manufactures or stimulate economic growth. The Ottoman Empire, then, is best understood as a land-based, agrarian, and bureaucratic state organized according to an economic model fundamentally at odds with the mercantilism and capitalism associated with the modern West. It is in large part the hegemony of this paradigm that has led scholarly attention to attribute a terrestrial constitution to Ottoman state and society.

There are also important theoretical issues with the paradigm. First, and most fundamental, the analysis must manage to take into consideration that the very concept of the economy, as Timothy Mitchell demonstrates, "came into being between the 1930s and 1950s as the field of operation for new powers of planning, regulation, statistical enumeration and representation."[51] So to speak of an "imperial economy" and an "economic mind" before then is conceptually problematic to begin with. Of course, the Ottomans did have concepts of wealth and scarcity, which they connected to political and social processes of multiple sorts (though how, and according to what logics and assumptions, have yet to be properly explored by historians), but they could not have thought of these questions in terms of modern notions of the economy as an external, representational object to be apprehended in thought.

A more concrete problem is the assumption of the omnipotence of the central state. The fixation on provisionism as the essence of the Ottoman mind leaves little room for economic activity outside the confines of formal transactions. Yet the central government simply did not have the means, or even the intent, of intervening thoroughly in the economy, whether at the levels of consumption, distribution, or even production. As Şevket Pamuk suggests, "Ottoman policy towards trade and the markets is best characterized not as permanent and comprehensive interventionism, but as selective interventionism."[52] This is echoed by Suraya Faroqhi, who affirms that the "general framework did not prevent trade conditions in Cairo or Aleppo, where long-distance merchants were accorded considerable leeway, from differing vastly from those prevailing in the sultans' rather over-administered capital."[53] Circumstances, then, varied greatly in time and space, so a unitary paradigm is inevitably reductive and biased toward the more disciplined capital.

It is a matter, also, of recognizing a whole range of transactions and types of exchange that do not fall within the purview of official or formal operations, from contraband to barter. In addition, there is the connected dimension of nonstate actors that often served as intermediaries between officialdom and the population, and whose role tends to be overlooked or ignored by the pull of provisionism: guilds, moneylenders, merchant collectives, brotherhoods, and social groupings of all kinds. For example, in his description of Istanbul, the famous Ottoman traveler and littérateur Evliyā Çelebī lists no fewer than 1,100 guilds.[54]

Related to the question of the omnipotence of the state has been the tendency to read Ottoman sources too literally, failing to integrate into the interpretation their conditions of production and consumption. Documents, ideas, phrases, even words do not operate independently from their diverse contexts and multiple grammars, and they do not bear a neutral relationship to reality or meaning—they are social acts, and they bear a performative function as much as a cognitive or informative one. Ottoman documents should therefore be read not as a mere reflection of some reality or another, however mediated, but as a core component of a discursive formation and an arrangement of power.

There is, to begin with, the simple fact that state archives tend to register evidence of state intervention rather than indications of its absence (grossly put, it is difficult to record what is not, whereas what is exists precisely as a result of its recording); this reinforces the sense of interventionism and control, especially to a reader seeking pure meaning rather than effect.[55] Archival documents served an ideological and political function for the state and bureaucracy that produced them. Composing a zone of great strategic, intellectual, spiritual, and commercial value, the lands surrounding the Red Sea generated especially acute legitimizing paperwork. Documents about the *hajj*, for example, are abundant, and they are all, as many scholars have shown, invested in demonstrating a particular node of imperial power, one that articulated its legitimacy in terms of the control, protection, and financing of the great annual pilgrimage to the Hijaz, on the shores of the Red Sea.[56] But this is only the most obvious instance, and it is generally explained away by the role played by the pilgrimage in the religious character of the state, as opposed to an essential dimension of the archival source per se. The case of coffee diffusion in the Ottoman world is another excellent, albeit unexplored, illustration of the performative component of writing and documentation and of the prejudice of the paradigm of provisionism. The performativity of archival documents can readily be grasped in the instance of a command coming from Istanbul to Cairo articulating its aim as the achievement of "abundance and plenty" of coffee supplies in Istanbul (*āsitāne-i ʿaliyeme kesret ve vefret üzere*), though in actuality it was precisely because the arrivals of the delectable commodity were not even sufficient to meet basic demand that the order was being sent.[57]

There were chronic coffee shortages in the capital city of the Ottoman Empire.[58] As a solution to this problem, the Ottoman government sought (among other measures, such as attempts to regulate the market with price controls) to mobilize all available resources toward the replenishment of the capital's supplies:[59] prohibitions were regularly issued on exports and even sometimes on internal sales to anywhere but Istanbul, and private merchant navies were appropriated by governmental order to transport the commodity on account of the state. Often, it would be a matter of shipping coffee from the Mediterranean ports of Egypt (Alexandria, Rosetta, Damietta) to Istanbul, but the rulings sometimes called for the seizing of the cargos of coffee arriving at or stored in commercial transit ports such as Izmir. This could very well be interpreted as a classic instance of the provisionist impulse: supplying the capital city was the absolute priority, above and beyond any other economic, financial, or political concern. But this would be a misreading of a more complex phenomenon. To begin with, the orders are always framed in a language that is purposefully oriented toward underlining that this is an *extraordinary* matter. In one case, for example, the reason for the shortage is attributed to a "*bidʿat-i muḥdeṣe*"—a recent innovation, that is—namely, oppressive exactions on merchants in Cairo.[60] Needless to say, coffee shortages were anything but recent, and their causes did not require particular innovations. Provisionism, therefore, for those who supposedly practiced it, was not seen as the natural or even accepted state of things; it was not an outgrowth of some economic mind, but rather a result of a special crisis. The sheer recurrence of these documents confirms this point: had it been the normal way, it should not need regular repetition; it would be the standard organization of trade. Furthermore, the chronic shortages of coffee in the capital city as well as the resulting extraordinary rulings give an indication of just how much of the trade in coffee was under the control of private merchants who carried out their transactions as, and where, they saw fit. Finally, the Ottoman government was simply incapable of following through on these orders and prohibitions. As Gilbert Buti explains, speaking of the increased prohibitions against coffee exports in the early eighteenth century on the basis of French consular records, "One can only take note . . . of the negligible effect of these official resolutions."[61] The maintenance of limitations on coffee exports toward Europe, it should be added, was to no little degree a result of popular pressure. The French consular reports from Egypt of the eighteenth century are replete with accounts of crowd actions in opposition to illegal exports of the commodity, taking aim at both corrupting foreign merchants and corrupted local officials.[62] Rather than the top-down, autocratic, and state-centered fixation of provisionism, then, the problem of coffee in Ottoman lands suggests alternative perspectives. Furthermore, on numerous occasions the commands emanating from the capital to provincial authorities articulate the suffering of the population of the capital due to shortages as integrally connected with the fate of the local merchants.[63] Provisioning the capital was thus projected as being in the natural interests of the merchants themselves, not despite their better options. In fact, the general objective of the Ottoman supply policies in Istanbul was to facilitate and expand *private* trade.[64]

The case of the coffee trade, and Red Sea commerce in general, undermines another staple assumption of the provisionism paradigm: that such a worldview neglected long-term economic interests by dealing mainly with issues of immediate political expediency, leading the Ottoman state to grant, for example, trading privileges to foreign merchants as a reward for their countries' friendly relations, without giving proper consideration to the ways in which these concessions might affect local merchants or the Ottoman economy as a whole. This assumption is belied by the fact that the Ottoman state never acquiesced, despite great pressure, to European merchants operating in the Red Sea north of Jiddah. France and England in particular repeatedly attempted to penetrate that important trading zone, but to no avail (before the nineteenth century, that is). This has been interpreted as a defense mechanism on the part of the Islamic power to prevent "the Infidels" from approaching the Holy Cities, but such an interpretation is absurd, since European ships came up to Jiddah, the port of Mecca itself. The fact that the religious-defensive argument simply does not hold water has long been recognized, but the falsity remains all the same, notably because of the idea that it was "*Christian* vessels" that were prohibited from sailing in the northern Red Sea. Even the great social historian André Raymond, who was steeped in the local sources, speaks in his classic *Artisans et commerçants* (1973) of the Sublime Porte being "determined to maintain the exclusion of the Christians from the Red Sea," although elsewhere he uses the more correct signifier *European*.[65]

The religious terminology is supported only by Western sources of the period. The British ambassador to Constantinople, Sir Robert Ainslie, used it often, speaking of the "Prohibition given to Christian Vessels from navigating the Red Sea beyond Gedda."[66] No evidence whatsoever of the use of the term *Christian vessels* in connection to the prohibition has been found in Ottoman sources. There, reference is made either to the particular state involved (in this case, *Ingiltere-i tüccār gemileri*) or to Christian Europe (*Efrenc gemileri*), an altogether different category.[67] Interestingly, the translation into English of the Ottoman official prohibition says, "English ships, *or by those of any Christian Power.*"[68] "Ships of any Christian Power" is quite different from "Christian vessels." This reference to "Christian states" does in fact appear in the Ottoman archival record, in the form *Düvel-i Naṣṣārā,* but the expression is strictly equivalent to "European states" (*Avrūbā devletleri*), and in some cases these two expressions are used interchangeably in the very same text.[69] Never is it made to imply Christians generally, and of course there were always many non-Muslim merchants in the region, and many owned vessels. In fact, the same André Raymond speaks of this period as one during which the "Syrian Christians" of Egypt came to dominate Red Sea trade.[70]

The archives are clear: it was local factors, and actors, that determined the policies that were eventually adopted, rather than the stubborn economic mind of the bureaucrats of the imperial center. The ban was primarily a result of the displeasure of the merchants and local governments of Jiddah, Suez, and Cairo, who monopolized the commerce in the northern half of the Red Sea and thus controlled in particular the lion's share of the distribution of coffee and all sorts of goods from the four corners of the Indian Ocean. It was especially the authorities of the Hijaz who made the government in Istanbul prohibit any non-Ottoman ships north of Jiddah and require that the Europeans enforce the prohibition among their subjects. Central Ottoman documentation ceaselessly (although ex post facto) accuses the perfidy of the deceased ʿAli Bey for causing the arrival of European ships at Suez, whereas the sultan would have reacted immediately to prohibit such an uncustomary state of affairs.[71]

A formal complaint, registered with Robert Ainslie in December of 1778, is particularly revealing: it emanated originally from the emir of Mecca, Sharif Surūr, but was formulated officially by the imperial divan, the highest body in the Ottoman government. It announced that, despite the ban, yet another English ship had arrived at Suez, loaded with a cargo of coffee from Yemen, and that the Ottoman state could afford no further tolerance of such behavior. It warned that with the beginning of the new year, if any non-Ottoman ship attempted to disembark at Suez, its cargo would be confiscated and its crew enslaved, regardless of whether it floated an English, or any other European, flag. The shipment of coffee from Yemen directly to Suez caused too great a prejudice to the customhouse of Jiddah, the letter stated, and there were "complaints and murmurs in the neighborhoods of Mecca and Medina."[72] This account, like so many others that may be gleaned from the historical record, runs against all the tenets of the provisionism paradigm. Supplying the imperial center was clearly not the priority. Imports (including that of an essential commodity, no less) were not facilitated at any cost. Foreign merchants were not treated irresponsibly well in exchange for political favors. And everything was done for the protection of the interests and rights of provincial officials and merchants.

Moreover, the story points to another serious problem with the provisionism paradigm: it locates historical agency squarely in the imperial capital and allows for no differentiation in space or time. Not only does the talk of the Ottoman economic mind fold four hundred years of tumultuous history into one essential principle, it also flattens a vast empire with wide-ranging internal variation into a broad but submissive periphery revolving faithfully around an all-powerful center. There is no room in this perspective for the possibility that economic choices and commercial practices may have differed from period to period, or place to place; that locales may have influenced the course of things independent from, and even contrary to, imperial desires; that state policies are not a simple product of bureaucratic, top-down initiatives. In short, it assumes the passivity of actors other than the central state authorities, whose decisions are envisioned as sui generis products of a despotic mind. This has been recognized by many historians for a long time—but at which point does the accumulation of exceptions amount to a scrapping of the rule?

The final issue with provisionism is one that is all too common in historical thinking: teleology. Accounts of premodern non-European economic policies in general, and that of the Ottoman state in particular, are always interpreted in relation to what happened later (the nineteenth century) and elsewhere (Europe), namely, the industrial revolution. "Why did the industrial revolution not happen here?" is the question to which provisionism is the answer.

Halil İnalcık concludes his study of the "Ottoman economic mind" by underlining its difference from its European (mercantilist) counterpart, from which emerged capitalism and modernity.[73] Mehmet Genç's book is explicitly formulated from the beginning as an explanation of the *absence* of industrialization in the Ottoman Empire.[74] The political implications of such a reading of history are laid out elsewhere, when Genç argues, with a value-laden choice of words, that the "classical reference system in the Ottoman economic mind" left "traces of its influence" in the Turkish republic and that it "was only in the 1980s, with Turgut Özal's premiership, that Turkey began to comply with the laws of a free market economy."[75]

The main problem with this mode of analysis is that it starts off by searching for what is not and therefore always finds the situation lacking—a lack of rationality, a lack of freedom, a lack of state investment, a lack of private entrepreneurship, a lack of capital accumulation, a lack of modernity. It begins with a set of naturalized concepts and essential laws and pastes them onto differing pasts. There is no flexibility, no potentiality. History in this mold is a prescripted, and indeed prescriptive, narrative: history everywhere is, in this sense, always already a history of Europe, with the ideas of Europe and of modernity themselves, of course, being the metaconcepts that structure much of historical thinking.

THREE

The Ottoman Red Sea does not exist because it lies at the frontier of a great disciplinary divide opposing the Arab to the African. Of nineteenth-century creation, this divide operates at many levels (political, of course, but also conceptual, archival, methodological, discursive) and remains dominant today. Recent works have provided some elements of deconstruction of the dichotomy by underscoring the vibrancy of the Sahara as a historical space and recasting Arabic-language literature and Islamic practices as integral to the continent just as African factors and actors were inherent in what subsequently became the Arab world, but even there the concepts and categories themselves continue to be operative.[76]

The production of the categories "Islam" and "Arab" passed through that of "the Orient," which the discipline of Orientalism undertook to elucidate through textual analysis. The objective was to extract the essence of Arab-Islamic civilization and its place in world history. The approach was always operating from a position of civilizational superiority, and central to it was a parabolic narrative arc that went from rise to greatness and decline. The entry on "Égypte" in the original *Encyclopédie* announces the colors with simple eloquence: "It was once a country to be admired, today it is one to be studied."[77] With the constitution of Orientalism as a discipline, the Orient becomes an object of study; those doing the studying are Europeans, who manage to pierce the layers of obscurity to unveil that new scientific object. But the Orient was also, once (*jadis* in the French original), an object of admiration (and fear) for the Christian West well into the early modern period, so that Orientalism also drew from and contributed to a whole series of tropes about Oriental fanaticism, intolerance, cunning, and cruelty. Marked by Christian tropes of a lost paradise and an ideal state of nature, the study of Africa produced a subject that was separate and inferior to, but ultimately more salvageable than, Islam and the Orient. The noble savage of the Dark Continent was childish, shameless, vulnerable, and irrational. These themes continue to shape the scholarly exploration of Africa and the Orient, though in a more surreptitious manner.

The persistence of the model is perhaps most evident in the continuing isolation of the fields, and the enduring legacy of the naturalization of ethnic, religious, linguistic, and geographical categories. Africa, just like the Orient (or Islam or the Arab world), was a cultural synthesis, a coherent and intelligible totality, whose laws, dynamics, and effects the disciplines would elucidate. The great barriers separating these worlds are the Sahara desert and the Red Sea—both, significantly, remain to this day without a proper history of their own. These racial-cultural taxonomies have rendered a Red Sea region unimaginable except in the strictest topographical sense. Segregated into African and Arab, its shores cannot be brought into a unitary frame of analysis.

Three sets of sources will suffice to illustrate the problem with the racial-cultural concepts that frame the discussion and with the mobilization of totally anachronistic and/or alien terminology in historical analysis. They are drawn from various archives and are of different periods, origins, and natures.

The first source, dated June 1789 and written by George Baldwin, the great lobbyist for the opening to the British of the route through Suez who will feature prominently in chapter 4, is entitled "Memorial Relating to the Slave Trade in Egypt."[78] It is a short text, and its relevance here lies mainly in the identitarian and moral categories through which the narrative is articulated. Baldwin begins by distinguishing among slaves in Egypt between "the Slaves of Asia, and those of Africa." This is clearly a continentalist vision, but it remains here a simple geographic locution. Interestingly enough, only Africa begets an adjectival form: whereas the "slaves of Asia," which "are brought from Georgia, Mingrelia, Circassia, and the Borders of Persia," are purchased to join the highest ranks of the military and bureaucratic order, "the *African* slaves, on the contrary, are brought to serve." The text then offers the possibility that Africa may be a coherent identity and a relevant analytical unit. This sense is reinforced by the definition of the "African slaves" in terms of their phenotypical appearance ("their Colour, diversified only by a few Shades, is Black") and by the affirmation that they are "Negroes of that same Nursery, from which our Plantations are Supplied." Nevertheless, the incipient Africanist consciousness remains here at the level of an uttering; it is not yet an organizing principle of the argument. It does, though, give an idea of the genealogy of the concept of Africa: inextricably linked to New World plantation slavery, it is articulated primarily in racial terms.

In Baldwin's account, the enslavers in Egypt are "the Turks," and they ought to be emulated by the Europeans, so as to "soften the Condition of the poor Men subject to our Service." The term *Arab* does in fact appear in the text, but it refers strictly to those people "who constantly encompass all fertile Countries bordering upon the Desart" and who supply the camels for the caravans within Egypt (especially between Suez and Cairo). Despite deriving a hefty profit from this transport service, "they are constantly finding Pretences for War, or more properly speaking for Rapine." A group equivalent to what would today be called "Bedouins," it is a translation of the words *ʿarab* or *ʿurbān,* a category that incessantly recurs in Ottoman sources, in terms similar to Baldwin's. This was the dominant meaning of the term *Arab* in western European languages for a long time, and well into the twentieth century.[79] By then, however, it had become thoroughly contested by a more racial derivation—in the contemporary sense of *race*, that is, a segment of the human species, defined by a certain number of hereditary traits, of both appearance (phenotype) and constitution (genotype).

In 1789, at the time when Baldwin was writing, the discourse on the Arab and the African was not hegemonic; indeed, it had not taken full form. Nowhere is there any evidence of an essential, indigenous African pitted against an invading, enslaving Arab, defining two separate worlds to be approached independently. On the contrary, the text quickly moves on to a discussion of the trade links throughout the region, freely flowing through the Sahara toward Darfour, Sennar, Fezan, and Abyssinia as well as toward Morocco, and over the Red Sea toward the Hijaz. The terms *Arab* and *African*, when at all used, simply did not carry the meaning that is ascribed to them today, and the historian must, at the very minimum, be conscious of such cognitive fluctuation and highly wary of the mobilization across time of categories claiming an essential, universal value.

The second archival source is taken from the Ottoman section of the Prime Minister's Archives in Istanbul. Classified under the Translation Unit of the Foreign Ministry (Hāriciye Neẓāreti, Tercüme Odası), it is the translation into Ottoman of a letter of complaint in French addressed to the Ottoman government by the French ambassador to Constantinople, dated May 1849.[80] In it are explained the reasons behind the recent closure of the vice-consulate of France at Jiddah: namely, the assault suffered by the vice-consul Mr. Fresnel at the hands of a drunken Ottoman soldier. There are a number of elements of historical interest in this episode (such as the articulation of the aggression in terms of fanatic Islamic hatred of foreigners), but of most direct relevance here is the adjective used to describe the disruptive individual in question, and its translation. Mr. Fresnel, the French letter reads, was assaulted by "un soldat nègre" (a Negro soldier), with all the implications and connotations that the epithet conveys: racial, of course, but also geographical, moral, psychological, behavioral. It is also revealing that the French officials thought this the most essential descriptive element through which to identify the person. The term is repeated later in the text, when the arrest of the "soldat nègre" in question is listed as one of the conditions posed by the French for the redress of the insult. Conscientiously translating the text for Ottoman consumption, the professional translator had to find a term that could most closely equate the French category *nègre;* and the word that was decided upon was *ʿarab.*[81] This choice was confirmed by the edits in a different color, which inserted it again when it appeared a second time in the French version.

This episode and its multiple representations demonstrate better than volumes of theory ever could the pitfalls of using concepts and identities across time and space, and without giving due attention to the context and grammar of their production and consumption. Who was this nègre/ʿarab? What was his "real" identity? Was he African, black, or Arab? Perhaps all, or none, of the above? These are questions without answers; or rather, they are questions with prefabricated answers, which do not derive from greater empirical data, because the framing of the question actually produces the data to begin with. It is not a matter of establishing what shade his skin color might have been, or to what ethnicity he belonged, even if this were possible. It is a question of taking this or that characteristic to be most relevant to the dynamics at play, of choosing this or that feature to determine belonging to this or that group that can assume the form of an analytical unit and a historical actor. What is indubitable, however, is that although the wording of French officials fits into a discursive formation based on a racial typology that would be recognizable today (for the French, the man had Negroid features and therefore belonged to that category of men prone to substance abuse and fearsome irrational behavior known as *nègres*), the Ottoman translators mobilized a terminology that destabilizes the very racial discourse that is European colonialism's legacy. Largely devoid as it was of institutionalized plantation slavery that required strict differentiation and hierarchalization of racial types, the Ottoman experience did not have the lexicon to reproduce adequately the term *nègre* without corrupting it by the introduction of elements from what should have been another category altogether. The Arab, the African, epithets understood to form not only a current political identity but also a cogent historical actor throughout time—this was simply untranslatable into Ottoman, even in the mid-nineteenth century.

The third source that will be briefly introduced here to complicate constructions separating Arab from African is the oldest extant treatise on coffee, by ʿAbd al-Qādir al-Jazīrī, already mentioned in the first chapter. At one point, though only in passing, the epistle mentions the land of origin of the coffee bean. Though the coffee bean was intimately related to Yemen, it was also acknowledged to have originated across the sea, somewhere in northeast Africa. Having narrated a story concerning the beginnings of coffee drinking (involving Aden), al-Jazīrī explains that it has been one hundred years since coffee was introduced in Yemen. However, he quickly clarifies: "This pertains to Yemen only, because, as for its appearance in the country of Ibn Saʿad al-Dīn and the lands of *al-Ḥabasha* and *al-Jabart,* and other places of the countries of *al-ʿAjam,* neither its time nor reason are known."[82] There is then clearly an indication that the beverage originated somewhere else, indeed somewhere non-Arabian (*ʿajam*) in one way or another, but there is simply no idea of Africa or African involved, nor indeed of Arab in the sense that it carries today. Most important, there is no sense that the original location of coffee is foreign or distant; there are simply no indicators of otherness mobilized. On the contrary, the narrative involves historical and geographical names from across the sea (Ibn Saʿad al-Dīn, al-Ḥabasha, al-Jabart) that had great resonance in a larger discursive tradition including Yemen, Arabia, Egypt, and beyond. The Horn of Africa (including Abyssinia), in this formulation, is not made to be apart from Arabia.[83] Much to the contrary, the assumption was clearly that these locations and peoples belonged to a common world, which took for granted the cross-pollination of plants and customs. This geographical imaginary, unpurposefully integrating western Arabia and northeastern Africa, would become a staple feature of most discussions of coffee's origins.

For al-Jazīrī, then, as well as for other narrators of coffee's beginnings, there is no barrier between the Arab and African worlds simply because there is no such thing as a concept of the Arab or the African that can accommodate their having a world, whether separate or not. The narrative here too flows through and beyond the Red Sea, and in fact this space is configured as a constitutive element of narrative trajectories rather than a self-contained, unitary obstacle.

FOUR

The Ottoman Red Sea does not exist because it has no nation. The hegemony of the nation-form makes it difficult for the historian to imagine alternative geographies that are not dependent on political borders. It is remarkable to notice how enduring the boundaries of the nation have been in the historical discipline, despite its recurrent and extensive theoretical critique. The typical monograph in history, at least in Ottoman or Middle Eastern history, still relies on anachronistic units of analysis that are assumed as objective, or at least normal. The problem with nation-centrism is not, however, one of greater or lesser empirical correctness, for there is no ready-made indication, in the past itself, of the adequate parameters that ought to structure works of history. These are introduced subsequently, by the historian as she crafts her story, according to varying criteria. The choice of the nation-form as structure for a historical narrative is neither more nor less political or real than any other. All histories of the past are always already also histories of the present. The essential question to be asked about the frame and form of history writing has to do with the modes of politics that they presume and produce and the genres of narrative structure that they assume and condone. In the case of the nation-form, the political dynamic that underlies it is anchored in a certain understanding of the modern, one that opposes it to the concept-frame of empire, to begin with. It assumes a specific, individualized type of subject who is called forth by the force of the law of the state. It is narrativized by a realist mode that runs along a teleology both linear and abrupt. This tone and structure serve precisely to bolster the status quo embodied in the present. It is, fundamentally, the same history that is constantly being written, the same story that has already been scripted, just with different actors and varying events.

Moreover, the nation, like the modern of which it is the incarnation in the political sphere, is always articulated *against* a particular Other. In the case of the post-Ottoman states, as this very expression indicates, the backward Other has systematically been the Ottoman Empire. From Bulgaria to Yemen, Iraq to Algeria, and including even Turkey, the Ottoman past was integrated in national self-portrayals as the ultimate Other. This Other could be rejected or recuperated, or, usually, both, but it remained always what *was,* before and against which the nation projected itself. In its crudest form, the anti-Ottoman stance takes on the appearance of virulent diatribes against the Turkish yoke that smothered the subject nations of the despotic empire. Nowadays, the discussion on the question is generally centered on the Ottoman roots of the modern nations and on the modernity of the late Ottoman state.

This, it should be repeated, has nothing to do with empirical matters; the Ottoman archives are filled with material relating to the Red Sea, and in fact for most of the period under consideration the coasts of the Red Sea almost in its entirety fell under the jurisdiction of the *vālī* based in Jiddah—making him governor of an eminently Red Sea province. During the Meḥmed ʿAlī period, the Ottoman Red Sea was administered from Cairo, which thus became the seat of the single largest administrative division in the history of the empire, and its southern flank was dominated by the Red Sea. But there is no history of the Ottoman Red Sea because there is no contemporary political unit or project to which it can be made to correspond: to be crude, there is today neither Red Sea nationalism nor a Red Sea identity, whether past or present.

One may object to this reasoning by saying that there is no Mediterranean nation-state, yet the Mediterranean has long been an established object of scholarly inquiry. The case of the Mediterranean Sea is quite different, however. First, there has been in the past what was seen as an eminently Mediterranean state: the Roman Empire (and the Greek thalassocracies before it). Moreover, the formulation of the Mediterranean as an object of scholarly inquiry also took place in conjunction with the projection of European (especially French and British) imperial ambitions. Finally, again during the same period, there emerged in the same circles the idea that the

Mediterranean Sea was the birthplace and fount of European civilization. In other words, the contemporary political unit to which the Mediterranean as a scholarly object was a corollary is colonial Europe.

That said, it is important to add here that the fact that the Mediterranean becomes identified as the source of European civilization does not prevent it also from being othered and despised, indeed, of being produced as an object in need of redemption by the grace of European colonial powers. Much to the contrary, even as it was thus constituted as the birthplace of Europe, the spirit of the Mediterranean was relegated to the past, along the pattern identified by Fabian as "the denial of coevalness." The Mediterranean might have been the origin of human civilization, but it had become decrepit and in need of salvation (by the new, transalpine or northern, European vanguards of humanity). This was the mechanism by which the Mediterranean could be both absorbed into and expelled from civilized Europe by its inventors, most if not all of whom, one cannot fail to notice, were of "northern European" affiliation: the British and the Germans, of course, but also the French—as Braudel in fact verbalized in those very terms in the opening words of the preface to the first edition of *The Mediterranean,* already cited above: "I have loved the Mediterranean, *as so many northerners before me* . . . " Of course, love and hate are never easily distinguished, and Ernest Renan, to take another example, famously claimed that the Orient, which he so reviled, began in that eminently Mediterranean city of Naples.

FIVE

The Ottoman Red Sea does not exist because it has no archive. There are innumerable sources, of course, that can provide information relating to the area and its past, but, simply put, there are, in the Ottoman archives, no constituted deposits labeled "Red Sea." This question of the archive is connected with the problematic of the nation-state discussed above. Archives, in the sense that the word carries today, were constituted alongside the disciplinization of history and the rise of the nation-state. They were made by the archivist, and seen by the historian, as the scriptural embodiment of the nation-state, a material substantiation of its claim to be both old and new, a testimony to its continuity, its longevity, and its novel, rational self-organization. It is no wonder that the archive holds such an important place in both Hegel's and Ranke's writings. It is precisely for *archival* reasons that the modern state is the central actor of history, of both history-as-past and history-as-writing. Only the modern state, claims Hegel, possesses a record of itself adequate to produce an account of its past—and only then do subjective and objective histories meet to create History. Before the modern state, there is no archive, and before the archive there is no history.[84]

A systematic engagement with the dynamics of the production of the archive and its connections with modern history writing in general is overdue. Regarding histories based on Ottoman source materials, the very basic elaboration of the concept of the archive, and the ways it relates to the state(s) (past and present) that it is meant to embody, is yet to be carried out, the appearance of some important work in Turkish notwithstanding.[85] The case of the Cevdet collections at the Prime Minister's Archive in Istanbul is a good example. In the 1930s, following an embarrassing disclosure of the sale to Bulgaria of Ottoman documents as scrap paper, the Turkish state commissioned the famed intellectual and educator Muallim Cevdet to organize the loose records from Ottoman times for archival consumption, building upon earlier archiving work by Ali Emiri, Ibnülemin Mahmud Kemal and others going back to the founding efforts of the famed reformer Mustafa Reşid Paşa.[86]

The Cevdet collections (this is the official appellation) were divided into seventeen state-centered categories compatible with the rationality of modernity: *Adliye* (justice), *Askeriye* (military), *Bahriye* (navy), *Belediye* (municipal affairs), *Dahiliye* (interior), *Hariciye* (exterior), *İkitisat* (economy), *Maliye* (finance), *Zaptiye* (police), and so on. It remains unknown to Ottomanist historians and archivists alike how exactly these records were assembled. According to what criteria were they chosen, and why? What kind of order were they in before? These are very basic questions indeed. Their solution would bring the argument barely to the threshold of the formulation of a problematic. Yet they have no clear answers.

A conclusive demonstration regarding the impact of archives on the scholarly production of Ottoman history must await further research and a different setting; still, it bears no doubt that, especially in terms of categories through which to channel the available records, the archive has played a significant role in the avenues of research. The literature on Ottoman Egypt is so large in part because of the numerous archival collections that are organized on a (supposedly) Egypt-centric basis: most importantly, the Mühimme-i Mısır, which have formed the documentary backbone of much scholarship on Ottoman Egypt, but also the collections of the Mısır Hazinesi (the Cairo

Treasury) of the Başmuhasebe Kalemi (Chief Treasury's Office), the Mısır Valiliği Kalemi of the Divan Kalemi (the Division of the Governorship of Egypt of the Chancery's Office), as well as the Eyalet-i Mümtaze Mısır (the Excellent Province of Egypt) section of the post-Tanzimat İrade and Sadaret series. Needless to say, the documents in these records cover matters that relate to the entire area surrounding the northern Red Sea and the southeastern Mediterranean, which had important connections with the province ruled from Cairo, rather than to some sort of Ottoman Egypt, in the sense that is given to the country today.

The absence of any collection in the Ottoman archives explicitly organized according to Red Sea–oriented categories has been prejudicial to the formulation of the very idea of a history of the Ottoman Red Sea. It has no archival presence as such, and this has further prevented it from becoming a guiding concept of research.

Revealingly, there is a significant section labeled "Red Sea" in the English, and to a lesser extent the French, archives for this period. At the National Archives (previously the Public Records Office) in Surrey, numerous series include the category "Red Sea" in their title, such as "Egypt Claims on the Red Sea" and "Reports and Minutes on French Designs in the Red Sea," or again, at the British Library, the East India Company series entitled "Factory Records: Egypt and the Red Sea." It is little surprise, then, that there appeared recently a collection of documents under the general rubric of "The Red Sea Region" gathered from the English national archives.[87] And, in turn, it is logical that there should be a fairly well articulated place for the Red Sea in Eurocentric histories of the region and the world, which tell the story of the penetration of Western capitalism, the expansion of scientific rationalism, the regulation of diseases, the control of native religious practices, and the clashes of great power rivalry, with the saga of the Suez Canal as symbolic linchpin. This approach is doubly mythical: it takes the Red Sea as an objective and natural setting that is almost quiescent throughout the ages until the irruption on the scene of the imperial Europeans, who are the only properly historical actors. The single existing book directly formulated as a "history of the red sea" (written by Roger Joint-Daguenet and published in 1995 in French) is a perfect case in point. Divided into two volumes, the first is devoted mostly to a description of the environment (geographical, linguistic, religious, with splashes of martial and political events) and ends with an eighteenth century whose only actors are European; the second begins with the Suez Canal as the true pivot of modern Red Sea history.

SIX

The Ottoman Red Sea does not exist because, quite simply, the Red Sea did not exist as such in Ottoman discourse during the period under consideration. Of course, this problem has never frightened historians, who have dabbled freely in making terms and expressions travel mind-stretching spans of time and space. Still, had an Ottoman discursive unit corresponded to that of modern scholarship known as "the Red Sea," surely it would have spurred a different approach to the place.

The catalogs of the Başbakanlık Osmanlı Arşivleri, the Ottoman repositories of the Prime Minister's Archive in Istanbul, contain only one document that makes use of the term Red Sea (in its Arabic-derived form, *Baḥr-ı Aḥmer*) before the mid-nineteenth century, when the expression gained more currency. It concerns the French invasion of Egypt and the Ottoman military and political endeavors to defeat it. Dated the first of *Şevvāl* 1213 AH (that is, March 8, 1799), it is a report from Sayyid ʿAlī Efendī, the permanent Ottoman ambassador to Paris. Following the defeat of the Mamluk and Ottoman forces and the successful conquest of Egypt by the French Armée d'Orient under the command of Général-en-chef Napoléon Bonaparte, it speaks of French desires to "control Indian trade by dominating the Red Sea" (*Fransīzlar'ıñ Hind ticāretini Baḥr-ı Aḥmer'e ḥaṣretmek nīyetleri*).[88] Revealingly, there is another document of the period that is recorded *in the catalog* of the Başbakanlık Osmanlı Arşivi as concerning the "Red Sea." Dated 10 *Cumādā I* 1215 AH (September 29, 1800), it is described as an imperial decree issued to the commander of Mekka, ordering him to "provide the necessary facilitations and assistance to the English navy located in the Red Sea so that the French invaders of Egypt do not attack Jiddah and Yanbu with a fleet procured at Suez."[89] The document itself, however, speaks, not of *Baḥr-ı Aḥmer,* but of *Baḥr-ı Süveys,* an altogether different category, as will be discussed below. The (extremely rare) use of the expression "Red Sea" in eighteenth- and early nineteenth-century Ottoman discourse is, then, related to, and derived from, European colonial projects in the region.

Otherwise, there were, for the Ottomans in the eighteenth and early nineteenth centuries, many seas in the space that is today called the Red Sea, and their names derived from port cities or lands with which they were associated. There was, first and foremost, *Baḥr-ı Süveys,* almost ubiquitous in the Ottoman archival record concerning the area in the north of the sea, especially in matters relating to relations and exchanges between the Hijaz and Egypt.[90] But there was also *Baḥr-ı Ḳulzum, Baḥr-ı Cidde, Baḥr-ı Mekka* in the north, *Baḥr-ı Muhā, Baḥr-ı Yemen, Baḥr-ı Ḥabeş* in the south, all named after adjoining places. This was in fact an old practice. The classical compiler of geographical lore Yāqūt al-Ḥamawī (d. 1229) explicitly articulates the idea, in the entry for *Baḥr al-Qulzum* of his famous *Muʿjam al-buldān*, that the sea takes the name of the various locations on its shores.[91] The Danish scholar-traveler Carsten Niebuhr reported this: "It is known that the Arabs do not call it *Red Sea* in their language. They name the northern arm thereof *Báhhr el Kolsum* or *Báhhr es Sues*, the arm which stretches eastward from *Râs Mohámmed*, *Báhhr el ákaba*, the middle part of the gulf, *Báhhr Hedsjâs*, *Báhhr Janbo*, *Báhhr Dsjidda*, or *Báhhr Mekke*, and the southernmost part thereof *Báhhr el Jemen*."[92] Such a multiplicity of names that mediate spaces by their constitutive places was still evident in Arabic geographical and historical works of the very late nineteenth century, which, however, sought precisely to undo it and standardize/homogenize an objective nomenclature. Aḥmad Zakī, for example, in his landmark bilingual (Arabic-French) *Dictionary of Ancient Geography (Qāmūs al-jughrāfiya al-qadīma)* relates the new master category of Red Sea/al-Baḥr al-Aḥmar as having been "for the Arabs, the sea of the Hijaz and the sea of Suez and the Arabian gulf and especially the sea of Qulzum."[93]

These are only the more common examples; there are more, and none are exclusive: they vary in geographical implication and can overlap. This toponomic multiplicity and polysemy should not come as a surprise, as it was a common feature of geographic knowledge until fairly recently.[94] It is not an absolute claim over space that is made with such appellations, but a fundamentally mediated one. This makes a significant difference on the cognitive level and, in view of the power-knowledge nexus, in the political-ideological field as well. Thus, even from the central imperial perspective, these maritime areas were viewed through the intercession of local intermediaries. Their definition and classification were produced, not as a limpid representation inscribed into abstract space from the desk of an imperial bureaucrat in Istanbul, but rather as connected to and dependent upon the presence of another locus of knowledge and authority. Once again, this is emphatically *not* a matter of greater or lesser empirical correctness. In many ways, as regards the prohibition on European ships to navigate the area, *Baḥr-ı Süveys*, for example, is more precise than the more abstract *Red Sea* (even when limited by the adjective *northern* or the qualifier *north of Jiddah*), because what was involved was access to the port of Suez and what it implied, not the right to navigate the waters of the Red Sea in and of itself.

The various potentialities of space are precisely what most of the scholarship on the region fails to acknowledge. For example, in one of the rare forays on the question, C. Edmund Bosworth is surprised that the great navigator Aḥmad ibn Mājid uses "no special term for the Gulf as a whole" even though he extensively describes the place.[95] From this, he infers "that the usage of such terms in Arabic as 'Sea of Fars' or 'Gulf of Fars' was so widespread and taken for granted that it was unnecessary to stress them."[96] Wouldn't it be more logical to conclude instead that it was unnecessary for Ibn Mājid to name and categorize "the Gulf as a whole" because neither he nor his readers had to conceive of space in that way?

The Ottoman projection of power over these spaces obviously followed a logic of control; it was, yes, divinely ordained, bound by imperial tradition, and upheld by the gun, but it was also, heavily and self-consciously, mediated. Space in this mold is imagined, not as a physical object over which there could or should be imperial rights, but as a plural network of relations. There was no place for the idea of the Red Sea in Ottoman discourse of the eighteenth and nineteenth centuries because there was no project to produce a clean breach between abstracted representation and material reality. It is a similar difference that underlies the dissonance between nationalist understandings of territorial space and the Ottoman naming of provinces through administrative centers (e.g., Mıṣır is the province ruled from Cairo, not some proto-national Egypt).[97] By contrast, over the second half of the nineteenth century, the Ottomanized version of "Red Sea" (mainly as *Baḥr-ı Aḥmer*) becomes omnipresent in Ottoman public discourse, and the use of the alternative nomenclature virtually disappears. Only then does it become a distinct object over which can be projected technopolitical power: a discrete part of a larger territorial whole that is commanded from the center.

The problematic issue of the naming of the Red Sea is reflected in contemporary European cartographic discourse. On the basis of the examination of the more common atlases and maps of the eighteenth and nineteenth centuries, it is clear that only in the 1860s do European maps, which systematically indicate at least one local name for the area, begin to use a vernacularized *Red Sea*—namely, in the form "ROTHES MEER arab. BAHR QOLSÚM od. B. el ÁHMAR (bei den Alten SINUS ARABICUS)" of the map entitled "Das Rothe Meer und die Wichtigsten Häfen seiner Westhälfte zur Übersicht der Ergebnisse von Th. von Heuglin's Reise, 1857" and published in Gotha by Justus Perthes in 1860. In this map, the term *Bahr Súes* remains present but is clearly limited to the maritime space on the west of the Sinai Peninsula that is today called the Gulf of Suez. Before then, all major European cartographers indicated alternative local renditions in addition to the *Red Sea* of their titles. Most often, this would be, or at least include, the classics *Baḥr-ı Ḳulzum* or *Baḥr-ı Mekka* (in various corrupted forms). The currency of this naming practice no doubt owes a great deal to its consecration in the notorious account by João de Barros of the first Portuguese foray into the Red Sea, in which it is said that "in general the Moors call this sea Bahar Corzum . . . ; they also call it the sea of Mecca, because of the house located there of their abomination Mahamad, and all are shocked that we call it the Red Sea."[98] Ortelius, in his *Theatrum orbis terrarum* (1573), indicates the Red Sea as "Mare de Mecca et Bohar Corsun, olim Sinus Arabicus." Hondius's *Turcici imperii imago* (1629) has it as "Mare de Mecca et Bohar Corsun et mare Rubru." Blaeu's *Atlas* (1662) similarly marks it "Mare Rubrum, Turcis Mare Mecca, olim Sinus Arabicus." Peter van der Aa's map entitled *Description de l'Arabie Heureuse, pétrée et déserte* (ca. 1729) includes "Mare Rubrum, Turcis Mare de Mocca et Boharcorsus, olim Sinus Arabicus." D'Anville's astonishingly meticulous map of 1765, *Golfe Arabique ou mer Rouge*, mentions only "Bahr Kolzum" in the main body of water, limiting it to its northern segment, and adds the names "Bahr Assuez" and "Bahr el Acaba" in the two northernmost extensions divided by the Sinai Peninsula. The southern part of the sea is left here nameless—although it remains ambiguous, for, as with maps in general, the reader is left to decide the extent of the area covered by the name inscribed. Still, the author of the map was clearly intent on placing his "Bahr Kolzum" toward the north. The equally scrupulous "Chart of the Arabian Gulf or Red Sea" drawn by L. de la Rochette in 1781 similarly indicates a "Sea of Suez" and "Sea of Akaba" in the two northern horns, "Bahr el Hedjaas *or* Bahr el Judda" in the middle, and "Bahr el Yemen" in the south.[99] The division of the globe's water surfaces into a strict set of definite oceans and seas is a rather late procedure, which finds growing hegemony with the institutionalization of the disciplines (of geography, of course, but also of botany and other natural sciences, as well as history) in early nineteenth-century Europe.

The history of the Ottoman Red Sea, therefore, does not exist; and its idea is anachronistic through and through. Still, thinking in terms of a history of the Ottoman Red Sea has its advantages. Because it does not exist, it tells us much about history as a discipline and a mode of writing, just as it opens the door for the telling of alternative narratives, histories that are not subject to the nation-state, to a certain model of the Ottoman economic mind, to a maritime form of Orientalism, to a division between Arab and African, to naturalized geographies. Thinking of a history of the Ottoman Red Sea frees space for the imagination and realizes the potentiality of history, and—why not—of the present and future as well.

THREE

Self-Portrait of the Ottoman Red Sea, June 21, 1777

IN ACCORDANCE WITH THE APPROACH that sees space, not as the foundational objective setting for the unraveling of time, but rather as a multitude of discursively constituted and lived places and landscapes, each with a poetics, a history, and a sense of its own, this chapter affirms the potentiality of alternative geohistorical compositions, governed by a different grammar than that of objective space and time.[1] If the Red Sea was invented only in the early nineteenth century as a scientific object, and if Ottoman public discourse did not frame the area in terms of that category before the 1850s, then how can one write the history of the region before European hegemony without subjecting it to teleological and absolutist notions of time and space? Formulated differently, do nonmodern Ottoman understandings of spatiality and temporality provide for an alternative narration? Or, in other words, how do Ottoman sources picture and speak of the Red Sea?

OVERREADING

Methodologically, this chapter advocates a form of slow overreading of even the most apparently unimportant of historical remains. For the purpose of evoking how some Ottomans themselves saw the Red Sea and its world in the late eighteenth century, a close exegesis of an official document reveals the special nature of that world as lived and imagined by its administrators and practitioners. An exploration of the various spatialities and temporalities embedded in the content and form of that document unveils a complex universe, involving local and global politics, the movement of tides and winds, the difficulties of shipbuilding and seafaring, the relationships within and between Ottoman state and society, various cycles of exchange and mobility, and other factors.

The chapter echoes recent works emphasizing the rich potential of overreading, which has been shown to reorient the very purpose of understanding in a radical way toward a certain reverence for the text itself. As Colin Davis has written: "This is why overreading is the precise opposite of the hermeneutics of suspicion. The aim of interpretation is to listen to the work rather than to demystify it. This willingness to submit to the text may be, of course, a further mystification. It is, however, the enabling self-delusion which makes possible the gains of overreading."[2]

However, the methodology of slow and deep reading advocated here does not limit itself to a hermeneutic exegesis of canonical texts of theory or philosophy or theology. On the contrary, it advances the rich potentiality of the overreading of quotidian or even trivial documents, salvaged from the mundane obscurity of the historical record. This is crucial in that it disturbs the foundational split that lies at the heart of the modern discipline of history: the separation between primary and secondary sources, and the attendant question of the archive. Such a methodological choice is also imperative in the effort to think of meaningful history outside or, for that matter, within Europe, because it shows that it is not only the canon of high culture that can provide insight into vital questions of epistemology and ontology.

The problem of the archive inevitably arises in thinking of how history makes its object, for it is a constitutive actor in the creation of the very idea of the past and the modalities by which it is apprehended.[3] And since the event requires, at the very least, a setting, a subject, and a plot to produce meaning, archivization can be said to contribute to the production of geography and history as a whole. But it is not only in this sense that the archive, as an institution, ought to be integrated into the field of historical analysis. It is also in the operational position it takes in the foundational split between primary and secondary sources that the archive plays a crucial role in molding the ways by which history creates its object. Roughly speaking, the division can be described as follows.

Primary sources are defined by their presence in an archive; secondary sources, by their presence in a library. Primary sources provide the raw material for an analytical reconstitution of the past; secondary sources offer the means to approach and contextualize that material and that past. Primary sources are read strictly to derive empirical data as unadulterated residues from the place and period under study; secondary sources are mediated and should be read critically, with an eye for the subjective penchants and rhetorical flourishes of the author. Primary sources are approached as evidence of materiality; secondary sources, as a function of literariness. Primary sources lead to reality; secondary sources, to its representation. Primary sources are the domain of science; secondary sources, of art.

The division has lent historical research its most efficient foundation of legitimacy. The typical monograph in history will claim to articulate itself upon or around a specific pool of primary sources, which serves both to define and to bolster its central subject and provide it with a concrete materiality. Speaking anthropomorphically, the pool of primary sources gives credence and weight to the existence of a particular subject, one whose memories and remains are encapsulated in that archival record. In this perspective, there seems little need to reflect upon the constitution of the subject of history as such: it is justified beforehand by its embodiment in that most definitive of tribunals, the archive.

Needless to say, this book does not base itself on such a split. To begin with, and to return to the original empirical observation, there is no such thing as a pool of sources in the Ottoman records that archivally embodies the Red Sea and thereby transforms it into a natural subject of history. The term is absent from the archival record. But, more fundamentally, given the quest for ways in which history makes its object, and since this object is in large part a function of the split between primary and secondary sources, the critique needs to target the very production of that separation. It is for this reason that there is no attempt here to discriminate fundamentally, in terms of constitution and nature, between primary and secondary sources. That most secondary of all sources, G. W. F. Hegel's *Lectures on the Philosophy of History*, is in this respect to be placed on the same plane as the fragmentary inscriptions of an unnamed scribe buried somewhere amid the numerous pages of a volume among many of a particular series from the Ottoman archives. The analysis of the supposed "primary sources" will pay attention to the literary and formal structure of the text that is similar to the attention paid to the presumed "secondary sources." No attempt will be made to derive straightforward, direct knowledge of the Red Sea from the primary sources with secondary sources lying still in the background. The primary sources will not be disguised as natural windows onto an unadulterated Ottoman past. They will be coaxed and abused into telling a story, as one would approach the interpretation of any secondary source, just as consciously, and with equal attention to the performative designs of the text. Secondary and primary sources are here both confronted as *texts,* inscriptions that need to be *read* with similar effort, for their hermeneutical value can be just as rewarding. Thus, after a brief discussion of some of the major references in Ottoman letters concerning the sea, the analysis will shift its focus to a seemingly prosaic archival document.

OTTOMAN VISIONS OF THE SEA

Seas feature prominently in many central references in the history of Ottoman discourse. As mentioned in the Introduction, the sea holds a central role in the Quran and its related corpus. The Hijaz is of course never far from water, and indeed the tribe to which the Prophet Muḥammad belonged, Quraysh, was named, according to one etymology, after an animal from the sea: the shark, in reference to its ferocity.[4] Well before Muḥammad and the Quran, the realm of the Arabs—it being understood that the ethnonym *Arab* signifies, from the very beginning, people of extraordinary diversity, who have as truly common identifiers only language, poetry, and genealogy (and even these, seemingly rather later than may be assumed, in the third or fourth century CE)[5]—is a space soaked by the maritime element, between al-Yaman (the south) to al-Shām (the north); that is, the Arabian *Peninsula* extended into greater Syria, surrounded on all sides by various seas and open, from the earliest times, to relations with the lands beyond the waves. The label in Arabic for the area—*al-Jazīra al-ʿArabiyya*—is even more explicit about the place of the sea around it, for here it is imagined as a full-fledged island (and not only in word; Aḥmad ibn Mājid, slotting the space in his discussion of islands, explains that only after Noah's flood did it become attached to the wider landmass).[6]

The caravan, crossing desert or sea, is its clichéd image, where oases are so many ports, and the camel merges with the ship—as in the famous verses of the legendary vagabond poet Ṭarafa ibn al-ʿAbd.[7] With the rise and expansion of the Islamic polity, this maritime factor would be extended further, and with it the geostrategic placement of this world: by the last third of the seventh century, virtually all interactions between the universes of the Mediterranean and the Indian Ocean and beyond would have to pass through one Islamic realm or another.[8]

More tangibly, the aquatic element holds pride of place in the thought system of Ibn Khaldūn (d. 1406), the great Tunisian scholar whose work would have an important impact on the Ottoman intellectual scene.[9] "In the books of philosophers [*ḥukamā'*] who speculated about the condition of the world," he writes in the second prefatory discussion of the *Muqaddimah,*

> it has been explained that the earth has a spherical shape and is enveloped by the element of water [*'unṣur al-mā'*]. It may be compared to a grape floating upon water. The water withdrew from certain parts of (the earth), because God wanted to create living beings upon it and settle it with the human species that rules as (God's) representative over all other beings. . . . The part of the earth from which the water has withdrawn is one-half the surface of the sphere of the earth. It has a circular form and is surrounded on all sides by the element of water which forms a sea called "the Surrounding Sea" (*al-Baḥr al-Muḥît*). It is also called *lablâyah,* with thickening of the second *l,* or *oceanos.* Both are non-Arabic words [*asmā' a'jamiyya*]. It is also called "the Green Sea" and "the Black Sea" [*al-Baḥr al-Akhḍar wa al-Aswad*].[10]

From the very beginning then, Ibn Khaldūn affirms the cosmological precedence of the sea; but he also mentions the difficult instability of naming the space, across and within cultural zones. Seas are thus both one and many, by nature. This is confirmed a few passages later, when Ibn Khaldūn discusses "the Mediterranean" (as Rosenthal freely translates it), which "is named the Roman and the Syrian Sea" (*yusamma hādhā al-Baḥr al-Rūmī wa al-Shāmī*).[11] Ibn Khaldūn thus conscientiously affirms the variability of nomenclature, and therefore the importance of this basic feature of the geographical discourse of the time. Almost equally interesting, however, is the fact that Ibn Khaldūn never uses any equivalent to "the Mediterranean," which leads the translator to incongruous taxonomical and syntactical constructions (such as "The Mediterranean is also called the Roman Sea or the Syrian Sea,"[12] when in fact it is called "the Roman Sea" to begin with). In addition, Ibn Khaldūn continues, two further seas extend from this sea—these are the Pontus Sea (*Baḥr Nīṭish*) and the Venetian Sea (*Baḥr al-Banādiqa*).[13]

The same operation is repeated for today's Indian Ocean, "a great and wide sea" (*baḥr 'aẓīm muttasi'*), which is "named the Chinese and the Indian and the Abyssinian sea" (*yusammā al-Baḥr al-Ṣīnī wa al-Hindī wa al-Ḥabashī*).[14] From this plural sea too emerge two others: "And from this Abyssinian sea, they say, come out two other seas."[15] These two, in turn, have a couple of names each: *Baḥr al-Qulzum* and *Baḥr al-Suways* (the Red Sea) in the first case, *Baḥr al-Akhḍar* and *Baḥr Fāris* (the Persian Gulf) in the second.

Like Hegel's and Carl Ritter's systems discussed in chapter 5, Ibn Khaldūn's version of geographical determinism is closely articulated through the aquatic element—though it follows, of course, a totally different grammar and logic (to begin with, it is organized according to a theory of climes, not continents). The centrality of the sea is perhaps most evident when he discusses the Arabian Peninsula, which, he repeats multiple times, is surrounded by seas on all sides. It is precisely for this reason (the preponderance of the maritime factor), he explains, that though this area finds itself in the first and second climes (usually intemperate in both climate and social/moral state), it is nonetheless temperate. "The inhabitants of the zones that are far from temperate," he writes, "such as the first, second, sixth, and seventh zones, are also farther removed from being temperate in all their conditions."[16] And this "is not contradicted," he then continues, "by the existence of the Yemen, the Ḥaḍramawt, al-Aḥqâf, the Hijâz, the Yamâmah, and adjacent regions of the Arabian Peninsula in the first and second zones. As we have mentioned, the Arabian Peninsula is surrounded by the sea on three sides [*faʾinna Jazīrat al-ʿArab kullahā aḥāṭat bihā al-biḥār*]. The humidity of (the sea) influences the humidity in the air of (the Arabian Peninsula). This diminishes the dryness and intemperance that (otherwise) the heat would cause. Because of the humidity from the sea, the Arabian Peninsula is to some degree temperate."[17]

The great Ottoman admiral and scholar Pīrī Reʾīs (d. 1553) was also highly conscious of the shifting sands of names and meanings. His celebrated *Kitāb-ı baḥriyye* (The Book of the Sea) is most famous for its intimate and detailed description of various corners of the Mediterranean coast. This part of the text is in prose, accompanied by numerous, remarkably beautiful map drawings. Before he delves into his favored domain, though, Pīrī Reʾīs explains his venture with a long and delightful introduction in verse, which frames the account in broad, global strokes. He justifies his narrative form (first verse, then prose) and his choice of a textual pilot over and above the maps, which, he notes, are helpful but insufficient for safe travel. He describes the manifold arts of his discipline (which he calls *deryā ʿilmi,* or the science of the sea) and his qualifications as a well-experienced seaman and an ethical Muslim subject. He also refers in passing to other ways of viewing the world. The Franks, he writes, divide the seas into four, like the inhabited parts of the earth (*rubʿ-i meskūn baḥrına nisbet bunu/dört bölükden biri dirler iy ğanī*),[18] yet these are not equivalent (*rubʿ-i meskūndan ğaraż dahi heman/cümle-yi deryā değüldür bil ʿayān*).[19] The White Sea is also known as the Black Sea, and even the Spanish Sea (*Aḳ Deñiz Ḳara Deñiz iy nāmudār/Baḥr-i Ispāniyye dahi iştihār*), he continues, "but these three are in fact one, so you should know that I say *Baḥr-ı Rūm* [the Sea of the Romans] for them all" (*bir ḳısımdur bu üçü bilün ānı/Baḥr-ı Rūm bu dur ki didüm cemʿini*).[20]

Another eminent Ottoman scholar, Kātib Çelebī (d. 1657), was also highly conscious of the conventional nature of geographical categories. In the opening of his influential *Tuḥfat al-kibār fī asfār al-biḥār,* he describes how (European) geographers divide the world into four parts (*bölük*) with an "imaginary/*hypothetical* line" (*ḥaṭṭ-ı farḍi*) running through the White Sea (*Aḳ Deñiz*), the Black Sea straits (*Ḳara Deñiz boğazı*), and the Azak Sea straits (*Azaḳ Deñiz boğazı*), and from the waters of the Ten (Don) toward the ocean of the northern region (*Ten ṣuyundan şemāl semtinde Baḥr-ı Muḥīṭa*): those places that fall to its west they call Europe, and those to the east they call Asia, the lands of Ethiopia and Egypt that separate the White Sea from the Sea of Ḳulzum they call Africa; as for the New World, they call it America.[21] "Thus," he adds, disturbing in one short phrase any stable intent of geographical divisions, "the Ottoman Well-Protected Domains have a share of the three parts" (*pes Mamālik-i Maḥrūse-i ʿOs̱māniye'nin üç bölükden ḥiṣṣesi vardir*).[22]

The most detailed treatment in Ottoman of the waters and shores of the Red Sea specifically is to be found in Evliyā Çelebī's famous travel narrative (mainly in the ninth volume, which covers the visits to Egypt, the Hijaz, and the Sudan). He discusses the types of boats used in navigating the sea, as well as the wind regimes by which they are propelled depending on the direction and the season, and he notes aspects of the social, architectural, natural, and cultural fabric of various places on his itinerary up the Nile and across the sea to Mecca and Medina, as well as some of the significant political and economic dynamics. He comments, for example, on the dependence of the Hijaz on foodstuffs from the Nile valley, much of it in the form of charitable donations from the special pious foundations earmarked for this. He clearly associates corals with this maritime space (which he actually calls *Şab deryāsı*—Coral Sea—at one point) and recounts a story that, though at creation the sea had no reefs at all, God answered the Prophet's supplications to defend him from his enemies by populating the sea with corals, upon which notably the cursed Portuguese fleet crashed.[23] It is from fear of the corals that the enemies of the faith do not venture toward Mecca. Of course, this also made navigation difficult for native vessels, and Evliyā Çelebī records a few shipwrecks in the year 1082 AH (1671 CE), concluding, "This *Baḥr-ı Süveys* is truly an unsafe sea" (*bu Bahri Süveys bîeman deryadir*).[24]

Evliyā Çelebī too notes the multiple names of the sea: having called it *Şab deryası,* he also uses *Bahri Süveys* and *Bahri Kulzüm* interchangeably. In any case, as Suraiya Faroqhi affirms, these features are "details which the author occasionally highlights, not elements of a coherent landscape description."[25] She then suggests, insightfully, that this stylistic mode be compared "to that of a miniature painter of the time, who also employed a realistic drawing of a flower, tree or monument to situate his story, while at the same time putting together his image according to non-illusionist criteria."[26]

SETTING THE STAGE

There was no Ottoman conception of that bounded coherent totality now called the Red Sea prior to European imperial expansion in the area. This does not mean that Ottoman subjects and officials of various sorts did not crisscross its waters for administrative, military, economic, religious, and other purposes. But just as the "sea of islands" evoked by Epeli Hau'ofa is not the same as the small islands of the Pacific Ocean historiography and cartography cannot conjure up a naturalized Ottoman Red Sea:[27] perspectives from the Porte were both more bounded and more far-flung. And the purpose here is not to preach any type of immanence to the construct, for there cannot be any. Nonetheless, this largely "Ottoman lake" reaches out and asks for a type of holistic representation that is frustratingly lacking in the academic literature. Indeed, despite the recent fashion of sea-centered studies, the Red Sea remains conspicuously absent as historical actor. It is therefore a challenge to be met, and this chapter endeavors to plumb the depths of the Red Sea, wresting from them a unit, which in Ottoman times was not one, by exploring the variety of implicit and explicit temporalities and spatialities raised through a close reading of an official document. Like any accused placed under cross-examination, it is seen to yield up a type of triangulation in the form of a fractal self-portrait: the Ottoman Red Sea. In the process, it will be shown that the historian's craft can go from the broadest to the most pointillistic strokes in its quixotic quest to give shape to that which until the ink has dried had none.

Too often, the *longue durée* frame of historical works rests on a geographical panorama composed in a thoroughly realist and naturalist tone as though written by an objective scientist with panoptical vision of both extended space and elongated time. The *longue durée* is usually *not* the place for an analysis grounded in archival material, normally the essential stuff of history writing. The present formulation of the Red Sea world as subject of history, by contrast, is anchored in a single document from the Ottoman archives. For the long span to be connected to the short, it must be ensconced in the historical artifact itself. There is no avoiding, otherwise, the treacherous split between reality and representation, nature and humanity, space and society, either of which (or a combination whereof) one would then have to choose from. It is not a matter of attempting to "let the archival record speak for itself" with the scholar as simple vehicle, as too many historians still claim their role to be. There is no fetishism of the "primary source" here. The document will be investigated, examined, interrogated, and tortured into confession, as Carlo Ginzburg might be abused into saying.[28] This allows one to avoid geographical determinism without seeking refuge instead in an illusory rationalist world of voluntarist closure, and it suggests the potentiality of the history of the Ottoman Red Sea by presenting a sketch of its self-portrait.

The arraigned document is not particularly remarkable in appearance. Dating from 1191 AH (1777 CE), it is simply a record among many others in the compilation of noteworthy commands and reports relevant to the governorship of Cairo and its environs that are collected in the Mühimme-i Mısır Defterleri (MMD), located at the Prime Minister's Ottoman Archive (Başbakanlık Osmanlı Arşivi, BOA) in Istanbul.[29] Labeled number 227, the entry appears on the lower and upper halves, respectively, of pages 129 and 130 in the ninth *defter* (tome). Totaling fifteen in all, running from the year 1119 AH (1718 CE), when the first tome begins, to the year 1333 AH (1915 CE), when the last ends, the *defters* of the Mühimme-i Mısır vary in length, ranging from 128 pages (the second *defter*) to 400 (the ninth). The style of the script, the rather difficult shorthand replete with unexpected ligatures between letters and missing many diacritical marks used in much official literature in the Ottoman bureaucracy known as *dīvānī,* is more or less the same until the middle of the nineteenth century, when codes of writing were standardized into a distinctly regular, simplified, and limpid handwriting.

Closely resembling the rest of the entries throughout the tome, the writing is monotone and slashed by every possible abbreviation, betraying clear signs of the haste and boredom, perhaps even annoyance, of the copyist, but also of his distinguished training as a scribe. The combination in these texts of the adherence to strict formal rules and the personal style of the scribe is astonishing, especially considering the obvious rapidity of the writing. Clearly written by different people, the various entries display unmistakable similarities (figures 1, 2, and 3).

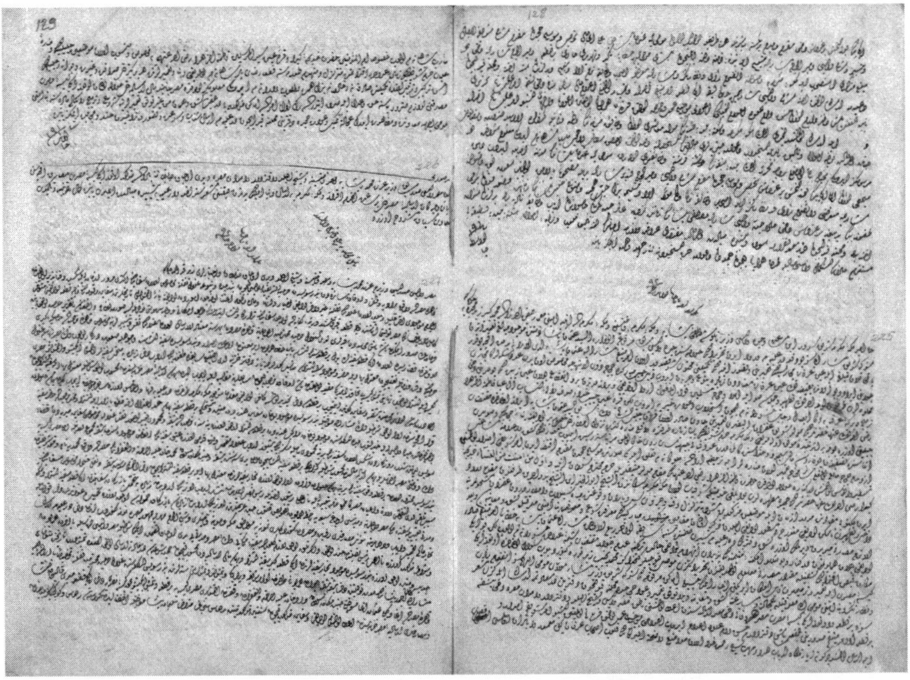

FIGURE 1. Mühimme-i Mısır. © Türkiye Cumhuriyeti Başbakanlık Osmanli Arşivi.

The entry—let us call it Document 227—begins, as these texts generally do, with the address: "To the governor of Egypt, former chief minister, my *vezīr* ʿİzzet Meḥmed Paşa, and to the judge of Egypt and to the *şeyh ül-beled* and the officers and elders of the Seven Corps, may their power be increased, has been ordered."[30]

Above the address, but in all evidence added subsequently, are two marginal notes, written, in typical fashion, at a sharp, here almost right angle to the main body of the text. The first of these indicates that "news and information [of the order] was given to the chief treasurer's office."[31] The second, dated a full year and half a month later than the order itself, affirms that "the order was repeated in writing."[32] Written after the fact, these notes were conscientiously highlighted for the reader by being placed before the beginning and by having divergent directionality.[33] The very first impression given, then, is one of recurrence and sedimentation. This provides a sense of order, continuity, and urgency to the issue at hand. It extracts it from its specificity, conferring upon it a higher order of abstraction, longer in time and larger in space.

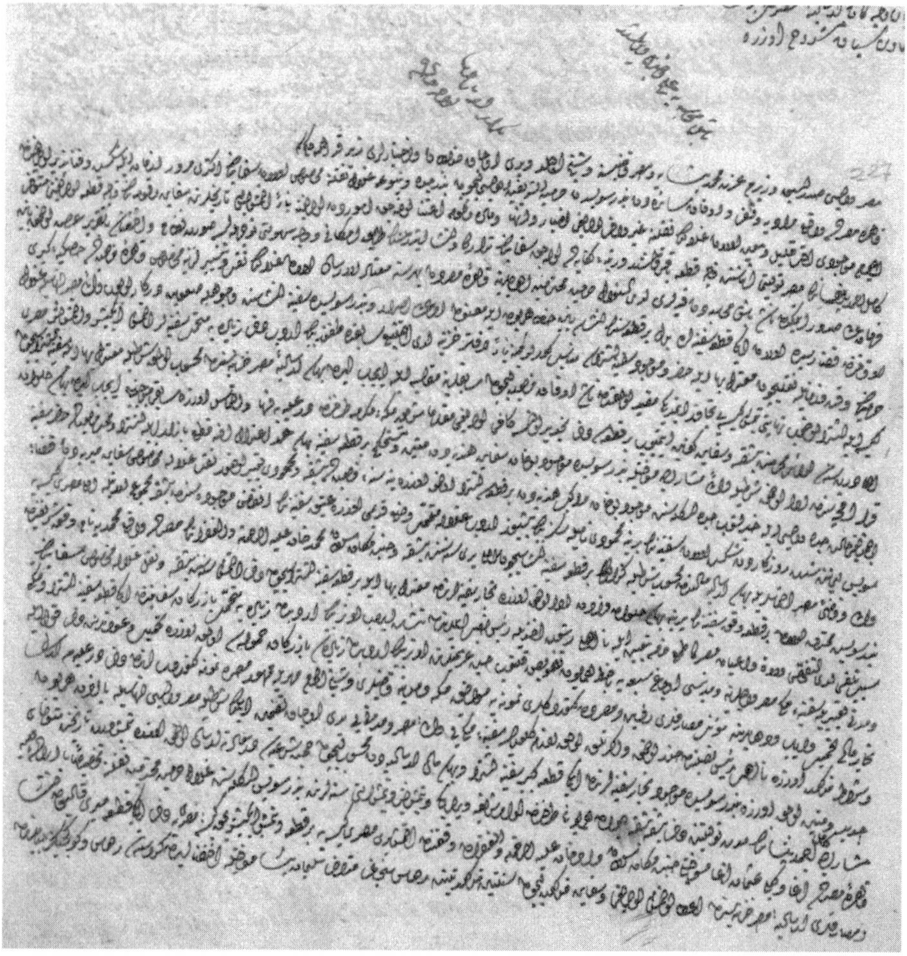

FIGURE 2. Document 227, Part 1. © Türkiye Cumhuriyeti Başbakanlık Osmanli Arşivi.

The crux of the matter is addressed from the very first line. The rest of the text is essentially a rhetorical reinforcement, accumulating weight and depth along the way. Indeed, the primary figurative-analytical mode of the piece as a whole is iterative (including even some use of alliteration): both its melody and argument are produced by incessant repetition. Directly following the address the essential concern is voiced:

> It has been reported and communicated that the majority of the ships belonging to the Murādiye *vaḳıf* located in the Cairo of Egypt and to the other *evḳāf,* which are meant for the transportation from the port of Suez to Yanbu

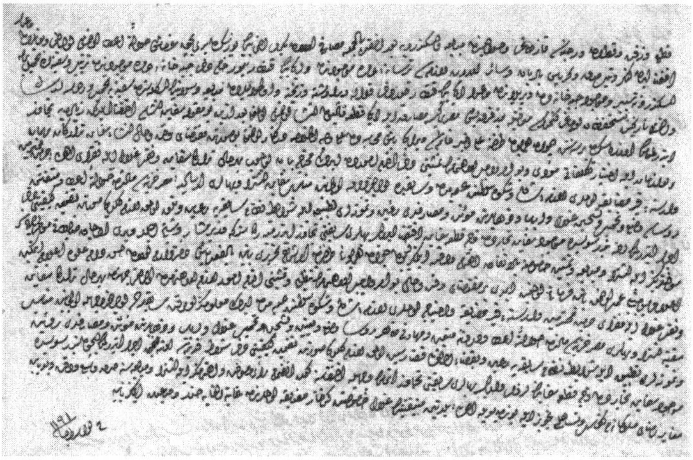

FIGURE 3. Document 227, Part 2. © Türkiye Cumhuriyeti Başbakanlık Osmanli Arşivi.

and to the port of Jiddah of the grains intended for the inhabitants of the Two Noble Sanctuaries, have, with the passing of time, suffered adversity and destruction, and, as a result, the ships still in existence today are extremely few, and these are insufficient for the transportation of the designated grains. The abovementioned matter is of those affairs that are to be given great attention.[34]

The rest of the text is entirely constructed upon its articulation to this initial passage by way of the conjunction *-a bināen,* meaning "building upon" in the sense of "considering the fact that," which comes at the end of the sentence.

CLOSE UP: SEASCAPE OF NECESSITIES

The opening problematic also provides the first and dominant stroke for a self-portrait of the Ottoman Red Sea: it was a world that remained largely dependent on the external provision of foodstuffs, just as it had been from antiquity. It was the special responsibility of officialdom to ensure the smooth and constant flow of these goods from their regions of production across land and sea to their various points of consumption and exchange dotted along the coast. Bearing this responsibility became particularly acute in the case for the Ottomans in relationship to the area containing the Twin Holy Cities. Indeed, so dramatic was the dearth of local resources that the provisioning of food supplies from beyond the waters was crucial just to keep normal prices from becoming prohibitive: "The delivery of grain from Egyptian foundations was of vital importance not only to the recipients of grain doles, but even to those inhabitants of Mecca and Medina who bought their own food, totally or in part; for the presence of grain in the city helped to keep market prices at a level that ordinary consumers could afford."[35] Indeed, a disruption in the maritime traffic across the northern Red Sea usually caused famine in the Hijaz.[36]

Regular navigation was thus absolutely necessary for the very survival of its surrounding population. And the existence of these populations and cities was of paramount importance to the central state and *its* subsistence. This was in large part a tradition that the Ottomans inherited from the past, and it was so central to the socioeconomic organization of the area that these Red Sea arrangements markedly diverged from policies elsewhere. Here, notably, the state was heavily involved in the provisioning of food supplies to the Hijazi populace, by the intermission of the pious foundations, of course. "As the inhabitants of the Hijaz," writes Suraiya Faroqhi concerning the era of Suleymān the Magnificent (second half of the sixteenth century), "had come to regard official subventions as a right and not in any way as alms, any attempt to discontinue support would have thoroughly discredited the newly-established Ottoman regime."[37] The same remained quite saliently the case in the late eighteenth century. The mutual dependence between state and population is the central message of the order of Document 227 as a whole, and it recurs throughout. The Red Sea world was one in which the sea was vital and pivotal—the beating heart of its long, narrow, and desiccated body.

This all points to another important characteristic of the place: its shores are contained by a series of mountain ranges of significant altitude, as described in chapter 1. These physical features had important consequences, in terms of water flows certainly, but also with regard to mobility and exchange: travel by land tended to follow the coastline in order to avoid the more dangerous and tiring escarpments. One clear example is found in the yearly pilgrimage caravan from Egypt to Mecca, which followed a series of set halts along the coastal plains.[38] The presence of steep mountains hugging the coast all around the Red Sea made the area difficult to control. The pilgrimage caravan routinely suffered assaults from marauding bands, usually referred to as *ʿurbān* in Ottoman documents. It was a logical prey, for to its spiritual pursuits were added commercial ones, ranging from big business involving global networks to small-scale trading to finance the pilgrims' travel and stay. But it was also a risky prey, since the pilgrims were always accompanied by a sizable armed escort. So difficult was it to secure the route that the role of safeguarding the caravan, heavily subsidized by the state, was one of the most prestigious and lucrative official positions to be obtained in Ottoman Egypt, that of the *emīr ül-ḥacc*. Moreover, records show that the Ottoman state calculated into its budget significant payments to local dignitaries along the way for guarantees of safe passage.[39]

BACKGROUND: LABYRINTH OF MIRRORS

All this is leading the narrative somewhat astray from Document 227, to which it must now return. Following the introductory statement of the actual problem (a need for more ships), the text recounts past predicaments of a similar nature, beginning with one almost thirty years previously. The problem is shown to be an endemic one, having been formally noted already, and thus placed in the perspective of "social time" and even the *longue durée*. There follows a chronological recounting of the problem, which gives it added weight.

"In the year [one thousand one hundred] sixty-five," Document 227 continues,

> an official report was presented concerning how many of the said ships were left, and how many were left remaining during the deceased Kāmil Aḥmed Paşa's governorship of Egypt, as well as the requirements and modalities of the possible paths and easiest ways to build and prepare ships so as to reach sufficient levels. Following on the exalted edict that appeared, on the basis of its clauses, and upon consultation of the records of the Chief Treasury, an exalted command inscribed with the imperial mark was issued for the construction of a ship in the place of the two accident-befallen ships meant for the dispatching and transporting of the grains that are sent by custom every year from Cairo of Egypt to the inhabitants of the Two Noble Sanctuaries and belonging to the *Hāṣṣekiye-i Kubrā vakıf* located in said Cairo. Also, as it became evident upon the communication of the governor of Egypt that construction of a ship in the port of Suez is difficult in many ways, it has been judged suitable to purchase at a reasonable price an existing and ready ship in order to transport the grains of the Two Sanctuaries in a timely fashion. In conformity with the treasury records, since it is registered that in the past ships carrying nine thousand *erdebs* and more were bought with sixty-two and sixty-five Egyptian purses apiece or at the very most the cost did not exceed seventy purses, and on the condition that the required price, comparable to the old ones, be deducted from the treasury of the annual remittance of Egypt, a ship should be bought at a reasonable price for the abovementioned *evḳāf*.[40]

The issue had then already elicited numerous responses from the highest authorities (including the notable weight of the *haṭṭ-i hümāyūn,* by the hand of the sultan himself). Beyond setting a clear legal and administrative precedent, this passage represents the performance of repetition, intended to engrave a sense of the matter's depth, continuity, and gravity. It also points to perennial difficulty in resolving the problem, something to which the text returns repeatedly. It is not by any means a question without an answer. The paragraph and indeed the entire text do come to a certain sense of closure in the command issued to the governor, thereby providing the sultan with a confirmed aura of legitimacy. But it is described as a difficulty nonetheless, in order, no doubt, to give a gloss of inevitability to the problem and to displace the guilt for its continuance from the authorities responsible for the well-being of the population and onto the natural order of things over the decades and, indeed, in the very *longue durée.* It thus provides another feature of the portrait of the Ottoman Red Sea. A world that does not yield sufficient foodstuffs, it is also one that does not contain the material required for the construction of ships.[41] Yet it was also a sea that *had* to be navigated consistently and efficiently: the grains destined for the Two Noble Sanctuaries, for example, simply could not be left unattended for fear of dramatic consequences. It was a matter of life and death for the people living there, but also a founding pillar of legitimacy of the state.

This thorny predicament was compounded by the fact that the sea and its environment presented grave dangers to navigation. Alluded to in the passage above (the two destroyed ships that had to be replaced had suffered accidents), the theme of the hazards faced by shipping reappears throughout Document 227.

At the core of the Ottoman Red Sea world thus lay a tense paradox: given the absence of trees locally, it could not produce urgently ships in sufficient quantities. Document 227 intimates this in passing: "It became evident that shipbuilding in the port of Suez was difficult in many ways." Ships were built at Suez, which functioned throughout the Ottoman period as the major port, shipyard, and arsenal. But such activities involved enormous effort and capital expenditure.

This leads to the second difficulty brought up by the command, involving petty finance. It is impossible not to notice the almost obsessive injunctions to obtain a moderate price for things.

The Ottoman government was undergoing economic difficulties. It had been defeated recently in a devastating and draining war with Russia. The harsh treaty of Küçük Kaynarca in July 1774 led to the transfer of significant portions of Ottoman territories to direct or indirect Russian domination, including access to warm-water ports and areas with large Muslim populations, ending the sultan's hegemony over the Black Sea and increasing the czar's influence in the region and beyond. Moreover, the treaty prefigured (though ambiguously) the idea of the authority of the Russian sovereign as the representative of Ottoman subjects of Christian Orthodox confession.[42] But in addition to these issues of sovereignty over territories and populations, it imposed a heavy financial burden on the Ottoman treasury for war reparations. At the same time, the Ottomans were incessantly involved in border disputes and military hostilities with Karīm Khān Zand in Iran, and Sultan ʿAbdülḥamīd even declared all-out war in 1776.

Because of the lack of local resources to sustain the construction of ships, the bargaining power of the state was now minimal. It had become concentrated in the hands of the merchant navies that crisscrossed the sea in search of profit. "As it became evident that construction of a ship in the port of Suez was difficult in many ways," the sentence continues, "it has been judged suitable to purchase at a reasonable price a ready and existing ship in order to transport the grains of the Two Sanctuaries in a timely fashion." There is here a threefold set of implications. First, unavoidable conditions forced the state to resort to the option of purchasing ships. Second, there existed enough "ready and existing ships" docked at Suez to purchase one, effective immediately. Finally, the state had to economize. Let it be remembered that the speaker is the Ottoman sultan, that alleged pinnacle of Oriental despotism, and he is requesting a "reasonable price"! The text goes on to define rather precisely what it considers such a value to be ("in conformity with the treasury records," no less) but then, in the same breath, undermines that precision by offering a range of prices differing by almost 9 percent, betraying surprising insecurity, timidity, and flexibility for a state said to be so controlling over its internal economy. The text seems almost to be pleading for an acceptable price, one that "at the very most . . . did not exceed seventy purses." In fact, the rest of the paragraph is entirely devoted to financial matters, noting once again, that the cost of the ship ought to be "reasonable" and "comparable to the old ones." It also sets the particular budget from which the cost should be deducted—in this case, the *irsāliye-i Mıṣır,* accountable yearly to the central imperial treasury in Istanbul, but mostly disbursed locally on various state-related matters. The sultan would thus pay for the purchase of the ship for the charitable goals of a *vaḳıf* from his own coffers, but the payment had to come from locally generated returns.

It was therefore not a case of an imperial center asserting its sovereignty over distant lands by certain public displays of spectacle. The Red Sea was the arena of complex webs of relations, networks, and nodes of power, which spanned the space of the local *and* the imperial (and even the global), and the time of the immediate *and* the long-standing (and even the eternal). The emerging portrait, though drawn from the written archive of the imperial center, was in fact lived as such by a plurality of people involved in the networks that defined the Red Sea world.

PROFILE VIEW: CENTRIPETAL NETWORKS, CENTRIFUGAL FISSURES

Such a multiplicity of perspectives emerges even more clearly in the section of Document 227 that immediately follows. "Also, in the beginning of Muḥarrem of the year [one thousand one hundred] fifty-four," the text reads, beginning now a linear chronological list of variations on the general theme,

> upon the communication and request from the former sharif of Mecca the Venerable to the Sublime Porte concerning the inadequate number of ships that would become sufficient if one additional unit were renovated, and in accordance with this, and on the condition that the necessary payments be deducted from the transfer money of the tax-farmed villages, a solid and reliable unit from the Indian ships present at the port of Suez should be bought, by way of the above-mentioned governor, at a price to be bargained strictly to the boundary of reason. In the case that a ready ship is not found in the said place, after consultation with the governor of Jiddah, one should be bought from the Indian ships available at the port of Jiddah.[43]

The elasticity of the webs entwined in the Red Sea world is here quite evident. The narrative flows seamlessly from one shore to the other, from one position to another, from one time to another, for they are all implicated and invested in the dynamics at hand. The complaint concerning the insufficiency of ships is here attributed to another major political personality of the region, the sharif of Mecca. Once again, it is concluded that a ship should be bought. And again, the issue of financial matters takes center stage and is repeated in a form strikingly similar to that of the previous segment. The weak bargaining power of the state vis-à-vis the merchants on the ground is further exposed, as it is ordered that the purchase be made "at a price to be bargained strictly to the boundary of reason." Finally, the origin and/or type of the ships, if not the merchants themselves, is referred to, dragging into the world of the Red Sea the larger universe of the Indian Ocean. The vessel is to be purchased from the "*Indian* ships" readily available in the region. The wording is clear enough: so present were these around the Red Sea, that if by misfortune such a unit—and a "solid and reliable" one at that, echoing again the risk involved in navigation—could not be found at Suez, then for sure the docks of Jiddah contained some. Although the text does not at all imply that the merchants on these boats themselves were "Indian," the presence of traders from the various parts of the Indian Ocean in the Red Sea region is well attested. Moreover, it was not only "Indian" traders that were pulled into the Red Sea world. A few months before the issuance of Document 227, another important problem, interlacing both global and local politics, had troubled the Ottoman sultan's court.

A sultan from Malabar (*aḳṭār-ı Hindiye'den Melībār ḥākimi olan sulṭān ʿAlī Rāca*), under threat from the British armies already well implanted in the surrounding areas, had sent an envoy to Istanbul to appeal to his fellow Muslim potentate for assistance against the European invaders. The Ottomans, it has been noted already, had just emerged from an exhausting and draining war and were in the midst of unending hostilities on their eastern borders, so their assistance could only be negligible. Moreover, having been on the wrong end of British support during the last war, and considering the increasing power of the British crown throughout the world, the Ottoman state was invested in not bruising its newly found amity. Still, it is simply incorrect to assert, as does Azmi Özcan in the introduction to his study on Ottoman-Indian-British connections, that the ambassador from Malabar returned empty-handed, except for words of sympathy and regret.[44] When the envoy of the sultan from Malabar was ready to return home, the Ottoman government sent word to wardens and officers all along the way from the fortresses on the Bosporus to Alexandria, as well as to the appropriate figures in Cairo, to ensure his safe passage along with the (rather limited) arms and munitions offered to him by the sultan.[45] The order is addressed to the "current governor of Egypt, former chief minister, the *vezīr* ʿİzzet Meḥmed Paşa, to the judge of Egypt, and the judges and deputies of the places and to the wardens and deputies of the fortresses along the coast from the Bosporus to Alexandria." The weapons are described as "three imperial cannons and their munitions" (*üç ʿaded şāhī topları mühimmātıyla*). The sultan in question is undoubtedly Ali Raja Kunhi Amsa II of Kannur and Arakkal, ruler of the small sultanate on the southwestern coast of the peninsula and the neighboring islands. Their capital city of Kannur would be completely overrun by the troops of the East India Company in 1790, and the dynasty continued to rule only as a British dependency. Another official document further orders the governor of Egypt to take the responsibility for arranging sea travel for the envoy and having him escorted safely to Jiddah by ship.[46] The wording of the command is clear and is made even clearer by the use of alliteration: the Egyptian authorities were to make sure that the envoy embark on an "adequate vessel" (*münāsib sefīneye irkāb*) at Suez and arrive "safe and sound" (*emīnen ve selīmen*) at his local destination (Jiddah).

This episode, along with the other documents relating to the region in the Ottoman archives, adds another theme to the portrait of the Red Sea, one that also relates to space, but internal space this time. Sultan ʿAli Rāca's embassy highlights the expansive global networks within which the Red Sea was articulated, but its treatment in the Ottoman records demonstrates how internally divided the sea was. Indeed, the order makes it clear that the governor of Egypt was accountable for the safe arrival of the envoy to Jiddah only, suggesting that this was, in a sense, the limit of the maritime sovereignty of the Ottoman sultan (since his guest was to continue his voyage all the way home). Of course, most of the shores of the Red Sea were under Ottoman control, and Ottomans were in fact present all around. But the sea itself was divided into two halves, with the separation line running more or less through Jiddah. The split is implicit in the Ottoman documents' focalization on Suez and Jiddah as polar reference points.

Over and above the compelling natural phenomena cutting the sea into north and south, described in chapter 1, the fundamental difference lies primarily in the political, discursive, and historiographic realms. Clearly, the Ottomans projected a special kind of power (political, military, economic, symbolic) over the area between Suez and Jiddah, and more precisely over the routes connecting Suez to Jiddah—as attested by the order concerning the return voyage of the Indian envoy. Control over the sea-lanes between Jiddah and Suez, between the Hijaz and Egypt, and the public display of such control, was crucial—hence the name *Baḥr-ı Süveys,* ubiquitous in Ottoman documents to refer to that space. This points to another factor in the production of the north-south division of the Red Sea, namely, the almost complete absence of mention of the southern portion of the sea from the Ottoman records for the period. Indeed, the region of Yemen on one side and the shores of Abyssinia on the other has a forceful presence in the Ottoman archives only in the earliest period following the conquest of those lands in the sixteenth century, and then after the reorderings of the nineteenth century. During the intervening period, by contrast, they make only rare, fleeting appearances, most of which have escaped the attention of scholars, who base themselves upon a different set of sources (such as chronicles and, mainly, European travel narratives, most notably those of Carsten Niebuhr, James Bruce, and John Burckhardt). Cengiz Orhonlu, an unequaled master of the Ottoman archives, is forced to rely almost exclusively on travel narratives when he discusses the eighteenth century in his classic account of the southern policy of the Ottoman Empire.[47] His sources of information here even include an Ottoman travel account, the *Tercüme-i Risāle-i Sūdān,* which is a fascinating document in its own right but one whose authenticity has been strongly put into doubt.[48]

The consensus regarding this intriguing archival absence is that it reflects the superficial nature of Ottoman sovereignty over these lands; but this is questionable. All sources indicate that, if perhaps "weaker," the Ottoman presence was significant and continuous (with the special exception of Yemen, of course). Burckhardt's account is often used to dismiss Ottoman rule as merely nominal, yet he himself reports, for example, the presence at Sawakin of an Ottoman governor, a garrison, and a customs chief to whom everyone in the region paid proper dues.[49] Moreover, he repeatedly signals the departure from there of numerous ships to different destinations across the sea, especially Jiddah, and mentions of sea-bound trade litter the account. The maritime connections were constant and easy. "No week passes without some vessel arriving from Djidda, or sailing for that port," writes Burckhardt, and Sawakin traders even had their own quarter in Jiddah, with huts resembling their own.[50] The cultural contact across the seas was so pervasive that people in the Hijaz could recognize he had been through Sawakin simply from the style of the sandals that Burckhardt had bought there.[51] He also noted the architectural commonalities between Jiddah and Sawakin, especially in the use of corals for building.[52]

Finally, it is important to note that these areas *do* make an occasional appearance in the archives for the period, in however rare and circumspect ways. For example, a record of the Chief Treasury's office in Istanbul mentions the revenues derived from Sawakin and Massawa for the year 1198 AH (around 1784 CE).[53]

Is this not sufficient evidence to warrant some form of full Ottomanity? And who is entitled to grant it? Is the historical imagination so limited that it is incapable of conceiving forms of politics and sovereignty outside either the despotic or the disciplinary regimes of power? Can analytical categories host only either direct and massive presence or complete autonomy/anarchy? These questions are all the more relevant considering the fact that the major references for the "only nominal sovereignty" view often had vested interests in the conclusions, since most were agents of foreign governments seeking footholds in the region. Of course, the point is not to reverse the claim and assert that the Ottoman state *was* present in full force during the period. In fact, the multiple plans for reassertion of central state control (from Cairo and/or Istanbul, among other locales) in the second half of the nineteenth century demonstrate well that it was not (or not in the way the reformers yearned for). On the contrary, the objective is to allow for alternative modes of governance and social interactions, which do not rely on an anachronistic understanding of state and society. Wael Hallaq's masterful analysis of the *shariʿa* presents a compelling model of an order that was fundamentally pluralistic and diverse, yet coherent, anchored largely in local self-rule, where the objective of the system was social harmony rather than social engineering.[54] Even in the case of the legally reformed state of turn-of-the-century Egypt, Will Hanley has recently demonstrated that sovereignty and citizenship remained divided and multilayered much longer than previously assumed, and that, since either/or models of citizenship did not apply, many people continued to assert a multiplicity of state affiliations and identities.[55] This stands in stark contrast to the project of universalizing norms of citizenship and legal personality: "In the preceding era of the disinterested state, when communities had the power of self-regulation, many individuals chose not to involve the state in their disputes, resolving them instead (or not resolving them, as the case may be) according to any number of informal or ad hoc means."[56]

FOREGROUND: GOD AND MAN AT SEA

Coming back to those documents that do exist, the repeated insistence on making sure the guest from Malabar made it safely through the voyage to Jiddah highlights the dangers of Red Sea navigation. Document 227 has much to say about this. The very next paragraph, in fact, speaks once more to the issue:

> Also, again in the same year [1154], a unit from the state flotilla named *Maḥmūdī* and reserved for the transportation of grains was destroyed by

calamity in the port of Suez due to the strength of the winds. Upon the request of the governor and chief judge of Egypt, a ship should be built in replacement of the ship by the name of *Maḥmūdī*, which in its old state carried a load of 8,500 *erdebs* of grains, on the condition that its price, reaching fifty Egyptian purses for all the equipment in addition to the remaining debris of the old ship, be deducted from the money of the treasury of the annual remittance.[57]

The text here makes a point of indicating that the ship was destroyed "*ḳażāen,*" that is, "by calamity," in the port of Suez, thereby seeking to explain the recurrence of such destruction, which is once more placed in the domain of the natural and supernatural order of things. This particular catastrophe is analyzed further as being "due to the strength of the winds" (*şiddet-i rüzgārdan*)—the force of divine nature par excellence when it comes to navigation, predictable yet ultimately unknowable.

The next allusion to the problem, in the following sentence, reinforces these same, unmistakable elements of the state's self-legitimizing argumentation: "Also, in the year [one thousand one hundred] fifty-seven, a ship belonging to the Muḥammediye named *vaḳf-ı şerīf* of Sultan Meḥmed Hān who dwells in paradise, mercy and compassion be upon him, burned in the port of Suez. In replacement for this *vaḳıf* ship, a vessel should be bought at a reasonable price from the merchant ships, on the condition that it be disbursed from the transfer money of the tax-farmed villages."[58] Here again a clear transfer of culpability is made from the all-too-human powers that be to a (super)natural order of things, nonetheless accompanied by a distinct assumption of responsibility on the part of the Ottoman state (on certain financial and budgetary conditions, of course, and in particular the incessant repetition of the need for the price to be reasonable, with the two possible treasury chests changing from paragraph to paragraph).

The references to the natural and supernatural were not unwarranted. Indeed, the difficulties of Red Sea navigation were notorious throughout the age of sail (and beyond, as will be discussed below in reference to the development of regular steam travel in the area). Travelers who left an account of their crossing of the sea invariably included mention of a traumatic experience, from Ibn Jubayr in the late twelfth century to Eyles Irwin in the late eighteenth century. The celebrated late fifteenth century navigator Aḥmad Ibn Mājid chided the common pilots of the Red Sea, who would follow routes hugging the coast in order to avoid the hazards of the high seas. This was "not the path of the true navigator," he noted, thus bringing greater honor onto himself and his fellow master captains (*muʿallims*) by affirming the dangerous intricacies of the venture.[59] "The dangers of this sea," warned Ibn Mājid, "are so numerous that they cannot be mentioned not even a few individual cases."[60] Shipwrecks were all too common, something Document 227 recurrently suggests and to which most relevant sources attest.

As described above (in chapter 1), wrecks were primarily a result of the natural, geological and climatic, configuration of the place—in particular, the treacherous currents, the abundance of underwater (and sometimes even emerging) reefs, and the unpredictable volatility of wind gusts. The latter factor is asserted in no unclear terms by Document 227: "destroyed by calamity . . . due to the strength of the winds." The unpredictable winds were particularly ferocious in the northern part of the sea, and the Gulf of Suez in particular—precisely the space covered by the Ottoman *Baḥr-ı Süveys*. In the words of the climatologist Frederick Edwards: "Most departures of the wind direction from the norm are associated with travelling disturbances of this type which generally only affect the Gulf of Suez and the northern part of the Red Sea."[61]

In any case, such difficulties of navigation were a well-known feature of these waters from antiquity onward, well before climatology emerged as an institutionalized science. At one point in his description of the region, Strabo writes of "a stretch of coast about one thousand stadia in length which is rugged and difficult for vessels to pass, for lack of harbours and anchoring-places, since a rugged and lofty mountain stretches along it. Then one comes to foot-hills, which are rocky and extend to the sea; and these, especially at the time of the Etesian winds and the rains, present to sailors a danger that is beyond help."[62]

This is only one passage in the text among many that evoke the danger of navigating these waters—and virtually all other accounts concerning the area mention it too. The description of the site of an ancient shipwreck off the coast of Eritrea by a contemporary archaeologist poignantly pictures the perils of the reefs: "Black Assarca, our base, is little more than an obstruction to shipping. Essentially, it is nothing but a massive sand-covered coral head lying two meters above sea level. Except for a sandy beach on its northern side, the island is nearly featureless. A reef, never more than a meter underwater, completely surrounds Black Assarca, forming a barrier to landing. At low tide, the highest tops of the coral protrude from the sea like pickets, as though defending the place from intrusion."[63] To quote the inimitable Evliyā Çelebī once again: "This *Baḥr-ı Süveys* is truly an unsafe sea" (*bu Bahri Süveys bîeman deryadir*).

PARALLAX VIEW: KNOWLEDGE AND POWER, GLOBAL AND LOCAL

All of these factors combined to create particular conditions that concentrated knowledge and power over navigation in the hands and minds of local pilots and captains, who had the unique training, skills, and perception that come from organic rearing in a place and profession. The reliance on local pilots and captains is manifest throughout the ages, making it also a distinctive feature of the personality of the sea in the *longue durée*. As for Document 227, in the very next segment it too raises the issue of the captaining and piloting of the ships, as well as the ever-thorny question of responsibility for the recurrence of wreckage and destruction. Departing from the appeal to the "natural order of things," it explicitly and directly orients itself, this time, to the most personal and individual of realms. "Also, in the year [one thousand one hundred] sixty," Document 227 continues, "the cause of the ruin of the ships meant for the transport of grains has, upon examination, been found to originate in the appointment of the ship captains on the basis of the receipt of improper bribes and in the ill-considered greed of the governors and notables of Egypt."[64]

Responsibility for the destiny of the ships lay quite firmly and logically in the hands of the captains (*reʾīs*). This theme that avarice and corruption are at the origin of the high rate of shipwrecks is a common one. It is echoed in Burckhardt's account: "The avidity of the masters in thus overloading their vessels often causes their ruin; about six months ago, two ships on their way from Djidda to Souakin, with a number of Negro pilgrims on board, were wrecked on the coast at a short distance to the north of Souakin; a few lives only were saved, and the cargoes were entirely lost."[65]

But culpability, at least in Document 227, was a more complex matter, relating to the political, social, and economic conditions of the region and the empire more largely. It was in the appointments of the ship captains, and in the operations behind them, that the problem lay. The extraordinary selfishness, the *ṭamʿ-ı hām* (an ill-considered or crude greed), of the region's dominant political class had caused the disasters at sea, along with the concomitant designation of ship captains on the basis of their compliance (through bribes) rather than efficiency or security. It is revealing that the text includes both the political elite appointed directly from Istanbul (the governors, *vülāt*) and the locally groomed ones (the notables, *aʿyān*), for the conventional narrative is one of fierce dichotomy between these two groups and orientations. The correct choice of ship captains was the crucial human element involved in the destiny of Red Sea navigation, and the Ottoman government therefore assumed its own responsibility to ensure that proper procedures were followed in this regard. How better to achieve this than by directly threatening the greedy where it hurt them most—in their pockets, as the popular expression goes? This solution had the added benefit of deflecting potentially heavy costs away from the state treasury. Thus, Document 227 announces, upon the heels of the discovery of the immediate reasons for the recurrent destructions,

> Two vessels from the merchant ships that can each carry loads of ten thousand *erdebs* and above should be bought, and labeled Meccan and Medinan. By way of an imperial command, the Meccan ship will be committed to the charge of the governors of Egypt and the Medinan one to the Seven Corps. They will be entrusted, upon the time of their departure, with the condition that their merchant loads be superior to ten thousand *erdebs* each, and also, upon their return, with the money of the merchants and the servants, and they will see to the maintenance costs of the coming and going. A certificate, sealed with the stamp of the judges of Mecca and Medina and the governor of the province of Medina, should be brought to Egypt that accords with the one that is brought from Egypt, and from there it should also be sent to my Sublime Porte. With the said conditions, precautions are taken against the appointment of improper ship captains. And if destruction must come, the governor of Egypt will bear the indemnity of the Meccan ship and the Seven Corps that of the Medinan. On such condition, and as per the request of the governor of Egypt, with imperial permission two large vessels should be bought from the merchant ships available at the port of Suez, on the condition that they be new and reliable. So that their price be calculated from money of the annual remittance, the legal title-deeds should be sent to the Gate of Felicity.[66]

Betraying annoyance and a certain loss of control over essential matters of state, the order exposes here the broad social and political networks implicated in the Red Sea, bringing in a panoply of officials and functionaries to serve as checks and balances over each other in order to ensure the proper conclusion of affairs. Ultimate authority, of course, lies, here and everywhere, in the person of the sultan himself and his court—but it is a distant authority, and the execution of the state's will must therefore follow indirect and highly sophisticated channels, with a paper trail traversing lands and seas and ending up, always, in Istanbul.

As the high rate of destruction was found to be due to local corruption, it was decided that the *financial* responsibility for the ships, and especially the cost of their potential indemnity, would rest with those culpable: on the one hand, the governors, appointed from Istanbul and eternally attempting to gain access to the revenues of the province that were increasingly monopolized by the Mamluks and their dependents; on the other, the Seven Corps, the locally groomed militiamen who formed the basis of the Mamluks' system of power and of their extensive social and economic networks. This ought to prevent the appointment of incompetent ship captains, in addition to enforcing closer and stricter surveillance of the assets on board. Furthermore, the examiners themselves were to be examined by way of the exchange of precise official documentation with various functionaries in the Hijaz, whose natural interests (unlike those of the officials in Cairo) would have made them favorable to the smooth and regular arrival of the customary provisions (upon which their fortunes and the sustenance of the local population depended), and therefore likely to enforce the required inspections. Finally, the certificates were all to make their way to the imperial capital. This was the imposition of an additional locus of ultimate surveillance for the actual transactions, of course, but also a performative affirmation of the emanating source of symbolic power, both in the flow of the text itself and in the regular dispatches that it called for.

This segment once again implicates the varying spatialities found in Document 227's idea of the Red Sea, but it also points toward a variety of differential temporalities. Indeed, in the Red Sea conjured by this text, just as in the case of Braudel's Mediterranean, the (super)natural and eternal flows through the sociopolitical and conjectural and into the petty and personal. Time in this text is anything but chronometric, and space anything but homogeneous. There is a clear sense that both of these concepts are tied to and mediated by many others.

These combined themes of passing time and expanding space return in the next segment as well, in what is perhaps the most interesting and revealing passage of all, as Document 227 dwells on the important question, to which it has alluded before, of the difficult and intricate modalities of shipbuilding on the shores of the Red Sea.

"In the year [one thousand one hundred] seventy-four also," the following sentence begins, driving the text closer and closer to its date of production (and completing an initial full circle by reaching the time of the very first example cited),

> during the period of the above-mentioned deceased Kāmil Aḥmed Paşa's governorship, noble decrees were repeatedly sent on the part of my Imperial

Chancery. In the years [one thousand one hundred] seventy-five and seventy-six, as per the command issued by the grand vizier, in the harbor of the port of Süveys, by way of Ağa Vekīli ʿO̱sman Ağa from Egypt's Cairo, one unit worth sixty-seven Egyptian purses and two other units worth each seventy-two and a half Egyptian purses of the state galleons type, reserved for the transport of grains for the Two Noble Sanctuaries, should be built for the *vaḳıf* of Sultan Meḥmed Hān, who dwells in paradise, mercy and compassion be upon him. Their costs were disbursed from the treasury of the yearly cash revenue of Egypt. During the said two years, by way of the governor of the district of Rhodes Süleymān Paşa, the necessary timber was cut from the mountains of Rhodes and Gökciğez and the necessary tar, pitch, and resin were purchased from Mount Ida and its environs for the purpose of the said ships. The total costs, 26,187.5 *ğurūş* including transport to Alexandretta, were sent. In addition to these, the necessary anchor, wool string, linen for the sails, and other required equipment have been arranged for from the material existing at the Imperial Dockyard, and two thousand *ḳınṭārs* of crude iron have also been arranged for from the material existing at the Imperial Arsenal. Loaded onto ships, they were immediately sent to Alexandretta. In addition to that given from the storage of the Arsenal, two thousand *ḳınṭārs* of pure iron were purchased from Kavala and Pravişte and Zihne and those environs and were loaded onto a ship in the port of Salonica and sent to Rhodes.[67]

This passage gives a good sense of the extensive efforts involved in the construction of ships on the Red Sea. It was clearly an affair that implicated impressively wide and efficient organizational networks in order to coordinate the necessary undertakings covering enormous distances during a significant period of time. Over the course of no less than two years, Suez was at the center of a costly enterprise involving the lands of the Mediterranean and the Black Sea coast, where lumber was plentiful, as well as the Balkans, which produced the necessary steel. The imperial center, stocked with gigantic productive capacity, also contributed to the material (and not only to the cash funds). Shipped from the various locations, the equipment was all centralized in Alexandretta on the southernmost Mediterranean coast of today's Turkey, before making its way to Suez (although this part is left to the reader's imagination). The breadth of the effort seems astounding—and that is exactly the rhetorical effect desired by the text. The time involved (two years) is mentioned twice, and the geographical stretch is sketched out in detail.

But most important, clearly, were the financial expenditures that such Red Sea shipbuilding set in motion—a point driven home yet again in the sentence immediately following, which goes back in time against the chronological flow of events precisely so as to mention once more the potential capital that the venture entailed: "And in the year [one thousand one hundred] sixty, by way of the chief of the reservist corps, and at the cost of 145 Egyptian purses, two galleons were constructed."[68]

FALL OF THE CURTAIN: WRITING SPACE AND TIME

In this way, Document 227 finally reaches the immediate issue at hand. Ships were needed for the provisioning of foodstuffs to the Hijaz, as the flotilla dedicated to this task had suffered losses of units, and it was the responsibility of the state to ensure their replacement. At the heart of the concern, then, was the question of the source of the new ships.

The first reaction, surely, would have been to appeal to the most logical solution at hand in terms of productivist protectionism and to build the ships at the Suez dockyard. It is, of course, anachronistic to speak of productivism or protectionism concerning this time and place. The terms are used here in full cognizance of this important problem and should not be seen to imply the fully fledged espousal by the Ottoman government of these economic and fiscal ideologies. Still, it is impossible not to notice the sense of need, on the part of the Ottoman state, to justify, along a most long-winded and convoluted argumentation, the decision to purchase private and even foreign ships rather than to construct them within Ottoman domains and under public auspices. This strongly suggests the existence and weight of an ideological spirit akin to some sort of productivist protectionism, which counters the standard trope regarding the "Ottoman economic mind."

The iterative accumulation of the recurrently mobilized cases and precedents, however, led to the conclusion that financial and political necessity produced its own logic, especially in the case of a state suffering severe economic duress and highly concerned by the symbolic weight invested in the problem. "On the basis of the preceding, the manner by which the costs for the construction of the said ships not be caused to increase was made clear by the summary of the receipt account submitted by the Chief Treasurer's Office to the Imperial Chancery in the year [one thousand one hundred] eighty-one. Thus, since it is of the oldest of matters, it needs no demonstration that utmost care and attention should be given to the building of ships in timely and proper fashion and to the procurement of the requisites and necessities at favorable costs."[69]

One senses Document 227 wanting to say that unfortunately it was probably cheaper and certainly quicker and easier to purchase the ships than to build them. And the issue was pressing and absolutely crucial. "In any case," the text asserts with grand solemnity, "that the poor among the population of the Two Noble Sanctuaries be free of the bonds of scarcity through the preparation of ships and the transportation of provisions is among the necessary corollaries of the glory and magnificence of my exalted sultanate."[70]

Thus has the text come full circle, addressing once again the fundamental problematic that it opened with: the Red Sea and its coasts formed a world utterly reliant upon the importation of foodstuffs from the outside. Furthermore, it was the noble responsibility of the state to ensure the constant flow of goods around the Red Sea. Finally, these were elements belonging to the natural, and supernatural, order of things—that is precisely why they were such a great source of its legitimacy and symbolic capital. They were purposefully inscribed in the *longue durée,* and this is another effect of the rhetorical flourish of examples. That is why the stylistic and symbolic weight of the constant principle of precedence and the recurrent appeal to the past is so integral to the text, not only in its prose, but also in its argument and meaning. Iterative diction here constitutes the very embodiment of time. It performs the space for time to grow. "Time does not pass," says literary critic Ian Baucom, "it accumulates."[71] The Ottoman state knew this. It discovered, further, that time in fact needs to be *made* to accumulate, for in order to accumulate it requires a structure, a body, a narrative. It is the accumulation of time, then, that is repeatedly inscribed in, by, and as Document 227. Thus the place of the past, its authority, its burden, is not, contrary to common wisdom, retrovisionary. It neither looks nor seeks to go back to a pristine golden age. It is about placing, grounding time so as to be, to act, to look forward. This is, on a different dimension, the basic thrust of the insight pioneered by Alasdair MacIntyre concerning the concept of tradition. "We are apt," he famously argues, "to be misled here by the ideological uses to which the concept of tradition has been put by conservative political theorists. Characteristically such theorists have followed Burke in contrasting tradition with reason and the stability of tradition with conflict. Both contrasts obfuscate. For all reasoning takes place within the context of some traditional mode of thought, transcending through criticism and invention the limitations of what had hitherto been reasoned in that tradition; this is as true of modern physics as of medieval logic."[72] And it is even true of punctual bureaucratic orders concerning the need to buy a ship, as Document 227 seeks precisely to perform tradition in the effort to create a space for common reasoning and behaving.

Ian Baucom credits as primary inspiration for the idea of the accumulation of time and the past the Martiniquan author Édouard Glissant, whose temporal perspective he contrasts with Walter Benjamin's more famous remarks on time, its past and its present, as a flash, a sudden image. Baucom, following Glissant, is, in the last instance, speaking about modernity and its temporality. The borrowing of the image of accumulating time here is a free one: it is not meant to engage the question of modernity, however conceived. Still, Glissant's vision as recaptured by Baucom is not completely absent from the issues at hand with Ottoman Document 227. Glissant's understanding of temporal accumulation contrasts with Walter Benjamin's famous vision of history as "seizing hold of a memory as it flashes," which is itself set against Ranke's *wie es eigentlich gewesen*.[73] For Glissant, Baucom explains, the lightning flash is "a figure of desire, the not-yet, and the impossible," whereas the accumulation of time operates "as a figure of necessity, the unending, and the unavoidable."[74] Where Benjamin's writings yearn for a messianic future, Glissant's have the weight of an elongated now: "The past with which a poetics of duration corresponds does not, however, await the future advent of a coming practice of historical materialism in order to detonate the charge of what-has-been. Rather, for Glissant the what-has-been *is,* and it is *lived,* and it is lived as the total environment linking together the 'histories of peoples.'"[75]

The expanse of time covered by Document 227 is in fact not particularly long—not even forty years, actually, from 1154 AH, the earliest moment mentioned, to 1191, when the text itself was composed (or 1192, taking into account the marginal note indicating the repeat of the order). But the sheer repetition in writing of the recurrence of the problem gives it a depth and breadth that far outweigh the chronological span. There was, of course, no strict analytical need to bring up previous cases, and certainly not with such detail of exposition. The order easily could have limited itself to the first paragraph before introducing the actual command. The significance of repetition lies elsewhere, in the symbolic and rhetorical spheres. On the one hand, it underlines how enduring a feature of the Red Sea's *longue durée* the problem was, how much people's lives and actions were constrained by it, and how everyone was conscious of the ensuing problem. On the other hand, it emphasizes how repetitively and extensively the Ottoman state was performing its noble duty by getting involved in the matter. The former element is necessary for the sustenance of the latter, since, if ultimately the problem could not be solved once and for all, it was not as a result of a deficiency on the part of a state that was doing its utmost, but precisely because it was an endless predicament. And conversely, the former depends on the latter, for it is only part of the *longue durée* because the state and the society were invested in it as a problem in the first place. Life, in the abstract, was not unsustainable in the Red Sea world at all, as demonstrated by the simple fact that most areas subsisted without support from any state structure. It was the particular form of life that the state and society supported, most notably urban agglomerations, that was unsustainable without external intervention.

The rest of Document 227 is the actual command, articulated mainly in the form of an assemblage of snippets from the previous segments, thereby embodying in its very structure the crucial element of precedence, and culminating in the order to purchase the ships so as to ensure the subsistence of the Red Sea world—the order itself involves a self-reiteration almost word for word (something that is not unusual in the genre):

> As it was done in the past, appropriate ships should be bought in those parts, and their costs transferred from the money of the treasury of the annual remittance of Egypt. The well-versed ship captains should see to the loading and carrying and transporting of the provisions as well as the maintenance and costs of the coming and goings. They should pay attention to follow the older procedures and precedents. In the case of destruction having to come, the modalities of the compensation should be carried out. On these conditions, the required number of ships should be purchased and bought from the merchant vessels, if available, at the port of Suez at a cost not exceeding the old ones. To this end, upon the notification made by my present chief treasurer Ḥasan, may his grandeur be enduring, my Imperial Chancery issued my noble command that you, who are the above-mentioned *Vezīr* and *Şayh ül-beled* and officers of the Seven Corps, should jointly pay attention and care to the advancement of the matter. Thus, in respect of the fact that the due attention to the matter of organizing and advancing this issue within the time and conditions required is of the oldest issues that require attention, and as you know that in any case the poor from the population of the Two Noble Sanctuaries are free of the bonds of scarcity through the preparation of ships and that the transportation of provisions is among the necessary corollaries of the glory and magnificence of my exalted sultanate, appropriate ships should be bought in those parts as it was done in the past, and their costs transferred from the annual remittance of Egypt. The appointed

> captains of manifest proficiency should see to the ships' cargo, to the loading and carrying and transporting of the provisions as well as the maintenance and costs of the comings and goings. They should pay attention to follow the older procedures and precedents. In the case of destruction having to come by God's decree, and on the condition that the modalities of the compensation be carried out according to the old practices, the required number of ships should be purchased and bought from the merchant vessels, if available, at the port of Suez at a cost not exceeding the old ones. You should act accordingly, use your knowledge, judgment, and ability, and devote paramount attention and care in buying and purchasing. Thus you are to avoid and evade at the extreme utmost the negligence and carelessness that lead to the population of the two illustrious cities being subjected to hardship, which is contrary to my sovereign approval.[76]

At the very end, providing the signal of termination of the order and separation from the text, comes the date: "in the middle of *Cumādā 'l-ūlā,* year 1191."[77] Thus, as if to provide a symmetrical contrast with the repetitive temporality and iterative style of the body of the text, the finale strikes a single, utterly simple note, trumpeting the direct authority of the command, which is so transparent that it is reducible to a pointillistic temporality. After the wearisome journey along the lane of the past littered with pit stops of varying lengths and differing meanings, the terminus arrives with the thump of a precise date. The differential effect is perhaps most visible on the level of analysis. Indeed, the final element gives reason to be interpreted, in evident distinction from the long-winded exegesis of the body of the text above, as follows: on June 21, 1777 CE, the Ottoman government ordered its functionaries in the province of Egypt to purchase as many ships as necessary to ensure the continued provisioning in grain of the Holy Cities in accordance with tradition.

Thus must this inquisition (in the form of a disquisition) of Document 227 come to a close as well, and with it, too, the Ottoman self-portrait of the Red Sea presented here. It is, admittedly, an impressionistic portrait; conspicuous are both its absences and presences. Among the former, first and foremost comes the lack of a coherent narrative of an embodied space along chronometric time. As for the latter, most noticeable surely is the crossing and overlapping of various spatialities and temporalities, which fold into the world of the Red Sea a multitude of places from Malabar to Istanbul (via, among others, Cairo, Alexandretta, Rhodes, and Kavala) according to a variety of rhythms: the immediate time of the command, the potential time of the purchase of the ships, the intermediate time of the construction of ships, the seasonal time of sailing, the cyclical time of pilgrimage, the eternal time of provisioning the Holy Cities, the catastrophic time of shipwrecks, the natural time of the dangers of navigation, the political time of provincial rebellion, the social time of bandits, the repetitive time of inscribing. As in the case of the Ottomans and their Red Sea, but in contrast to the age of the world picture, it is not an absolute claim over time and space that is asserted here, but a fundamentally mediated one, overdetermined by the effusive-yet-diffuse space of reading and the endless-yet-finite time of writing, with Document 227 as pilot, reference, native informant, and victim all in one.

FOUR

The Scientific Invention of the Red Sea

THE RED SEA WAS CAPTURED textually before any of its shores were subjected to enduring colonial control, though this was executed in the context of a rapidly expanding British dominance over the region in particular, and the globe more largely. Just as the Crown's navy was gaining greater and greater control of the Indian Ocean, so too did it seek to reinforce its position in the Mediterranean.[1] It was only logical for the connecting Red Sea to be appropriated as well.

Clearly printed, easily accessible, and widely reproduced, the *Sailing Directions for the Red Sea* has been heralded since its publication in 1841 as the first scientific charting of the space in question, a true breakthrough in the knowledge of the region.[2] The title was unwittingly deceptive, for it purported simply to provide navigational directions to a known quantity. But there was in fact something radically new about the text, since, rather than constituting a linear increase in knowledge, it did much to create the space that it claimed to describe: the Red Sea, seen as a clearly delineated scientific object, about which particular truth claims could be made. In stark contrast to Ottoman Document 227 analyzed in the previous chapter, it asserted an absolute, homogeneous notion of space (not a mediated one), no matter what fissures and aporias such a claim would have to contend with.

The title of this chapter consciously echoes that of a volume devoted to the Mediterranean, *L'invention scientifique de la Méditerranée,* which itself evokes the classic article on the question by Anne Ruel, who opened "L'invention de la Méditerranée" with a pioneering insight: "It is only with the beginning of the nineteenth century that one can speak of a Mediterranean."[3] Likewise, one cannot properly speak of a Red Sea until the same period. The fundamental theoretical impulse is shared, namely, that far from being out there to be unveiled, geographical regions require a particular kind of historically bound treatment for them to be produced in the first place. Scientific objects in general, and the spatial categories of the geographical discipline in particular, cannot be taken as pregiven but ought rather to be explored as the heterogeneous and power-laden outcomes of specific genealogies.

Just as the objectification of the Mediterranean was connected, in many ways, to an eminently French imperial project, so was the Red Sea an especially British object of imperial attention.[4] This point should not be overstated. There certainly exists a distinctly British genealogy of the Mediterranean too, running, say, from Lord Byron to Lawrence Durrell, from the protectorate over the United States of the Ionian Islands to the protectorate over Cyprus, and there is also a German strand (with Goethe and Hegel at the helm), and yet others.

Still, it is no coincidence that the charting of the Red Sea was performed by employees of the Indian navy. That said, such an imperial production of the Red Sea did not take place in a vacuum. There were numerous competing claims in the region, both big and small. These are excavated in Isa Blumi's work, which brings to life the multiplicity of actors that constituted the historical dynamics around the area.[5] Throughout the nineteenth century, there was a "scramble to secure reliable, local allies," without which it was impossible for merchants or administrators of whatever affiliation to settle throughout the region of the Red Sea and the Persian Gulf.[6] It was precisely these types of connections that facilitated the subsequent extension of state power, as "these attempts to gain control over territorial assets prove to be the pillars of the Tanzimat reforms evolving during this crucial period of comparative imperial history in which all major state-centralization reforms in neighboring empires took place."[7] This is an important corrective to the assumption of the omnipotence of the modern imperial state, which, as with the scientific saga discussed here, was much more muddled than later master-narratives are wont to admit.

APPLIED METAPHYSICS

The problem of the scientific fact was addressed in a now classic work of the new science studies. To a poetically evocative title, *Laboratory Life* (1979), authors Bruno Latour and Steve Woolgar adduced a more mundane, though no less radical, explanatory subtitle: *The Construction of Scientific Facts*.[8]

Scientific facts, they show by an ethnographic examination of the workings of a laboratory, are produced by the quotidian activities of scientists. This does not, however, make them any less real. Their conclusion is confirmed by an etymological detour: the word *fact* derives from a Latin root *facere,* meaning "to make or do," whence also the term *artifact.* Of the two, only the latter has maintained the sense of being created. "Facts and artefacts," they argue, "do not correspond respectively to true and false statements. Rather, statements lie along a continuum according to the extent to which they refer to the conditions of their construction. . . . *Our argument is not just that facts are socially constructed. We also wish to show that the process of construction involves the use of certain devices whereby all traces of production are made extremely difficult to detect.*"[9]

An appeal to a sovereign reality simply cannot provide for a stable basis of scholarly practice. "At the frontier of science," Latour and Woolgar's ethnography reveals, "statements are constantly manifesting a double potential: they are either accounted for in terms of local causes (subjectivity or artefact) or are referred to as a thing 'out there' (objectivity and fact)."[10] The importance of this observation is that it dissolves the distinction between the fact and the artifact, between reality and psychological conditions. In other words: "'Reality' cannot be used to explain why a statement becomes a fact, since it is only after it has become a fact that the effect of reality is obtained."[11]

Reality, then, is an effect, and it must be *obtained.* Roland Barthes had explored this principle in a famous 1968 essay carrying that title ("L'effet de réalité") by subjecting to semiotic analysis the "useless details" that are inevitable in realist narratives, both fiction (Flaubert) and nonfiction (Michelet).[12] What Barthes shows is that in the discursive formation to which both writers belong, "'Reality' becomes the essential reference in historical narrative, which is supposed to report 'what really happened': what does the nonfunctionality of a detail matter then, once it denotes 'what took place'; 'concrete reality' becomes the sufficient justification for speaking."[13] And here, history takes central stage: "History (historical discourse: *historia rerum gestarum*) is in fact the model of those narratives which consent to fill in the interstices of their functions by structurally superfluous notations, and it is logical that literary realism should have been . . . contemporary with the regnum of 'objective' history."[14]

What is radically transformed, then, in the wake of such studies, is the very notion of reality. Reality can no longer be understood in absolute terms, counterpoised to its contrary in proper Cartesian dualism. This profound breakthrough in the study of scientific practice and its history comes in the wake of a radical reorientation of philosophical attention identified by Foucault as a shift from the "philosophy of experience, of meaning, of the subject" dear to Sartre and Merleau-Ponty, to a "philosophy of knowledge, of rationality, of the concept" formulated by Canguilhem, Bachelard, Cavaillès, or Koyré.[15] It is this deep transformation of the locus of scholarly attention that Lorraine Daston has named "applied metaphysics."[16] The modifier *applied* is opposed to *pure* metaphysics, which "treats the ethereal world of what is always and everywhere from a God's-eye-viewpoint" (1). By contrast, applied metaphysics "studies the dynamic world of what emerges and disappears from the horizon of working scientists" (1). It thus avoids the pitfalls of a conventional historiography based on the assumption of the constancy of historical objects. The scholar's objects do not exist "always and everywhere" to be defined in their essence once and for all; rather, they come into being through the scientific practice itself, and when it shifts its attention they can even disappear. This argument reorients the analytical lens onto the scientists themselves, the discipline embodied in their practice, the rhetoric inhabiting their texts, the power embedded in their ideas, the grammar organizing their concepts.

Daston too makes insightful use of etymological exploration, evoking an era when *invention* and *discovery* were synonyms, not antonyms. Only in the eighteenth century, she shows, did "the distinction between what is and what is made bec[o]me unavoidable, a metaphysical axiom" (4). Then an essential distinction came to separate the "novelty" inherent in both invention and discovery into a "novelty revealed, as an explorer fills in a blank spot on the world map," and a "novelty contrived, as an artisan manufactures a device." Other words radically changed meaning around the same time, such as *realism*, *objective*, and *fact*. Perhaps the trajectory of the word *objective* is the most revealing: it "performed a volte-face, from its fourteenth-century meaning referring to objects of consciousness to its late eighteenth-century meaning referring to objects external to consciousness" (4).

Of particular relevance to the arguments made throughout this book, the approach of applied metaphysics shakes the very concept of reality, for the assumption becomes "that reality is a matter of degree and that phenomena that are indisputably real in the colloquial sense that they exist may become more or less intensely real, depending on how densely they are woven into scientific thought and practice" (4). Thus the Red Sea obviously existed before its scientific charting, but it was real in a different sense—and what needs to be explored is precisely the ways in which it was real, according to what criteria, and to what effect. Transcending the sterile polemics regarding the "reality" versus the "social/historical construction" of certain concepts or things, this new idea of reality "posits that scientific objects can be simultaneously real *and* historical" (3). There is thus a difference between a quotidian object and a scientific one that has been transformed by the process of scientific scrutiny: a scientific object has a solid coherence, molded by a clear interior and exterior, defined by specific and recurrent criteria. It is then not a case of arguing that the objects under study were not real and suddenly became so; much to the contrary, the goal is to explore "how a heretofore unknown, ignored, or dispersed set of phenomena is transformed into a scientific object that can be observed and manipulated, that is capable of theoretical ramifications and empirical surprises, and that coheres at least for a time, as an ontological entity" (5).

This is why it is important to take seriously the absence of the category "Red Sea" in Ottoman discourse and its sudden appearance in the mid-nineteenth century. *Baḥr-ı Süveys* (the Sea of Suez) was not just another term for the same object. Rather, it molded a different reality, now no more, with varying contours and genealogies, and alternative effects. It implicated its authors and practitioners in intricate webs of mutual interactions, from the most abstract and cosmological to the most practical. The invention of the Red Sea as a scientific object asserted a notion of space that was absolute and homogeneous, unlike the spatiality of the *Baḥr-ı Süveys* in the Ottoman text analyzed in the preceding chapter. Thus not only do ideological, political, and social elements enter scholarly practices, but these themselves open up the field of possibility for ideology and politics of a particular kind.

Applied metaphysics thus urges the scholar to pay attention to the *practice* and *rhetoric* of scientific inquiry: rather than the epic of the revelation of a reality that was always already there just waiting to be unveiled, science becomes a matter of producing new objects imbricated in material and ideational structures of power relations. It also leads to the realization that making truth claims about the world is not simply a constative act but a performative one, in J. L. Austin's parlance; or, as Ian Hacking has it, science is not merely a matter of representing the world but of intervening in it.[17] That is, scientific utterances are never merely statements that can be measured in correspondence to pregiven facts but are also acts of creation that elicit the facts themselves and lead to real changes. It is an explicitly parallel feature that Dominick LaCapra develops in his distinction between the "documentary" and the "worklike" aspects of texts: "The documentary situates the text in terms of factual or literal dimensions involving reference to empirical reality and conveying information about it. The worklike supplements empirical reality by adding to, and subtracting from, it."[18] "With deceptive simplicity," he adds, "one might say that while the documentary marks a difference, the worklike makes a difference—one that engages the reader in recreative dialogue with the text and the problems it raises."[19] The molding of a particular object of scientific attention thus not only creates the object itself but also has an impact on the world around it.[20]

The scientific invention of the Red Sea not only brought it into being as an object that could be defined textually and pictorially, and therefore subjected to imperial power from afar. It also indicated by its own spectacle which power ought to dominate that new space. Creating the Red Sea as a *legible* and *scripted* space was necessary for the exercise of imperial power upon it, just as the very performance of science was integral to the constitution of imperial power.[21] This is why Edward Said defined imperialism as "an act of *geographical* violence through which virtually every space in the world is explored, charted, and finally brought under control."[22] At the same time, modern colonial science could not help but involve elements that undermined its own claim to difference. Like the clichéd return of the repressed, the traditional, the local, the non-European, the nonscientific, the irrational, the nonscriptable, surreptitiously erupt at various points of the self-narrative of modern European written science.[23] This ambivalence is partly why modern science, however objective and rational it claims to be, is never sufficient unto itself and usually comes accompanied by guns, bombs, and warships, along with other disciplinary institutions and infrastructures of all kinds.

Such a genealogical exploration of the Red Sea is important for reasons both epistemological and ethical: not only because a particular convention is shown to be not the only or best way to describe the world but also because such classifications are not merely descriptions but acts in the world, with serious material consequences, and also, finally, because it ineluctably opens the way to engage *other* traditions (nonmodern, non-European) on their own terms rather than as deficient or primitive renditions of the modern. In other words, it is crucial to realize that the Red Sea is not the same object as the Ottoman *Baḥr-ı Süveys*, not only because the two denominations classify the world differently, but also because the dichotomy forces us to think through a different overall way of representing and intervening in the world.

What follows draws from these insights to explore the scientific invention of the Red Sea: its subjection to disciplined scrutiny, its charting as a discrete space on the map, its transformation into an object of scholarly attention. The Red Sea obviously existed before its scientific invention (though differently for different people), but it had not crystallized into a coherent epistemological and ontological entity. The term *invention* should be taken in its nonmodern meaning, as akin, not opposed, to *discovery*.[24]

MUDDLED BEGINNINGS

The story of the scientific invention of the Red Sea is a part of the saga of cartography and empire in the wider Indian Ocean world, which reached its zenith with the launching of the Great Trigonometrical Survey of British India that spanned the entire nineteenth century. Anchored in the novel method of triangulation, which saw itself as establishing "an exact equivalence between the geographic archive and the world," this grand cartographic project sought to "reduce India to a rigidly coherent, geometrically accurate, and uniformly precise imperial space, a rational space within which a systematic archive of knowledge about the Indian landscapes and people might be constructed."[25] Crucially, the historian Matthew Edney adds that "the meaning of empire is inscribed into each map," so that, in the end, what was cartographically captured was not an eternal geographical entity called India but *British* India specifically.[26] The charting of the Red Sea as well was imbricated from the very beginning in its imperial setting, just as it was thoroughly intertwined with other technological, commercial, and political changes of the age, such as the introduction of steam power in long-distance navigation, itself a central actor in the nineteenth-century imperial reorderings.

The first thing to note about the transformation of cartography and geography into scholarly practices is their muddled beginnings, seamlessly blending literary, artistic, and scientific operations. The hybrid origins of the practices are perhaps most evident in the multiplicity of genres within which the results of the surveys were published at the time. The surveyors were thus also authors, in addition to being often administrators or military men—and they would produce simultaneously, often with identical data, travel narratives, governmental/military reports, and articles in one of the newly founded scholarly journals. Thus the most up-to-date surveying of the Red Sea in the early nineteenth century (executed under the command of Captain Court) was in fact published as a chart in the travel account of Lord Valentia, who accompanied him. Apart from this three-volume narrative, Valentia penned numerous governmental letters and memos now kept in the National Archives.[27] This multiplicity of genres that eventually crystallized into the absolutist scientific practice of cartographic surveying was taken for granted by the great nineteenth-century chronicler of the Indian Surveys Clements Markham. Though obviously enraptured by the positivistic truth of geographical science, he begins his foundational account of the Indian Surveys with a platitude that carries more meaning than first strikes the eye: "The Surveys of India began along the coasts, and the sailors preceded the shore-going surveyors by nearly 200 years. . . . Before India could be measured, it was necessary to get there."[28] There follows an extended discussion of the many ventures to chart multiple parts of the Indian Ocean, the references shifting with ease from travel narratives to archival documents and scholarly journals.

Further muddling any idea of pristine science, the hybrid quality of the Red Sea's scientific invention was compounded by the signal fact that the process was deeply embedded in a context both bellicose and colonial: the first serious stab at charting those waters came on the heels of the British military expedition to oust the French Armée d'Orient from Egypt. This too was gladly acknowledged by Markham: "The expedition to the coast of Egypt led to an examination of the Red Sea in 1799–1800, and Sir Home Popham, who commanded the fleet, drew up some sailing directions for its navigation."[29] But the results remained limited, and Lord Valentia complained to the governor-general of British India, Lord Wellesley, that it was "a national disgrace that the western coast of the Red Sea should be a perfect blank on our charts."[30] Finding a supportive ear in the ambitious governor-general, he took the initiative of rectifying the national disgrace himself, an effort that led ultimately in 1809 to the publication of his *Voyages and Travels*, which included the chart by Captain Court. Only with his death, and replacement by Daniel Ross, known as "the Father of the Indian Surveys," did the surveying practice obtain Markham's approval as operating according to "a really scientific method."[31] This was in 1823, and the said scientific method was the trigonometrical approach of triangulation, aided by astronomical observations.[32]

This was also, and it is no coincidence, the beginning of the era of long-distance steam navigation. A great debate took place in British imperial circles regarding the value of launching a regular steam service from the Isles to

India by way of the Red Sea. The single most important fixation of the British long nineteenth century was the famed route to India; and the greatest difficulty on the way, when it came to steam navigation, was that of gaining regular access to coal. Though a presentist bias makes it seem that the supremacy of steam must have been immediately evident and inevitable, it did not appear so at the time. Indeed, the domination of steam navigation in many parts of the world did not make itself felt until the late nineteenth century, and even then it often continued in tandem with sail transport. This was especially the case in such dangerous waters as the Red Sea, where the fierce winds made steam much less efficient. Meantime, local sailing traditions and expertise had established regular and constant contact between the shores for millennia in intimate collaboration with the environment, both human and natural. In the first half of the nineteenth century, steam navigation to India was not a foregone conclusion. Much to the contrary, the East India Company, for example, remained unconvinced. Various parties staked their positions (ranging from complete rejection of the technology to an ardent, almost chiliastic belief in its potentially world-transforming effects), based on a number of arguments centering on cost, feasibility, and rapidity. Three main routes were discussed: one, exclusively maritime, rounded the Cape of Good Hope; the two others were amphibious, one passing through the Persian Gulf and the other through the Red Sea.

The question of the preferable route was in fact derived from similar discussions dating back to the second half of the eighteenth century, when the Red Sea found its first iteration as a distinct object of public attention. The Red Sea in this case was mainly conceived as a *route* rather than a distinct place. Nonetheless, heightened interest in the Red Sea set the stage for its eventual constitution as a discrete object of scientific scrutiny.

THE WAY TO THE JEWEL: WAR, COMMERCE, AND SCIENCE

The main protagonist of the saga of the Red Sea route in the late eighteenth century was the merchant and diplomat George Baldwin.[33] Already before him, both the traveler James Bruce and the governor-general of Bengal Warren Hastings claimed to have established agreements with the leading Mamluk bey of Egypt, Muḥammad Abū al-Dhahab, allowing the British to trade directly through Suez.[34] The great advantage of the Red Sea route was its shortness. The issue of distance had come to a head in the context of the late eighteenth-century wars dominated by the Franco-British imperial rivalry, and Baldwin claimed that he had saved the Crown by ensuring the swift transfer to India of the news of the declaration of war in 1778, giving the British a decisive advantage that allowed them to overrun French possessions there.[35] Baldwin even suggested that his actions had partly inspired the French invasion of Egypt itself.[36]

Ottoman officials sought to maintain the northern Red Sea ports free of European vessels. The British ambassador to Constantinople, Sir Robert Ainslie, advised repeatedly against infringing on this directive from the Porte.[37] However, in the mid-1780s, the Red Sea would gain renewed attention in British circles, as news was heard of a treaty having been agreed between Mamluk beys and an envoy of the French king, the Chevalier de Truguet, obtaining the right of French vessels to navigate the Red Sea. French designs on India constituted one of the dominant themes of British foreign policy throughout the period.[38] As a direct result of this Franco-Mamluk agreement (whether the Ottoman government approved is highly unlikely), the British authorities were suddenly spurred into sending a consul to Egypt, with the primary duty of securing the safe passage of vessels through the Red Sea and spying on French activities in the region.[39] That consul was George Baldwin. He had convinced both the British government and the newly formed India Board of his competence and of the value of monitoring, if not dominating, the Red Sea.[40] Following his appointment by royal command, four senior British statesmen drafted a series of instructions delineating the functions of the new consul general in Egypt.[41] "The great end of Mr. Baldwin's Residence at Cairo," they announced, "is the opening [of] a communication to India through Egypt."[42] They then discussed the repeated barring of European ships as challenges to legal precedent, which make no exception of the Red Sea. "Your Lordship will recollect," continued the authors, "that complaint was made by the Porte in the year 1777, that 'the English carried on a Trade contrary to custom up to the Port of Suez, with a view to make a conquest of the Country.'"[43] Indeed, this issue appears repeatedly in the Ottoman records in the late 1770s, and the sultan warned in the fiercest of terms those who might contravene the orders for European ships not to disembark at Suez (in one instance, he threatened them with his mighty imperial wrath, *ğażab-ı şāhānem*).[44]

To the defensive deductive logic of the Ottomans, the British opposed a conciliatory inductive approach, assuring that there had been "no ill consequences" elsewhere and that there would be none here. So George Baldwin moved to Alexandria to push for British interests in the Red Sea, though his mandate there did not last as long as he would have liked: after a few eventful years, involving mainly internal Egyptian struggles for power, the plague, and attempts at exporting natron, but also eventually a treaty permitting navigation for purposes of correspondence only, the post of consul general in Egypt was abolished in 1793.

In March 1798, an ill George Baldwin decided to leave Egypt permanently, not knowing that only a few months later the question of the control of the Red Sea would once again erupt, this time permanently, into the arena of global geopolitics. Following the peace of Campo Formio in October 1797, which cemented French victories against the Habsburgs in Italy and the Low Countries, General Napoleon Bonaparte was ordered to invade Egypt. The First Coalition against the new revolutionary order in France had collapsed, and only the British were left in the fight. The French thus moved for a head-to-head confrontation with the British, and how better to do this than to attack their vast and wealthy possessions in the East? The invasion of Egypt was therefore a first step in the projected conquest of the British Empire in Asia. The logic of the expedition had been floating in Paris for quite a while (as evidenced in the flustered report on a 'Mémoire sur l'Inde' by a British spy in France),[45] and it would gain increasing momentum as the First Coalition was unraveling. In August 1797, Bonaparte wrote to the Directoire, "The times are not distant when we feel that, in order really to destroy England, it will be necessary to seize Egypt."[46] In the summer of 1798, a vast fleet assembled at Toulon, sailed through the Mediterranean, and disembarked its troops at Alexandria. The troops went on to rout a Mamluk army at the so-called Battle of the Pyramids and triumphantly enter Cairo.

Just as Horatio Nelson and Sidney Smith commanded the fleets that harassed the French in the waters and shores of the eastern Mediterranean (most famously Alexandria and Acre), some vessels were sent from India all the way up the Red Sea, to Suez and Qusayr, where Napoleon had ordered garrisons to be established. Two gunboats made a show around Suez harbor for a couple of months in the spring of 1799, Qusayr was bombarded in the summer, and troops were landed on the shores of Upper Egypt to support the campaign against the French there.[47] Beyond the ephemeral agreement that Baldwin claimed to have achieved with the Cairene beys, an express imperial command (*emr-i şerif*) capped by the sultanic seal ordered the sharif of Mecca, Ghālib ibn Musāʿid, along with other Hijazi authorities, to provide amenities and necessities to the English navy all along the shores of the *Baḥr-ı Süveys* and around Jiddah, in order to help thwart French naval preparations in and around Suez.[48] This formalized the entry of the British into the Red Sea, which they would not leave.

In 1801, two other British squadrons arrived in the Red Sea for the final showdown with the French, which would lead to the capitulation of Alexandria proposed by the French general Menou and formally accepted by the British and the Ottomans in the first days of September 1801. Of the two detachments that made their way up the Red Sea, only the first, landing at Suez, managed to make it in time to partake in any significant fighting; the other, dropped off at Qusayr, arrived in Cairo after the city had already surrendered.[49]

Home Popham, captaining the *Romney,* was head of the squadron that deposited the troops at Qusayr. Henry Dundas, longtime president of the Board of Control for Indian Affairs and War Secretary, had appointed Popham to oversee the British naval presence in the Red Sea but also, on behalf of a secret committee of the East India Company, to establish a permanent British presence in the region, notably by establishing "some system of permanent commercial negociation with the Imaum of Sennah and the Sheriffee of Mecca."[50]

Popham's mission was military and commercial. It was also scientific. Indeed, as he himself explained, since the area was unexplored he took the initiative at his own expense to bring on board a draftsman and the appropriate instruments, which enabled him to compose a chart of the Red Sea.[51] This cartographic venture was celebrated at the time and marked a new stage in the formation of the Red Sea as a distinct object.[52]

From that moment on, the Red Sea assumed a permanent place on the geostrategic and scientific map of imperial politics. Popham, like Baldwin before him (and many others thereafter), embedded in his writings explicit recommendations to enforce a permanent British presence in the area.[53] He also advocated setting up an oven at Qusayr, which would produce biscuits "as cheap as at Calcutta," to sustain such a permanent British naval presence in the Red Sea.[54]

Clearly there had developed a thirst for further details on the region. Valentia thus set out, with Captain Court and Henry Salt at his side, to cover the Red Sea in a thorough manner. The result was a long travel narrative/scientific account, full of anecdotes, data, and the most up-to-date maps. Valentia too advocated a permanent British presence in the Red Sea to consolidate

British hegemony over the region and to bar the path to French encroachment. His suggestion was to take advantage of the connection established by Salt and the Abyssinian authorities to establish the British on the southwestern shores of the sea.[55] This was essential, for the "terrible eagles of regenerated France threaten universal destruction to ancient establishments."[56]

STEAM, FREE TRADE, AND BRITISH HEGEMONY

The first half of the nineteenth century was fortuitous for British imperial politics on a global scale. Indeed, if the urgings of Baldwin, Popham, and Valentia to install permanent British establishments in Egypt and the Red Sea did not get as quick a response as they would have liked, the results in the Mediterranean were instantaneous: Malta became a British possession by the Treaty of Paris itself (1814), and the Ionian islands fell under the "amical protection" (and military administration) of the United Kingdom at the Congress of Vienna the following year. These colonial outposts, along with Gibraltar, which had been granted in perpetuity to Great Britain already by the Treaty of Utrecht in 1713, went a long way in extending British hegemony in the region.[57] In this, the British were following in the footsteps of Napoleon. Both Malta and the Ionian Islands had been occupied beforehand by the French on their way to Egypt. About the Ionian Islands, Napoleon had reported to Paris that "they are more interesting to us than all of Italy combined."[58] Having taken possession of the Ionian Islands, Napoleon then wondered, in a letter to the minister of foreign relations (Talleyrand), why Malta would not be conquered as well, for, "with the island of St-Peter, which has been ceded to us by the king of Sardinia, Malta and Corfou, we will be masters of the entire Mediterranean."[59] It was in this same letter that he advocated the invasion of Egypt.

This period also heralded a number of fundamental changes in global affairs directly affecting the Red Sea, of which only three of particular relevance will be introduced here. The first concerns an initial phase of state-driven transformations in the Ottoman realm, including elements of militarization and industrialization, manifested as regards the Red Sea region in the figure of Meḥmed ʿAli and his expansionist governorship. The growing power of the paşa of Cairo over the eastern Mediterranean and the Red Sea troubled the British and was one of the immediate reasons for their increased attention to the Red Sea and their eventual occupation of Aden.[60] It is no coincidence that the direct British implantation in the area coincided with the acme of Meḥmed ʿAli's power and the imposition of the 1838 Treaty of Balta-Liman on a threatened Ottoman government, which fixed commercial duties and prohibited all monopolies, to the great benefit of the British.

The content of the Treaty of Balta-Liman echoes the second major theme that needs to underlined here, namely, the newfound creed of free trade. It led, notably, to the abolition of the East India Company's trade monopolies. These laws have been much debated, but one thing is clear: they affirmed the sovereignty of the Crown (as opposed to the Company) over the Indian territories and contributed to the ways in which "the Indian economy was being shaped to meet the needs of the British economy."[61] This required a centralization, expansion, and diffusion of knowledge production on the region and particularly on its major waterways.

The third new dynamic in the early nineteenth century that played a dominant role in the constitution of the Red Sea was the gradual development of maritime steam travel in the Indian Ocean. The debate concerning steam travel would become very acrimonious, involving complex politics from London and all along the way to Bombay. Among the public at least, support for the establishment of a steam connection to India was distinctly gaining ground in the 1830s.

These structural changes combined with shifts in scientific practice to promote the centralization of the cartographical production of space in the larger Indian Ocean world. James Horsburgh already had built on the pioneering work of Alexander Dalrymple to produce a navigational guide of the seaways to the east, which would be published in two volumes in 1809 and 1811.[62] This guide, constructed from the meticulous analysis of numerous ship logs and memoirs, was comprehensive and would become the fundamental reference for navigators. Regarding the Red Sea, the first editions of *The India Directory* built mainly on the accounts of the journeys mentioned above, and the information remained quite scant.

All of these factors together prompted the decision by the governor of Bombay Sir John Malcolm, along with his brother Sir Charles, commander-in-chief of the Bombay Marine (soon to be renamed the Indian Navy), to fund and coordinate a proper survey of the Red Sea that would facilitate the establishment of regular connection by steamship from Bombay to Suez. Commander Moresby, who had already gained esteem for earlier surveys, was sent aboard the *Thetis* to "determine the best course at all seasons for steamers proceeding from Suez," accompanied by another ship that carried a supply of coal to be deposited at strategic points on the coast.[63] But on its return voyage, the collier accompanying Moresby's *Thetis* suffered a common fate: it was wrecked on a reef and lost in an unknown location. Since the reason for the disaster was deemed to be the lack of proper maps, this "untoward incident had the effect of hastening plans for a complete survey and charting of that long body of water."[64] A thorough, in-depth survey of the Red Sea was ordered.

THE COMING INTO BEING OF THE RED SEA

This time, the charting would be done right: once and for all, according to the new and proper scientific methods, and with all the necessary equipment. Captain Moresby was sent to cover the northern half of the sea aboard the *Palinurus*, and Captain Elwon was sent to the southern half aboard the *Benares*. The dividing line, cutting off north from south, went through Jiddah. Though the processes of data collection, interpretation, and writing were carried out separately, the space that emerged as the object of the scientific gaze of the project was unitary and coherent: these were sailing directions for the Red Sea as a whole, with indications of the one way in and out. The mandated officers were a select group, hand-picked for their special skills, and "Almost all who survived the exceedingly trying conditions under which the work was carried on distinguished themselves later in the cause of steam communication."[65] They were aided by a numerous crew and staff, along with the most advanced equipment. In the words of Markham: "No expense was spared in fitting out the expedition, and all the surveying appliances of the day were provided, besides ample supplies of well-found boats and tenders. The latter were native craft with Arab crews. The sea was then practically unknown, and great dangers and privations were inseparable from such a service."[66]

The stage was set for a revolutionary moment. The actors involved were talented, the outlay was impressive, and the method employed corresponded to the most up-to-date standards, recently pioneered in the Indian context by Daniel Ross: "The first base was measured by a chain at Suez by Captain Moresby in 1830, by a system of triangulation down either shore. The work was verified by frequent bases, by almost daily azimuths, by latitudes by the sun and stars observed on shore with artificial horizons, and by chronometric differences."[67]

And a revolutionary moment indeed it was in the formulation of the Red Sea as a distinct and knowable object, which can be subjected to scholarly scrutiny of a specific type. A simple glance at the difference between two editions of Horsburgh's *India Directory* before and after the appearance of the *Sailing Directions for the Red Sea* (which were included wholesale) suffices to get a sense of the difference between a quotidian object and a scientific one: the tone of the writing is more authoritative; the assertions are bolder; the details are starker; the effects are enduring. The Red Sea would get here an internal consistency, with sharp contours and regular features. The editors of the sixth edition of the *India Directory* admit as much in the introduction to the segment by Moresby and Elwon: "The notice of the Red Sea given in the former editions of this work was, from the scantiness of our information, necessarily brief and imperfect; but full directions by Captains Moresby and Elwon, of the Indian Navy, to accompany their four-sheet Chart of this Sea, having been published by the East-India Company, we are now enabled by the liberal permission of the Honourable Court of Directors, to give these valuable directions verbatim."[68]

As Lorraine Daston explains, scientific objects "grow more richly real as they become entangled in webs of cultural significance, material practices, and theoretical derivations."[69] Certainly, Markham and many other commentators after him down to the present day viewed the *Sailing Directions* as a major turning-point, both scientifically and practically speaking, especially with regard to the penetration of steam travel in the region: "The noble resolution of all the officers was that the Red Sea Survey should be as perfect as labour and skill could make it; and it has served well to guide thousands of steamers up and down one of the most important and, at the same time, one of the most intricate routes in the world."[70]

Subsequent surveying expeditions would always hearken back to Moresby and Elwon as the point of beginning: the "Advertisement to the Fifth Edition" of the *Red Sea and Gulf of Aden Pilot,* the constantly updated official navigational guide of the British Admiralty, refers back to the original compilation of the pilot "from sailing directions drawn up by Commanders R. Moresby and T. Elwon, and published in 1841, by order of the Court of Directors of the East India Company."[71]

The foundationalist ambitions of the project, explicit from its very conception as an expedition to chart those treacherous uncharted waters, are perhaps most evident when Moresby and Elwon decide to revert to more "authentic" names rather than the explicitly ideological appellations of their recent surveying antecedents. Implicitly decrying the narcissism of their most famous predecessor, they mention that "Lord Valentia gave the name of Valentia Island to Dissee Island, and he describes Goob Ducnoo under the name of Ansley Bay."[72] By this scripted maneuver Moresby and Elwon wiped the slate clean, as it were, in order to construct a new spatial structure all their own, according to the neutral and objective methods of modern science.

Of this scientific adventure, a few primary accounts were left to posterity. These include, of course, the *Sailing Directions* themselves, published in 1841 to complement the two charts that had appeared about three years earlier, and celebrated as having reached unprecedented cartographical heights. When an international scientific commission gathered in 1855 to discuss the question of the Suez Canal, "It was found that all the charts hitherto published of the roadstead of Suez were inaccurate with the exception of that by Commander Moresby, published in 1837."[73] Both the charts and the sailing directions were signed by the names of the first commanders of the ships, Captains Moresby and Elwon. But equally important were the travel narratives and scientific memoirs of other participants of the survey: especially Wellsted's *Travels in Arabia,* a compelling two-volume narrative of the journey that appeared in 1838 (well before the sailing directions themselves), but also articles in one of the leading scholarly journals of the time, the *Journal of the Royal Geographical Society.*[74] To reiterate, the mixity of genres in the early productions of scientific practice was very much the norm, and all of these accounts were cited as important contributions in the history of the Indian surveys by Markham.[75]

The most striking feature of the *Sailing Directions* is perhaps the endemic references to corals, reefs, and shoals on almost every page. The reader of the text cannot but gain the sense that the abundance of coral reefs is the dominant feature of the space described. This is to be expected: the event that led to sending the Red Sea survey team in the first place was the wreckage of yet another ship on a reef, so the objective of the venture was in large part to chart precisely such (mostly) submerged hazards. And this charting had to appear in the textual product, not only to make it useful as a practical guide, but primarily to display the taming of the danger by the valiant scientists. Needless to say, however elaborate and groundbreaking the *Sailing Directions* may have been, they did not succeed in preventing shipwrecks from occurring in the Red Sea. Perhaps the most famous is the *SS Carnatic,* which ran aground a coral reef and sank near Shadwan Island in 1869.

The theme of coral reefs and the shipwrecks associated with them was not new—indeed, it is a common trope in any evocation of these seas (as mentioned recurrently above, the connection between these waters and the hazards of navigation begins already with the earliest extant sources, including the Bible itself), but the prominence given to it in this text is truly out of the ordinary. Not only is much of the text devoted to the detailed localization and description of as many reefs as possible, but this maritime character is transferred onto the land as well, so that local coral-based architecture is repeatedly remarked upon. The production of a space as organic and coherent is a precondition for such effortless back-and-forth movement from local ecology to culture. With the *Sailing Directions,* the Red Sea becomes a geographical world in its own right.

Indeed, so dominant was the presence of corals and reefs in the production of the Red Sea as a scientific object that subsequent iterations of the space would render it even more defining. The British Hydrographic Department's *Red Sea and Gulf of Aden Pilot* of 1900, for example, which acknowledges its debt to Moresby and Elwon's pioneering sailing directions, introduces the general remarks on the Red Sea from the outset with a special entry entitled "Coral Reefs": "The Red Sea, though, generally speaking, of considerable depth (in some places over 1,000 fathoms), is in parts studded with rocky islets and hidden coral banks, which extend far into the channel used by ships. . . . The reefs in the Red Sea are, perhaps, more numerous and extensive than in any other body of water of equal size."[76]

As in Moresby and Elwon's text, much of the subsequent discussion concerns the description of as many reefs as possible throughout the volume. As for the coral-based buildings found in various coastal towns of the Red Sea, these were labeled by Derek Matthews as belonging to a distinct "Red Sea Style" of architecture, which notably blends various types of corals into the building materials.[77] Thus with the *Sailing Directions* the Red Sea comes to cohere as a space, marking out particular features that define its sovereign geohistorical character. In other words, the Red Sea was being turned anthropomorphic and given features that encompassed both its shores and its waters, which would define its particular place in history and geography.

In the case of currents, there was also a concerted attempt to carve out the specificities of the Red Sea. Captain Moresby explains that "the currents in the Red Sea, from Jiddah to Ras Mahommed, are various all the year; no particular direction can be assigned to them."[78] This he saw as a special feature of the place that required mention. Here too, the *Sailing Directions* opened the way for the theorization of a special kind of *Red Sea variety* of currents and tides, the prime specificity of which seems to relate to their variability and irregularity.[79] Elsewhere, the particularities of the Red Sea are further elaborated: "The specific gravity and temperature of the Red sea have a character of their own."[80] And of course, comments abound concerning the particular wind regimes of the Red Sea, their plurality and their fierceness. The Red Sea had come into its own. A few years later, Dr. George Buist published what can be seen as its first identity card. In an article in the *Journal of Royal Geographical Society of London* entitled "On the Physical Geography of the Red Sea," Buist captured the object by organizing the accumulated data in a series of abstract entries with the specific details filled in (Boundaries, Depth, Tides, Islands, Temperature, Appearance and Saltness of Its Waters, Climate and Winds, Shores).[81]

The navigational hazards that derive from the special natural conditions of the Red Sea are also often noted in the *Sailing Directions*. This is generally done by the addition of the adjective *dangerous* to the reference to a specific reef, but sometimes by the mention of the fear of wreckage or even the reference to a narrow escape from destruction. In the entry on Yembo (Yanbu), for example, when discussing the possible difficulties in approaching the harbor, the authors recall that one of their own ships almost perished.[82] Elsewhere, concerning the Ushruffee Islands, they mention that it was on their reefs that "the Indian ship *Samdang* was wrecked in 1831."[83] Or again, the "extensive reef" west of Ras Roway is described as that "on which the Honourable Company's sloop of war Nautilus was wrecked in 1833."[84] The sense of constantly being on the brink of disaster when navigating the Red Sea is even more evident in the more fully narrativized account of the surveying expedition given by Wellsted in the second volume of his *Travels in Arabia*. So recurrent are the references to near-fatal occurrences due to the unpredictability of winds, currents, and reefs in the area that Wellsted felt the need to justify himself: "I now dismiss, with unfeigned pleasure, all further allusion to our nautical mishaps: four years in the Red Sea, amidst the numerous reefs with which its waters are studded having rendered the perils of its navigation familiar to us, I have not dwelt on them; but in this Gulf, in a course of only ninety miles, the incidents are so numerous and varied, that I trust the reader will pardon my prolixity."[85]It is revealing, in this regard, that Wellsted even evokes the idea of some sort of native Red Sea people: "On the Arabian and Nubian coast we found a race of fishermen, which bear the general designation of Huteïmí, and from the similarity of their present habits, are, I have little doubt, a remnant of the Ichthyophagi, described so minutely by Diodorus Siculus."[86]

A parallel transformation is discernible when it comes to nomenclature: the scientific becoming of the Red Sea calls forth a new platform of definitional discussions. Though debates about this origin of the appellation existed well before the nineteenth century, following the postulation of the Red Sea as a scientific object, the discussion about its naming takes on a noticeably different character: more quantitative in tone, it often relates the name to a particular feature of that organic body of water that the Red Sea is assumed to be. George Buist is of the opinion that the sea most probably derives "its name from large portions of it, as well as of the Arabian Sea, being covered with patches, from a few yards to some miles square, of a blood-red colour, derived from a species of animalculae."[87] Although his argument contains echoes of the millennial debate, he couches it very distinctly in scientific terms, notably acknowledging in a footnote an earlier study by a certain Ehrenberg that he read only after finishing his own study, which also demonstrates, on the basis of straightforward empirical observation, the bloody color specific to the sea and connects it to the presence of algae.[88] The scientifically couched and empirically observable explanation then enters the domain of general knowledge, as exemplified by its inclusion in common encyclopedias of the time, such as M. W. Duckett's *Dictionnaire de la conversation et de la lecture,* whose entry on the Red Sea has this to say about the origin of the name:

> One finds, furthermore, near its coasts, innumerable coral banks, often reddish, and which most likely gave it the name *Red Sea,* because people will have thought that they communicated to the water the particular tint which it sometimes offers to the eyes of navigators. But based on very recent observations, this particular coloration is due to the presence of an algae, of the tribe of the oscillaries, to which the botanic name of trichodesmium has been attributed, and whose distinctive characteristics are: simple, membrane-like, blood-red filaments, still, enclosed, kept together in small bunches or bouquets by a mucilaginous substance, and floating on the surface of the seas, of which they color immense spaces.[89]

In 1912, Sarah Hoyt mobilized an arsenal of scientists in support of the algae theory as the origin of the name of the Red Sea, connecting it all the way back to Strabo, no less.[90] Such classical references contributed to the rhetoric of scientificity. European colonial powers of the nineteenth century sensed well the special power of naming, so that imperialism has been described as a "territorial writing-machine" that imposes itself through a process of "palimpsestual inscription and reinscription."[91] In terms of the

Red Sea world, this principle was most evidently established when the Kingdom of Italy gradually established itself on the southwestern shores of the sea, and eventually called the colony *Eritrea* in reference to the most famous ancient name for the waters of the northwestern Indian Ocean. With its explicit classical Roman sonorities, the new denomination, which, as has been suggested, was unfamiliar to the local population in reference to their land (and sea), appropriated the region into a flatly Eurocentric metanarrative, whereby the late nineteenth-century Italian king was portrayed as the culmination of a long, noble tradition and Italian colonization was cast as a simple recovery of ancient rights, by that most evident and implacable of logics: onomastics.

RETURN OF THE REPRESSED

Yet despite the scientific tone and objective pretense of the *Sailing Directions,* a number of elements reveal the aporias of such claims. First, there are the regular reminders, at various points in the text, of the biases of the particular perspective put forward. This, as many have argued, is in fact part and parcel of its scientificity: it is a perfect example of the creation of a breach between reality and its representation that lies at the heart of modern knowledge and power. As in many other cases of the early phases of the coming into being of scientific objects, Moresby and Elwon's *Sailing Directions* constantly reminds its readers that what is presented is merely a *model* of what is truly out there. Indeed, the *Sailing Directions* integrate the breach into the very structure of their analysis, repeatedly providing explanations for the conditions and biases of their representation only to reinforce the existence of a reality of which it is the model. This element is indeed the exclusive purpose of the "Introduction," which first attributes appropriate authorship (explaining that the sections concerning the Red Sea north of Jiddah were composed by "Robert Moresby, of the East-India Company's ship Palinurus, by whom that part of the survey was executed," and that the sections concerning the Red Sea south of Jiddah were composed "by the late Commander Thomas Elwon, of the East-India Company's ship Benares, to accompany his portion of the survey," and crediting a Mr. Rassam for the Arabic transcriptions), before highlighting the parameters that render the text simply a representation, a model of something else (namely, reality): "The longitudes have been determined by chronometric measurements from Bombay to Maculla, Maculla to

Mocha, and from Mocha to Jiddah, made during the years 1829, 30, 31, 32, 33, and 34, an abstract of which is given by Captain Moresby—Bombay being considered in 72° 54′ 36″. The trigonometrical survey of India, based upon the longitude of Madras, which is considered to be 80° 17′ 21″, placed the longitude of Bombay about three minutes more west, viz. 72° 51′ 15″."[92] A footnote is further added to the survey regarding the longitude of Madras, which remarks that "recent observations make it in 80° 14′ 0″, which, if confirmed, will of course affect the position of Bombay, as well as all those places depending upon it.—The longitude of Bombay is now determined to be 72° 49′ 40″ E."[93] After the introduction comes the "Abstract of Chronometric Measurements," providing in numbers the various measurements of the *Palinurus* and *Benares* watches, organized by location (such as "From Bombay Apollo Pier to Maculla"), by year (ranging between 1829 and 1834) and serial (first, second, etc.). Only then can the text properly commence.

More specific perhaps to this text in particular is the recurrent frank admission of the continued reliance on native pilots for sailing. This had much to do, clearly, with the specific natural features characteristic of the Red Sea as a space, described above. By determining the modalities of sailing in the Red Sea, all of those factors combined to create particular conditions that concentrated the knowledge and power over navigation in the hands and minds of local pilots and captains, who had the unique training, skills, and perception that come from the organic rearing in a place and profession. Navigating the Red Sea was their *habitus,* and only within particular parameters of altered power-knowledge dynamics could this be transferred to modes of operating that bypassed these intermediaries. The reliance on local pilots and captains is manifest throughout the ages. When the crusader knight Reginald of Châtillon launched his infamous maritime raid on the Hijaz in the winter of 1182–83, contemporary sources indicate that he was dependent upon locals, both to carry his ships to the coast and especially to navigate them once they were at sea.[94] These, it is reported, "presumably were pirates familiar with the difficulties of Red Sea navigation."[95] The twentieth-century scholar rationalizes the reliance of "Europeans" on "non-Europeans," which must obviously be an oddity for him, by repeatedly explaining (two lines before the previous quote) that "this was an unknown world to the Franks" and (at the very beginning of the article) that "this was the first European penetration of the Red Sea in force since 24 B.C. when Aelius Gallus led an expedition of Romans as far as southern Arabia."[96] Six hundred years after Reginald, when Europeans confidently believed themselves to have achieved immeasurable advance over their civilizational rivals, Eyles Irwin, in narrating his own grueling travels and travails on and around the Red Sea, still repeatedly referred to the dependence of crossers of those seas on indigenous pilots.

Most revealing in this regard is the fact that the scientific charting of the Red Sea itself, ordered by the most powerful state of its time, which controlled the most advanced technical, military, and discursive tools and mechanisms, and dominated the sea-lanes essentially of the entire globe (and certainly of the Indian Ocean), rested entirely on the use of local intermediaries as pilots, as reported by the British captains. Betraying an enormous dependence on their local guides, the *Sailing Directions* announce at the end of the section entitled "Winds and Currents between Suez and Jiddah": "The native pilots being acquainted with the reefs and anchorages from eyesight are always able to take a vessel among them with safety; a stranger, not acquainted with the localities, would feel alarmed in navigating among the reefs; they are all safe to approach, taking the precaution to be on the fore-topsail-yard with the native pilot, and keeping a good look-out for sunken rocks, the eye, and not the lead, being the only guide."[97]

Indeed, the deference to "native pilots" (and their "eyesight") is omnipresent throughout these *Sailing Directions.* The overall reliance on local intermediaries as a locus of power (to sail) and knowledge (of sailing) is so complete that the authors-surveyors are made to admit that their empirical data remain inferior to the knowledge locally produced and transmitted. More than once, the text dutifully acknowledges that the author found himself incapable of charting this or that reef, and even an entire area or another, that were said to exist by their informants. And this knowledge is not simply dismissed, or even just acknowledged. It is integrated wholesale into the empirical dimension of the charting of the sea. The approach to Mocha from the south, for example, is described thus: "Ships having entered the Straits of Bab-el-mandeb and passed Perim Island, should steer along the Arabian coast about N. by W. ½ W. or N.N.W. (*true*), keeping without the depth of 12 fathoms, in order to avoid a shoal said to exist between Cape Bab-el-mandeb and Zee Hill, but which the surveyors could not discover; and also to keep clear of the sand and rocky banks which project from Mocha Roads."[98]

Such deferral of authority, it should be repeated, is not an uncommon occurrence in the text. It reappears, in fact, on the very next page, when the authority of "the pilot" is appealed to in reference to the presence of habitations inland off of Billool Bay, which appeared from the boat to be completely deserted. What is *said to exist* (by the native pilots) is included on a par with the actual soundings made to chart the passages safe for navigation. Like the census map of Egypt that replaced the preceding system of organization of knowledge on the basis of local intermediaries, carefully analyzed by Timothy Mitchell, the *Sailing Directions,* by their authors' own admission, constituted, not an increase or an advance in the precision or efficiency of knowledge along the linear path of progress that the very idea of scientific charting conjured, but rather a new *locus* and organization of the production of knowledge, and therefore a novel configuration of power.[99]

In fact, local knowledge is at one point in the text explicitly and favorably compared to previous European accounts. Concerning the "Centurion Shoal," the *Sailing Directions* states that it is "mentioned by Horsburg [*sic*] to be situated in lat. 25° 20′ N., and lon. 35° 56′ E."[100] This supposed "Centurion Shoal," the text continues,

> certainly does not exist in this situation, or near it; having been on the spot assigned to it, and often about it, nothing has been seen. Once, when on the situation assigned to it, a shoal was reported from the masthead, and it was not until we sailed over the spot that we found it was not a shoal, but a strong rippling, caused by currents, appearing in light winds exactly like a shoal. When in the rippling we sounded 200 and 400 fathoms, but found no bottom; on the North side of this rippling, which extended several miles to the N.E. and S.W. in a narrow line of breakers, we found the current setting to the S.E. one quarter of a mile per hour, and on the South side of the rippling 1½ miles per hour to the N.W., the wind then very light or nearly calm. This appearance, so deceitful to us, having been three years constantly in sight of coral shoals, at once proves that former navigators must have seen the same, and placed them down as shoals, without examining them; which fully accounts for the numerous dangers in the old charts. None of the Arab pilots have any oral information of this shoal, nor do they believe it to exist.[101]

In one clear stroke, the *Sailing Directions* dismisses, almost ridicules, the previous standard European accounts, which are recast as prescientific, and, in stark contrast, celebrates the more empirically precise "information" of the "Arab pilots," which is, however, compromised by being "oral." Thus does this text establish itself as the new ultimate center of knowledge (and power, of course, which is never far away: many of the descriptions of places along the coast discuss matters that can be of value only for military purposes, and it should not be forgotten that the authors-surveyors were in the service of the Indian Navy).

The dependence on indigenous pilots is even personalized in Wellsted's narrative, where a particular pilot is named, "old Seroor, deservedly accounted the most skillful as well as undaunted seaman that ever sailed upon its waters."[102] Succumbing to a wave of lyricism on this theme, the British captain confirms his own role as mere spectator rather than actor of the navigation: "At these moments, the sturdy old helmsman stood with his head bared, his few grey locks streaming in the breeze, and his face completely drenched with the spray that incessantly dashed over the boat. In this manner, he directed our course with admirable skill and coolness over seas and through violent gusts that menaced us with destruction. To the spectator, who contemplated our progress from a place of safety, this scene could not fail of presenting a striking and admirable picture of human skill successfully contending against the fury of the raging elements."[103]

Connected to this trope and also participating in somewhat undermining the pure objective scientificity of the text are repeated affirmations that navigation in the Red Sea can be performed only by continuous and active observation, because many of the reefs can be avoided only by sight. In other words, however extensively charted and profoundly surveyed, the Red Sea remains as hazardous as ever, and the navigator can still rely only on the age-old power of the ocular. This is set forth persuasively in the *Sailing Directions,* as evoked above in reference to the pilot's *vision* "being the only guide," and would be elaborated upon in subsequent scientific formulations of the Red Sea as a space for navigation. The *Sailing Directions* often advocates that knowledge of the sea be based on immediate perception rather than fixed data (enshrined in charts and directions, for example). This is perhaps most apparent when it speaks of the particular color of the sea or the shoals. It mentions the "different shades of green on the coral rock" that give a sense of the water's depth and therefore the right place to drop anchor.[104] Elsewhere, it states: "When the sun shines, a green shade is reflected from the rocks, by which they may be avoided" (351). At multiple locations, the surveyors also mention that direct observation is indeed requisite for safe arrival. The only way to reach Jiddah is by the naked eye, "for the channels are so narrow, that the marks will be found of little use, except in approaching the place" (306). This also determines the optimal time for going in: "towards noon . . . as, owing to the transparency of the water, the sunken rocks then appear as a dark green shadow on the surface" (306). As for the channel near Farsan Island, "The eye must be the principal guide to a vessel entering either way" (292). Almost the exact same wording (with "only" replacing "principal") is used for the area near Salaka, and again for Dohana Bay (334, 335).

The placement of the pilot's perception above scientific data is confirmed at various points in Wellsted's textual capture of the Red Sea, both explicitly and implicitly. At one point Wellsted even felt the need to spell it out as clearly as possible: "In the neighborhood of, and amidst the clusters, a chart can avail the mariner no further than in marking the outer boundary, to which our attention was therefore especially directed; within this, the navigator must be directed by the eye, as the only and the best pilot; and a short acquaintance with the manner of proceeding here laid down will enable him to distinguish the dangers, and also to estimate from the various shades the changes in the depth of the water."[105]

This theme would be elaborated in subsequent instantiations of the Red Sea as a scientific object, perhaps nowhere more forcefully than in the third edition of the US Navy's own *Sailing Directions for the Red Sea and the Gulf of Aden,* the contents of which were largely derived from the British guide, itself building on Moresby and Elwon. Having discussed the particularity of the abundance of coral formations in the Red Sea, the guide moves on to provide explicit directions for *seeing:*

> Navigation among coral reefs is often dependent on the eye, and it is well to note the conditions under which the reefs are most easily seen. They are more easily seen from the masthead than from the deck or bridge, and when the sun is high rather than when it is low; the most favorable position of the sun is behind the observer. Colored glasses of a greenish-yellow tint are found to be very useful for eliminating sun glare, and the effect produced by wearing them brings out the contrasts between the blue and the gray; glasses of any other color should not be used. A considerable difference has been observed in the light on the water from 5 hours before noon to 5 hours after noon; this may be caused by the eye accustoming itself to the light after the darkness of night.[106]

The suggestions for the best times, angles, and modes of perception continue for a few more paragraphs before the text moves on to geographical and topographical directions, of which a large part concern charting reefs and corals in detail.

Finally, another dimension of the text that highlights the aporias of the objectivist and scientific rhetoric of Moresby and Elwon's *Sailing Directions* is the sheer variety of information involved in the survey. This echoes the medley of genres that connect to these charting expeditions. The data mobilized in the text are anthropological, archaeological, architectural, commercial, historical, military, and religious, in addition to the more strictly geographical and topographical records provided.

These multiple holes in the pristine and elevated construction of modern science should not come as a surprise. The charting itself had crude pragmatic ends from its very origin: the avowed purpose was to pave the way for the institution of steam travel through the region. Wellsted devotes an entire segment to underlining the importance of establishing regular steam navigation through the Red Sea. And here too colonization is urged: "I have, however, always contemplated that Egypt, the highway between Europe and India, must, sooner or later, be ours."[107] Though Egypt would not come under direct British control for another half century, Aden did, just a few years thereafter, in 1839. Dominating the antechamber leading to the entrance of the Red Sea, it would become a crucial coaling hub for British steamers.

OTTOMAN CONVERSION

The actual regularization of steam travel in the Indian Ocean would take a few decades. This was in large part due to technical matters that maintained the superior efficacy of sail over steam. As Daniel Headrick has shown, it was only in the 1850s and 1860s that "four innovations . . . lowered costs and improved the competitive position of steamers vis-à-vis sailing ships: the screw-propeller, the iron hull, the surface condenser, and the compound engine."[108] In the early 1850s, steam navigation in the Red Sea was still a rarity. The sixth edition of the *India Directory* admits as much in the preface to the reproduction of the *Sailing Directions,* as it seeks to justify that work's inclusion.[109] This chronology corresponds well with the larger expansion of European/British dominance over the wider Indian Ocean and Mediterranean worlds, a dominance that was manifested in the increasing indebtedness, both financial and conceptual, of non-European states and societies.

Before this time, the use of the expression "Red Sea" in Ottoman discourse was extremely rare and always connected to European projects in the region. After the report of the Ottoman ambassador from Paris during the Egyptian expedition, the term next shows up in the Ottoman archives only in a document dated April 21, 1841, and this is, again, a European-induced text. It is the translation of a letter to the British foreign secretary Lord Palmerston concerning, once again, French ambitions, and their arrangements with Meḥmed ʿAlī over sailing in the Red Sea in the effort to dominate the area, and indeed, the coasts of all of Africa.[110] After this episode, it is only with the potential generalization of steam navigation in the Red Sea and the rise to global hegemony of Western cartographic practices that the category becomes regularly operational in the Ottoman archives. Indeed, the other archival record from before the middle of the century that uses the category of "Red Sea," giving an idea of the provenance of its eventual hegemony, is (as the inset caption on the map reads) the "exact translation drawn by His Majesty's office of the Navy of a map of the Red Sea surveyed by a rear-admiral in India named Elwon in the year one thousand eight hundred and thirty four of the Gregorian calendar" (figures 4 and 5).[111] The actual date of the Ottoman map is unclear, as is the original of which it is the "exact translation," but its source is unmistakable.[112]

The actual adoption of the term *Red Sea* in Ottoman discourse can be dated back to the 1850s and the discussions surrounding the creation of an Ottoman steamship company under the aegis of the governor of Egypt (first Meḥmed Saʿīd Paşa and then Ismāʿīl Paşa), which speak of connecting the various parts and ports of the sea, as well as establishing links between the sea and various spaces beyond it. The numerous documents concerning this venture systematically use the same vocabulary to define the spatial parameters of the steamship company's field of operations, speaking notably of "*Baḥr-ı Aḥmer'de vāḳıʿ banāder*," that is, "the ports lying on the Red Sea"—and here the literal translation of the name of the basin is used.[113] The Mecidiye company for steamboats was born in 1856, at about the same time as the Ottoman and Egyptian authorities took out their first debts to European banks.[114] In due time, and after a few name changes, it would be sold to a British company, after the Cairo and Istanbul treasuries went bankrupt.[115]

In many ways, the Ottoman authorities were quite right to associate travel and mapping with colonial expansion, as illustrated by the explicit logic underpinning communications with the British ambassador in relation to the question of navigation to Suez. The survey of the Red Sea was followed shortly by the conquest of Aden. Eventually most of the Ottoman territories surrounding the Red Sea would come under British influence. The Ottomans were highly conscious, then, of the danger of maps and realized that imperialism was first and foremost an act of "*geographical* violence." The sultan regularly reminded the Cairene authorities of this, invoking the precedent of India, where Europeans had arrived under the guise of commerce and science before conquering those lands.[116] In addition to ruining the customs revenues of Jiddah, says an imperial command to Cairo, the Frankish ships measure, survey, and map the area inch by inch. And, as past events and history books make clear, the command continues, the Frankish nations have sailed the globe and, under the guise of commerce, penetrated the lands. The text then describes the appearance of the English and the Dutch in the Indian Ocean, recounting the famous story of the Arabian sailor (here said to be from Yemen, "a malignant person, Muslim in appearance but unbeliever in intention," who first took them, around the year 900 (AH, i.e., the mid-1490s CE) from the coasts of East Africa to the shores of India.[117] Having learned and secured the route to the coasts of Bengal and Malabar, the Franks returned with an excellent navy and all of a sudden surrounded strongholds such as Surat, Ahmadabad, Bengal, and Burhanpur, and even subjugated some of these.[118]

In a highly conscious shift of authorial voice, the narrative moves into direct speech: "We do not wish you any harm, we are here only to obtain merchandise and do commerce. We will pay the proper tariffs. Leave the forts in our hands, for we need them just as safe harbors for our ships. With these words, the Franks occupied the lands." Bringing more and more soldiers and weapons, the Portuguese and the English and other Christian nations divided up and subjugated the entire Indian coast, completely removing Muslim control over any port there, and seizing unprecedented numbers of Muslims as subjects.

These precedents were clearly meant to make the Cairene elites understand the urgency of preventing the Franks from sailing the *Baḥr-ı Süveys,* which was the actual order involved in the command (as made clear repeatedly throughout the text). Moreover, most important was to maintain unity—and for this the sultan also mobilized a historical precedent. In the late 400s (AH, i.e., the late 1090s), the command continues, following the discussion of the more recent conquest of India, again under the guise of commerce, the Frankish nations began to come and go on the Syrian coasts. As a result of the incapacity of the Fatimid kings of Egypt and the Abbasid caliphs' quarrels with them, the Franks started attacking the forts of the Syrian coasts, eventually conquering Acre, Ḳalʿat ul-cedīd ("New Fort/City," specific location unclear), Safad, and Beirut, and ultimately even occupied the first *ḳible* and the source of saints, the holy city of Jerusalem. The command then moves to extol Ṣalāḥ al-Dīn, the Ayyubids, and the Mamluks for their role in cleansing the

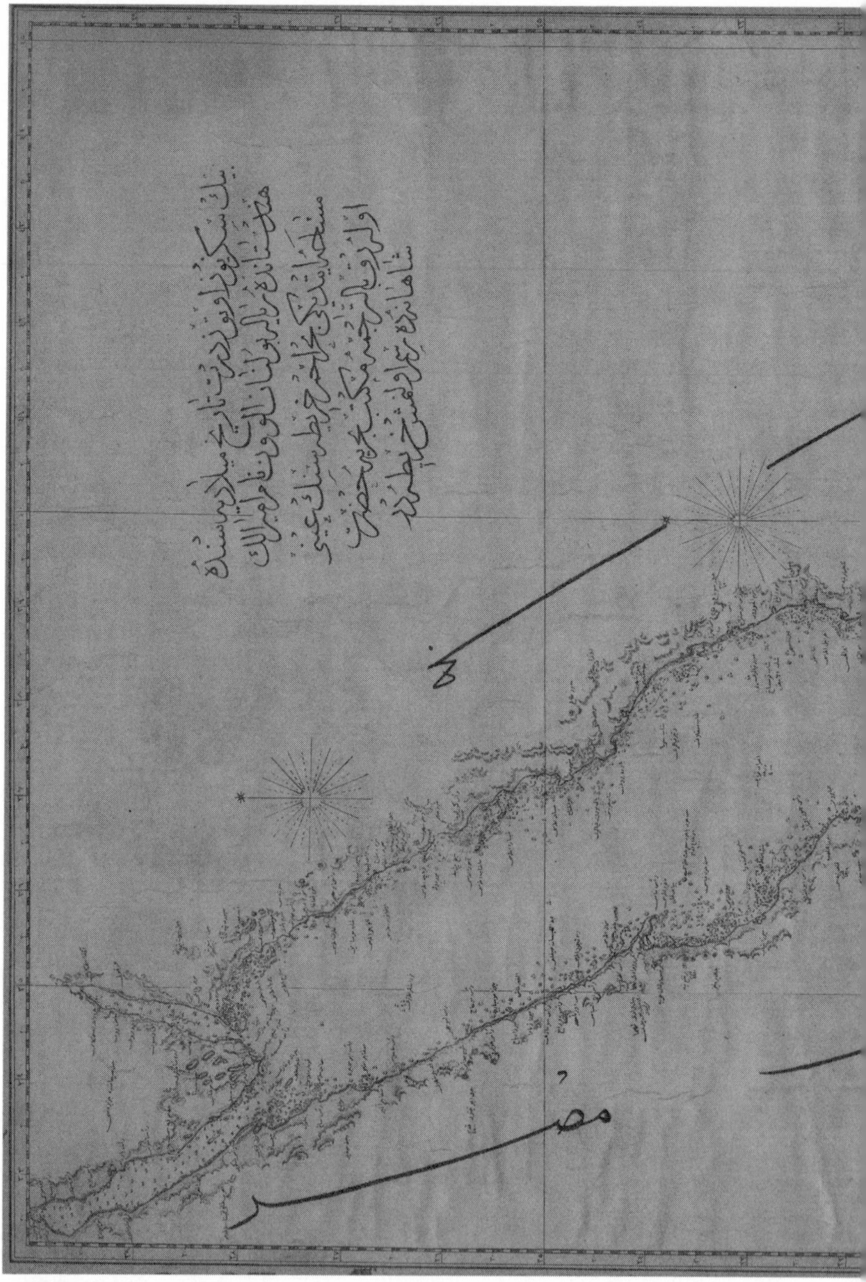

FIGURE 4. *Baḥr-ı Aḥmer,* North (*left*) and South (*right*). © Türkiye Cumhuriyeti Başbakanlık Osmanli Arşivi.

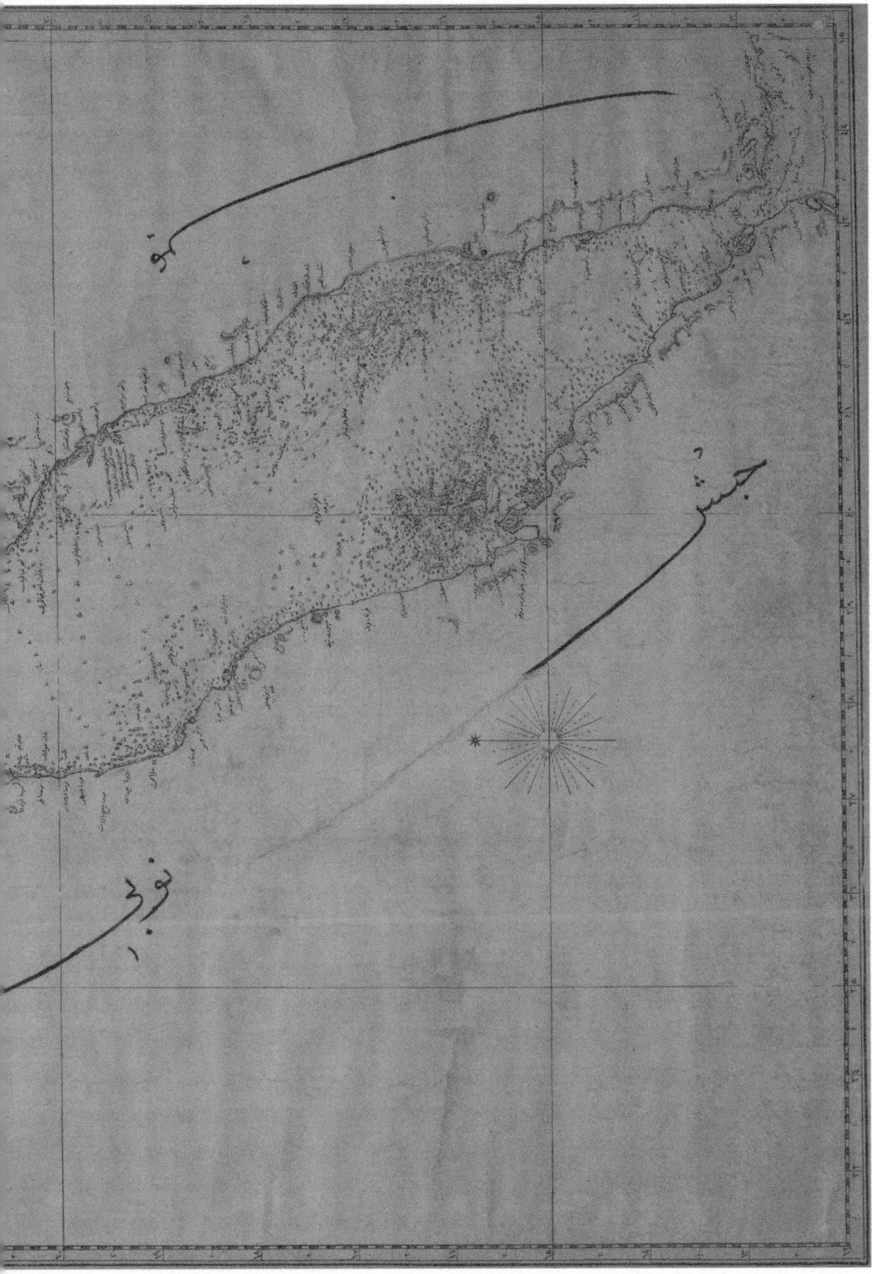
حبش

Franks from the area and to repeat the acute danger involved in the matter at hand. With the advantage of hindsight, it is easy to confirm the sultan's intuition: in whichever part of the world western Europeans showed up as tradesmen and surveyors, there was a good chance of its being colonized soon.

When the Ottomans suddenly sought to get into the world-as-picture, it was all too late: to do that, they had to take out loans from those very people who would make sure that they were kept well out of the picture. In the same way, when the Ottoman state attempted to get involved in colonial-style politics, at around the same time, the dice were already loaded (in favor of the master version, of course—especially Britain and France). It is not a coincidence that the assumption of the sea's sovereign integrity would occur just as the state was formulating a modern colonial discourse whereby ruled populations required the assistance of the state to move along the trajectory of progress. The adoption of modern homogeneous space and linear time was itself a process of colonization that excluded the non-European by definition. In other words, by internalizing the framework of progress along which different civilizations could be placed, the Ottomans set themselves up to be constantly playing catch-up: just as Ottoman bureaucrats found some tribesmen to be savage, so did European Orientalists and politicians deem the Ottoman state itself to be backward and in need of reform.

The greatest irony of all, perhaps, is the startling fact that, just as the Red Sea crystallized as a coherent object, it was colonized by multiple processes that culminated in the perforation of the Suez Canal, which, literally and symbolically, destroyed the Red Sea as an integral lived space and fundamentally transformed its internal and external flows. Not only did the digging of the canal, at enormous cost of life (mainly Egyptian peasants conscripted by a regime of forced labor), lead to the direct exchange of fluids and biota with the Mediterranean,[119] but it also affected the urban landscape of the region, with the creation and development of new cities such as Port Said, Ismaïlia, and Port Sudan, and led to the entrenched imagination of the Red Sea as simply a corridor, a passageway, a funnel, always leading somewhere else. It also gave a crucial advantage to steamboats, which could pass through it more easily than their wind-powered competitors, thereby ringing the death knell of long-distance, interoceanic commercial sailing.[120]

In this way was the Red Sea both invented and dissolved in the same grand imperial gesture, with the expansion of Europe to swallow the waters of the

Mediterranean first and then to penetrate other seas.[121] A sexual, even reproductive, metaphor for the process was fantasized by the European advocates of the canal: the Saint-Simonians, who would have a major impact on Ferdinand de Lesseps, envisioned the piercing of the canal as the climax of the mating between a male Occident and a female Orient.

Like the charting of the sea and other modernizing projects, nothing about the making of the Suez Canal was a smooth, self-assured imposition of imperial will. The whole affair was the object of great strife and tension, both local and global, intra-European, extra-European, and in between.[122] This is no simple triumphalist story, especially considering the "paradoxical fact," in Marwan Buheiry's words, "that Western technological breakthroughs in communications (the press, railways and steamship navigation, the Suez Canal, and the telegraph)" both "facilitate[ed] colonial dominance" and "served to tie" colonized societies together.[123] Moreover, as Valeska Huber has recently shown, the increased mobility spurred by the opening of the canal produced "a force that was difficult to control and which was connected with problems such as the worldwide propagation of disease or the movement of unruly individuals or groups."[124] Indeed, it changed the modes of mobility and exchange in the region in multiple ways. If for some people it accelerated movement, for others it decelerated it. Thus the Suez Canal must be read as a part of the larger "differentiation, regulation and bureaucratisation of different kinds of movement."[125] Even further, On Barak demonstrates in compelling fashion that those "Western technological breakthroughs" were suffused by "non-Western" and even "non-human" actors, so that the founding terms themselves (Europe, the West, the human, science, etc.) must be read as conceptual end-products (as opposed to points of departure), resulting from camouflages, silencings, and violences of multiple sorts.[126] "Indigenous knowledge, materials and actors originating from the colonies," he writes, "remade the metropole in significant if unacknowledged ways."[127]

Still, with the opening of the Suez Canal, the destiny of Egypt was now linked to Europe (and especially Great Britain) in intimate ways, and indeed the canal would figure prominently in the subsequent history of Egypt, taking central stage at multiple crucial junctures of its colonial and postcolonial predicament, from the British bombardment of Alexandria in 1882 to the Tripartite aggression of 1956 (both of these invasions of Egypt were explicitly linked to the canal). The historic event also transformed the relationship of Egypt to its Ottoman suzerain in Istanbul.

Meḥmed ʿAlī apparently sensed all this. Keen politician that he was, he (according to the French historian Pierre Crabitès) "took the view that if a waterway were cut from the Red Sea to the Mediterranean, the blending of their waters would swamp the independence of Egypt."[128]

It is in the wake of these structural transformations that the Khedive Ismāʿīl is said to have pronounced his country "no longer in Africa" but rather "now a part of Europe."[129] This story may be apocryphal, and it was not necessarily connected to the opening of the Suez Canal (though in subsequent literature it is often associated with it),[130] but it speaks to the imbricated discursive and material constitution of geography, and to the simultaneous constative and performative dimension of spatial categories—and of course, it indicates the formidable pull of the European modern.

FIVE

Thalassomania

MODERNITY AND THE SEA

FROM THE POINT OF VIEW of modern geography, the world appears clear and simple. This is somewhat paradoxical, since one of the special qualities of modernity is deemed to be complexity (complex societies, complex personality, complex logic, and so forth). But with the advent of modern geography, every schoolchild should know that the world is divided into a set number of landmasses and seas: there are seven continents, just as there are five oceans, and a set number of seas, all made up of salt water, some completely bounded, others almost so.

The claims to objectivity of modern geography have been subjected to severe critique. The historical geographer Martin Lewis opens his important article "Dividing the Ocean Sea" by decrying the fact that "global geography operates under a widespread assumption of naturalism."[1] By this, he means that the "continents and oceans that constitute the most basic divisions of the world are generally regarded—to the extent that they are considered at all—as nonproblematic features of the natural world, features that have been discovered rather than delimited by convention."[2] Referencing his own 1997 book *The Myth of Continents* (coauthored with the historian Kären Wigen), he suggests that continental distinctions "are as much intellectual constructs as they are given features of the natural world."[3] Such critiques of what the authors call metageography are important and have opened fresh grounds to think through the question of the geographical assumptions that lie at the root of some of the most commonly used categories.

The present book has derived crucial inspiration from such works but seeks to go beyond a logic grounded in the mere unveiling of convention, expanding the rejection of naive geohistorical naturalism to encompass a contestation of geohistorical realism as a scholarly practice. This requires a move beyond approaches (such as the one focused on social construction) that take for granted the simple division between a mental world of concepts and a material world of things. Here is precisely the subtle power of modern knowledge: it is the very unreal dimension of the representation that conjures the effect of the real. This is why one can believe both in the naturalism of geographical concepts and in their conventional origins. The fact that an object of some sort is drawn by convention rather than nature does not diminish its claims to realism, nor does it affect its purchase on reality. It is rather the very condition of the production of an understanding of material reality that appears separate from representation, from language, from science, from the imagination, and, most importantly, from power.

To begin with, most schoolchildren also know that the categories of geographical thought are "as much intellectual construct as they are natural features of the given world." They know that the boundaries between continents and between oceans are merely conventions. They are often taught, for example, that in some countries other schoolchildren learn that there are only six continents, because they conceive of the Americas as a single entity rather than two, or that still others speak of a five-plus-one model, to single out the uninhabited Antarctic landmass. They are also conscious that the oceans of the world constitute one large connected body of water, and that separating them from each other is difficult. What works of critical historical geography show is of course much more: that these conventions have serious and profound (sometimes even unconscious) consequences regarding the manner in which the world is seen, scholarship is produced, and lives are lived. They also show that there have been different ways of dividing and classifying, ways that may be less connected to conquering and stereotyping.

The division of the world into a strict set of theoretically comparable units crystallized into the form still current today only in the Europe of the nineteenth century. However much they are made to appear of ancient vintage and objectively natural in their features, the continents and the oceans of the world held numerous names and various contours before modernity. At some point in the early nineteenth century, a particular fixed picture of the world was formalized into objective units, each with specific features and, perhaps most importantly in the age of progress, distinct destinies. In other words, each unit was defined *both* as a geographical object and as a historical one in mutual constitution.

Through his intervention in the debate over social constructionism, Ian Hacking makes a helpful distinction between "Objects" and "Ideas." Objects, he writes, are "'in the world' in a commonsensical, not fancy, meaning of the word."[4] He cites a list of items as examples of this category (people, states, conditions, practices, actions, etc.), after which he adds, "and homes, landlords, housecleaning, rent, dry rot, evictions, bailiffs, squatting, greed, and the Caspian Sea" (22). By way of further clarification he suggests that Objects can be "ontologically subjective but epistemologically objective," using rent as an example: "It is ontologically subjective, because without human subjects and their institutions there would be no such object as rent. But rent is epistemologically objective. You know full well (there is nothing subjective about it) that $850 is due on the first of the month" (22).

So what about that last example on his list—the Caspian Sea? It is clearly, in a commonsensical meaning, in the world. But jumping off the docks in Baku, does one instinctively know that one is bathing in the Caspian Sea, thereby making it an "epistemologically objective" category?

The Caspian Sea is an Object, then, but it is one entirely produced by an institutionally embedded discipline of knowledge. Furthermore, it may, at least in part, belong to another one of Hacking's types of things: Ideas, by which, in explicit contrast to Objects, he means "ideas, conceptions, concepts, beliefs, attitudes to, theories. They need not be private, the ideas of this or that person. Ideas are discussed, accepted, shared, stated, worked out, clarified, contested" (22). As examples, he mentions "purposes, groupings, classifications (ways of classifying), and kinds" (22). Is not the expression "the Caspian Sea" a classification, a way of classifying, and/or a kind? It is.

The Caspian Sea, then, in addition to being an Object is an Idea—one that depends on a series of discursively enabled parameters, including, at the very least, that the Caspian Sea is a self-evident and sovereign entity and that it may be apprehended as a particular instance of a general classificatory set. How it is that "the sea" may nonchalantly slip into a list of straightforward

Objects in this world, along with genes, quarks, landlords and bailiffs, is the subject of this chapter.

In analyzing the discussions of social construction in the various disciplines, Hacking identifies *interactivity* as constituting one basic difference between the natural and the social sciences (32). As he explains: "The classifications of the social sciences are interactive. The classifications and concepts of the natural sciences are not. In the social sciences there are conscious interactions between kind and person. There are no interactions of the same type in the natural sciences" (32). Earlier in the paragraph, he had given the contrasting examples of refugee women and quarks: the former, a category of the social sciences, "interacts with things of that kind, namely people, including individual women refugees, who can become aware of how they are classified and modify their behavior accordingly"; quarks, however, "are not aware that they are quarks and are not altered simply by being classified as quarks" (32). In other words, "The idea of the quark does not interact with quarks" (32). This distinction is insightful, even though, as Hacking also mentions, there remain "plenty of questions about" it (32). Furthermore, what about the case of a science such as geography, sitting as it does at the cusp of the natural and the social? The Red Sea is obviously not aware of itself as such, nor does it interact with the idea of the Red Sea, but what of the people who live around its shores? Geographical classifications and categories, even in their most natural scientific iterations, cannot but be interactive with the inhabitants that populate their landscapes. Moreover, geographical notions are interactive in the sense that particular classifications and indeed modes of classification eliminate other types of classifying, seeing, and being in the world. These questions are particularly salient since modern history, from its very birth as a discipline, has attached itself to geographical categories and concepts. Thus the Mediterranean Sea is not aware of itself as such, but it does interact with things of that kind, namely, Mediterranean people(s), who are indeed "altered simply by being classified as such." As Michael Herzfeld has repeatedly shown, the term *Mediterranean* must also be understood as "a formidable weapon of present-day *Realpolitik,*" a power-laden tool meant to distance backward southern European societies from the advanced, civilized north.[5] However, this does not mean, he explains, that the category is immaterial: "To say that the Mediterranean 'does not exist' is as silly as to argue that facts themselves 'do not exist.'"[6] The reference to facts is revealing, but factuality here is understood as "always a constitutive act," so that "claims that the Mediterranean 'exists' are performative in Austin's sense; they do not so much enunciate facts as create them."[7] Attention is thus shifted away from an empirical evaluation of the validity of the category and invites one "to determine what conditions make these utterances persuasive as statements of fact."[8]

This chapter is precisely a genealogical exploration of those very conditions that Herzfeld speaks of. It reveals the discursive parameters that permit affirmations of Mediterranean unity in particular, and the coherence of maritime basins in general, to be "persuasive as statements of fact." It explores an epistemic shift that occurs not *within* a discipline of knowledge but *across* disciplines. Indeed, the idea of a sovereign sea becomes the center of scholarly attention in numerous disciplines, in both the natural and the social sciences. This should not come as a surprise, since it is a characteristic of such epistemic ruptures that they should operate at the level of discourse as a whole, rather than individual disciplines—indeed, it is the same epistemic break that created the disciplines as such in the first place.[9] The sovereign sea emerges to take on a crucial role in the newly institutionalized disciplines of history and geography, the joint monarchs of the novel order of things. The sea turns out to be at the very center of the cosmos of modernity, just as the modern episteme was a condition for the idea of the sovereign sea to make its appearance.

A FREE SEA FOR FREE TRADE

The sea appeared suddenly and forcefully in the Western European intellectual scene when the youthful jurist Hugo Grotius was commissioned to write an apologia for the capture by the Dutch East India Company (VOC) of the Portuguese vessel *Sta. Catarina* off the coast of Singapore in 1603. It led to the drafting, first, of an expansive commentary on the law of booty, *De jure praedae comentarius,* which remained unpublished (and was almost lost), except for the twelfth chapter, which appeared anonymously in 1609 as *Mare liberum.* This was the first salvo in the constitution of the sea as a coherent concept; it was, in short, the first projection of the thalassological imagination. Grotius's political insight was quite simple, though ingenious and erudite; its impact was extensive, giving rise to applause but also critiques throughout the centuries, and making it a foundational moment for the

Western legal, political, and philosophical tradition in general and the question of international jurisprudence in particular.[10]

Evoking the ancient Stoics, Grotius maintained that the fundamental natural right was self-preservation. From this derived two primary laws of nature: first, self-defense ("It shall be permissible to defend one's own life and to shun that which threatens to prove injurious") and second, appropriation ("It shall be permissible to acquire for oneself, and to retain, those things which are useful for life").[11] To interpret the latter precept, Grotius echoes Cicero: "Each individual may, without violating the precepts of nature, prefer to see acquired for himself rather than for another, that which is important for the conduct of life."[12] The next step, then, was to explain the right to acquisition and property according to a logic grounded in nature, much of which appeared in the work that was published as *Mare liberum.*

The argument was based on a foundational dichotomy between land and sea—one that was to become a central feature of modern thought. The difference between them was that only land could be made property or claimed as dominion. Since God had bestowed the earth upon humanity as a whole and in common, only by extended attachment, occupation, or seizure could it become individual. By way of human labor and industry, what belongs to all may be turned into personal property; by way of possession and use, ownership claims could be made. Natural laws were thus divinely ordained but understandable by the workings of human reason.

The sea, however, cannot be possessed, for it cannot be fixed or made static. Dynamic, unstable, and infinite by nature, the sea cannot be owned, since "those things which cannot be occupied or were never occupied can be proper to none because all propriety hath his beginning from occupation."[13] Just as air is "common to all and proper to none . . . both because it cannot be possessed and also because it oweth a common use to men," so too is the sea "so infinite that it cannot be possessed and applied to all uses, whether we respect navigation or fishing."[14] In other words, the sea "is in the number of those things which are not in merchandise and trading, that is to say, which cannot be made proper."[15] And from this, Grotius concluded that "no part of the sea can be accompted in the territory of any people."[16] In short, the sea is *free* by its very nature, and "servitude be not imposed on the sea, which cannot serve."[17] There was something infinite and eternal about maritime space that gave it added weight in its pure, natural liberty.

John Locke, incidentally, would retrace the steps of Grotius's argument with striking similarity toward the end of the seventeenth century in the

Second Treatise of Government ("God, by commanding to subdue, gave authority so far to *appropriate:* and the condition of human life, which requires labour and materials to work on, necessarily introduces private possessions")—and he too would describe oceanic space as "that great and still remaining common of mankind," even as he made himself the advocate of endless appropriation and enclosure in his famous fifth chapter "Of Property."[18]

This sense of limitless freedom and the infinite, this oceanic feeling, first theorized by Grotius, would fundamentally mark the thalassological imagination, and indeed the Western tradition more largely. Romain Rolland appropriated it to describe the sense of religious attachment, as made famous by Sigmund Freud in *The Future of an Illusion* and *Civilization and Its Discontents.* Baudelaire would evoke it to celebrate the intimate connection of freedom, man, and the sea: "Man—a free man—always loves the sea/ and in its endlessly unrolling surge/ will contemplate his soul as in a glass/ where gulfs as bitter gape within his mind."[19] And Hegel would involve it directly in the very march of Spirit.

Grotius had thus theorized the inherent *freedom* of the sea. And this freedom was of the most abstract and general variety (the difference between things that can be owned and things that cannot)—but it also embodied a very particular type of freedom: free trade. Let it not be forgotten that it was probably the VOC that commissioned Grotius to compose his commentary in the first place, and certainly the VOC that had *Mare liberum* published—the objective being to intervene in a matter concerning the freedom to trade, particularly in the Indies.

The sea would indeed find pride of place in the works of the grand theoretician of free trade Adam Smith. Smith grounded his entire analytical system on the principle of the division of labor: labor was at the origin of all value, and the extent of its division indicated the stage of social development. The first three chapters of *The Wealth of Nations* outline this primary feature of human exchange: the first chapter affirms the centrality of the division of labor as the singular cause of progress, and the second insists that its origin is due to mechanical nature rather than to human intentionality. The third chapter moves from the abstract to the empirical by focusing on the actual geohistorical development of the division of labor, and it is here that the aquatic element makes its entry: "As by means of water-carriage a more extensive market is opened to every sort of industry than what land-carriage alone can afford it, so it is upon the sea-coast, and along the banks of navigable rivers, that industry of every kind naturally begins to subdivide and improve itself, and it is frequently not till a long time after that those improvements extend themselves to the inland parts of the country."[20]

As the editors intimate, Smith probably derived the idea from Richard Cantillon, who greatly influenced the circle of Parisian physiocrats that Smith frequented. In his *Essai sur la nature du commerce en général,* Cantillon too insisted on the greater efficiency of water-carriage, which for him explained the presence of big cities on navigable routes.[21] In any case, the idea is well implanted in *The Wealth of Nations,* where it is repeatedly advanced not only as a microeconomic principle but indeed as a world historical force: "The nations that, according to the best authenticated history, appear to have been first civilized were those that dwelt round the coast of the Mediterranean sea" (34). It is "by far the greatest inlet that is known in the world," it has no tides (and therefore lesser waves), it has many islands, and the neighboring shores are close—so it facilitated naturally "the infant navigation of the world; when, from their ignorance of the compass, men were afraid to quit the view of the coast, and from the imperfection of the art of ship-building, to abandon themselves to the boisterous waves of the ocean" (34).

Laying another brick in the mansion of the thalassographic imagination, Smith thus associates the sea with civilization. Though he puts forward the Mediterranean Sea in particular as the locus classicus of civilization, Smith is not committed fully to a Eurocentric vision: he credits Egypt especially but also Bengal and the eastern provinces of China as the first to progress in civilization (35). This aquatically stimulated progress he contrasts directly with "all the inland parts of Africa, and all that part of Asia which lies any considerable way north of the Euxine and Caspian seas," which "seem in all ages of the world to have been in the same barbarous and uncivilized state in which we find them at present" (35–36). And this frozenness in time, this lack of progress, is a direct consequence of the absent aquatic element.

Even in the case of ancient Egypt, India, and China, though these may have been the "the wealthiest [states], according to all accounts, that ever were in the world," they do not naturally progress for want of foreign trade, largely because of their ambivalence toward the sea. At least in the case of the first two, Smith explains the lack of progress explicitly through their thalassophobia: "The antient Egyptians had a superstitious antipathy to the sea; a superstition nearly of the same kind prevails among the Indians" (367). Smith comes back yet again to the superiority of water-carriage, and the determinant feature of maritimity (a particular territory's relationship to the sea) further on in his text, to explain the advantage and dominance of England, which "on account of the natural fertility of the soil, of the great extent of the sea-coast in proportion to that of the whole country, and of the many navigable rivers which run through it, and afford the conveniency of water carriage to some of the most inland parts of it, is perhaps as well fitted by nature as any large country in Europe, to be the seat of foreign commerce, of manufactures for distant sale, and of all the improvements which these can occasion" (424).

In his earlier *Lectures on Jurisprudence,* Smith had already connected maritimity with progress and civilization. This time, it concerned (ancient) Greece primarily, and then Europe more largely, a continent perhaps for the first time defined in its essence by its special connection to the sea. In his explanations of the "great difference" between barbarous and civilized nations, and in particular of the reasons why there is "little probability" that "[republican] government will ever be introduced into Tartary or Arabia," Smith turns to geography.[22] These places are constituted by arid hills and deserts, whereas "The contrary of this is the case in these countries where republican governments have been established, and particularly in Greece."[23] Most importantly, "Two thirds of Attica are surrounded by the sea," and "most of the European countries" benefit from similarly privileged natural conditions: "They are divided by rivers and branches of the sea, and are naturally fit for the cultivation of the soil and other arts."[24] And this, in turn, is favorable to the organic blossoming of republican government.

Though it remains rather undeveloped in Adam Smith and, significantly, does not enter the analysis in *The Wealth of Nations,* this particular formulation of Europe's identity will become a staple of the rising self-understanding of the West, which appears at the nexus of the constellation made up by the sea, progress, civilization, and freedom. And one specific sea is particularly important to the story.

MEDITERRANEANISM

Although it is now taken for granted, the idea of a coherent Mediterranean uniting the shores of the sea was just beginning to be formulated at the turn of the nineteenth century. Augustin Pyramus de Candolle, celebrated as one of the founders of modern botany, was probably the first to think of that body of water as a unit. In 1805, already, he had used the adjective *Mediterranean* to describe a portion of France in a personal addendum to a re-edition of Jean-Baptiste Lamarck's *Flore française.*[25] In an 1820 article entitled "Botanical Geography" for the *Dictionnaire classique des sciences naturelles,* Candolle spoke of a "Mediterranean region" that ought to be addressed separately as a function of its floral and climatic homogeneity—a region that "includes all of the geographical basin of the Mediterranean: that is, the part of Africa above the Sahara, and the part of Europe that is sheltered in the north by a more or less continuous chain of mountains."[26]

Naturalist, botanist, and geographer of great renown, military man, leader of the scientific expeditions to Morea (1829–31) and Algeria (1839–42), and editor of the important *Dictionnaire classique des sciences naturelles* (of which he also wrote much of the content), Bory de Saint-Vincent appropriated Candolle's suggestion of a "Mediterranean region" defined by its botanical coherence and systematized it. In the entry "The Sea" in his *Dictionnaire,* Bory described the "littoral of the Mediterranean" as "form[ing] a natural basin of the most characterized kind, and one that is so to the extent that the coasts of France on this side resemble in their physiognomy and their productions much more the Barbary or even the Syriac shores than they display the aspect and productions of the oceanic beaches of the same land."[27] Ten years later, in the opening pages of the first volume of the section on the physical sciences of the Expédition scientifique de Morée that he supervised, he famously related his feeling of estrangement already when reaching the south of France. "Everything around me," he says, following a long list of features ranging from the architectural to the geological, "had a character in which nothing at all remained of that of the other, even temperate, parts of France. It was that one we can call Mediterranean, but of a reinforced kind."[28] By 1836, then, as Jean-Marc Drouin argues, the nomenclature of the Mediterranean to describe a landscape (both human and natural) had gained sufficient traction to accommodate gradations in degree.[29]

Bory goes even further with the idea of a coherent Mediterranean, in an analytical move that will have considerable consequences. He moves with ease and purpose from the particular to the universal, transforming the idea of the Mediterranean from a specific water basin to a *type* of basin. Here is the opening of the section on the Mediterranean of the same dictionary entry, which follows a discussion of the oceans: "Mediterranée, *Mediterranea.* Is used . . . to describe that which is enclosed by land. This name of *Mediterranean* will therefore be reserved here to designate any sea that, not being an immediate part of an ocean, communicates through one or even several straits with one of the great previously established maritime divisions"

(378). Bory then defines a total of nine of these mediterraneans, such as "the Scandinavian Mediterranean or Baltic Sea," the "Erythrean Mediterranean or Red Sea," the "Persian Mediterranean or Gulf," the "Sinitic (*Sinique*) Mediterranean," and the "Colombian Mediterranean" (in which is included "the Gulf of Mexico and the Sea of the Antilles").

The point is not to suggest that Bory innovated simply by transposing the term to describe any almost enclosed body of water; other writers of the early nineteenth century (and indeed before) did the same.[30] What is capital in Bory's argument is that these are autonomous, organic units constituted by a set of specific internal criteria related to each other and to other units within a strict system of classification. There are five, and only five, oceans, just as there are only five continents; there are nine, and only nine mediterraneans. The symmetry of the oceans and continents is not coincidental; it is a function of the strong conviction that the natural world is a harmonious, organic entity, divided into two pairs and an odd one: Bory amalgamates Europe and Asia to serve as counterpoint to northern America, detached from a southern America that mirrors Africa. Australasia is apart (378). This is not to say that Bory sees these entities as eternal or unchanging; much to the contrary, he is very sensitive to the historical nature of things, and of seas in particular as they contract over time, so that parts of oceans become mediterraneans just as parts of these become caspians, the generic term for a wholly enclosed body of salt water. Some of these caspians, in turn, dry up completely. It is for this reason, Bory explains, that one finds many more traces of seas than there are actually existing seas (389). A most impressive example of such vestiges of earlier seas is constituted by those "sterile, briny, even" deserts, of which the surrounding mountains were the "antique shores" (389). The Sahara, then, to highlight one of the many examples provided by Bory, is just a mediterranean, or, to be more precise, a caspian, without water. Its coherence as an analytical unit is not obscured by the fact that it is left to the imagination of the reader. In short, the Mediterranean, with Bory, has truly become a concept; and this is an essential step for it to be able to have an independent history.

Indeed, Bory theorizes the harmonious coherence of *all* of the sea units that he defines and describes in his entry. This is due, he explains, to the particularities of nonterrestrial geographies, void as they are of the political vagaries of their earth-bound counterparts. "The Sea is unlike the land," he writes in anticipatory echo of the new thalassologists' claims to neutrality and novelty, "where human domination, having usually been established and perpetuated through force and tyranny, the natural limits of each country have long since disappeared, making place for political limits, where citadels were erected, the way we place markers around our properties" (371). This is a true windfall for the geography of the seas, one that should be acted upon by mobilizing a science that in its ideal form is both methodologically total and utterly impartial: "Given this community of the sea, geography may therefore, over its entire surface, not admit the kind of divisions that caprice and violence establish on the enslaved face of the earth" (372). The distinction at sea being "purely geographical," the scientist can "place markers rationally," as a ratio of water to land, the influence of temperature, and the distribution of botanical and zoological species (372).

Setting himself against the "arbitrar[y] divi[sion] of previous geographers and mapmakers," Bory states clearly, "We will admit here of only five great oceanic regions." The wording is unequivocal, for the conclusions are derived from unadulterated scientific rationality. The borders of the units are drawn with the complete arsenal of the natural sciences; the units themselves therefore have perfect internal coherence. Thanks to the absence of artificial terrestrial meddling, the domains are coterminous, and the limits produced in the mind of the scientist are limpid reflections of those in the world's waters. Thus it is not only the Mediterranean specifically, or even the mediterraneans in general, that have internal coherence and therefore should serve as units of analysis. It is the reverse. It is the very homogeneity that makes this or that stretch of water a *body* of water. Uniformity, then, is what defines *all* seas—as long, of course, as they are ascertained "rationally," according to the rigorous demands of a geographic science untouched by the artificial borders that corrupt the earth because of state politics. In fact, the first such internally coherent body of water described by Bory is an ocean: "The traveler who crosses the Atlantic from one end to the other recognizes in it, whatever may be the change in temperature that he experiences, a certain resemblance among all things" (375). Like Hegel and Ritter, he affirms that the opposite coasts of oceans resemble one another more than do those of continents: Senegambia has much less in common with the Red Sea than it does with the Orinoco and the Amazons, and these river zones are more compatible with West Africa than with the coastal areas of Chile and Peru.

Not only is oceanic unity here contrasted with continental diversity, the *shores* themselves relate to one another. It is not only a matter of strict marine unity: the consistency emerges from the waves and swallows the coast, transforming the conventional and biased land-based visions of nations and continents into the scientific and apolitical aqua-centric perspective of thalassology.

Thus, while the harmony is greatest in the liquid depths, land animals and plants, indeed geology and landscapes, are no less defined by their association with a given sea. The pull of the water engulfs much more than simply the coasts: in some cases, seas (all of them mediterraneans) are matched with one of the races of man, of which there are also only a finite number, defined and classified according to strict criteria. Although it is never conceptualized as such, there are unmistakable intimations that the body of water actually creates the body of humanity. Vagueness notwithstanding, the "mer Méditerranée proprement dite" is defined, at the very outset, as that mediterranean "on the shores of which developed the civilization of the Japetic species of the human genus" (379); the "Méditerranée Sinique" for its part has "coasts peopled by our Sinitic [*Sinique*] species of the human genus" (383), just as "the humans of the Colombian species occupy the perimeter" of the "Méditerranée Colombienne" (385). Well over a century before Braudel, then, Bory conceptualized large ecological areas, scientifically derived and centered (or modeled) on the sea, that were to serve as the primary unit of analysis for a science of nature and humanity untainted by the false boundaries set up by a science that limited itself to territories and their political events.

GEOHISTORICISM

The concept of the sea took center stage in the founding moments of the modern order of knowledge as a whole. As Foucault demonstrated in *The Order of Things*, the disciplines of the new "human sciences" can be thought of only in relation to each other, so that it is not mere accident that makes history and geography become institutionalized at the very same time and place (the University of Berlin in the 1820s, where the founding fathers of the modern disciplines of history, philosophy, and geography, Ranke, Hegel, and Ritter, were colleagues).

For Hegel, Europe is defined by its relationship to the sea. Europe is totality, it is where contradiction provides the conditions for reaching a higher synthesis, unlike Africa, where there is no contradiction at all, and Asia, where it is inert. It is the sea that, only in Europe, combines with uplands and river valleys to form a genuine antithesis to the land and therefore provides that blessed continent with a special spatial essence: History.

Hegel establishes three geographical principles, which "are to be regarded as essential, rational distinctions, in contrast with the variety of merely accidental circumstances": "1) the arid elevated land with its extensive steppes and plains; 2) the valley plains—the Land of Transition permeated and watered by great Streams; 3) the coast region in immediate connection with the sea."[31] Each principle comes loaded with a particular spiritual configuration, and they determine the essence of the three primary units of the globe "with which History is concerned." Africa, from which the part north of the desert (renamed "European Africa") and the Nile valley (truly of Asian spirit) have been extricated, is defined by the Upland principle: it is the isolated "land of childhood, which lying beyond the day of self-conscious history, is enveloped in the dark mantle of Night" (95). Asia is dominated by the principle of the valley plains (lined by zones of the Upland principle). In that land of contradictions, for the first time, "arose the Light of Spirit, and therefore the history of the World" (104). The oppositions find no resolution, however, and it is to Europe that the Spirit moves. Asia "presents the origination of all religious and political principles, but Europe has been the scene of their development" (106). Europe is defined by totality, and therefore history; all three geographical principles find in it their harmonious combination.

However, the correspondence between the geographical principles and the empirical units is not a one-to-one relationship. Africa is one large and compact elevated land, isolated from both river and sea; Asia is where uplands and river valleys clash, though it is defined by rivers; and Europe is the harmonious combination of all three, but its geohistorical soul is especially derived from the spirit of the sea, the third principle. Moreover, the spatial units themselves hover between approximation and precision. "Every country," Hegel admits, "is both east and west in relation to others," but countries also possess an absolute value: Europe is "the centre and end of the Old World" and therefore "absolutely the west," where the sun peaks and sets into the horizon, whereas Asia is "absolutely the east," for "it is there that the light of the spirit, the consciousness of a universal, first emerged, and with it the process of world history."[32]

Geography was thus not simply made up of abstract, geometrical calculations; it was anchored in History, and vice versa. And both geography and history were fundamentally tied to theology. "What we call continents," Hegel says elsewhere, are the "organic divisions of the Earth's individuality," and in them "there is an element of necessity, the detailed exposition of which belongs to geography."[33] The continents too are both absolute and relative. Since each continent embodies a specific natural and spiritual essence, Hegel can, and indeed must, detach from "Africa proper" both its northern tier abutting the Mediterranean Sea and the Nile valley: he states in *Lectures on the Philosophy of History* that "*Africa* must be divided into three parts: one is that which lies south of the desert of Sahara,—Africa proper,—the Upland almost entirely unknown to us, with narrow coast-tracts along the sea; the second is that to the north of the desert,—European Africa (if we may so call it),—a coast-land; the third is the river region of the Nile, the only valley-land of Africa, and which is in connexion with Asia" (95).

Having been thus amputated, Africa is *absolutely* the Upland. Other places also display the characteristics of the Upland, such as "middle Asia inhabited by Mongolians," "the deserts of Arabia and of Barbary," or "in South America the country round the Orinoco, and in Paraguay" (92), but none in the way that Africa does. For that continent, it is the "leading classical feature" (95). "What we properly understand by Africa," Hegel writes in conclusion to his discussion of the continent before "eliminating this introductory element" and moving to true History, "is the Unhistorical, Undeveloped, Spirit, still involved in the conditions of mere nature" (103).

Africa, that "substantial, unvarying, metallic, elevated region, intractably shut up within itself," is thus captured by the Upland principle (92). It is at the "threshold of world history" and is only "adapted to send forth impulses over the rest of the world" (92). The "peculiarity" of the inhabitants of these arid zones is patriarchal pastoral life; their regions bearing little productivity, they hold property not in land but in animals; they are "careless" and do not know of legal relations (92–93). They do not genuinely participate in the world-historical, but they do sometimes "cohere together in great masses, and by an impulse of one kind or another, are excited to external movement" (93). It is then that, "as does an overwhelming Forest-torrent,—possessing no inherent principle of vitality," they appear on the stage of history and "rush as a devastating inundation over civilized lands" (93). A "revolution" does come out of such irruptions, but it has "no other result than destruction and desolation"—and this, even though such people may have been of "peaceful disposition" (93).

Thus Africa's main historical feature, for Hegel, is its essential isolation. "Africa," he declares, "as far as History goes back, has remained—for all purposes of connection with the rest of the World—shut up; it is the Gold-land compressed within itself" (95). This is not a particularly original thesis; interesting about it, however, are the causes that he adduces to this secluded state of Africa. It is an essential product of "its geographical condition" (95). It is its natural, organic, spatial being that leads to its isolation, for Africa proper forms a triangle that "is on two sides so constituted for the most part, as to have a very narrow Coast Tract, habitable only in a few isolated spots" (95–96). The inaccessibility of the seashore is compounded by a "girdle of marsh land with the most luxuriant vegetation, the especial home of ravenous beasts, snakes of all kinds" (96). This repugnant border ("whose atmosphere is poisonous to Europeans") is reinforced by "a cincture of high mountains" to create a true citadel shrouded in mystery, which Europeans have only very rarely reached, and which even "the Negroes have seldom made their way through" (96).

Africa proper, then, is an impregnable, elevated, and secluded fortress. Both its general spirit and the particular character of its inhabitants are products of this desolate state. But what is it isolated from, exactly, and by what? *It is isolated, by its very geography, from the sea.* That is what makes Africa proper ahistorical. All of Hegelian philosophical-historical discourse rests on a certain understanding of geography, with the sea holding a place of choice within it.

The peculiar character of the African is the result of his lack of access to the sea. Hegel explains that in "Negro life the characteristic point is the fact that consciousness has not yet attained to the realization of any substantial objective existence,—as for example, God, or Law,—in which the interest of man's volition is involved and in which he realizes his own being" (97).By symmetry, what makes the European spirit so distinctly European is precisely its relationship to the sea, its inherent maritimity. This sentiment is perhaps most succinctly and clearly expressed in the *Philosophy of Mind,* where in the *Zusatz* to paragraph 394 Hegel connects the "unchangeableness of the national character" to climate and geography, underscores the special importance of the sea in connection to this, and says: "In the interior of Africa proper, surrounded by high mountains in the coastal regions and in this way cut off from this free element of the sea, the mind of the African remains shut up within itself, feels no urge to be free and endures without resistance universal slavery."[34]

The decisive impact of the sea is confirmed in a passage of the *Lectures on the Philosophy of History,* when Hegel recounts, at some point in the sixteenth century, "outbreaks of terrible hordes which rushed down upon the more peaceful inhabitants of the declivities" (96). The reasons behind these movements are unclear, he explains, but what is most interesting is the reversal of these hordes from showing "the most reckless inhumanity and disgusting barbarism" upon their wild descent to being "mild and well disposed towards the Europeans" afterwards. The logic could not be clearer. Even the most primitive pack of savages in an impulsive fit of particular barbarity can be tamed by their contact with the sea. What is important in this tale, what makes it a crucial example in Hegel's argument and an integral element of his larger philosophical system, is that these hordes were pacified, made calm, almost civilized, upon their settling on the coasts, just as their isolation from the sea dissolved. The sea is civility, morality, universality; it is everything Africa proper is not. And the sea implies the European, as the passage flows without notice from one to the other.

Many of these basic ideas, especially those connected to the question of land and sea, find a striking echo in the writings of Hegel's esteemed colleague Carl Ritter, who is, indeed, Hegel's "only explicitly mentioned source for geography."[35] Ritter's most important contribution toward opening the space to theorize the place of the sea in history lies in his formulation of the purpose and nature of geography, and the basis from which it can be systematized as a holistic science. Ritter, while amassing formidable amounts of information about the globe (for his gargantuan, if unfinished, *Erdkunde*), conceived of the world as a harmonious organism that was the setting of humanity's progress. Each continent and every people, or rather each and every spatial category, had an inherent meaning and a special role to play in the great drama of the world. These "terrestrial units" were imagined as smaller organisms blending to form the organism that was the world, and each of them embodied a specific spirit, the realization of which was the duty and destiny of its inhabitants. This sentiment appears, with greater or lesser precision, in all of the authors that have been discussed here, but in Ritter it is most clearly formulated and theorized as the organizing principle of his system of thought.

Derived from a Christian understanding of the earth and its peoples as a perfect creation, and of their evolution as fixed and predetermined according to God's plan, Ritterian geography assigned an ideal fit between man and his environment and assumed as its objective the elucidation of the relationship between the body (earth) and the soul (humanity). "This earth was to him," Ritter's American biographer and translator William Gage says, "not a mere dwelling-place for nations; it was the material out of which life is woven; it was the garment in which the soul clothes itself, the body wherein the spirit formed by God must move."[36]

It was therefore the goal of humanity, and of human knowledge, to fulfill the divine plan through the achievement of its potential, in symbiosis with its natural surroundings. "In the totality of natural and historical phenomena," Ritter announces, "the effects of the constitution and qualities of the earth appear everywhere, since it was established from the beginning as the bearer of peoples, as the home, dwelling place, and temporary nursery of the human species."[37] This was an anthropocentric system through and through, and unabashedly so: as a devout Christian, Ritter could not have been embarrassed by his belief in divine providence. "Creation and creature," he responded to a critic who disapproved of his speculative and spiritual meanderings in favor of a strictly physical approach to geography, "cannot be separated from each other without shattering their essential fundamental relation. My critic calls the shattering of this great mutual relation a precise definition of science; but wrongly, in my opinion. For all science, however manifold it may be and however sharply it may be divided, is nevertheless at bottom only one, on which all others rest; it can be only the creature's hymn of praise to its Creator; and the contemplation of God is to me the highest, the only absolute science."[38]

It was a perspective centered on Man, but, paradoxically, it was also one that shunned the humanly constructed political units as the basis for the organization of geographical study in favor of a focus on natural factors. Relief, ecology, geology, landscape—these were the domains from which stemmed the framing parameters of Ritter's novel discipline. This is not to suggest that Ritter ignored nation-states; much to the contrary, he saw them as integral to the divine plan and their history as determined by the fulfillment of a particular spirit, but the political map of the world was no longer the explanatory grid for geographical knowledge. The relationship was inverted: it was geographical knowledge of the local and regional relief that defined the nature and purpose of political units, whose destiny, then, was the realization of those capabilities. The environment (and again, included in this term were both human and nonhuman, animate and inanimate constituents), as opposed to politics, became the enduring, permanent basis of the organization of knowledge. In the words of his disciple and translator William Gage:

> To him, the earth was like a tree, with root, trunk, branch, leaf, blossom, fruit, each necessary to the perfection of the whole; or like the human form, with chest, head, and limbs, none of which can be removed without obvious injury to the vitality of the organism. Sometimes he went so far as to use a still more forcible expression, saying that the globe has a life of its own—

> the winds, waters, and landmasses acting upon one another like animated organs, every region having its own function to perform, thus promoting the well-being of all the rest. To him these were no fanciful analogies. They were living truths.[39]

This critical reorientation was not unrelated to political developments of the time; indeed, as John Leighly suggests, the "obsolescence of traditional political boundaries in Europe [caused by the Revolutionary and Napoleonic wars] prepared the ground for Ritter's reorganization of descriptive geographic data by divisions of the continents according to their major relief features."[40]

The relationship between humanity and its natural environment was not exclusive, however. Ritter was highly sensitive to the historical nature of things: after all, his masterwork's full title reads, "The Science of the Earth in Relation to Nature and the History of Mankind; or, General Comparative Geography as the Solid Foundation of the Study of, and Instruction in, the Physical and Historical Sciences." Before the creation of the chair in geography in Berlin, he held a position in Frankfurt teaching history, and indeed, he even theorized what he saw as the necessary and complementary relationship between the two disciplines, most explicitly in an 1833 lecture entitled "The Historical Element in Geography as a Science."[41] Ritter always insisted on the historical nature of geographic knowledge and on the ways in which different conceptions of space and time are governed by particular contexts, which are themselves defined by specific spatial and temporal configurations. He practiced, not a strictly physical geography, but one of a more holistic kind in which the human, and therefore historical, element was central. Environmental features appeared to him not simply in their geological or ecological structure but also, and perhaps primarily, as a function of their interaction with human development. Geography's role was not just to treat environmental features from a naturalist perspective but to integrate them in a totalizing historical framework, where so many physical elements (mountains, valleys, waterways, etc.) contributed to or inhibited the circulation of people and goods, established barriers or passages to communication, promoted borders or subverted them. In return, he saw environmental parameters as fundamentally dynamic and as responsive in particular to the progress of human population. For example, he suggested that the world was shrinking as a result of increased connectivity.[42]

Ritter thus laid the foundations for the historical turn in geography and the geographical turn in history, of which Braudel's study of the Mediterranean in particular was a famous moment. The historical revolution of the Annales school was anticipated and enabled by Ritter more than a century earlier. His reorganization of geographical knowledge according to environmental criteria, as opposed to the reification of the political boundaries of the status quo, would also be influential, as was his articulation of geographical units having a specific spirit. All of these parameters were connected, and they all intersected in the focus on the notion of the natural region in his geography and that of his successors. A region was not the product of such an ephemeral feature as political boundaries, it was not merely a section of the earth. It was an organic whole, defined by a particular set of elements derived from the natural and human sciences (at the intersection of history and geography), and characterized by a specific form, arrangement, and location in relation to other units, all of which provided it with a special essence that was integral to the universal divine plan. Although the transcendental aspect of such a scheme was (arguably) to fade alongside the accelerating transformation of Western Christendom into its secularized self, this configuration of the fundaments of geographical knowledge would have a most enduring legacy and a most profound impact on today's thalassology.

This was especially the case because the sea was at the very center of Ritter's system, just as it was in Hegel's. As he writes in his methodological introduction to the *Erdkunde:* "It is the fluid elements, everywhere met, and compassing heights and depths alike, which have the highest significance in relation to the globe. . . . Water seems not only in geology and vegetation, but in the history of animals and nations, to be the first condition of increase or improvement, from lands well watered by rivers, coast regions, and internal seas, up to the great union of the world by oceans."[43] It is no surprise then, that the continents, by then firmly objectified and naturalized, would come to be defined by their relationship to the sea, with complexity decreasing as one moved from Europe to Asia and finally to Africa, which was "the most compact and unrifted continent of all" and had "the most simple coast-line," and with which he therefore began his masterwork.[44]

In an 1826 lecture entirely devoted to the continents, Ritter also focuses on this maritimity to help define the organic terrestrial units that are the continents. Europe, though "the smallest of the three continents of the Old World," is "the most varied and rifted and divided up of all."[45] This leads to the unique "individuality, not only of its coast outlines, but of the countries which these inclose."[46] At this point there enters a measurement that will have a long life in the scholarship: the ratio of the shoreline to the surface area, which is greatest in Europe and defines its natural and spiritual character.

Europe is thus "the continent most approachable of all from the sea."[47] And this was all a matter of revealing the geographical determinants of civilization, history, and politics and explaining the "remarkable fact, that the smallest continent should be the field for the greatest deeds of history, and that the smallest, too, should gain the mastery of the whole."[48]

THE ENCLOSURE OF THE SEA

Ritter's natural-theological geography was the essential inspiration for an entire generation of geographers, and particularly the North American avid promoter of thalassology, also designated as founder of a discipline (oceanography), Matthew Fontaine Maury. A naval lieutenant from Virginia, a most devout Christian, and an admirer of Humboldt and Ritter, Maury was, in scholarly matters, an autodidact who quickly developed a great reputation for his work in charting winds, currents, and navigation routes and was consequently appointed as the first superintendent of the US Naval Observatory in 1842.[49] In 1855, he published what was to become the foundational text of oceanography and a terrific commercial success, *The Physical Geography of the Sea*.[50]

Unlike Alexander von Humboldt, whom Maury credits with the origin of the expression "the physical geography of the sea,"[51] Carl Ritter goes unmentioned anywhere in Maury's published work, but his overall stamp is unmistakable. What Ritter had done to land, Maury thought to execute for the sea. Nature was to Maury a harmonious whole, and its perfect design followed a divine plan. Therefore the liquid domains of the earth had a fundamental order akin to their terrestrial counterparts, the laws of which were regular, uniform, and intelligible and could be elucidated by dedicated efforts to unravel God's scheme. In the words of a contemporary describing this "brilliant thought": "The waves, the winds, the storms, the currents, the depths and the temperatures of the sea were believed by Maury to constitute a system, a complex of cause and effect, constant in its regularity, perfect in its orderliness, and so mathematically interrelated that the mind of man could by patient investigation understand its phenomena and even forecast its processes."[52]

Maury was a dedicated proponent of the argument of design, and his text is suffused with quotations from and references to the scriptures, something that engendered great disapproval by later scholars, and even the discomfort of some contemporaries. The only escape would be to find a way to forcibly separate the theological/religious from the positive/scientific. This is precisely what John Leighly attempts to do, at length, in the introduction to a 1963 re-edition of *The Physical Geography of the Sea,* where he criticizes Maury so severely that he feels impelled to supply a corrective. Concerned with having "overemphasized the scientific weaknesses of *The Physical Geography,*" Leighly states, "There is in fact a great deal of sound information in the book, but the reader now, as a hundred years ago, must weigh each paragraph and sort out its content of objective fact, of material selected to support Maury's interpretations, and of fantasy."[53] The goal, then, is to cordon off the purely empirical from the fantastical—a distinction that is reported to have a long genealogy going back, ironically, to Ritter himself. Leighly is irked most especially by the appeal to the metaphysical and theological, an enduring tendency of geographical thought that he spent most of his life denouncing. Thus Ritter too suffers fierce condemnation on similar counts in one of Leighly's first articles on the history and nature of the discipline of geography.[54]

Still, by no means can Maury's work be seen simply as a literary, philosophical, or moral appendage to a more grounded, factual, scientific collection of data. To begin with, one just cannot easily discriminate between these spheres. The desire to compartmentalize knowledge, and the act of doing so, are themselves a function of particular power dynamics that have nothing to do with the empirical nature of things but attempt to escape scrutiny through precisely such dissections. Moreover, Maury's dedication to some form of natural theology and his inspiration from the scriptures were common to virtually all geographers, scientists, and scholars of the period. Leighly, for example, mobilizes as the most "forthright" contemporary criticism of the devotional tendencies of Maury's text a passage by a French naval officer, Captain Bourgois, but it is rather remarkable to note how *concordant* they actually are in the general tenor of their conceptual frame with regard to the divine. Captain Bourgois's problem is not that Maury's worldview identifies the goal of scholarly inquiry as the revealing of God's plan, but simply that Maury confuses "some ephemeral system born of his own imagination" for "the immutable laws of Providence."[55] Maury is wrong not in his approach but simply in his conclusions, the weakness of which are compensated for by use of the scriptures. Bourgois and Maury could not be closer on that front: the disagreement is one of exegesis. References to the harmonious laws of nature can at this time be a question only of degree and not kind, as can be readily seen in the divine shadows and specters that often mark the quotes cited throughout this chapter.

Finally, and counterintuitively, it is through his general (speculative) framework, rather than his "empirical" data, that Maury's legacy is most enduring and that he made his most profound scientific discoveries. Few will remember Maury for his factual assertions regarding the Gulf Stream or the atmosphere; what is significant about his work is that it renders the sea a totally domesticated and tamed entity, which is entirely overtaken by terrestrial epistemology. The same can be said about Carl Ritter, or indeed Hegel, whose "empirical data" matter little but whose abstract, and theologically inspired, systems had an enormous impact.

With Maury, the sea enters the modern scientific world with its laws, regulations, topographies, and routes—with, in short, a physical and quasi-territorial *geo*graphy. The sea is not just shown to be a coherent analytical unit; that is taken for granted. The sea, as a unit, is here scientifically dominated from a desk in Washington, D.C., for the explicit betterment of the commercial and military interests of the land power. Maury's "special charts and forms for recording observations," for example, were "used first on vessels of the Navy and then on American merchant ships."[56]

This domesticated nature of the sea is perhaps most evident in Maury's promotion of the idea of a (potential) "American Mediterranean," roughly corresponding to Bory de Saint-Vincent's Colombian Mediterranean. Not only does the sea here become a space upon which power can (and ought) to be projected, but its very concept is one that can belong to a state, in contradiction to Bory, who associated his seas with distinctly nonstate epithets. In fact, Maury's parlance implies European ownership of the master copy, for an *American* Mediterranean can be meant only in symmetry with a *European* one. A "Pacific railroad" combined with a "thoroughfare across the Isthmus," and allied with the traditional policy of preventing any non-American interference in the Western Hemisphere, would create, he explained in a plea for the opening of the Panama Canal, a coherent and self-enclosed body of water connected to the major poles of world commerce and belonging to the United States.[57]

The sea is, then, completely terrestrialized by Maury and made into a distinct and self-evident object of scientific knowledge and of state power. It is only a step away from Alfred Thayer Mahan's formal introduction of thalassology into history with his illustrious *The Influence of Sea Power upon History, 1660–1783*.[58] And indeed the lexical and cognitive fields of Mahan's writing are quite indebted to Maury, as is evident from the beginning of the first chapter: "The first and most obvious light in which the sea presents itself from the political and social point of view is that of a great highway; or better, perhaps, of a wide common, over which men may pass in all directions, but on which some well-worn paths show that controlling reasons have led them to choose certain lines of travel rather than others. These lines of travel are called trade routes; and the reasons which have determined them are to be sought in the history of the world."[59]

For Mahan too, the sea is turned into a scientific object to be dominated like a territory. He too advocated the opening of the Panama Canal, along a familiar thalassological model. The Mediterranean Sea, he writes, has played "a greater part in the history of the world, both in a commercial and a military point of view, than any other sheet of water of the same size."[60] Therefore, studying the conditions and configurations of power on its waters and shores will be particularly rewarding, he explains, especially considering the potential opening of a canal in Central America. Mahan's historical exploration had direct geopolitical consequences: with the establishment of the right strategic naval bases coupled with the sustenance of constant military preparation, "the preponderance of the United States on this field follows, from her geographical position and her power, *with mathematical certainty*."[61]

As Christopher Connery has shown, "Mahan relentlessly underscores his conception of the ocean as definite space, and as space to be mastered."[62] It is the "strength of Mahan's terrestrial-oceanic hybrid vision," Connery continues, "his notion of an ocean crisscrossed by figurative highways and bridges, a great Common requiring the commanding presence of a dominant power, [that] has ensured his continued influence on U.S. Pacific strategy."[63] It has also secured the enduring legacy of Maury, the quite aptly named "Pathfinder of the Seas."

THE ANTHROPOMORPHIC SUBJECT OF HISTORY

Before Mahan, however, another historian, Jules Michelet, consolidated the thalassological imagination by articulating a vision of the sea that distilled the essence of the cognitive and conceptual moves evoked above. *La mer* was first published in 1861, and it, too, rapidly became a best-selling classic, going through many editions and translations.[64]

Space, for Michelet, as for Hegel and Ritter before him, was not simply a static setting; it partook of history and it had a history. "Without a geographical basis," he once wrote, "the people, the makers of history, seem to be walking on air."[65] In *La mer* this insight is taken to its logical conclusion. Appealing explicitly to both Bory de Saint-Vincent and Matthew Fontaine Maury, Michelet adopts as central actor of his historical narrative the sea. Long thought of as fixed, eternal, and dark, it is placed on the stage of science and history and found to be the origin (and future) of all life. The work begins with the evocation of the atavistic sense of the sea's sinister mystery, but that is only a formalistic ploy (and historical allegory) to heighten the increasing domestication of the sea as the text moves along, culminating in the plea for a "Renaissance by the Sea" that would lead to a thalassocentric "*Vita Nuova* of nations."[66]

From Bory, Michelet retrieves a vision of the globe that is organized according to bodies of water rather than terrestrial features, with each maritime unit forming a coherent and intelligible whole. "The principle of geographical unity, and the elements of classification," he predicts, "will be more and more sought in the *maritime basin,* where the waters, and those faithful messengers the winds, found the affinity and assimilation of opposite coasts."[67] In Maury, he finds inspiration for a vision of the sea as a harmonious organism that combines science, naturalism, and theology. What he cannot reveal by mechanical or physical causes, writes an admiring Michelet of the author of the *Physical Geography of the Sea,* he explains with "physiological laws," endowing "Ocean with pulse and arteries—ay, even with a heart" (52–53).

The "feeling of the personality of the Sea," Michelet explains in a most revealing terminology, is "the secret of his genius" and the reason for the power of Maury's treatise (52–53). Before it, "the Sea was a thing for the use of the sailors who ploughed its waters"; thanks to it, the sea is "an individual being" (*une personne*), within whom everyone senses there lies "an impetuous and formidable mistress whom they adore, and would fain to subdue" (*une violente et redoutable maîtresse qu'on adore, qu'on veut dompter*) (53).[68] Michelet's text is suffused with such taming of the sea, where even the most ferocious storms become part of an explicable, even predictable whole. It is also replete with organic metaphors: molecular attractions, mucus, aortas, and hearts pulsate in harmony through the descriptions and depictions of *La mer,* a sea that has espoused the form of a person, a mother figure in fact, the source of all life: "the great female [*femelle*] of the globe, whose indefatigable desire, permanent conception, and prolific birth never cease" (91).[69]

"Three forms of Nature expand and elevate our soul, lift it above itself, and carry it into the infinite," reads the final subsection of the book with distinct

Hegelian resonance (299). The ocean of the Air, the ocean of the Earth, and the ocean of the Waters, "these three forms compose the gamut, or musical scale, by whose means Infinity speaks to the soul" (299). The ocean of the waters is unique among the elements, however, for only it can reach the human sense of hearing and cognition, only it carries the human faculty of speech. The Air "shifts so constantly, that we can scarcely observe it," and "the Earth is dumb," but "the Ocean speaks" (299–300). "Ocean," Michelet continues,

> is a voice. It speaks to the distant stars, responds to their motions in its grave and solemn eloquence. It speaks to the earth and the shore with a pathetic accent, and holds a dialogue with their echoes; alternately plaintive and menacing, it roars or sighs. Before all, it addresses itself to Man. As it is the prolific crucible wherein creation began and wherein it is continued, in all its potency, it possesses a living language; it is life speaking to life. . . . What says it? It speaks of *life,* and the eternal metamorphosis. It speaks of the fluid existence. It puts to shame the petrified ambitions of terrestrial movement. (300–301)[70]

Michelet is concerned with a sea that is not just a character but a soul—the soul not only of an individual person but of whole nations and indeed humanity: it is the Self. The author had, after all, announced the colors from the very beginning: "Ocean breathes as we do—in harmony with our internal movement, with that from on high" (31).[71]

The sea here has become fully anthropomorphic, and it thereby naturally merits, and indeed begets, its own historians and its own histories. Thalassological epistemology is consolidated, and the stage is set for the proliferation of formulations of histories and politics of the sea in the twentieth century (and beyond): Mahan, Mackinder, Schmitt, Braudel, the protagonists of the "new thalassology," all of these authors depend on the thalassological pioneers discussed above as a condition of possibility for their arguments.

And *this* is the greatest lesson of the genealogical exploration of thalassological history. To become a legitimate subject of a historical inquiry, the sea had to be domesticated and turned into an anthropomorphic character, just as a novelist would present the story's main protagonist. Hence the importance of the state in post-Hegelian historiography, since only it had a *self*-conscious attitude to its past and present, very much as an individual might, and therefore produced a record of itself.

Braudel's work on the Mediterranean exemplifies this necessity for the subjectification of the object of the historian's gaze—the production of a *subject,* that is, intended here in the meaning ascribed to it usually in relation to the individual's relationship to the disciplinary regimes of power. Thus, despite the oft-repeated pretensions of the social scientific basis of *The Mediterranean and the Mediterranean World in the Age of Philip II* (brilliantly parodied, graphs, tables, maps, and all, by J.H. Hexter in his 1972 review "Fernand Braudel and the *Monde Braudellien*), Paul Ricoeur in particular has shown that Braudel's three-tiered text relies on a deeper structure in the form of an "overall plot" (if only a "virtual" or "quasi-" one) that is obviously related in nature to novelistic fiction.[72]

More so even than his maritime magnum opus, the short collection entitled *La Méditerranée: L'espace et l'histoire,* edited by Fernand Braudel and containing four chapters by himself (entitled "Mediterranée," "La terre," "L'aube," and "L'histoire") along with one by Filippo Coarelli on "Rome" and one by Maurice Aymard on "Espaces," is insightful in this regard.[73] Essentially, all of these chapters, and especially Braudel's, take part in formulating "the Mediterranean" as a historical actor, in domesticating the idea of "the Mediterranean" for it to become a subject of history. It is, one might say, a sort of "writer's guide" to Mediterranean history. Three themes that emerge from this study are particularly revealing. First, it is striking to notice that Braudel relies explicitly on *common sense* knowledge of the object "the Mediterranean" to build his argument. This is a regular feature of studies of Mediterranean history, however unacknowledged. Perhaps the greatest insight of Pedrag Matvejevic's work is that it gracefully bears the weight of rumor and common sense.[74]

In fact, Braudel opens the problematic of the entire book by wondering, "This evident unity, this profound being of the Mediterranean, how to explain it?"[75] And again, before addressing the earliest history of the region, he declares, "*Everybody says, everybody knows* that the 'first civilizations' were born in the eastern Mediterranean of the Near East."[76] The history of the Mediterranean is, he complains, "a mass of knowledge defying any reasonable synthesis."[77] Perhaps, but it is the very existence of this critical mass of knowledge, both lay and specialized, that produces the space as analytically meaningful and historically relevant, indeed, as commonsensical. Other places, such as the Great Rift Valley, the Sahara, or the Red Sea, are recognized geological and geographic entities but have no history of their own because they simply have not mobilized the critical mass of knowledge required.

Second, the specific temporality of the coherent Mediterranean is premodern, preindustrial time. It therefore relies on a particular understanding of modernity that follows a linear trajectory of the decreasing domination of nature over man, which produces a romanticized notion of the past. This is not spelled out in such terms, but it is unmistakable, especially in the use of ethnographic data, as in the following passage: "It is thus in the hills and the high country that one finds best preserved the images of the past, the tools, habits, dialects, costumes, superstitions of traditional life. All of them very old constructions, which perpetuated themselves in a space where the old agricultural methods could hardly yield to modern techniques. The mountain is *par excellence* the conservatory of the past."[78]

Finally, the last theme is the one of most direct concern to the question of the *subject* of historical writing. As "guide" for his synthetic vista on Mediterranean history, Braudel chooses the concept of civilization, "the only long-lasting destinies that may be followed without interruption through the meanderings and the accidents of Mediterranean history."[79] This allows him to slip effortlessly into anthropomorphic analogies, speaking of "three enormous and vivacious civilizations, three cardinal ways of thinking, believing, eating, drinking, living," and even more explicitly, "three monsters always ready to show their teeth, three characters with an interminable destiny."[80] The concept of civilizations fits well into the Braudellian universe, since, being "immobile, or quasi-immobile, in time and in space," they are particularly suited to the favored *longue durée,* indeed "they triumph over duration." Though they are "imperturbable" to the passage of time, "they remain mistresses of their space, because the territory they occupy may vary on its margins but in the heartland, in the central zone, their domain, their lodging remain the same."[81]

There is Christendom, that "Latin, then Catholic universe" centered in Rome, against which emerges Islam, and the anthropomorphic is here accentuated by the mobilization of a zoomorphic metaphor and the use of the active verb "to do," surely the most characteristic feature of the fully formed subject: "Islam facing the West is like the cat facing the dog. . . . But what enemies, what rivals! What one does, the other does."[82] Islam is Christendom in reverse (a "Counter-Occident," a "Counter-Mediterranean"), and it even has its own personal "cuisine," in which there is supposedly little room for products from the sea.[83]

In the case of the third and final civilization of the Mediterranean, the anthropomorphic is so salient that there may be room for something Oedipal in the analysis: "The third actor does not immediately unmask its face. It is the Greek universe, the Orthodox universe. But which center can one find for it? The Orthodox world today, is it a world without a father?"[84]

SCIENTIFIC THEOLOGY

With Hegel and Ritter already, the World Spirit espouses both Time and Space. It would, by the time of Maury, very comfortably inhabit the arts and sciences more generally and infiltrate further geographical, historical, and perforce political Reason. This is best exemplified by Élisée Reclus, one of the least religiously inclined of God's creatures, a late nineteenth-century libertarian anarchist. In his preface to the translation of a text by Ritter, which is generally seen as a decisive moment in the history of the French geographical tradition, Reclus explains Ritter's importance as he "who taught us as an immutable dogma the life of our globe."[85] It is precisely through his theographic insights that Ritter laid the foundational cornerstones of the modern science of geography, as Hegel did for history and Maury for oceanography.

This is a theme that underlies the questions visited throughout this chapter, relating to the thinking of historians and geographers down to the present time, even though it would come to be repressed. In other words, an important conclusion needs to be drawn from this on the place of the (broadly defined) theological in the modern disciplines. For all the authors addressed here, there is a large measure of intelligent design, of providential plan to the physical structure of the earth. The role of geography (or history, botany, philosophy, etc.) was essentially to reveal the Creator's design and the laws according to which it operated. Once explicitly divine in appeal and inspiration, this element gradually developed an exclusively geohistoricist indentation as God lost analytical traction. Hence the absolutism of the theo-scientific: there is a Plan, and it is knowable and provable in positivistic, empirical terms. Reality is split from its representation, and referents become fixed, absolute, and directly knowable, precisely because they are set apart.

A nonmodern appeal to the divine breeds a certain form of relativistic restraint, for knowledge can only be a human interpretation of an ultimately unknowable because totalizing God. The tenth-century scholar al-Masʿūdī, for example, asserts such a voluntary relativism: "Most people count four seas in the inhabited parts of the world, others count them as five, yet others make them six, and some see them as seven, each separate and disconnected."[86]

Al-Muqaddasī is equally unassuming as to the division of the world's water surfaces. As Bosworth relates, al-Muqaddasī showed doubt about a common interpretation of *sura* 31 of the Quran, which suggested that the seas were eight in total; "However, he says, if one has to find eight of them, they would comprise the seas around the Arabian peninsula, i.e., those of the Hijaz, Yemen, Oman, Makran, Kirman, Fars, and Hajar."[87] For scholars like these, knowledge remains always hermeneutically complex and rhetorically constituted, as opposed to the strict, straightforward representation of reality proposed by Ritter and Bory.

The analysis of various strands of the genealogy of the thalassological imagination has revealed geography's rise to a position of equality and sometimes preeminence in relation to history, a highly modern struggle between time and space. This development entailed the transformation of the earth in general, the sea in particular, into an actual actor, that is to say, its anthropomorphic evolution. The seas became persons; they continued to be mirrors of a divine order. This overt theological bent became anathema to thinkers in the late industrial age, who, while affirming the scientific qualities of the discipline (and the anthropomorphic nature of the oceans), repudiated the divine inspiration of what was to be seen as a positive social science. Other than that, the image of the seas and continents given by the previous generations of God seekers remained in place. This is shown in the case of the universally and rightly revered dean of thalassology, Fernand Braudel, for whom the historically established structures of the seas and oceans is a given. These had been completely naturalized, and Braudel in turn passed on the set of acquired truths to successive generations of thalassologists, all of whom have lost contact with the theo-scientific roots of the discipline. Take the text that accompanies Braudel's map of the Mediterranean in its regional context, seen with the south on top: "Nous avons choisi l'orientation inhabituelle qui, plaçant le Sahara au-dessus de la Méditerranée, souligne combien la mer est écrasée par l'immensité désertique. Celle-ci va de la mer Intérieure aux forêts tropicales d'Afrique. Le rôle de l'eau méditerranéenne est de border ces terres inhumaines, de les séparer de l'Europe méridionale (qui va, pour sa part, jusqu'aux forêts Nordiques) et, si l'on ajoute mer Rouge, océan Indien et golfe Persique, d'en briser la masse)."[88]

The Agent who has assigned this "role" to the Mediterranean may be unspoken, but He is patently immanent. The standard English translation does not convey the full range of meanings of Braudel's prose: "The unusual orientation has been chosen to illustrate how the great Sahara desert dominates the sea, stretching from the shores of the Mediterranean to the tropical forests of Africa. The Mediterranean both acts as a frontier between these deserted lands and southern Europe (which reaches to the forests of the North) and, along with the Red Sea and the Persian Gulf punctuates them."[89]

The English version leaves out the subject that caused the Mediterranean to act as a frontier, since someone had to give it its "role" in this regard. It retains the sense of the anthropomorphic (the Mediterranean "*acts*") but loses the obvious, if implicit, conviction that the action is preordained by an unmoved mover. In Braudel's case, one can say there is a very Christian trinity of time. The *longue durée* is divine in nature, since it is so long that it is nearly unchanging. It has the beard of God the Father. As for social time, it is the length of a generation, the life of God the Son (Jesus lived to his early thirties). The time of events, like the Holy Ghost, inhabits every individual's consciousness. All conjecture aside, one is dealing in modern thalassology with a clear case of scientific theology. This scientific theology is unabashedly Eurocentric: what defines the very essence of the European continent and its spirit, where progress, reason, and proper religion have their abode, is the maritime principle. A rewriting of the Gospel of John in light of the modern disciplines of geography and history would perhaps open like this: "In the beginning was the sea, and the sea was with Europe and the sea was Europe."

CONCLUSION

Rigging the Historian's Craft

FOR AN EPISTEMOLOGY OF COMPOSITION

rig·ging *noun* \ˈri-giŋ, -gən\
a : lines and chains used aboard a ship especially in working sail and supporting masts and spars
b: a similar network (as in theater scenery) used for support and manipulation

craft *noun* \ˈkraft\
1: skill in planning, making, or executing
2: an occupation or trade requiring manual dexterity or artistic skill
3: skill in deceiving to gain an end
4: the members of a trade or trade association
5: a boat especially of small size

AT THE HEART OF THIS book is a basic question that has heretofore largely eluded serious attention: How does history make its subject? Clearly, not all subjects are deemed historical at all times—that much has been clear from the beginnings of the discipline. What is required, then, for a particular object to become a proper subject of history? And what are the implications of such constraints for the history that is being written? In other words, what this book explores is the *rigging* involved in the safe sailing of the historian's *craft,* that is, as per the Merriam-Webster definitions quoted above, it interrogates the network of discursive lines and conceptual chains that both support and manipulate the writing of history, conceived as a skilled trade combining dexterity and deceit.

The point is not simply to denounce such history writing as ideological, in order then to move on to something free of constraints. The result is a rather more complicated one, seemingly paralyzing at first but ultimately invigorating: all history writing is rigged from the outset in multiple ways. Such rigging is indeed the condition of possibility of the craft's steady sailing/writing.

This does leave history all at sea, without a sovereign anchor outside ideology and an easy prey to the sharks of petty politics. But by the same token, it reconnects the discipline of history with other ones, such as geography, law, philosophy, anthropology, and literary criticism, as well as its longer-term past practice, when the historical arts belonged to the domain of rhetoric. It also injects an ethical dimension into the practice of history writing and reading. This need not necessarily mean falling back onto an abstract model of history as providing strict moral lessons from the past; rather, it can mean reimagining a world in which scholarship of all kinds is "a way of life."[1] What it certainly does imply is a move away from a naive reality effect, from history's pose as just mimicking a simple truth out there "as it really happened," and closer to a practice of historical interpretation that seeks to create, in Hayden White's beautiful formulation, "perplexity in the face of the real."[2] And thus can, nay must, history be reborn in an age after deconstruction.

• • •

> Where are your monuments, your battles, martyrs?
> Where is your tribal memory? Sirs,
> In that grey vault. The sea. The sea
> Has locked them up. The sea is History.
>
> DEREK WALCOTT

This opening fragment from Walcott's poem lends eloquent expression to the vagaries of the relationship between the discipline of history and the concept of the sea. Indeed, this poem, and especially its title, "The Sea Is History," have often been invoked in strategic justification of scholarly projects that aim to centralize maritime history and focus on the history of the sea.[3]

Certainly, Walcott makes a strong case for looking to the sea as an alternative setting for the writing of history, especially the history of those deemed without history, the subalterns par excellence: slaves forcibly taken across the Atlantic in a voyage of historical defilement, during which the very basic elements of collective existence and therefore of history (the monuments, the battles, the martyrs, the tribal memories), and even, when it was more profitable, the human commodity itself, were thrown overboard along the way. The sea is History, says Walcott, in which case a focus by historians on the sea would, indeed should, reveal such histories and allow them to be retrieved from oblivion and written. But it is never so simple, and Walcott himself senses the ambivalent implications of his pronouncement, for the sea, in his poem, is not a repository of sources at the disposal of historians for the production of historical narratives. On the contrary, the sea has *locked up* the memorial indices of past times, which serve as the standard symbol-bearers of accounts of history. The claim that "the sea is History" is thus something of a conscious paradox. It contains all the founding elements that make up traditional History, but it is a history that cannot be written, at least not in the traditional mode. And this, in turn, makes it no longer really History, for history-as-past and history-as-writing are indissoluble. Introducing the poem many years later, Walcott explained that the question in the poem was the word *history* itself:

> I'm talking neither about the idea of revisionist history, from the reverse view of the victim now becoming articulate, nor about the idea of history from the view of the ex or current master, or ex or current slave. I'm talking about the idea of history becoming a deity. History obviously has to do with the idea of time, and the idea of time varies. People who have confidence to dominate the idea of time, or nations who have ideas of dominating the future, or of hallowing the past, do it under the name of this alleged force called history.[4]

So Walcott's poem does indeed hit home, reaching the heart of the thorny nexus where history and the sea meet. The sea is an awkward setting for historians: it is, certainly, a space upon which the presence of History cannot but be felt and thought out. Indeed, the very essence of History seems to follow the waves of the oceans and seas, since ultimately History is about communication and exchange, and the sea is the dominant platform of travel and commerce. But it is a space that has enormous difficulty taking the form appropriate for an historical account. Most notably, it simply does not contain, let alone produce, an archive of its own.

Furthermore, the sea will never be able to *make* history. It will never be a true subject of history in the full Hegelian sense, despite all the valiant efforts of thalassologists old and new. History may be made upon it, within it, through it, by means of it, but it will never make History. The sea just cannot, or can no longer, in the absence of Poseidon, assume anthropomorphic features in the long term, something the research for this project has revealed to be essential to the production of subjects of history. The sea, that is, can be subjected to History but cannot be subjectified into history. Hegel, in this sense, was ultimately right: only the state can assume the burden of producing history—if by *state* is meant an entity, an apparatus that is able to coagulate and consolidate in such a way as to produce the effect of its own memory. The sea, by contrast, dislocates, disperses, dissolves—all that remains, all that washes up to the shore, are fragments.

Braudel attempted, with great effort, to transform the Mediterranean into an anthropomorphic subject that had a body, a heart, and a head and that sustained a memory of some sort, and his endeavor, it must be admitted, achieved a certain success. But it was a success strictly delimited in time, in a time long past, which could not be maintained into the present. His Mediterranean is a human personage, there is no doubt, but it is a long dead one. Its development was arrested in the sixteenth century. After that, the Mediterranean is no longer unitary, no longer coherent, no longer intelligible as such—in short, it is no longer sovereign. How that may accord with the geological time of the *longue durée* is unclear. Rather than *anthropo*morphic, his Mediterranean is *necro*morphic. Hence his use of ethnographic data and his attachment to those rural mountainous communities around the sea in which can supposedly be seen remnants of that long lost primeval identity. The contrast could not be more evident than with Braudel's last (unfinished) major scholarly project, eminently terrestrial, indeed territorial, *Identity of France,* in which the subject of the narrative is properly eternal, with neither an identifiable date of birth nor, for sure, of death. Indeed, it runs up to the present day, catapulting the subject into the future.[5]

This is confirmed by Peregrine Horden and Nicholas Purcell's differentiation between a "history in" the region and a "history of" it, not only synchronically, but also diachronically. At the very outset of their work, *The Corrupting Sea: A Study of Mediterranean History,* a standard-bearer of sea-centered histories, they separate a "history *in* the region, contingently Mediterranean," from a "history *of* it—history either of the whole Mediterranean or of an aspect of it to which the whole is an indispensable framework."[6] But the authors explain that a "history of" the Mediterranean is no longer thinkable when the threshold of modernity is reached. The Mediterranean is no longer a unitary whole, no longer a coherent subject of history after a certain point in time. "It was tempting, therefore," they admit, "to indicate our revised chronological scope by somehow including 'traditional' (or 'pre-modern') in the subtitle of this book as a substitute for 'Antiquity and the Middle Ages.'"[7] And they too move freely "between prehistory, history, and ethnography."[8]

This contradiction between the claims of a geographical basis of history brought forth by the very appeal to the idea of Mediterranean history, and its dissolution with the onset of modernity, is also echoed in Faruk Tabak's critique of the historiography of the Mediterranean for ceasing to pursue seawide, holistic accounts following the sixteenth century.[9] Instead, he argues *contra* Braudel that the Mediterranean died, not with Philip II (it might have waned), but much later, around the middle of the nineteenth century. Tabak's problem with the existing scholarship on the question, then, is essentially one of chronology. Proposing, instead of the usually posited end to Mediterranean unity in the late sixteenth century, to pursue it further in time, he proceeds to present an impressive portrait of the Inner Sea in the early modern age. Hence his grievance against the "perverse fashion" through which "the very paucity of holistic accounts of the basin has eventually turned into one of the distinguishing features of its age of twilight."[10] In other words, the historiography has determined the actual dynamics and forms of the history in question. But there is in fact nothing perverse about this process at all. History is by definition a *mise en scène,* a theatrical representation—that is precisely what differentiates it from the documentary or the chronicle. All that Tabak seeks to achieve—and it is a formidable achievement indeed—is to extend the length of the act.

. . .

The act of representation is by definition invested in its own staging as distinct from reality. This is truly the conundrum of modernity: however mimetic it seeks to be (in its science or politics or literature), it must simultaneously avow itself as not quite integral. The *Sailing Directions* definitely claimed to be a scientific breakthrough (and therefore universal, textual, and rational), but it also had to recognize the contribution of local, non-European, oral, and experiential modes of knowledge in its very constitution. Triangulation promised, as Edney emphasized, that it could produce a map perfectly mimetic of reality. But the claim was not, as he inferred, that "the map *is* the world."[11] It means exactly the reverse: the map *is not* the world, it is only its representation. However positivist, objectivist, naturalizing, or otherwise reductive, that is modern science's maximum claim. Indeed, this is the reason for the constant anxiety of realism of whatever nature: once rhetoric has been banished from the realm of science and the real, so that as a result reality = verisimilitude, then reality must be split from representation, and, as a result of that split, representation cannot be directly realistic. This is why triangulation in no way promised a 1:1 map—it claimed that it could *represent* it, that is all. A long time ago already, the inimitable Borges brilliantly satirized the conundrum of the realist's desire. In one of his shortest stories, a report by Suárez Miranda from the mid-seventeenth century is quoted, describing an empire where "the Art of Cartography attained such Perfection that the map of a single Province occupied the entirety of a City, and the map of the Empire, the entirety of the Province."[12] Eventually, even these "Unconscionable Maps" were not sufficient to quench the thirst for precision, so "the Cartographers Guilds struck a Map of the Empire whose size was that of the Empire, and which coincided point for point with it." But the succeeding generations lost interest in the science, and the map was left to decay. "In the Deserts of the West, still today," ends the piece, "there are Tattered Ruins of that Map, inhabited by Animals and Beggars; in all the Land there is no other Relic of the Disciplines of Geography." The reason Borges's satire is so powerful is that it disrupts the reality effect that is at the very heart of the modern disciplines of geography and history. This was recognized by Umberto Eco in "On the Impossibility of Drawing a Map of the Empire on a Scale of 1 to 1." Here, the Italian semiotician heightens the Borgesian disturbance of normality by detailing, soberly and with utmost seriousness, the difficulties that would arise in the making of such an imperial map. In a series of deductive maneuvers, he touches upon the map's impossibility, not really at the practical level (though he suggests numerous obstacles there too), but on a theoretical plane: "The map's transparency would eliminate its semiotic function, since it would be functional as sign only in the presence of its own referent."[13]

The problem of the 1:1 map is precisely the one Roland Barthes identified in his critique of narrative realism, of which modern historical discourse was the model. The crucial maneuver of the reality effect, he explained on the basis of an analysis of the "useless details" found in realist texts, is to expel the signifier from the sign and to collapse the space between signifier, signified, and referent.[14] Thus can the referent (reality) be advanced as speaking for itself, and a 1:1 map fantasized. Barthes, like Eco, demonstrated that the maneuver is ultimately impossible and that the most realist narrative could still be subjected to semiotic analysis—precisely because it must, by its very own operations, remain only a narrative, a map, a representation, and *not* reality. In other words, form matters, as Hayden White has tirelessly argued.

• • •

> The classical author who composes his tragedy by observing a certain number of rules he knows is freer than the poet who writes whatever goes through his head, and who is a slave to other rules of which he is unaware.
>
> RAYMOND QUENEAU

All attempts to transcend the contradictions that are placed upon the discipline of history have been vain. Here is a discipline mired between the dictates of the present and the quest for an authentic past, between scientific objectivity and artistic inspiration. Instead, historians should take on these contradictions unabashedly; indeed, perhaps think of them as creative—and this may be done by giving epistemological primacy to the practice of *writing* history itself. Constraints in writing are thus neither bad nor good, neither positive nor negative, they *are,* period. Texts can simply not escape structure, and neither can their creation.

Thalassology is a good place to think about discipline and constraints precisely because it is so often touted as lacking the constraints of tradition, be it historical, political, ideological, or disciplinary. Indeed, the sea, as we have seen, produces no archive of its own, and for this very reason it easily appears to be free from the biases of traditional history, which is associated so intimately with that archive-producing apparatus par excellence, the state. Quite logically, then, the sea is less obviously the elected domain of politics, and the political, in these post-Braudellian times, seems inimical to the properly historical. But such claims, as this book has shown at length, are overstated: they dismiss too swiftly the problem of the archive and its crucial position in the epistemology of history, and they limit too narrowly the extent and depth of the idea of the political. In the end, thalassological history is just as political, just as traditional, and just as problematic as any old other type of history. The reason for this is that the politicalness of history writing derives not only from its content (explicitly reflecting the political) but also from its form. The analytical perspective must therefore shift from posing a problem of pure metaphysics, of simple epistemology, being and thought, to discovering that it is always already a question of grammatology, always already turning into a reflection primarily about genealogy, practice, and writing. This denotes a reorientation of analytical perspective away from authorial intention toward an emphasis on textual intention and the conditions of possibility and discursive implications of writing. The critical stance is fundamental, as it "relocates meaning (for the reader) from the mind of the author to the expressive properties of the text and acknowledges that the historian's language of communication is not inert and plastic, but always already filled with its own messages."[15]

. . .

> I have loved the Mediterranean with passion, no doubt because I am a northerner like so many others in whose footsteps I have followed. I have joyfully dedicated long years of study to it—much more than all my youth. In return, I hope that a little of this joy and a great deal of Mediterranean sunlight will shine from the pages of this book. Ideally perhaps one should, like the novelist, have one's subject under control, never losing it from sight and constantly aware of its overpowering presence. Fortunately or unfortunately, the historian has not the novelist's freedom. The reader who approaches this book in the spirit I would wish will do well to bring with him his own memories, his own vision of the Mediterranean to add colour to the text and to help me conjure up this vast presence, as I have done my best to do. My feeling is that the sea itself, the one we see and love, is the greatest document of its past existence. If I have retained nothing else from the geographers who taught me at the Sorbonne, I have retained this lesson with an unwavering conviction that has guided me throughout my project.
>
> FERNAND BRAUDEL

With this remarkable declaration of love, Fernand Braudel famously opened his preface to the first edition of his first, and arguably still most influential, book. An inciting statement of passion, it is also an interesting methodological position and even a profession of faith of sorts. As in other parts of the book, Braudel infuses his compelling prose with seemingly contradictory postures. He advocates both affective reading as a compositional act and the grounding of historical narratives in social scientific, quantitative data that ought to defy emotive responses. He appeals simultaneously to love, passion, joy, sunlight, feeling, vision, color, and the unmediated, raw power of the sea itself, as a natural, organic geographical space that is both sign and referent folded into one, which needs no external consecration, and to which one can only vow unwavering conviction. In other words, reality and its representation are set apart, one made of solid stone, the other of affective streams. Yet even that presumably fundamental distinction dissipates as the reality in question endlessly expands and contracts throughout the text and indeed is contingent on the participation of the reader, who must be swayed into adding more color and substance.

It has been two-thirds of a century now since Fernand Braudel finally published his revised dissertation as *La Méditerranée et le monde méditerranéen à l'époque de Philippe II* in 1949. It instantly became a classic (a second, wholly reworked and updated edition appeared in 1966) and remains to this day one of the most influential contributions to the discipline of history, the primary reference point of any interrogation on the history of the sea.[16] Indeed, *all* of the interventions without exception of the *AHR* forum "Oceans in History" invoke the French master, with Horden and Purcell calling his book "the prototype sea history" and the other two feature articles actually opening with him.[17] Incidentally, Braudel himself, in the preface to the first edition of his *Mediterranean,* asserted the novelty of the approach in terms similar to those of his latest avatars, as he decried the absence of existing works that could help guide his quest: "A historical study centred on a stretch of water has all the charms but undoubtedly all the dangers of a new departure."[18] Yet in the fantastic annotated bibliography appended to the second edition Braudel tells his readers that he "cannot pretend to draw up an exhaustive catalogue of the literature devoted to the Mediterranean: it would fill volumes and the list would still not be complete."[19] Notable in particular is the sixth subsection, containing references on "The General History of the Mediterranean," such as Carl Rathlef's *Die welthistorische Bedeutung der Meere, insbesondere des Mittelmeers,* dating back to the mid-nineteenth century, or the more contemporary book by the historical biographer Emil Ludwig simply entitled, in French, *La Méditerranée.* In the general bibliography, an even more startling figure makes an appearance: Leopold von Ranke. Indeed, as mentioned in the introduction, Ranke too was taken by the allure of the Mediterranean and formulated a volume centered around the Inner Sea. Thus even the supposed originator of the much-reviled event-based, political, narrative history against which the *Annales* as a whole took form is in a sense a precursor of Braudel in his Mediterraneanism.

Clearly, then, Braudel did not invent the idea of the historical becoming of seas, or even the idea of the Mediterranean as a coherent space, the subject of a world-historical drama. Still, looking back on the enduring legacy of his analysis, Braudel mentioned precisely "two major truths [that] ha[d] remained unchallenged": the first was "the unity and coherence of the Mediterranean region," and the second, its "greatness."[20] In this, most of his successors, whether disciples or critics, were in full agreement.

Indeed, *The Mediterranean* has long been the ultimate reference and model for historians seeking to produce innovative accounts of various regions of the world, whereby the focus on the sea, the *longue durée*, and the *annaliste* methodology allow one to transcend artificial political boundaries and superficial event-based narratives. This, however, means letting oneself be taken by Braudel's self-portrayal as the initiator of Mediterranean unity and thalassology. And it would be to misunderstand the peculiar nature of the innovativeness of Braudel's project, which, *contra* common knowledge, does not lie in the assumption of Mediterranean unity or the invention of the idea of the Mediterranean as a coherent space. Rather, as Hans Kellner has shown in his brilliant exegesis, the originality of *The Mediterranean,* and its enduring appeal, are related to the formal genre to which the text belongs, namely that of the anatomy (or Menippean satire), making Braudel a sort of historian's Rabelais.[21]

As noted above, there had been in fact much laborious intellectual foraging and scholarly taming of the Mediterranean that preceded Braudel by over a century. Indeed, from a visual and cartographic perspective at least, the idea of a unitary Mediterranean was produced and reproduced over centuries, in the form of highly stylized representations of the basin.

A realization of the extent of preparatory work involved in the production of the Braudellian idea of the Mediterranean leads one to understand the largely unexplored fact, basic enough though it should be, that geography too is discursively constituted. It was not until the early nineteenth century, and only by a conceptual sleight of hand, following extensive analytical labors, that geographical regions were produced and turned into naturalized, objective categories. Braudel's thesis thus represents the culmination of a long tradition, scientific and artistic, that had transformed the idea of the Mediterranean into both a scientific object and a notion of common sense.

What is more, this tradition of viewing seas in general and the Mediterranean in particular as coherent entities with distinct destinies (what has here been called the "sovereign sea") occurred under specific historical conditions: the expansion of European colonial power. A main argument here is that the making of the sovereign sea is articulated at the deep level of the larger epistemic formation, along lines roughly similar to Foucault's dissection of modern thought in *The Order of Things,* though it is crucial to keep in mind the political contexts within which these developments occur, as Edward Said always urged. The challenge is thus to account for both the deep discursive structures that cross over disciplines and borders *and* the immediate political factors. Together, they form the conditions of possibility of the emergence of the idea of the sovereign sea. In other words, if it is certainly not a coincidence that the idea of a coherent Mediterranean region emerges simultaneously in the works of English, French, and German philosophers, botanists, historians, and so on, but rather a feature of the nascent epistemic formation that produced the human sciences more largely, neither is it a coincidence that these developments occur alongside a new sort of colonial order of things. This is perhaps most evident in the case of the French adventures in the Mediterranean, which accompanied the constitution of a solid notion of a Mediterranean region, but it also applies to the British in the Red Sea.

This conjugation of the birth of the human sciences with the launching of the new imperialism is critical because it demonstrates the labor that went into the sudden production of the Mediterranean as a coherent object, while showing that the colonial encounter was central to that intellectual effort. The objective is not to decry the colonial roots of the particular idea but to reflect upon the colonial dimension of the modern episteme as a whole. The colonial was not incidental to modern knowledge but constitutive of it. In other words, there is more than simple happenstance to the fact that the appearance of the sea as a coherent unit coincides with the institution of the disciplines of history, geography, and Orientalism, along with a new colonial encounter. The organizing categories of these new disciplines are thus not neutral or innocent; rather, they carve out particular horizons of possibilities for the various actors that find themselves interpellated (or not) by them. This is as true of the ubiquitous Mediterranean as of the spectral Red Sea.

• • •

The disciplines of history and geography and cartography do not only describe reality. Nor do they simply interpret it. In part, they also make it.

NOTES

The following are abbreviations used in the Notes:

BL	British Library, London
BOA	Başbakanlık Osmanlı Arşivi, Istanbul
EI2	*Encyclopedia of Islam*, 2nd ed., edited by P.J. Bearman, Th. Bianquis, C.E. Bosworth, E. Van Donzel, and W.P. Heinrichs (Leiden: Brill, 1960–2005)
IOF	India Office Records, BL
LPH	*Lectures on the Philosophy of History*, by G.W.F. Hegel, translated by John Sibree (London: Henry Bone, 1857)
LPWH	*Lectures on the Philosophy of World History—Introduction: Reason in History*, by G.W.F. Hegel, translated by H.B. Nisbet (London: Cambridge University Press, 1975)
MMD	Mühimme-i Mısır Defterleri, BOA
NA	National Archives, Kew Gardens

INTRODUCTION

1. Denis Diderot and Jean d'Alembert, *Encyclopédie, ou Dictionnaire raisonné des sciences, des arts et des métiers* (Lausanne: Société Typographique, 1782), vol. 11, http://encyclopedie.uchicago.edu (accessed December 13, 2012).

2. Kātib Çelebī, *Tuḥfat al-kibār ʿan duwal al-biḥār* (Istanbul: Dār al-tibāʿa al-maʿmūra, 1729), 72, and *The Gift of the Great Ones on Naval Campaigns*, ed. Idris Bostan (Ankara: Prime Ministry Undersecretariat for Maritime Affairs, 2008), 210. The former is the famous published copy printed by Ibrāhīm Mūteferriḳa; the latter

is a facsimile reproduction of a beautiful manuscript version of the text, preceded by an introduction and translation in English, which, however, sacrifices too much of the original wording for the sake of simplicity. An amended version of this passage is cited in Ismāʿīl Sarhank's late nineteenth-century chronicle *Ḥaqāʾiq al-akhbār ʿan duwal al-biḥār*, vol. 1 (Cairo: Bulāq, 1894), 664.

3. See notably Palmira Brummett, "The Ottomans as a World Power: What We Don't Know about Ottoman Sea-Power," *Oriente Moderno* 20, no. 1 (2001): 1–21.

4. Johannes Fabian, *Time and the Other: How Anthropology Makes Its Object* (New York: Columbia University Press, 1983).

5. Quoted in Edward Casey, *The Fate of Place: A Philosophical History* (Berkeley: University of California Press, 1997), 296.

6. Michel Foucault, *Discipline and Punish: The Birth of the Prison* (1977; repr., New York: Vintage Books, 1995). See further Timothy Mitchell, *Colonising Egypt* (1988; repr., Berkeley: University of California Press, 1991).

7. Edward Said, *Orientalism* (New York: Vintage, 1979), 55.

8. Bernard Bailyn, *The Idea of Atlantic History* (Cambridge, MA: Harvard University Press, 2005); Alison Games, "Atlantic History: Definitions, Challenges, and Opportunities," *American Historical Review,* 111, no. 3 (June 2006): 741–57.

9. K.N. Chaudhuri, *Trade and Civilization in the Indian Ocean: An Economic History from the Rise of Islam to 1750* (Cambridge: Cambridge University Press, 1985), and *Asia before Europe: Economy and Civilisation of the Indian Ocean from the Rise of Islam to 1750* (Cambridge: Cambridge University Press, 1990).

10. Matt Matsuda, *Pacific Worlds: A History of Seas, Peoples, and Cultures* (Cambridge: Cambridge University Press, 2012); Donald Freeman, *The Pacific* (New York: Routledge, 2009); Merja-Liisa Hinkkanen and David Kirby, *The Baltic and the North Seas* (New York: Routledge, 2000); Alan Palmer, *The Baltic: A History of the Region and Its People* (Woodstock, NY: Overlook Press, 2006); Charles King, *The Black Sea: A History* (New York: Oxford University Press, 2005).

11. Roger Joint Daguenet has authored an *Histoire de la mer Rouge* (published in two volumes by Perrin in Paris in 1995), but it is not a scholarly work.

12. The Mediterranean is called the White Sea in Turkish (*Akdeniz*) and Arabic (*al-Baḥr al-Abyaḍ*).

13. As termed in the conference held at the University of California Riverside, "The Oceanic Turn in the Long 18th Century: Beyond Disciplinary Territories," November 20, 2009, sponsored by the University of California's Humanities Research Institute.

14. For an insightful elaboration of nonsynchronous time and fractal space, see Paul Gilroy, *The Black Atlantic: Modernity and Double Consciousness* (Cambridge, MA: Harvard University Press, 1993).

15. For more on this subject, see my "Narcissus: Woman, Water and the West," *Feminist Review* 103 (2013): 42–57.

16. Edward Peters, "*Quid nobis cum pelago?* The New Thalassology and the Economic History of Europe," *Journal of Interdisciplinary History* 34, no. 1 (2003): 61.

17. Claudio Magris, foreword to *Mediterranean: A Cultural Landscape*, by Pedrag Matvejevic (Berkeley: University of California Press, 1999), 1–6.

18. See Ludovico Marini, "On the Method of Studying Thalassology," *Geographical Journal* 25, no. 2 (1905): 191–97.

19. Peters, "*Quid nobis cum pelago?*" 56.

20. Ibid., 49.

21. Markus Vink, "Indian Ocean Studies and the 'New Thalassology,'" *Journal of Global History* 2 (2007): 41–62. Horden and Purcell themselves are keen to have the term adopted, as indicated by their use of it in the title of their survey of the field as it relates to the Mediterranean ("The Mediterranean and 'the New Thalassology'") in the forum "Oceans of History" in *American Historical Review* 111, no. 3 (June 2006).

22. Kären Wigen, "Oceans of History: Introduction," AHR Forum, *American Historical Review,* 111, no. 3 (June 2006): 717.

23. Horden and Purcell, "Mediterranean," 722.

24. Ibid., 723.

25. Ibid.

26. Hayden White, *The Content of the Form: Narrative Discourse and Historical Representation* (Baltimore: Johns Hopkins University Press, 1987), 62.

27. Martin Heidegger, "The Age of the World Picture," in *The Question Concerning Technology and Other Essays,* ed. William Lovitt (New York: Harper, 1977), 115–54.

28. The anthropomorphism of historical subjects was once fully assumed, as in the words of Hegel: "In world history, however, the individuals we are concerned with are nations, totalities, states" (*LPWH,* 36).

29. See especially the essays collected in White, *Content of the Form.*

30. On seminars and archives as constitutive of modern historical practice, see Bonnie Smith, *The Gender of History: Men, Women, and Historical Practice* (Cambridge, MA: Harvard University Press, 1998), chap. 4, "The Practices of Scientific History."

31. *LPWH,* 19.

32. Leopold von Ranke, *The Theory and Practice of History,* ed. Georg G. Iggers and Konrad von Moltke (Indianapolis, IN: Bobbs-Merrill, 1973), 33–46.

33. Ibid., 38. In this lecture, Ranke mentions Fichte's approach as the example of philosophical history. Elsewhere, he also names Hegel as the continuator, "with greater vigor," of Fichte's type of philosophical history (49).

34. Ibid., 38.

35. On which see the still unsurpassed George Nadel, "Philosophy of History before Historicism," *History and Theory* 3, no. 3 (1964): 291–315. Ranke's disapproval of exemplar history is well known, enshrined in the preface to his first book, "Preface: Histories of Romance and Germanic Peoples" (reprinted in *The Varieties of History: From Voltaire to the Present,* ed. Fritz Stern [New York: Vintage Books, 1973]). Hegel was no less dismissive: "There is nothing so insipid as the constant appeals to Greek and Roman precedents we hear so often" (*LPWH,* 21). This stands in striking contrast to Adam Smith just a few decades before, who, however much he most certainly influenced all of these later authors (especially Hegel), maintained

an understanding of history as being exemplary in function. See J. G. A. Pocock, "Adam Smith and History," in *The Cambridge Companion to Adam Smith,* ed. Knud Haakonssen (Cambridge: Cambridge University Press, 2006), 270–87.

36. This was expertly theorized by Hegel, who set the tone for much subsequent geohistorical discourse: "The universal premise of this investigation is that world history represents the Idea of the spirit as it displays itself in reality as a series of external forms. . . . Every people which represents a particular stage in the development of the spirit constitutes a *nation*; its natural characteristics correspond to the nature of the spiritual principle within the series of spiritual forms" (*LPWH*, 153).

37. For Ranke's Eurocentrism, see, for example, the preface to his massive *Universal History,* unfinished at his death (*Universal History: The Oldest Group of Nations and the Greeks,* ed. G. W. Prothero, trans. D. C. Tovey [New York: Charles Scribner's Sons, 1884]), as well as the piece from the early 1830s, in which the "scope of world history" is limited to Europe (*Theory and Practice*, 46).

38. Leopold von Ranke, *The Ottoman and the Spanish Empires, in the Sixteenth and Seventeenth Centuries* (Philadelphia: Lea and Blanchard, 1845), 1.

39. Ibid.

40. Ibid., 4.

41. *LPH*, 91.

42. Ibid., 94.

43. Ibid., 94–95.

44. Ibid., 94. Emphasis in original.

45. Wigen, "Oceans of History," 718; Horden and Purcell, "Mediterranean," 724.

46. Fernand Braudel, "Toward a Serial History: Seville and the Atlantic, 1504–1650," in *On History* (Chicago: University of Chicago Press, 1980), 93. This piece was first published in *Annales: Économies, Sociétés, Civilisations* 18, no. 3 (1963): 541–53.

47. Louis Althusser, "The Object of *Capital*," in *Reading "Capital,"* by Louis Althusser and Etienne Balibar (London: NLB, 1970), 101. Emphasis in the original.

48. Epeli Hau'ofa, "Our Sea of Islands," in *We Are the Ocean: Selected Works* (Honolulu: University of Hawai'i Press, 2008), 30.

49. Ibid., 31.

50. Ibid.

51. Following "Our Sea of Islands," Hau'ofa went on to publish many other important contributions along similar lines, subsequently collected in *We Are the Ocean.* On Epeli Hau'ofa's intellectual project and its impact, see the essays in his honor in Vicente M. Diaz and J. Kehaulani Kauanui, eds., "Native Pacific Cultural Studies on the Edge," special issue, *Contemporary Pacific* 22, no. 1 (Spring 2010). For further elaborations on the lands and seas of Oceania in historical perspective, see Margaret Jolly, "Imagining Oceania: Indigenous and Foreign Representations of a Sea of Islands," *Contemporary Pacific* 19, no. 2 (2007): 508–45; Paul D'Arcy, *The People of the Sea: Environment, Identity, and History in Oceania* (Honolulu:

University of Hawai'i Press, 2006); Patrick Kirch, *On the Road of the Winds: An Archaeological History of the Pacific Islands before European Contact* (Berkeley: University of California Press, 2002); Patrick Nunn, *Vanished Islands and Hidden Continents of the Pacific* (Honolulu: University of Hawai'i Press, 2008).

52. Many of the most relevant recent titles in this regard are mentioned in Virginia Aksan's review article "Theoretical Ottomans," *History and Theory* 47 (February 2008): 109–22.

53. For an exemplary study that evokes oceanic space without fetishizing modern categories by focusing on the Hadhrami "local cosmopolitans" distributed over much of the Indian Ocean, see Engseng Ho, *The Graves of Tarim: Genealogy and Mobility across the Indian Ocean* (Berkeley: University of California Press, 2006).

1. THE PLACE IN THE MIDDLE

1. See in particular the sections "Place-Names: The Name" and "Place-Names: The Place," respectively in the volumes *Swann's Way* (1913) and *Within a Budding Grove* (1919) of his *In Search of Lost Time*. The general topic of the place-name nexus has produced an ever-increasing literature. Most stimulating remains the classic by Gaston Bachelard, *The Poetics of Space,* trans. Maria Jolas (Boston: Beacon Press, 1994), who credits Proust as an inspiration.

2. As per Matvejević's suggestions, for example: "Scholars familiar with dead languages have pointed out that civilizations using colors to indicate the cardinal points tend to call our sea green or white. The Arabs have preserved the name White Sea (*al-bahr-al-abyad*), white being used for designating its western part. The Turks and Bulgarians use White Sea as well. The early songs of the South Slavs refer to the sea as white in addition to blue—and not only when the waves are up. Nor is the reference completely alien to modern Greek, despite its strong ancient tradition. The Red Sea (Erythros Pontos) once referred to the Indian Ocean, red being used to designate the East." Pedrag Matvejević, *Mediterranean: A Cultural Landscape,* trans. Michael Henry Heim (Berkeley: University of California Press, 1999), 146. Léopold de Saussure was one of the first to formulate this theory, though in his account red indicated south; see "L'origine des noms de mer Rouge, mer Blanche et mer Noire," *Le Globe* 63 (1924): 23–36.

3. On Ptolemy and his Green Sea, see, for example, Jean Baptiste Bourguignon d'Anville, *Compendium of Ancient Geography,* 3 vols. (New York: R. M'Dermut and D.D. Arden, 1814), 2:182. Ibn Khaldūn discusses *al-khalīj al-akhḍar,* which he describes as one of two branches of the Abyssinian Sea (the other being the Red Sea, which he names only as it reaches its northern parts as the Sea of Qulzum and the Sea of Suez), in *Muqaddimat Ibn Khaldūn,* ed. Khalīl Sheḥāda (Beirut: Dār al-fikr, 2001), 60. Ibn Khaldūn also describes (part of) the Atlantic as a Green Sea.

4. Lionel Casson, ed., *The Periplus Maris Erythraei: Text with Introduction, Translation, and Commentary* (Princeton, NJ: Princeton University Press, 1989), 94.

5. G. W. B. Huntingford, ed., *The Periplus of the Erythraean Sea, by an Unknown Author, with Some Extracts from Agatharkhides "On the Erythraean Sea"* (Farnham: Ashgate, 2010), 1.

6. The remaining fragments of this work were translated by Stanley Burnstein in his edition of Agatharchides of Cnidus, *On the Erythraean Sea* (London: Haklyut Society, 1989). No actual manuscript is extant; the text is derived from a number of sources that quote Agatharchides at length. On these sources, see Burnstein's introduction to the translation.

7. Huntingford, *Periplus*, 178.

8. Ibid., 179.

9. Strabo, *The Geography of Strabo,* vol. 7 (16.4.20), trans. H. L. Jones (London: William Heinemann, 1930), 351. Pliny the Elder recounts some of these data in abridged form in his *Natural History* 6.28, to take another example.

10. Carsten Niebuhr, *Beschreibung von Arabien aus eigenen Beobachtungen und im Lande selbst gesammleten Nachrichten* (Copenhagen: Möller, 1772), 417–18.

11. John Towers, "The Red Sea," *Journal of Near Eastern Studies* 18, no. 2 (1959): 150–53.

12. Maurice Copisarow, "Ancient Egyptian, Greek and Hebrew Concept of the Red Sea," *Vetus Testamentum* 12, no. 1 (1962): 5.

13. William Facey, "The Red Sea: The Wind Regime and Location of Ports," in *Trade and Travel in the Red Sea Region,* ed. Paul Lunde and Alexandra Porter (Oxford: Archaeopress, 2004), 7.

14. The preceding three sentences are loosely translated and fitted from a paragraph by Fernand Braudel in *La Méditerranée: L'espace et l'histoire* (1977; repr., Paris: Flammarion, 1985), 48.

15. For a holistic introduction to the Red Sea as an analytical space, see Stephen Head's introduction to *Red Sea*, ed. Alasdair Edwards and Stephen Head (Oxford: Pergamon Press, 1987), 1–21. For the foundational treatment of the oceanography of the Red Sea, see S. A. Morcos, "Physical and Chemical Oceanography of the Red Sea," *Oceanography and Marine Biology: An Annual Review* 8 (1970): 73–202.

16. Colin Braithwaite, "Geology and Paleogeography of the Red Sea Region," in A. Edwards and Head, *Red Sea*, 22–44.

17. Ibid., 23.

18. Head, introduction to A. Edwards and Head, *Red Sea*, 5.

19. Huntingford, *Periplus*, 177.

20. See entry for "t-h-m" in Muḥammad Ibn Manẓūr, *Lisān al-ʿarab* (Beirut: Dār Ṣādir, 1968), 12:72–74; G. R. Smith, "Tihāma," in *EI2*; and for more philological suggestions, A. Grohmann's entry for "Tihāma" in *Encyclopedia of Islam, First Edition (1913–1936)*, ed. M. Th. Houtsma, T. W. Arnold, R. Basset, and R. Hartmann, Brill Online, accessed March 12, 2015.

21. Head, introduction to A. Edwards and Head, *Red Sea*, 3.

22. Frederick Edwards, "Climate and Oceanography," in A. Edwards and Head, *Red Sea*, 48.

23. Under the order of Augustus, Aelius Gallus, Roman prefect of Egypt in the first century BCE, led an expedition into the Arabian Peninsula that ended in disaster. The campaign was recounted by Strabo, the prefect's intimate friend, and then subsequently by Pliny the Elder, Josephus, and Cassius Dio. The failure of the campaign is attributed to the treachery of the Romans' Nabatean guide, who, writes Strabo, "pointed out neither a safe voyage along the coast nor a safe journey by land, misguiding him through places that had no roads and by circuitous routes and through regions destitute of everything, or along rocky shores that had no harbours or through waters that were shallow or full of submarine rocks." *Geography of Strabo,* vol. 7 (16.4.23), trans. Jones, 355. Romain Gary's book was published by Gallimard in Paris in 1971.

24. F. Edwards, "Climate and Oceanography," 46.

25. See Ludwig Karbe, "Hot Brines and the Deep Sea Environment," in A. Edwards and Head, *Red Sea*, 70–89.

26. J. S. King, "The Red Sea: Why So Called," *Journal of the Royal Asiatic Society of Great Britain and Ireland* 30, no. 3 (July 1898): 617.

27. See, for example, the entry for *ṣāb* in James Redhouse, *A Turkish and English Lexicon*, 3rd ed. (1890; repr., Istanbul: Çağrı Yayınları, 2006), 1106, and Şemseddin Sami, *Ḳāmūs-ı Turkī* (1900; repr., Çağrı Yayınları, 2007), 761.

28. F. Edwards, "Climate and Oceanography," 49.

29. Ibid., 48.

30. A. F. Mohamed, "The Egyptian Exploration of the Red Sea," *Proceedings of the Royal Society of London, Series B, Biological Sciences* 128, no. 852 (February 1940): 306–16.

31. J. Luksch, "The Austro-Hungarian Expedition to the Red Sea," *Geographical Journal* 12, no. 6 (December 1898): 571–72.

32. Head, introduction to A. Edwards and Head, *Red Sea*, 3. Emphasis added.

33. On this subject, see especially Michel Tuchscherer, "Les échanges commerciaux entre les rives africaine et arabe de l'espace mer Rouge-golfe d'Aden aux XVIe et XVIIe siècles," in Lunde and Porter, *Trade and Travel*, 157–63.

34. Quran, 14:37, English interpretation by A. Yusuf Ali, cited in the original Arabic by Muḥammad ʿAlī Fahīm Bayyūmī, *Mukhaṣṣaṣāt al-ḥaramayn al-sharīfayn fi Miṣr ibān al-ʿaṣr al-ʿuthmānī fi al-fatra min 923–1220h/1517–1805m* (Cairo: Dār al-Qāhira li-l-kitāb, 2001), 7.

35. Eyles Irwin, *A Series of Adventures in the Course of a Voyage up the Red-Sea, on the Coasts of Arabia and Egypt, and of a Route through the Desarts of Thebais hitherto unknown to the European Traveller in the year M.DCC.LXXVII in Letters to a Lady* (London: J. Dodsley, 1780), 4.

36. See René Cappers, "Trade and Subsistence at the Roman Port of Berenike, Red Sea Coast, Egypt," in *The Exploitation of Plant Resources in Ancient Africa*, ed. Marijke van der Veen (New York: Kluwer Academic/Plenum, 1999), 195.

37. For a good introduction to the question, see the various chapters in Michel Tuchscherer, ed., *Le commerce du café avant l'ère des plantations coloniales* (Cairo: Institut français d'archéologie orientale, 2001).

38. See, for example, George Hourani, *Arab Seafaring in the Indian Ocean in Ancient and Early Medieval Times* (Princeton, NJ: Princeton University Press, 1995); Lionel Casson, *Ships and Seamanship in the Ancient World* (Baltimore: Johns Hopkins University Press, 1995).

39. Lionel Casson, *The Ancient Mariners: Seafarers and Sea Fighters of the Mediterranean in Ancient Times* (New York: Macmillan, 1959), 4.

40. See Caroline Vermeeren, "The Use of Imported and Local Wood Species at the Roman Port of Berenike, Red Sea Coast, Egypt," in *The Exploitation of Plant Resources in Ancient Africa*, ed. Marijke van der Veen (New York: Kluwer Academic/Plenum, 1999), 199–204.

41. Casson, *Ancient Mariners*, 2–3.

42. G. R. Tibbetts, *Arab Navigation in the Indian Ocean before the Coming of the Portuguese, Being a Translation of Kitāb al-Fawāʾid fī uṣūl al-baḥr waʾl-qawāʾid of Aḥmad b. Mājid al-Najdī* (London: Royal Asiatic Society of Great Britain and Ireland, 1981), 264.

43. John Meloy, *Imperial Power and Maritime Trade: Mecca and Cairo in the Later Middle Ages* (Chicago: University of Chicago Press, 2010), 45.

44. Lucy Blue, "The Red Sea," in *The Oxford Handbook of Maritime Archaeology*, ed. Alexis Catsambia, Ben Ford, and Donny L. Hamilton (Oxford: Oxford University Press, 2011), 497.

45. Mark Horton, "The Human Settlement of the Red Sea," in A. Edwards and Head, *Red Sea*, 340; Blue, "Red Sea," 497.

46. Meloy, *Imperial Power*, 41.

47. Timothy Power, *The Red Sea from Byzantium to the Caliphate, AD 500–1000* (Cairo: American University in Cairo Press, 2012), 17.

48. Huntingford, *Periplus*, 180.

49. See notably Richard Bulliet, *The Camel and the Wheel* (New York: Columbia University Press, 1990), and Steven Sidebotham, *Berenike and the Ancient Maritime Spice Route* (Berkeley: University of California Press, 2011).

50. On the various calendars and the "times of business," see Michel Tuchscherer, "Le commerce en mer Rouge aux alentours de 1700: Flux, espaces et temps," *Res Orientales* 5 (1993): 175–76.

51. Fernand Braudel, *Civilization and Capitalism, 15th-18th Century: The Wheels of Commerce* (London: William Collins Sons, 1982), 2:405.

52. As Li Guo writes: "it is rather curious that spices . . . are rarely mentioned in the Quseir documents as a whole." *Commerce, Culture and Community in a Red Sea Port in the Thirteenth Century: The Arabic Documents from Quseir* (Leiden: Brill, 2004), 43.

53. Marshall Hodgson, *The Venture of Islam: Conscience and History in a World Civilization* (Chicago: University of Chicago Press, 1974), 2:541.

54. Meloy, *Imperial Power*, 19.

55. Albert Dietrich, "Afāwīh," in *EI2*.

56. For example, Shihāb al-Dīn al-Qalqashandī sometimes speaks of the *bahār* that merchants stored and traded, but elsewhere he uses other typologies. *Subḥ al-aʿshā fī kitābat al-inshā* (Cairo: al-Maṭbaʿa al-amīriyya, 1914), 3:461.

57. For an extended discussion of the *kārim,* see Eric Vallet's *L'Arabie marchande: État et commerce sous les sultans rasūlides du Yémen, 626–858/1229–1454* (Paris: Publications de la Sorbonne, 2010).

58. Arrian, *The Anabasis of Alexander, or, The History of the Wars and Conquests of Alexander the Great,* trans. by E.J. Chinnock (London: Hodder and Stroughton, 1883), 408.

59. Sidebotham, *Berenike,* 230.

60. Ibid., 225.

61. André Raymond, "Le commerce des épices au Caire, du XVIe au XVIIIe siècle," in *Herbes, drogues et épices en Méditerranée,* ed. Georges J. Aillaud et al. (Marseille: CNRS, 1988), 115–24, http://books.openedition.org/iremam/3135.

62. On the variety of commodities traded, see, for example, Sidebotham, *Berenike,* and Guo, *Commerce, Culture and Community.*

63. Sidebotham, *Berenike,* 247.

64. Tuchscherer, "Commerce," 159.

65. Agius writes that, expectedly, "Wherever it was possible shipbuilders reverted to local wood," such as for the ribbing and joints of small vessels, but also for masts, yards, oars, and anchors. Still, these are exceptions that prove the rule: most of the construction material was imported from abroad. Dionisius A. Agius, *Classic Ships of Islam: From Mesopotamia to the Indian Ocean* (Leiden: Brill, 2008), 147–48. That ships were constructed in local shipyards is attested at various ports in the region in different ages.

66. See Roxani Margariti, *Aden and the Indian Ocean Trade* (Chapel Hill: University of North Carolina Press, 2007).

67. Huntingford, *Periplus,* 29–30, chaps. 15–16.

68. Muḥammad Ibn Jubayr, *Riḥlat Ibn Jubayr* (Beirut: Dār Ṣādir, 1980), 47.

69. Powers, *Red Sea,* 53.

70. Ibid., 56–59.

71. Cited in ibid., 59. The brackets are Powers's own.

72. The question of the lexical borrowing in the Quran is an old topic of interest in both the Islamic and the Orientalist traditions.

73. K.A.C. Creswell, "The Kaʾba in A.D. 608," *Archaeologia* 94 (1951): 97–102. The twentieth-century scholar argues for the Ethiopian identity of the builder/carpenter, *contra* the explicit position of classical Arabic sources, which suggest a Greek (*rūmī*) or Coptic affiliation.

74. Taqī al-Dīn al-Maqrīzī, *Al-Mawāʿiẓ wa al-iʿtibār bi-dhikr al-khiṭaṭ wa al-āthār* (Cairo: Maktabat al-thaqāfa al-dīniyya, 1987), 1:70–71.

75. John Meloy, "Imperial Strategy and Political Exigency: The Red Sea Spice Trade and the Mamluk Sultanate in the Fifteenth Century," *Journal of the American Oriental Society* 123, no. 1 (2003): 1–19.

76. On the continuation of these Mamluk practices of provisioning the Hijaz by way of Egyptian endowments, see Suraya Faroqhi, "Trade Controls, Provisioning Policies and Donations: The Egypt-Hijaz Connection during the Second Half of the Sixteenth Century," in *Süleymân the Second and His Time,* ed. Halil Inalcik and

Cemal Kafadar (Istanbul: Isis Press, 1993), 131–44. Selmān Reʾīs, in his well-known report of 1525 on the Red Sea and the Indian Ocean (about which see further below), speaks of *awqāf* dedicated for the sustenance of Mecca and Medina, which had been abundant, but were now not fulfilling the duty they had been created for as a result of the chaos in Yemen. See Michel Lesure, "Un document ottoman de 1525 sur l'Inde portugaise et les pays de la mer Rouge," *Mare Luso-Indicum* 3 (1976): 137–60.

77. Doris Behrens-Abouseif, "Waḳf," in *EI2*.

78. Albert Kammerer, *La mer Rouge, l'Abyssinie, et l'Arabie depuis l'antiquité—Essai d'histoire et de géographie historique*, vol. 2, pt. 1 (Cairo: Société royale de géographie d'Égypte, 1935), x.

79. See the detailed narrative of the Ottoman conquest in Ibn Iyās's famous chronicle, with the account of Ṭumān Bāy's death at Muḥammad Ibn Iyās, *Badāʾiʿ al-zuhūr fī waqāʾiʿ al-duhūr*, ed. Muḥammad Muṣṭafā (Cairo: al-Haiyʾa al-misriyya al-ʿāmma li-l-kitāb, 1984), 5:176.

80. Qutb al-dīn al-Nahrawālī, *Al-Barq al-yamānī fi al-fatḥ al-ʿuthmānī*, ed. Ḥamad al-Jāsir (Riyadh: Manshūrāt dār al-yamāma li-l-baḥth, 1967), 18–30, with the account of his death on p. 29.

81. For discussions of the global political and economic context of this period, see Andrew Hess, "The Ottoman Conquest of Egypt (1517) and the Beginning of the Sixteenth-Century World War," *International Journal of Middle East Studies* 4, no. 1 (January 1973): 55–76; Palmira Brummett, *Ottoman Seapower and Levantine Diplomacy in the Age of Discovery* (Albany: SUNY Press, 1994); Giancarlo Casale, *The Ottoman Age of Exploration* (Oxford: Oxford University Press, 2010).

82. On Selmān's career and Ottoman Indian Ocean policy, see Casale, *Ottoman Age of Exploration.*

83. On this episode, see Jean-Louis Bacqué-Grammont and Anne Kroell, *Mamlouks, Ottomans et Portugais en mer Rouge: L'affaire de Djedda en 1517* (Cairo: Institut français d'archéologie orientale, 1988).

84. For a consummate analysis of the changing *nomos* of the earth from a Euro-universal perspective, see Carl Schmitt, *The* Nomos *of the Earth in the International Law of the* Jus Publicum Europaeum (New York: Telos Press, 2003).

85. For a facsimile of the document, accompanied by a transcription and translation, and a general introduction, see Lesure, "Document Ottoman."

86. Ibid., 156. The transcription is Lesure's.

87. See the chapter "The Pepper Trade" in Part II of Fernand Braudel, *The Mediterranean and the Mediterranean World in the Age of Philip II*, trans. Siân Reynolds (Berkeley: University of California Press, 1996), 1:543–69. In fact, the very title of the first section of the chapter announces the point forcefully: "Mediterranean Revenge: The Prosperity of the Red Sea after 1550." A foundational statement on the question can be found in Frederic Lane, "The Mediterranean Spice Trade: Further Evidence of Its Revival in the 16th Century," *American Historical Review* 45, no. 3 (1940): 571–90.

88. Raymond, "Commerce des épices."

89. On Egyptian policies and ambitions in the Red Sea arena, see Ṭariq ʿAbd al-ʿĀṭī Ghunaym Bayyūmī, *Siyāsat Miṣr fī al-Baḥr al-Aḥmar fī al-niṣf al-awwal min al-qarn al-tāsiʿ ʿashar* (Cairo: Al-haiʾa al-miṣriyya al-ʿāmma li-l-kitāb, 1999).

90. Fred Lawson, *The Social Origins of Egyptian Expansionism during the Muhammad ʿAli Period* (New York: Columbia University Press, 1992).

91. Ibid., 135.

92. Khaled Fahmy, *All the Pasha's Men: Mehmed Ali, His Army and the Making of Modern Egypt* (Cairo: American University in Cairo Press, 1997), 44–45; Braudel, *Mediterranean,* 1:110. Braudel was writing about Spain, which should have fulfilled, but did not fulfill, its "geographical mission" by invading North Africa following the fall of Granada.

93. ʿAbd al-Raḥmān al-Jabartī, *ʿAbd al-Rahman al-Jabartī's History of Egypt: ʿAjāʾib al-āthār fī'l-tarājim wa'l-akhbār*, vols. 3 and 4, ed. Thomas Philipp and Moshe Pearlmann (Stuttgart: Franz Steiner, 1994), 4:178.

94. Isa Blumi, *Foundations of Modernity: Human Agency and the Imperial State* (New York: Routledge, 2012), 40–41 and passim.

95. Heinrich Eduard Jacob, *The Saga of Coffee: The Biography of an Economic Product* (London: George Allen and Unwin, 1935), 115; Silvestre de Sacy, *Chrestomathie arabe* (Paris: Imprimerie impériale, 1806), 1:179.

96. Al-Jabartī, *ʿAbd al-Rahman al-Jabartī's History*, vols. 1 and 2, 2:233, 234, both relating to occurrences in the month of Ramadan 1201 AH/June-July 1787.

97. This notable "lower-class" aspect may have been an Ottoman particularity. In France, by contrast, coffee seems to have been, until fairly recently, a distinctly upper-class affair. Braudel mentions the story of the famous early eighteenth-century bandit Cartouche, who requested wine instead of the coffee he was offered just before he was about to be put to death (Braudel, *Civilization and Capitalism,* 1:260). A century later, one of the features of the local social landscape that Rifāʿa Rāfiʿ al-Ṭahṭāwī noticed from his time in France was the fact that "the coffee houses in this country are not the meeting places of riff-raff, but of decent people. Indeed, these places are decorated with such beautiful and precious things that they are suited only for the very rich. The prices there are very high, so only wealthy people can go there." *An Imam in Paris: Account of a Stay in France by an Egyptian Cleric (1826–1831),* ed. and trans. Daniel Newman (London: Saqi, 2004), 151.

98. Braudel, *Civilization and Capitalism*, 1:256.

99. An early version of this legend, particularly popular in European accounts of the discovery of the drug, can be found in Jean de la Roque's influential *Voyage dans l'Arabie Heureuse* of 1716.

100. Braudel, *Civilization and Capitalism*, 1:249. Braudel's startling sentence is ably critiqued by Ross Jamieson, "The Essence of Commodification: Caffeine Dependencies in the Early Modern World," *Journal of Social History* 35, no. 2 (Winter 2001): 269–94.

101. Frédéric Mauro, *Histoire du café* (Paris: Desjonquères, 2002); William H. Ukers, *All about Coffee,* 2nd ed. (New York: Tea and Coffee Trade Journal, 1935).

102. Tuchscherer, *Commerce du café*, 1.

103. Charles Schaefer, "Coffee Unobserved: Consumption and Commoditization of Coffee in Ethiopia before the Eighteenth Century," in Tuchscherer, *Commerce du café*, 24.

104. Carsten Niebuhr, *Travels through Arabia and other Countries in the East,* trans. by Robert Heron (Edinburgh: Morison and Son, 1792), 1:291; 2:357–58.

105. Mutsua Kawatoko, "Coffee Trade in the al-Tur Port, South Sinai," in Tuchscherer, *Commerce du café*, 52.

106. For an introduction to the main texts on the history of coffee, see Ralph Hattox, *Coffee and Coffeehouses: The Origins of a Social Beverage in the Medieval Near East* (Seattle: University of Washington Press, 1985), and Jean-Louis Bacqué-Grammont, "Autour des premières mentions du café dans les sources ottomanes," in Tuchscherer, *Commerce du café,* 17–21. The Frenchman Antoine Galland already addressed some of these sources in his *De l'origine et du progrès du caffé* from 1699.

107. The Arabic text, drawn from the Paris manuscript at the Bibliothèque nationale, appears in the first volume of the 1806 edition (177–224); the French translation appears along with notes in the second volume (224–78).

108. Entry "ḳahwa," in *EI2*.

109. Jean-Paul Pascual, "Café et cafés à Damas: Contribution à la chronologie de leur diffusion au XVIème siècle," *Berytus* 42 (1995–96): 144.

110. Kātib Çelebī, *Kitāb-ı Cihānnūma* (Istanbul: Dār al-ṭibāʿa al-ʿāmira, 1732), 534–36. Here Shaykh ʿUmar al-Shādhilī is given a fidgety ball by his master and told to settle wherever it would be still. He proceeds from Sawakin to Mocha, where the ball finally stops moving, so there he builds a house and digs a well. Eventually, following a convoluted story of sickness and healing in which coffee is discovered, the shaykh sends one of his sons, Abū al-Futuḥ, back to Sawakin to establish himself there.

111. Nancy Um, *The Merchant Houses of Mocha: Trade and Architecture in an Indian Ocean Port* (Seattle: University of Washington Press, 2009), 21.

112. Michel Tuchscherer, "Coffee in the Red Sea Area from the Sixteenth to the Nineteenth Century," in *The Global Coffee Economy in Africa, Asia and Latin America, 1500–1989*, ed. William Gervase Clarence Smith and Steven Topik (Cambridge: Cambridge University Press, 2003), 57.

113. De Sacy, *Chrestomathie arabe*, 191–92. Remarkably, al-Jazīrī's chronology corresponds with the earliest material evidence in the vicinity of Cairo (the 1497 invoice at Tor in Sinai).

114. Ibid., 192.

115. Ibid., 192–93. Al-Jazīrī is here quoting another author, who writes in the first person, as a member of the said audience.

116. Tuchscherer, "Coffee," 51.

117. De Sacy, *Chrestomathie arabe*, 1:193.

118. Ibid., 1:193–97.

119. This is a recurrent theme in accounts of coffee in Ottoman/Islamic history and lies at the very heart of the only scholarly monograph on the subject, Hattox's *Coffee and Coffeehouses.* Most of the interpretations focus on the anxieties of

the state concerning the subversive potential of the coffee shop as a space. What remains to be properly explored is the form, content, function, and purpose of the recurrent arguments for or against coffee in the Islamic discursive tradition. In the eighteenth century, for example, Shaykh Iskandar argued for the illicit nature of coffee, on account notably of its addictive properties (al-Jabartī, *'Abd al-Rahman al-Jabartī's History*, 1:256), whereas Shaykh Murtada al-Zabidi composed a treatise advocating for its legitimacy, a copy of which can be found in the National Library in Cairo.

120. See Pascual, "Café et cafés"; Suraya Faroqhi, "Coffee and Spices: Official Ottoman Reactions to Egyptian Trade in the Later Sixteenth Century," *Wiener Zeitschrift für die Kunde des Morgenlandes* 76 (1986): 87–93.

121. Faroqhi, "Coffee and Spices," 89.

122. In eighteenth-century Egypt, the rulers most commonly took out loans from the great coffee merchants. See, for example, al-Jabartī, *'Abd al-Rahman al-Jabartī's History*, 2:139, 220, 249. The French, after the invasion of Egypt in 1798, continued the practice and took out a loan, mostly from coffee merchants (3:20).

123. On a coffee shop serving as a meeting-place for a popular religious movement and another as a cabaret/brothel, see respectively al-Jabartī, *'Abd al-Rahman al-Jabartī's History*, 1:46–47; 3:77. On coffeehouses as a nodal point of information and politics, see Cengiz Kirli, "Coffeehouses: Public Opinion in the Nineteenth-Century Ottoman Empire," in *Public Islam and the Common Good*, edited by Armando Salvatore and Dale F. Eickelman (Leiden: Brill, 2004), 75–97.

124. Mouradgea d'Ohsson, *Tableau général de l'empire Othoman* (Paris: Imprimerie de Monsieur, 1791), 4/1:80.

125. Selma Akyazici Özkoçak, "Coffeehouses: Rethinking the Public and Private in Early Modern Istanbul," *Journal of Urban History* 33, no. 6 (2007): 965–86.

126. Cemal Kafadar, "How Dark Is the History of the Night, How Black the Story of Coffee, How Bitter the Tale of Love: The Changing Measure of Leisure and Pleasure in Early Modern Istanbul," Kamal Salibi Memorial Lecture, May 17, 2013, American University of Beirut.

127. Michel Tuchscherer, "Coffee," 56.

128. Here is al-Jabartī on the question: "A large amount of coffee beans had arrived from Europe. These beans are larger and greener than the Yemeni beans coming to Egypt on Hijazi boats. He [Meḥmed 'Alī Paşa] took it all paying for it with grain. He sold them to the coffee merchants in Cairo at 23 French *riyal* a *qintar*. The merchants mixed it with Yemeni beans and sold it for a higher price. When [this coffee] had first been introduced, it sold cheaply because it was inferior to the Yemeni beans in flavor and not as enjoyable to drink. There is an obvious difference between the two types apparent to the connoisseur" (al-Jabartī, *'Abd al-Rahman al-Jabartī's History*, 4:202).

129. For a case involving a French merchant, and the need not to mix Yemeni beans (*yemen ḳahvesi*) with the European imported beans (*frenk ḳahvesi*), see BOA, C.HR 64/3157. See also Mouradgea d'Ohsson, *Tableau général,* 4/1:84–85.

130. References to the Red Sea trade in coffee abound in the chronicles of the time. See, for example, al-Jabartī, *'Abd al-Rahman al-Jabartī's History*, 3:60, 62, 405; 4:283.

131. See, for example, ibid., 4:189.

2. THALASSOLOGY *ALLA TURCA*

1. G. W. F. Hegel, *Lectures on the Philosophy of World History*, vol. 1, *Manuscripts of the Introduction and the Lectures of 1822–3,* ed. and trans. R. F. Brown and P. C. Hodgson, with the assistance of W. G. Geuss (Oxford: Clarendon Press, 2011), 477.

2. Herbert Gibbons, *The Foundation of the Ottoman Empire* (New York: Century, 1916). This is the crux of the very first chapter, revealingly entitled "Osman: A New Race Appears in History."

3. See, for example, Colin Heywood, review of *The Ottoman Empire, 1300–1650: The Structure of Power*, by Colin Imber, *Reviews in History*, no. 431, November 2004, www.history.ac.uk/reviews/review/431.

4. Aksan, "Theoretical Ottomans," 109.

5. Cemal Kafadar, *Between Two Worlds: The Construction of the Ottoman State* (Berkeley: University of California Press, 1995), xii.

6. Gabriel Piterberg, *An Ottoman Tragedy: History and Historiography at Play* (Berkeley: University of California Press, 2003), 6.

7. Aksan, "Theoretical Ottomans," 109.

8. Murat Dağlı, "The Limits of Ottoman Pragmatism," *History and Theory* 52 (May 2013): 212.

9. Blumi, *Foundations of Modernity.*

10. All these quotations are from *LPWH*, 196.

11. G. W. F. Hegel, *Philosophy of Mind—Being Part Three of the Encyclopaedia of the Philosophical Sciences, Together with the Zusätze,* trans. William Wallace and A. V. Miller (Oxford: Oxford University Press, 1971), 46.

12. Ibid.

13. Abraham Udovitch, for example, speaks of "an ambivalence toward and wariness (almost rejection) of the sea" on the part of "medieval Islamic culture." "An Eleventh Century Islamic Treatise on the Law of the Sea," *Annales Islamologiques* 27 (1993): 38.

14. *LPH*, 370.

15. Ibid., 369. Emphasis in original.

16. Ibid., 371.

17. André Servier, *L'Islam et la psychologie du Musulman* (Paris: Augustin Challamel, 1923).

18. Braudel, *Mediterranean*, 1:187. It should be noted here, though, that Braudel, great anatomist that he is, then continues with the following caveat: "But we should be wary of oversimplifying something so complex. Islam is the sum of human realities implied by the desert, harmonious or discordant, the whole family of geographi-

cal problems we have noted: the great caravan trails; the coastal zones, for Islam lived off these *Sahels,* fringes of settled civilization along the shores of the Mediterranean, the Persian Gulf, the Indian Ocean, or the Red Sea, and also bordering the countries of the Sudan; the oases and their accumulated power, which Hettner thinks was the essential factor. Islam is all that, a long road cutting through the strong and rigid mass of the Ancient World. Rome, when she achieved the unity of the Mediterranean, did no more" (1:187).

19. Xavier de Planhol, *Les fondements géographiques de l'Islam* (Paris: Flammarion, 1968).

20. *LPH,* 371.

21. Paul Rycaut, *The Present State of the Ottoman Empire* (London: J. Starkey and H. Brome, 1668), 213.

22. Ibid., 216.

23. Ibid. Emphasis in original.

24. Ibid.

25. Quoted in Casale, *Ottoman Age of Exploration*, 199.

26. Ibid.

27. See the Introduction for the actual quote.

28. BOA, Nāme-i Hümayün Defterleri, 9, 80, 77 (beginning of *Şaʿbān* 1189/late September 1775).

29. Muḥammad Ibn Iyās, *Badāʾiʿ al-zuhūr fī waqāʾiʿ al-duhūr,* ed. Muḥammad Muṣṭafā (Cairo: al-Haiyʾa al-misriyya al-ʿāmma li-l-kitāb), 5:148.

30. See J. H. Kramers and C. E. Bosworth's entry for *sulṭān* in *EI2*.

31. See C. E. Bosworth's entry for *laḳab* in *EI2*.

32. See the various relevant entries in Ḥasan al-Bāshā, *al-Alqāb al-Islāmiyya fī al-tārīkh wa al-wathāʾiq wa al-āthār* (Cairo: Maktabat al-nahḍa al-miṣriyya, 1957), 334.

33. See, for example, Brummett, *Ottoman Seapower,* 12–13.

34. Michel Mollat du Jourdin, *Europe and the Sea* (London: Blackwell, 1993); Xavier de Planhol, *L'Islam et la mer: La mosquée et le matelot, VIIe-XXe siècles* (Paris: Perrin, 2000).

35. Mollat du Jourdin, *Europe and the Sea*, 3.

36. Ibid., 4.

37. Ibid.

38. Ibid. The translation has been altered to preserve the meaning of the French original, rendered nonsensical in the English edition.

39. Ibid. Amazingly, the arithmetical analysis does not prevent the conclusion from enshrining a purely aesthetic line from a Paul Claudel poem that says: "The West looks to the sea and the East to the mountains."

40. The French original, *nette* (clear-cut, neat, clean), is even more unmistakable.

41. Xavier de Planhol, "The Geographical Setting," in *The Cambridge History of Islam,* ed. P. M. Holt, Ann K. S. Lambton, and Bernard Lewis, vol. 2B (Cambridge: Cambridge University Press, 1970), 443.

42. Ibid.

43. Cited in David Livingstone, "Race, Space and Moral Climatology: Notes toward a Genealogy," *Journal of Historical Geography,* 28, no. 2 (2002): 171.

44. Ernest Renan, "The Religions of Antiquity," in *Studies of Religious History and Criticism,* trans. O. B. Frothingham (New York: Carleton, 1864), 103.

45. De Planhol, *L'Islam et la mer,* 9. Subsequent page citations to this work are given parenthetically in the text.

46. Giancarlo Casale, "The Ethnic Composition of Ottoman Ship Crews and the 'Rumi Challenge' to Portuguese Identity," *Medieval Encounters* 13 (2007): 139.

47. The most forceful critic of the model remains Brummett's *Ottoman Seapower.* Other critics include, for example, Suraiya Faroqhi, Rhoads Murphey, and Şevket Pamuk. The model itself, however, remains steadfast *as a model.*

48. Fernand Braudel, *Civilisation matérielle, économie et capitalisme, XVe-XVIIIe siècle,* vol. 2, *Les jeux de l'échange* (Paris: Armand Colin, 1979), 110–11.

49. Halil İnalcık, "The Ottoman Economic Mind and Aspects of the Ottoman Economy," in *Studies in the Economic History of the Middle East,* ed. Michael Cook (Oxford: Oxford University Press, 1970), 207–18.

50. Mehmet Genç, *Osmanlı İmparatorluğu'nda Devlet ve Ekonomi* (Istanbul: Ötüken Neşriyat, 2000). See also Mehmet Genç, "Ottoman Industry in the Eighteenth Century: General Framework, Characteristics and Main Trends," in *Manufacturing in the Ottoman Empire and Turkey, 1500–1950,* ed. Donald Quataert (Albany: SUNY Press, 1994), 59–86.

51. Timothy Mitchell, "Fixing the Economy," *Cultural Studies* 12, no. 1 (1998): 91.

52. Şevket Pamuk, *A Monetary History of the Ottoman Empire* (Cambridge: Cambridge University Press, 2000), 15.

53. Suraiya Faroqhi, introduction to *The Cambridge History of Turkey,* vol. 3, *The Later Ottoman Empire, 1603–1839,* ed. Suraiya Faroqhi (Cambridge: Cambridge University Press, 2006), 8.

54. Evliyā Çelebī, *Seyāhatnāmesi,* vol. 1, ed. Ahmed Cevdet (Istanbul: Iḳdām matbaʿasī, 1896), 512.

55. Pamuk, *Monetary History,* 15.

56. See in particular Suraiya Faroqhi, *Pilgrims and Sultans: The Hajj under the Ottomans* (London: I. B. Tauris, 1994).

57. BOA, MM 8, 215, 426 (middle of *Cumādā I* 1180 AH/mid-October 1766 CE).

58. References to shortages are legion in the archives. The following is a sample taken at random, from various periods and concerning different places (and located in separate collections), BOA, HAT 749/38393 (a request from 1136 AH/1724 CE) to send coffee from Izmir to palliate the demand in Istanbul), BOA, C.IKTS 22/1054 (dated 1214 AH/1799 CE, addressed to Iznikmid's judge and customs official, it commands that all arriving coffee be sent directly to Istanbul), BOA, C.BLD 138/6881 (dated 1255 AH/1840 CE, this order for coffee to be sent immediately to Istanbul shows that the problem of shortages continued well into the mid-

nineteenth century, despite the increasing production of coffee in the European colonies). Coffee shortages in the capital city and their remedying constitute perhaps the single most common subject of the commands in the Mühimme-i Mısır series.

59. On attempts to regulate the coffee market, see Mehmet Genç, "Contrôle et taxation du commerce du café dans l'Empire ottoman fin XVIIe–première moitié du XVIIIe siècle," in Tuchscherer, *Commerce du café*, 161–80.

60. BOA, MM 8, 268, 508 (beginning of *Rebīʿ II* 1181 AH/late August 1767).

61. Gilbert Buti, "Marseille entre Moka et café des îles: Espaces, flux, réseaux, XVIIe-XVIIIe siècles," in Tuchscherer, *Commerce du café*, 222.

62. Ibid.

63. See, for example, BOA, MM 8, 268, 508 (beginning of *Rebīʿ II* 1181 AH/late August 1767), or again BOA, MM 8, 352, 659 (end of *Şaʿbān* 1188 AH/early November 1774).

64. Faroqhi, "Trade Controls," 139.

65. André Raymond, *Artisans et commerçants au Caire au XVIIIe siècle*, 2nd ed. (Cairo: Institut français d'archéologie orientale, 1999), 1:153–54.

66. See, for example, "Extract of a Letter from His Exc. Sir Robert Ainslie, to Lord Viscount Weymouth, Dated Pera of Constantinople 17th Dec. 1778," BL, IOR/G/17/5, p. 197.

67. See the official complaint reiterating the prohibition for European ships to disembark directly in Egypt sent by the Ottoman government to the English ambassador (BOA, MM 9, 3, 1), as well as a discussion of it sent to the sultan (BOA, MM 9, 3, 2), both dated on the last day of *Z̲ī 'l-ḳaʿde* 1192 AH/December 19, 1778 CE.

68. BL, IOR/G/17/5, pp. 208–10, emphasis added.

69. E.g., BOA, MM 9, 114, 201 (beginning of *Şaʿbān* 1191 AH/beginning of September 1777 CE).

70. Raymond, *Artisans et commerçants,* 1:155.

71. See, for example, MM 9, 150, 261 (middle of *Receb* 1191 AH/middle of August 1777 CE): "maḳtūl ʿAlī Bey'iñ hengām-i tuğyānında muğāyır-ı rıżā-yı şāhānem Ingiltere gemileriniñ Süveys'e vürūd eylediği sāmiʿa-ı güzār-ı hüsrevānem olduğu saʿat menʿ ve defʿilerini ḥāvī Mıṣır cānibine ve Cidde vālīsine evāmir-i ekīdem taṣdīr ve keyfiyet Der ʿaliyemde mūḳīm Ingiltere elçisine ifāde . . ."

72. This is the wording used in "Translation from the Italian. Representation of the Sublime Porte Sent by His Excy the Reis Efendi to His Excy Sir Robert Ainslie His Britannick Majesty's Ambassador" (BL, IOR/G/17/5, pp. 208–10). The Ottoman version of this text reads "*aḳṭār-ı Ḥicāziye'de güft ü şenīd hudūs̲una bādī*"; see BOA MM 9, 3, 1, last day of *Z̲ī 'l-ḳaʿde* 1192 AH/December 19, 1778 CE.

73. İnalcık, "Ottoman Economic Mind," 218.

74. See, for example, Genç, *Osmanlı İmparatorluğu'nda*, 76.

75. Mehmet Genç, "State and the Economy in the Age of Reforms: Continuity and Change," in *Ottoman Past and Today's Turkey*, ed. Kemal Karpat (Leiden: Brill, 2000), 187.

76. For a groundbreaking volume, see Scott Reese, ed., *The Transmission of Learning in Islamic Africa* (Leiden: Brill, 2004).

77. Diderot and d'Alembert, *Encyclopédie,* vol. 11.

78. A manuscript version of this text, dated Alexandria, June 21, 1789, can be found in the Foreign Office series of the National Archives in Kew Gardens (FO 24/1, 161–66). It was subsequently printed as well.

79. Nadine Picaudou, "'Les Arabes' comme catégorie du discours mandataire britannique en Palestine," in *Temps et espaces en Palestine: Flux et résistances identitaires,* ed. Roger Heacock (Beirut: Institit français du Proche Orient, 2008), 235–45.

80. BOA, HR.TO 192/9.

81. Incidentally, such connotations of the term persist in a number of post-Ottoman countries, including notably contemporary Turkey and Greece.

82. De Sacy, *Chrestomathie arabe,* 1:189.

83. And indeed why should it be, other than in a racialized world that only emerged in the late eighteenth-century West?

84. See *LPWH,* 12–13, and especially 134–36.

85. The best introduction to the Prime Ministry's Ottoman archives remains their regularly updated official guide, which also contains a basic bibliography of the existing literature at the end. Başbakanlık Devlet Arşivleri Genel Müdürlüğu, *Başbakanlık Osmanlı Arşivi Rehberi* (Istanbul, 2010).

86. On Muallim Cevdet, see Osman Ergin, *Muallim M. Cevdetin Hayatı, Eserleri, ve Kütüphanesi* (Istanbul: Bozkurt Basımevi, 1937).

87. Stephen Smith, ed., *The Red Sea Region: Sovereignty, Boundaries and Conflict, 1839–1967* (Cambridge: Archive Editions, 2008).

88. BOA, HAT 141/5855.

89. The document is BOA, C.HR 6/287.

90. Less common versions based on Turkic constructions, such as *Süveys Deñizi,* can also be found in some documents (e.g., BOA, MM 9, 114, 201, dated early *Ṣafer* 1191 AH/middle of March 1777 CE). The occurrence of the name is too frequent to reference. Even foreign representatives in Istanbul used it, as in the case of the US ambassador requesting an authorization for two of his compatriots to travel through a number of places in the Ottoman lands, including *Baḥr-i Süveys,* which is listed right after *Mıṣır-ı Ḳāhire* and before *Ṭarāblus-i Şām.* BOA, C.HR 150/7466, dated 7 *Receb* 1249 AH/19 November 1833 CE). *Süveys Körfüsü* was also used, seemingly in the more restricted reference to what would be called today the actual Gulf of Suez (e.g., BOA, MM 9, 21, 33, dated early *Receb* 1189 AH/end of August 1775).

91. "Wa fī aqṣāh madinat al-Qulzum qurb Misr, wa bi-thālik summīya baḥr al-Qulzum, wa usammā fi kul mawḍiʿ yammurru bih bi-ism thālik al-mawḍiʿ." Yāqūt al-Ḥamawī, *Muʿjam al-buldān* (Beirut: Dār Ṣādir, 1977), 1:344.

92. Niebuhr, *Beschreibung,* 418.

93. Aḥmad Zakī, *Dictionary of Ancient Geography/Qāmūs al-jughrāfiya al-qadīma* (Cairo: Bulāq, 1899), 7.

94. On the question of the naming of seas, see, more globally, Martin Lewis, "Dividing the Ocean Sea," *Geographic Review,* 89/2 (April 1999): 188–214, and more locally, C. Edmund Bosworth, "The Nomenclature of the Persian Gulf," *Iranian Studies* 30, nos. 1–2 (Winter-Spring 1997): 77–94.

95. Bosworth, "Nomenclature," 88.

96. Ibid.

97. This critical point is made in passing by Timothy Mitchell in *Rule of Experts: Egypt, Techno-Politics, Modernity* (Berkeley: University of California Press, 2002), 180. For a concise formulation of the general argument as related to the problematic of modernity, see Timothy Mitchell, "The Stage of Modernity," in *Questions of Modernity*, ed. Timothy Mitchell (Minneapolis: University of Minnesota Press, 2000), 1–34.

98. João de Barros, *Da Asía de João de Barros—Dos feitos, que os Portuguezes fizeram no descubrimento, e conquista dos mares, e terras do Oriente. Decada Secunda. Parte Secunda.* (1553; repr., Lisbon: Regia Oficina Typografica, 1777), 259.

99. The thoroughness is of course not innocent: the map was to be used by the British government for military designs. It is no doubt for these reasons that a copy of the map can be found in the State Papers Office series at the National Archives, SP 112/69, "A Chart of the Arabian Gulf and the Red Sea by L. S. De la Rochette."

3. SELF-PORTRAIT OF THE OTTOMAN RED SEA, JUNE 21, 1777

1. For a particularly inspiring introduction to these questions, see Casey, *Fate of Place*.

2. Colin Davis, *Critical Excess: Overreading in Derrida, Deleuze, Levinas, Žižek and Cavell* (Stanford, CA: Stanford University Press, 2010), 186.

3. Much has been written on the subject; for a recent stimulating example, see Ann Stoler, *Along the Archival Grain: Epistemic Anxieties and Colonial Common Sense* (Princeton, NJ: Princeton University Press, 2009).

4. See the entry for *q-r-sh* in Ibn Manẓūr, *Lisān al-ʿarab* (Beirut: Dār Ṣādir, 1968), 6:334–36. The fact that there are other possible etymologies changes nothing to the point here, which is simply that maritime references saturate the discursive tradition to which the Ottomans belong.

5. On the influence of Ibn Khaldūn in the Ottoman world, see Cornell Fleischer, "Royal Authority, Dynastic Cyclism, and 'Ibn Khaldunism' in Sixteenth Century Ottoman Letters," *Journal of Asian and African Studies* 18, nos. 3–4 (1983): 198–220.

6. G.R. Tibbetts, "Arabia in the Fifteenth-Century Navigational Texts," *Arabian Studies* 1 (1974): 87.

7. See Michael Sells, "The *Muʿallaqa* of Ṭarafa," *Journal of Arabic Literature* 17 (1986): 21–33. Maritime imagery appear repeatedly in the poem, beginning with the first section (the *nasīb*): "As if, yesterday / the *howdas* of a Málikite / were a ship, free-floating, / in the wide wadi beds of Dádi, / The ship of an *ʿAdawlíyann* / or the Yemenite, / the mate tacking at times / then bringing her around, / She cleaves the rippled waves, / bow breast submerged, / like the hand of a child at play, / scooping through the soft soil" (24).

8. The designator *Islamic* is somewhat misleading, since the individuals involved, at practically all levels, are extraordinarily varied (in faith, mother-tongue, culture, etc.). Still, what may be termed in a loose sense "Islamic" did provide for something of a broad linguistic and juridical coherence to the space under consideration, with Arabic as a sort of lingua franca. Roxani Margariti relates a particularly revealing example from the domain of the Cairo Geniza documents: an Adeni Jew sent to his brother-in-law who lived on the Indian coast of Konkan a letter of introduction *in Arabic script* for the local collaborators (their other communications usually taking place in Judeo-Arabic written in Hebrew letters). Margariti, *Aden*, 158.

9. See Robert Hoyland, *Arabia and the Arabs: From the Bronze Age to the Coming of Islam* (London: Routledge, 2001).

10. Ibn Khaldūn, *The Muqaddimah: An Introduction to History,* trans. Franz Rosenthal (New York: Pantheon Books, 1958), 1:94–96, and *Muqaddimat Ibn Khaldūn,* ed. Sheḥāda, 57. The transliterations in parentheses and directly in the text are Rosenthal's; those in square brackets are my own.

11. Ibn Khaldūn, *Muqaddimah,* trans. Rosenthal, 98, and *Muqaddimat Ibn Khaldūn,* ed. Sheḥāda, 59.

12. Ibn Khaldūn, *Muqaddimah,* trans. Rosenthal, 98.

13. Ibn Khaldūn, *Muqaddimat Ibn Khaldūn,* ed. Sheḥāda, 59.

14. Ibn Khaldūn, *Muqaddimah,* trans. Rosenthal, 99, and *Muqaddimat Ibn Khaldūn,* ed. Sheḥāda, 60.

15. Ibn Khaldūn, *Muqaddimat Ibn Khaldūn,* ed. Sheḥāda, 60. Rosenthal renders it as the "Indian Ocean" (Ibn Khaldūn, *Muqaddimah,* trans. Rosenthal, 99).

16. Ibn Khaldūn, *Muqaddimah,* trans. Rosenthal, 168, and *Muqaddimat Ibn Khaldūn,* ed. Sheḥāda, 104.

17. Ibn Khaldūn, *Muqaddimah,* trans. Rosenthal, 169, and *Muqaddimat Ibn Khaldūn,* ed. Sheḥāda, 105.

18. "The Franks," *Efrenc,* was the generic Ottoman term for western European Christians.

19. Pîrî Reis, *Kitab-ı Bahriye,* ed. E. Z. Ökte (Istanbul: Historical Research Foundation, 1988), 83.

20. Ibid., 83–84.

21. Kātib Çelebi, *Tuḥfat al-kibār fi asfār al-biḥār,* 2b. The Sea of Qulzum is a common name given to the Red Sea (or parts thereof) in Arabic and Ottoman geographical works, derived from the name of the town that was eventually replaced by Suez.

22. Ibid.

23. Evliya Çelebi, *Evliya Çelebi Seyahatnamesi,* vol. 9, *Anadolu, Suriye, Hicaz (1672–1672)* (Istanbul: Devlet Matbaasi, 1935), 805–6.

24. Ibid., 806. The transliteration follows the published version, as the later volumes of the travelogue were published in Latin script.

25. Suraiya Faroqhi, "Red Sea Trade and Communications as Observed by Evliya Çelebi (1671–72)," in *Making a Living in the Ottoman Lands, 1480 to 1820,* ed. Suraiya Faroqui (Istanbul: Isis Press, 1995), 251.

26. Ibid.

27. Hau'ofa, "Our Sea of Islands" (discussed in the Introduction above).

28. The theme of *making* the archive speak is a recurrent one in Ginzburg's work. In one intervention, he states that his intention is "to demonstrate that the *hors-texte*, what is outside the text, is also *in* the text, nestling in its folds: we have to discover it, and make it talk;" to which is adduced a footnote that reads: "I have been working in this direction from the time of my *I benendanti* (1966); see, especially, "The Inquisitor as Anthropologist," in *Clues, Myths and the Historical Method* (Baltimore, 1989), pp. 156ff." Carlo Ginzburg, *History, Rhetoric, and Proof* (Hanover, NH: University Press of New England, 1999), 23; 37 n. 103.

29. BOA, MMD, 9, 129–30, 227 (middle *Cumādā I* 1191 AH/middle June 1777 CE). The document will be quoted in translation in the text with the transliteration added in footnotes. Of course, the original has neither capital letters nor punctuation. These have been added as seen fit to facilitate the task of the reader. The Mühimme-i Mısır is a regionally specific variation on the general Mühimme series, analyzed in depth as a pool of sources by Uriel Heyd in *Ottoman Documents on Palestine, 1552–1615: A Study of the Firman According to the Mühimme Defteri* (Oxford: Clarendon Press, 1960).

30. "Mıṣır vālīsi ṣadr-ı esbaḳ vezīrim ʿIzzet Meḥmed Paşa'ya ve Mıṣır ḳāżīsina ve şayh ül-beled ve yedi ocaḳ ḍābiṭān ve ihtiyārları zīde ḳadruhumā hüküm ki."

31. "Başmuḥāsebe'ye ʿilm u haberi verilmişdir."

32. "Tekrār emir yazılmışdır. Evāhır-ı Cā [Cumāda 'l-ūlā], S[ene] [11]92."

33. It is fairly common for the orders to have marginal notes of this format and content.

34. "Ḳāhire-i Mıṣır'da vāḳıʿ Murādiye vaḳfı ve evḳāf-ı sāʾireden Bender-i Süveys'den Ḥarameyn el-Şerīfeyn ahālīsi içün Bender-i Cidde ve Yenbūʿ'a ğılāl naḳline mahṣūṣ olan sefāyiniñ ekṡeri mürūr-i ezmān ile şikest ve fenā-pezīr olduğundan el-yevm mevcūdu eḳall-i ḳalīl ve muʿayyen olan ğilāliñ naḳlına ğayr-i vāfī olduğu ihbār ve inhā ve mādde-i merḳūme iʿtinā olunacaḳ umūrdan olduğuna bināen."

35. Faroqhi, "Trade Controls," 138.

36. For example, al-Jabartī affirms that at a certain point in the Ottoman-Wahhabi war, "Most of the inhabitants of Medina had died of hunger because of the dearness of foodstuffs," which had been "due to the stoppage of imports" (*ʿAbd al-Rahman al-Jabartī's History*, 3:460–61).

37. Faroqhi, "Trade Controls," 142.

38. See chap. 6, "L'itinéraire du Caire à La Mecque," in Jacques Jomier's *Le Maḥmal et la caravane égyptienne des pélerins de La Mecque (XIIIe-XXe siècles)* (Cairo: Institut français d'archéologie orientale, 1953), 170–204, as well as the accompanying map.

39. Fees dedicated for payments to personalities along the pilgrimage route are often explicitly listed in the *ṣurres* (for examples from the same period as Document 227, see BOA, MAD 4980 (1193 AH/1779 CE) and MAD 7396 (1203 AH/1788–89 CE), in which the recipients are described as "*ʿurbān ve ʿaşāʾir sheyhleri*"). See more

generally Stanford Shaw, *The Financial and Administrative Organization and Development of Ottoman Egypt, 1517–1798* (Princeton, NJ: Princeton University Press, 1962), as well as Faroqhi, *Pilgrims and Sultans.*

40. "Altmiş beş tārīhlerinde sefāyin-i merḳūmeniñ ḳaç ḳıtʿa olduğunu müteveffā Kāmil Aḥmed Paşa'nıñ Mıṣır tevlīyeti es̱nāsında ḳaç ḳıtʿa bāḳī ḳalmışdır ve rütbe-'i kifāyede olacaḳ sefāyiniñ tedārük ve inşā etdirilmesiniñ ṭarīḳ-i imkānı ve vech-i sühūleti nevechle ise ṣūret-i niẓām ve iḳtiżāsı bā taḳrīr ʿarḍ olunmaḳ bābinda firmān-ı ʿālī ṣudūr etmekden nāşī Başmuḥasebe'den ḳeydlerı ladā al-suʾāl Ḥarameyn-i Muḥteremeyn ahālīlerine Ḳāhire-i Mıṣır'dan beher sene muʿtād ül-irsāl olan ğılālıñ naḳl ve tesyīrlerine mahṣūṣ Ḳāhire-i mezbūrede Hāṣṣekiye-i Kubrā Evḳāfı'ndan ḳażā-resīde olan iki kıṭʿa sefīnelere bedel bir kıṭʿasınıñ inşāsı bābında haṭṭ-i hümāyūn ile muʿanven emr-i ʿālī ıṣdār ve Bender-i Süveys'de sefīne inşāsında vücūhla ṣuʿūbet derkār olup vālī-i Mıṣır inhāsıyla ğılāl-ı Ḥarameyn'iñ vaḳt ve zamānıyla naḳliyçün muʿtedil bahā ile ḥāżır ve mevcūd sefīne iştirāsı münāsib görüldügüne bināen defter-i hazīne ladā al-tetebbuʿ sābıḳda dokuz biñ erdeb dahi zīyādeye müteḥammil sefīneler altmış ikişer ve altmış beşer Mıṣrī keyse ile iştirā olunup nihāyeti yetmiş keyseyi tecāvüz etmediği muḳayyed olmaḳdan nāşī evḳāf-ı mezbūre içün sābıḳlarına muḳāyese ile īcāb eden bahāsı irsāliye-i Mıṣır hazīnesinden maḥsūb olmaḳ şartıyla muʿtedil bahā ile sefīne iştirasıyçün."

41. As shown in chapter 1, this was a very old issue throughout the region. So acute was the problem that access to timber has long been assumed to be one of the primary objectives of Meḥmed ʿAlī Paşa's invasion of Syria (something that is evident in the sources of the period, Egyptian, Ottoman, and European). See, for example, the relevant passages in Lawson, *Social Origins*; Fahmy, *All the Pasha's Men*; and Alan Mikhail, *Nature and Empire in Ottoman Egypt: An Environmental History* (Cambridge: Cambridge University Press, 2011).

42. The precise nature and extent of this clause of the treaty have been the subject of significant debate and revision. See notably Roderic Davison, *Essays in Ottoman and Turkish History, 1774–1923* (Austin: University of Texas Press, 1990), chaps. 2 and 3.

43. "Elli dört senesi evāʾil-i Muḥarremi'nde başḳa ve sefāyin kifāyet etmeyüb bir ḳıṭʿası dahiḫi tecdīd olunsa kāfī olduğu muḳaddemen Şerīf-i Mekke-i Mükerreme ṭarafindan Der-i ʿAliye'ye inhā ve iltimās üzere sābiḳī mūcebince īcāb eden bahāsı Ḥulvān-i ḳurā aḳçesinden edā olunmaḳ şartıyla vālī-'i muşārun ileyh maʿrifetiyle Bender-i Süveys'de mevcūd bulunan sefāyin-i Hindiye'den metīn ve müstaḥkem bir ḳıṭʿa sefīne bahāsı ḥadd-i iʿtidāl üzere ḳaṭʿ-ı bāzār ile iştirā ve maḥall-i mezbūr'de ḥāżir sefīne bulunmadığı ḥālde Cidde vālīsi ile haberleşüp Cidde iskelesi'nde mevcūd bulunan merākib-i Hindiye'den bir ḳıṭʿası iştirā olunmaḳ üzere."

44. Azmi Özcan, *Pan-Islamism: Indian Muslims, the Ottomans and Britain, 1877–1924* (Leiden: Brill, 1997), 11.

45. BOA, MMD, 9, 149, 260 (middle of *receb* 1191AH/August 1777)

46. BOA, MMD, 9, 147, 253 (early *receb* 1191AH/August 1777).

47. Cengiz Orhonlu, *Osmanlı İmparatorluğu'nun Güney Siyaseti: Habeş Eyaleti* (1974; repr., Ankara: Türk Tarih Kurumu Basımevi, 1996).

48. See P. M. Holt, review of *Le livre du Soudan*, by Cheykh Muḥammad ibn ʿAlī ibn Zayn al-ʿAbidīn, *Bulletin of the School of Oriental and African Studies* 45, no. 3 (1982): 582–83.

49. John Lewis Burckhardt, *Travels in Nubia* (London: John Murray, 1822).

50. Ibid., 398, 399.

51. Ibid., 281.

52. Ibid., 389.

53. BOA, D.BŞM.d 5213A (1198 AH/1783 CE).

54. Wael Hallaq, "What Is Shari'a?," in *Yearbook of Islamic and Middle Eastern Law*, vol. 12, *2005–2006*, ed. Eugene Cotran and Martin Lau (Leiden: Brill, 2007), 151–80.

55. Will Hanley, "When Did Egyptians Stop Being Ottomans? An Imperial Citizenship Case Study," in *Multilevel Citizenship*, ed. Willem Maas (Philadelphia: University of Pennsylvania Press, 2013), 89–109.

56. Ibid., 107.

57. "Yine sene-ʾi mezbūrede başḳa ve Maḥmūdī taʿbīr olunur ve naḳl-i ğılāla maḥṣūṣ sefāyin-i miriyeden ḳażāen Süveys Limanı'nda şiddet-i rüzgārdan şikest olan sefīneniñ yerine Maḥmūdī nāmıyla sekiz biñ beş yüz erdeb ğılāla müteḥammil vaḍʿ-ı ḳadīmi üzere ʿatīḳ sefīneniñ enḳāż-ı mevcūdesinden başḳa mecmūʿ ālātıyla elli Mıṣrī keyseye vālī ve ḳāżī-ʾi Mıṣır iltimāslarıyla bahāsı irsāliye mālından maḥsūb şarṭıyla keẕālik bir ḳıṭʿa sefīne inşāsıyçün."

58. "Elli yedi senesinde başḳa ve cennet-i mekān Sultan Meḥmed Hān ʿaleyhi-el-raḥmetü ve el-ğufrānıñ Mıṣır'da vāḳıʿ Meḥmediye nām vaḳf-ı şerīfinden Bender-i Süveys'de muḥteriḳ olan bir kitʿa vaḳıf sefīneniñ yerine bahāsı Ḥulvān-i ḳurādan edā olunmaḳ üzere tüccār sefīnelerinden muʿtedil bahā ile bir ḳitʿa sefīne iştirāsıyçün."

59. Tibbetts, "Arab Navigation," 325.

60. Tibbetts, *Arab Navigation*, 249.

61. F. Edwards, "Climate and Oceanography," 49.

62. Strabo, *Geography of Strabo*, vol. 7 (16.4.18), trans. Jones, 345.

63. Ralph Pedersen, "Under the Erythraean Sea: An Ancient Shipwreck in Eritrea," *INA Quarterly* 27, nos. 2/3 (Summer/Fall 2000), 3.

64. "Dahi altmış senesinde başḳa ve naḳl-ı ğilāla maḥṣūṣ sefāyiniñ sebeb-i telefi ladā al-tafaḥḥuṣ vülāt ve aʿyān-ı Mıṣır'ın ṭamʿ-ı hāma tebʿīyet ile nā-ehlī rüşvet ahẕıyla reʾīs naṣb eylemelerinden neşʾet edib."

65. Burckhardt, *Travels in Nubia*, 413.

66. "Onar biñ erdebden ziyādeye müteḥammil bāzargān sefāyininden iki ḳıṭʿa sefīne iştirā ve Mekkī ve Medenī taʿbīriyle sefīne-i Mekkī Mıṣır vālīlerine ve Medenī'si ocağ-ı sebʿaya bā haṭṭ-ı hümāyūn tefvīż ḳılınıb ḥīn-i ʿazīmetlerinden onar biñ erdebden ziyādesi bāzargān ḥamūlesi olmaḳ üzere taḥmīl ve ʿavdetlerinde dahi ḳūl ve tüccār mālı taḥmīl ve iyāb ve ẕihāblarında meʾunet maṣārifleri rüʾyet ve Mıṣır'dan getirdikleri numūneye muvāfıḳ Mekke ve Medīne ḳāżīleri ve Şeyh ül-ḥarem mührüyle memhūr Mıṣır'a nümūne getirib ve ondan dahi Der-i ʿaliyeme irsāl ve şurūṭ-i meẕkūre üzere nā ehl reʾīs naṣbından ḥaẕer olunmaḳ ve eğer telef olmaḳ lāzim gelir ise sefīne-i Mekkī'yi vālī-i Mıṣır ve Medenī'yi yedi ocaḳ tażmīn

eylemek şarṭıyla Mıṣır vālīsi inhāsıyla bā izn-i hümāyūn cedīd ve metīn olmaḳ üzere Bender-i Süveys'de mevcūd tüccār sefīnelerinden iki ḳıṭʿa kebīr sefīne iştirā ve bahāsı māl-ı irsāliyeden maḥsūb içün hüccet-i şerʿiyesi Der-i saʿādetime irsāl olunmaḳ üzere."

67. "Yetmiş dört tārīhinde müteveffā-yi müşārun ileyh Kāmil Aḥmed Paşa'nıñ müddet-i tevlīyetinde dahi başḳa başḳa Dīvān-ı Hümāyūnum tarafından evāmir-i şerīfe verildiği ve yetmiş beş ve yetmiş altı senelerinde Bender-i Süveys iskelesinde ğilāl-ı Ḥarameyn-i Muḥteremeyn naḳlına tahṣīṣan bā irāde-i ʿaliye Ḳāhire-'i Mıṣır'da Ağā Vekīli ʿOs̱mān Ağā maʿrifetiyle cennet-mekān Sulṭān Murād Hān ʿaleyhi el-raḥmet ve el-ğufrān vaḳfından altmış yedi Mıṣrī keyseye bir ḳıṭʿa ve yetmiş ikişer buçuḳ keyse-'i-i Mıṣrī'ye dahi iki ḳıṭʿa miri ḳalyun inşā ve maṣārıfları irsāliye-'i Mıṣır hazīnesinden iʿṭā olunmuş olduğu ve sefāyin-i mezkūre içün seneteyn-i mezkūreteynde Rodus sancağı mutaṣarrif Süleymān Pāşā maʿrifetiyle iḳtiżā eden kerestesi Rodus ve Gökciğez cibālından ḳaṭʿ ve zift ve ḳaṭrān ve reçinesi Ḳāzṭağı ve ḥavālīsinden mubāyaʿa ve Iskenderūn'a baʿd el-naḳl bi'l-cümle maṣārifi olan yirmi altı biñ yüz seksen yedi buçuḳ ğurūş havāleten iʿṭā olunmuş olduğu ve bunlardan mā ʿadā iḳtiżā eden lenger ve til-i ṣāf ve kırpas-i bādbān ve sāʾir ālāt-ı lāzimesi Tersāne'-i ʿĀmire mevcūdundan ve iki biñ ḳinṭār timur-i hām dahi Cebehāne-'i ʿĀmire mevcūdundan tertīb ve sefīnelere taḥmīl birle Iskenderūn'a tesyīr ve mevcūd-ı Cebehāne'den verilenden mā ʿadā iki biñ ḳınṭār timur-i ṣāf Ḳavala ve Preveşte ve Zihne ve ol havālilerinden mübāyaʿa ve Selanik Iskelesi'nden sefīneye taḥmīl ve Rodus'a irsāl [olunmuş]."

68. "Ve altmış tārīhinde mustaḥfiẓān ocağı kethudası maʿrifetiyle yüz kırk beş Mıṣrī keyse maṣārıf ile iki ḳıṭʿa ḳalyun inşā olunmuş." The final conjugated verb here serves as auxiliary for the entire preceding segment as well. The whole passage is connected with the following section by the phrase of conjunction (*olmağla baʿd-ı ezīn*), in the sense of "on the basis of the preceding."

69. "Olmağla baʿd-ı ezīn bu maḳūle sefāyin inşāsi iḳtiżā eyledikde ziyādeye tecāvüz etdirilmemek üzere seksen bir senesinde Dīvān-ı Hümāyūn ṭarafına ʿilm ve haber ḳāʾimesi verildiği Başmuḥāsebe'den ʿalā vech el-hulāṣa derkār olunmağla bu ṣūretde muḳteża-yi vaḳt ve ḥāl inşā-'ı sefāyin tedārükāt-ı mühimmāt ve levāzimāt ile ihtiyār-ı tekellüfātı müʿeddī ve bu emr-i vācib el-ihtimāmıñ temşīyeti dahi aḳdem-i umūrdan idüğü muḥtāc-i beyān olmayıb."

70. "Beher ḥāl tedārük-i sefāyin ve naḳl-ı ğılāl ile fuḳarā-yı ahālī-'i Ḥarameyn-i Muḥteremeyn vāreste-i ḳayd-i mużāyaḳa olmaları lāzime-i şān ve şükūh-ı salṭanat-i ʿaliyemden."

71. Ian Baucom, *Specters of the Atlantic: Finance Capital, Slavery, and the Philosophy of History* (Durham, NC: Duke University Press, 2005), 34.

72. Alasdair MacIntyre, *After Virtue* (1981; repr., Notre Dame, IN: University of Notre Dame Press, 2007), 221–22.

73. Walter Benjamin, "Theses on the Philosophy of History," in *Illuminations*, ed. Hannah Arendt, trans. Harry Zohn (New York: Schocken Books, 1968), 255.

74. Baucom, *Specters of the Atlantic*, 319.

75. Ibid.

76. "Ve sābiḳda olduğu vechle ol cānibde münāsib sefāyin iştirā ve bahāları irsāliye-'i Mıṣır hazīnesi mālından havāleten i'ṭā ve mütefennin rü'esā vaḍ' ve taḥmīl ve teşḥīn-i ğilāl ve iyāb ve zihāblarında me'unet ve maṣārıfları rü'yet ve nümūneleri taṭbīḳ ile şerā'ıt-ı niẓām-ı sābıḳaya ri'āyet ve telef olmaḳ lāzım geldiği ṣūretde tażmīn keyfiyeti dahi icrā etdirilmek üzere Bender-i Süveys'de mevcūd sefāyin-i tüccārdan ḳaç ḳıṭ'a sefāyin iḳtiżā eder ise bahāları sābıḳını tecāvüz etdirmeyerek siz ki vezīr-i muşār ve şayh ül-beled ve yedi ocaḳ żābitānı mūmā ilayhimsiz ma'rifetleriniz ile iştirā ve mübāya'a ve temşīyet huṣūṣuna bi'l-ittifāḳ ihtimām ve diḳḳat eylemeniz içün Dīvān-i Hümāyūnum tarafından emr-i şerīfim taḥrīri bābında bi'l-fi'l bāşdefterdārım olan Ḥasan dāme 'ulūvuhu i'lām etmeğin i'lāmi mūcebince 'amel olunmaḳ bābında fermānım olmağın imdi ber muḳteżā-yı vaḳt ve ḥāl bu emr-i vācıb ül-ihtimāmıñ tanẓīm ve temşīyeti aḳdem-i umūr-i lāzım ül-ihtimam olduğu cihetden beher ḥāl tedārük-i sefāyin ve naḳl-ı ğılāl ile fuḳarā-yı Ḥarameyn-i Muḥteremeyn vāreste-'i ḳayd-i mużāyaḳa ve ihtiyāc olmaları lāzime-' i şān ve şükūh sulṭanat-i 'aliyemden idüğü ma'lūmunuz olduḳda sābıḳlarda olduğu vechle olcānibde münāsib sefīne iştirā ve bahāları irsāliye-'i Mıṣır hazīnesi mālından havāleten i'ṭā ve derūnuna müte'ayyin ve mehāreti ẓāhir rü'esā vaḍ' ve ta'yīn ve teşḥ īn ve taḥmīl-i ğılāl ve iyāb ü zihāblarında me'unet ve maṣārıfları rü'yet ve nümūneleri taṭbīḳ ile şerā'ıt-ı niẓām sābıḳaya ri'āyet ve bi-ḳażā' Allāhi ta'ālā ḳażā-resīde olmaḳ lazım geldiği ṣūretde tażmīn keyfiyeti dahi şürūt-ı ḳadīmesi üzere icrā etdirilmek içün Bender-i Süveys'de mevcūd sefāyin-i tüccārdan ḳaç ḳıṭ'a sefāyiniñ lüzūmu var ise bahāları sābıḳını tecāvüz etmemek vechile iḳtiżāsına göre inżimām-ı re'yī ve ma'rifet ve ihtimāmınız ile iştirā ve mübāya'asına ṣarf-ı vus' ve diḳḳat ve bu bābda muğāyir-i rıżā-yi mülūkānem tekāsül ve tesāhülü tecvīz ile bundan böyle ahāli-'i Beldeteyn-i Münīfeteyn'iñ ğılāl huṣūṣında giriftār-ı mużāyaḳa olmalarından ğāyet ül-ğāye haẕer ve mubā'adet eylemeniz bābında."

77. "Fī evāsıṭı Cā. S 1191."

4. THE SCIENTIFIC INVENTION OF THE RED SEA

1. For one of the rare accounts of the British Mediterranean, see Sakis Gekas, "Colonial Migrants and the Making of a British Mediterranean," *European Review of History* 19, no. 1 (February 2012): 75–92.

2. *Sailing Directions for the Red Sea* was published independently in 1841, and in various formats subsequently, including in the (posthumous) sixth edition of the standard for navigation of the times, James Horsburgh, ed., *The India Directory, or, Directions for Sailing to and from the East Indies, China, Australia, and the Interjacent Ports of Africa and South America*, 6th ed., vol. 1 (London: W.M.H. Allen, 1852), which is used here.

3. Marie-Noëlle Bourguet, Bernard Lepetit, Daniel Nordman, and Maroula Sinarellis, eds., *L'invention scientifique de la Méditerranée—Égypte, Morée, Algérie* (Paris: École des hautes études en sciences sociales, 1998); Anne Ruel, "L'invention de la Méditerranée," *Vingtième Siècle* 32 (October–December 1991): 7.

4. See notably the very detailed Thomas E. Marston, *Britain's Imperial Role in the Red Sea, 1800–1878* (Hamden, CT: Shoe String Press, 1961).

5. See in particular Blumi, *Foundations of Modernity*.

6. Ibid., 35.

7. Ibid.

8. See Bruno Latour and Steve Woolgar, *Laboratory Life: The Construction of Scientific Facts*, 2nd ed. (Princeton, NJ: Princeton University Press, 1986). The first edition (Sage, 1979) had appended the modifier *social* to the word *construction* in the subtitle. In the new postcript of the second edition, the authors explain the "demise of the 'social.'"

9. Ibid., 176. Emphasis in original.

10. Ibid., 180.

11. Ibid.

12. Roland Barthes, "The Reality Effect," in *The Rustle of Language*, trans. Richard Howard (Berkeley: University of California Press, 1989), 141–48.

13. Ibid., 146.

14. Ibid.

15. Michel Foucault, "La vie: L'expérience et la science," in *Dits et écrits*, vol. 4, *1980–1988* (Paris: Gallimard, 1994), 263–76.

16. Lorraine Daston, "The Coming into Being of Scientific Objects," in *Biographies of Scientific Objects*, ed. Lorraine Daston (Chicago: University of Chicago Press, 2000), 1. Subsequent page citations to this work are given parenthetically in the text.

17. J. L. Austin, *How to Do Things with Words* (Oxford: Clarendon Press, 1962); Ian Hacking, *Representing and Intervening* (Cambridge: Cambridge University Press, 1983).

18. Dominick LaCapra, "Rethinking Intellectual History and Reading Texts," *History and Theory* 19, no. 3 (October 1980): 252. The parallel to Austin's construction is acknowledged in the footnote.

19. Ibid., 52.

20. This is equally true of artistic objects, something W. J. T. Mitchell has tirelessly taught, as in the case of landscape, for example, which he seeks to change "from a noun to a verb" so that it may be thought "as a process by which social and subjective identities are formed." *Landscape and Power*, ed. W. J. T. Mitchell (Chicago: University of Chicago Press, 2002), 1.

21. Timothy Mitchell, *Colonising Egypt* (1988; repr., Cambridge: Cambridge University Press, 1991). See also Derek Gregory, "Scripting Egypt: Orientalism and the Cultures of Travel," in *Writes of Passage: Reading Travel Writing*, ed. James Duncan and Derek Gregory (London: Routledge, 1999), 114–50.

22. Edward Said, *Culture and Imperialism* (New York: Vintage Books, 1994), 225. Emphasis mine.

23. On this point, see especially Gyan Prakash, "Science 'Gone Native' in Colonial India," *Representations* 40 (1992): 153–78.

24. On such semantic genealogies, see Daston, "Coming into Being," 4.

25. Matthew Edney, *Mapping an Empire: The Geographical Construction of British India, 1769–1843* (Chicago: University of Chicago Press, 1997), 21, 319–20.

26. Ibid., 2.

27. See, for example, NA, FO 1/1: Abyssinia/Lord Valentia and Mr Salt, September 1808 to December 1813.

28. Clements Markham, *A Memoir of the Indian Surveys* (London: W. H. Allen, 1871), 1.

29. Ibid., 6.

30. Ibid. Valentia begins the second volume of his travels with precisely this point of the astounding ignorance of the shores of the Red Sea on the part of British surveyors, using identical language ("perfect blank in our charts") as Markham's reconstituted exchange between him and Wellesley in Calcutta. George Annesley Valentia, *Voyages and Travels to India, Ceylon, the Red Sea, Abyssinia and Egypt, in the Years 1802, 1803, 1804, 1805, and 1806* (London: F., C., and J. Rivington, 1881), 2:2. This second edition was supplemented by a fourth volume of maps.

31. Markham, *Memoir,* 9.

32. Ibid., 10.

33. For his letters of appointment as consul general in Egypt, see the opening texts of FO 24/1. For an introduction to this interesting character, see Rosemarie Said Zahlan, "George Baldwin: Soldier of Fortune?," in *Travellers in Egypt,* ed. Paul and Janet Starkey (New York: I. B. Tauris, 2001), 24–38.

34. See BL, IOR/G/17/5, much of which concerns issues relating to the general theme.

35. England declared war against France when it signed treaties of alliance and amity with the newborn United States of America during the Revolutionary War.

36. George Baldwin, *Political Recollections Relative to Egypt* (London: W. Bulmer, 1802), 23–24. This is a composite text, containing documents of different types written at various points over the preceding two decades.

37. See, for example, NA, FO 78/1 (Turkey. To and From Robert Ainslie, 1780), and BL, IOR/G/17/5, where the issue is recurrent.

38. This is evident in the 1772 document "French Memorandum on India" (NA, SP 78/284), and even more explicitly in the "Report and Minutes by Sir James Outram on French Designs in the Red Sea" of 1862 (NA, FO 881/1100, with supplement volume, WO 106/6234).

39. Certainly the Porte constantly disavowed such treaties when confronted by the British ambassador to Constantinople, Robert Ainslie. See "Sir Robert Ainslie's Extracts Concerning the French Establishment in Egypt," in BL, IOR/G/17/5, pp. 131–34. The Ottomans suggested to the British that they use Ottoman ships for transport and communication, which would be made available when needed.

40. A draft of the royal appointment signed "Carmarthen" opens the volume of NA, FO 24/1, pp. 3–6. The ascriptions are added in the margin of p. 3b.

41. The letter is signed Dundas, Wallingham, Grenville, and Mulgrave and is dated Whitehall, May 19, 1786 (NA, FO 24/1, pp. 9–17).

42. Ibid., 9.

43. Ibid.

44. BOA, MMD, 9, 150, 261 (middle of *Receb* 1191 AH/mid-August 1777 CE).

45. NA, SP 78/284, pp. 212–33 (the memorandum itself is dated 1767 CE, but the letter to which it was annexed is dated March 10, 1772 CE).

46. "Lettre du général Bonaparte au directoire exécutif, en date de Milan le 16 août 1797," partially reproduced in Le Baron I. de Testa, *Recueil des traités de la Porte Ottomane,* vol. 1 (Paris: Amyot, 1864), 516. This quote is also cited in Halford Hoskins, *British Routes to India* (1928; repr., London: Frank Cass, 1966), 55.

47. Wm. Laird Clowes, *The Royal Navy: A History, from the Earliest Times to the Present* (London: Sampson Low, Martons and Cie, 1899), 4:405–6.

48. BOA, C.HR 6/287 (10 *Cumādā I* 1215/29 September 1800, according to the catalogue).

49. Clowes, *Royal Navy,* 4:457. The Ottoman sultan rewarded the English troops, including the "navy admiral who came to Suez," with a variety of lavish furs as ceremonial presents (*teşrīfāt*); see BOA, C.DH 132/6577 (15 *Rebīʿ II* 1216 AH /25 August 1801).

50. Henry Popham, *Concise Statement of Facts* (London: John Stockdale, 1805), 82.

51. Ibid., 26–27.

52. *Eclectic Review* 1, pt. 1 (January–June 1805): 73.

53. Popham, *Concise Statement,* 85.

54. Ibid., 63.

55. Valentia, *Voyages and Travels,* 3:252–53.

56. Ibid.

57. To these possessions would be added, in due time, Cyprus (1878) and then Egypt itself (1882). For an illuminating work of colonial geography of colonization, see C. P. Lucas, *A Historical Geography of the British Colonies,* vol. 1, *The Mediterranean and Eastern Colonies,* 2nd ed., rev. R. E. Stubbs (Oxford: Clarendon Press, 1906).

58. "Lettre du général Bonaparte au directoire exécutif, en date de Milan le 16 août 1797," partially reproduced in de Testa, *Recueil des traités,* 516.

59. "Lettre du général Bonaparte au ministre des relations extérieures, en date du quartier-général de Passariano le 13 septembre 1797," partially reproduced in ibid., 516.

60. There are two volumes at the British National Archives entirely devoted to the subject of Egyptian "claims to sovereignty in the Red Sea, Africa, and Arabia" (NA, FO 78/3185 and FO78/3186), which speak to British anxiety regarding Meḥmed ʿAlī's menace to the Red Sea. The series begins with a letter from Consul Henry Salt from Alexandria in 1825, which mentions rumors in Mocha and Aden of an Egyptian invasion. Such a fear is made even more explicit and indeed public in Captain James Mackenzie's published account of his trip to the region in 1837, which advocated the immediate conquest of Aden, "whose noble harbours would be of the greatest benefit to us in the prosecution of our Indian steam navigation plans." "One thing is certain," warned Mackenzie, "either Mohammed Ali, or some other powerful state, will

take possession of Aden, and all the other sea-ports in that quarter." James Mackenzie, "Egypt and Arabia," *Literary Gazette; and Journal of Belles Lettres, Arts, Sciences, &c.* (London), no. 1072, August 5, 1837, 490. See also more largely R. J. Gavin, *Aden under British Rule, 1839–1967* (London: C. Hurst, 1975).

61. Anthony Webster, "The Political Economy of Trade Liberalization," *Economic History Review* 43, no. 3 (1990): 411.

62. Andrew Cook, "Establishing the Sea Route to India and China: Stages in the Development of Hydrographical Knowledge," in *The Worlds of the East India Company*, ed. H. V. Bowen, Margarette Lincoln, and Nigel Rigby (Woodbridge: Boydell Press, 2002), 135.

63. Hoskins, *British Routes*, 187.

64. Ibid., 188.

65. Ibid.

66. Markham, *Memoir*, 14.

67. Ibid.

68. Horsburgh, *India Directory*, 278.

69. Daston, "Coming into Being," 13.

70. Markham, *Memoir*, 14.

71. *The Red Sea and Gulf of Aden Pilot,* 5th ed. (London: Hydrographic Office, 1900), iii.

72. Horsburgh, *India Directory*, 312.

73. Barthélémy St-Hilaire, cited in Hoskins, *British Routes*, 188 n. 15.

74. James Wellsted, *Travels in Arabia,* 2 vols. (London: John Murray, 1838). Wellsted also published numerous articles in the *Journal of the Royal Geographical Society* derived from his time on the Red Sea survey.

75. Markham, *Memoir*, 14–15.

76. *Red Sea and Gulf of Aden Pilot,* 5th ed., 2. In later editions, the comparative judgment is excised, but not the reference to reefs as being constitutional to the Red Sea. See, for example, *The Red Sea and Gulf of Aden Pilot,* 16th ed. (London: Hydrographic Office, 2009), 17.

77. Derek Matthews, "The Red Sea Style," *Kush* 1 (1953): 60–86. Specimens from Sawakin were beautifully sketched by Jean-Pierre Greenlaw in *The Coral Buildings of Suakin* (London: Oriel Press, 1976).

78. Horsburgh, *India Directory*, 347.

79. Alexander Brownlie, "Varieties of Tides: The Red Sea Variety," *Bulletin of the American Geographical Society* 35, no. 1 (1903): 17–23. *Red Sea and Gulf of Aden Pilot*, 16th ed., 17, also speaks of the "great variability of the currents within [*sic*] Red Sea."

80. *Red Sea and Gulf of Aden Pilot,* 5th ed., 2.

81. George Buist, "On the Physical Geography of the Red Sea," *Journal of the Royal Geographical Society of London* 24 (1854): 227–38.

82. Horsburgh, *India Directory*, 309.

83. Ibid., 316.

84. Ibid., 335.

85. Wellsted, *Travels in Arabia,* 2:141.

86. Ibid., 258.

87. Buist, "On the Physical Geography," 229.

88. The reference must be to C. G. Ehrenberg, also a pioneering scientist of the Red Sea, who addressed the question of the observation throughout history of red waters before adding and explaining his own observations of the redness of the Red Sea in a two-part article entitled "New Observations on the Blood-like Phenomena Observed in Egypt, Arabia, and Siberia; with a View and Critique of the Early Accounts of Similar Appearances," in *The Edinburgh New Philosophical Journal, Exhibiting a View of the Progressive Discoveries and Improvements in the Sciences and the Arts . . . October 1830 . . . April 1831,* ed. Robert Jameson (Edinburgh: Adam Black, 1831), 122–36 and 341–52.

89. M. W. Duckett, *Dictionnaire de la conversation et de la lecture,* vol. 15 (Paris: Comptoirs de la Direction, 1857), 567.

90. Sarah Hoyt, "The Name of the Red Sea," *Journal of the American Oriental Society* 32, no. 2 (1912): 115–19.

91. Robert Young, *Colonial Desire: Hybridity in Theory, Culture and Race* (London: Routledge, 1995), 173–74.

92. Horsburgh, *India Directory*, 279.

93. Ibid.

94. See Gary Leiser, "The Crusader Raid in the Red Sea in 578, 1182/83," *Journal of the American Research Center in Egypt* 14 (1977): 87–100.

95. Ibid., 94.

96. Ibid., 94, 87.

97. Horsburgh, *India Directory*, 347.

98. Ibid., 281.

99. For Mitchell's analysis, see especially the chapter "The Character of Calculability," in Mitchell, *Rule of Experts*, 80–122.

100. Horsburgh, *India Directory*, 343.

101. Ibid.

102. Wellsted, *Travels in Arabia,* 2:116.

103. Ibid.

104. Horsburgh, *India Directory*, 347. Subsequent page citations to this work will be given parenthetically in the text.

105. Wellsted, *Travels in Arabia*, 2:246.

106. *Sailing Directions for the Red Sea and the Gulf of Aden* (Washington, DC: Government Printing Office, 1943), 16.

107. Wellsted, *Travels in Arabia,* 2:294.

108. Daniel Headrick, *The Tentacles of Progress: Technology Transfer in the Age of Imperialism, 1850–1940* (Oxford: Oxford University Press, 1988), 24.

109. Horsburgh, *India Directory*, 278.

110. BOA, Y.EE 42/144 (April 21, 1841).

111. "Biñ sekiz yüz otuz dört tārīḫ-i mīlādiyesinde Hindistan'de riyāle bulunan Elvon nām amirallık mesāḥe eyttiği Baḥr-ı Aḥmer harīṭasınıñ ʿaīnī olaraḳ

bi'l-tercüme mekteb-i baḥriye ḥażret-i şāhāne'de resm olunmuş harīṭadır." BOA, HRT.h 717.

112. The Ottoman map closely resembles but is not identical to the maps by Moresby and Elwon in the British archives, NA, FO 925/3018, "Chart of the Red Sea Comprising Part above Jiddah, Surveyed by Cmdr Moresby and Lt. Carless," and FO 925/286, "Map of the Red Sea, Surveyed by Cpt Elwon and Others, 1830–34."

113. On this matter, see especially the imperial decree sent to the vālī of Egypt concerning the creation of the company in BOA, MM 15, 48–9, 22 (middle of *Rebī' I* 1272 AH/late November 1855 CE), as well as the collection of documents BOA, İ.MMS 28/1205 (1280–1283 AH/1864–1866 CE), which contains letters exchanged between the Sublime Porte in Istanbul and the governorship of Egypt. The documents further specify the setting as such: "Baḥr-ı Aḥmer'de vāḳı' banāder ve sevāhil-i Hicāziye ve Yemāniye ile Muṣavva' ve Sevākin ve Ḳuṣeyr ṭaraflarina ve Baṣra körfüzüne islettirilmek üzere bir vapur kumpaniyası teşkīlī muḥsenāttan olacağına ve huccāc ẕu ul-ibtihāc naḳl ve īsālında dahi teshīlāt-ı kulliyeyi istilzām eyliyeceğine." Already a few years earlier (1268 AH/1852 CE), an Indian merchant had brought up the idea of a steam connection between Suez and Jiddah to the imperial court, spurring extended bureaucratic discussions on the matter involving the Red Sea (*Baḥr-ı Aḥmer*). See BOA, İ.MVL 265/10084.

114. Nubar Paşa claimed paternity of the idea of launching an Egyptian steamboat company; see Nubar Nubarian, *Mémoires de Nubar Pacha* (Beyrouth: Librairie du Liban, 1983), 159–62.

115. See Gülden Sarıyıldız, "Misirda Kurulan Mecidiye Vapur Kumpanyasi ve Faaliyetleri," *Türk Kültürü Incelemeleri Dergisi* 9 (2003): 17–36.

116. This is the crux of the command sent to the elites of Cairo reproduced in BOA, MM, 9, 190–91, 331 (dated the beginning of *Ẕi'l-ḥicce* 1192 AH/late December 1778), that will be cited and paraphrased directly in the text. It is not an isolated document; rather, it forms part of a common trope that develops a connection between knowledge, trade, and colonization in Ottoman public discourse of the time.

117. This story has been a staple of both Western and Ottoman accounts of the voyage of Vasco da Gama from the very beginning. The sixteenth-century chronicler of the Ottoman conquest of Yemen Qutb al-Dīn al-Nahrawālī famously accused the great navigator Aḥmad ibn Mājīd of being the culprit who, in a state of inebriation, showed the Portuguese the way across the sea, though recent scholars have denied the connection.

118. Another city is mentioned, though its precise spelling is unclear.

119. The numbers of Egyptian laborers involved vary greatly. Use of the *corvée* was eventually stopped in mid-1864, after Ismā'īl came to power. On the question of forced labor in the making of the canal, see 'Abd al-'Azīz Muḥammad al-Shinnawī, *al-Sukhra fi ḥafr qanāt al-Suez* (Cairo: al-Hai'a al-misriyya al-'āmma lil-kitāb, 2002).

120. In terms of regional trade, sailboats remained important well into the twentieth century: they required a smaller initial capital outlay, their schedule was flexible, their source of energy was free and available everywhere. In the words of the

pilot with whom Alan Villiers sailed in the late 1930s: "Allah is great and merciful and His winds are free. Therefore His faithful use them." Villiers's informants estimated "the total fleet of seagoing Arab craft" in 1939–40 to be in the range of 2,000 to 2,500. Alan Villiers, *Sons of Sindbad* (1940; repr., New York: Charles Scribner's Sons, 1969), xx.

121. For the place of the Suez Canal in the history of technology, commerce, and imperialism, see Headrick, *Tentacles of Progress*, especially chap. 2.

122. The history of the Suez Canal from the Ottoman standpoint remains to be written, though the idea of a canal joining the seas (most often via the Nile) has a long presence in Ottoman public discourse (Evliya Çelebi speaks about this, for example), and the eventual project itself was much discussed in Istanbul, as evidenced by the extensive documentation about it in the archives.

123. Marwan Buheiry, "Colonial Scholarship and Muslim Revivalism in 1900," *Arab Studies Quarterly* 4, nos. 1–2 (1982): 3.

124. Valeska Huber, *Channelling Mobilities: Migration and Globalization in the Suez Canal Region and Beyond, 1869–1914* (Cambridge: Cambridge University Press, 2013), 3.

125. Ibid.

126. On Barak, *On Time: Technology and Temporality in Modern Egypt* (Berkeley: University of California Press, 2013).

127. Ibid., 40.

128. Pierre Crabitès, *Ismail, the Maligned Khedive* (London: George Routledge and Sons, 1933), 9.

129. Quoted in ibid., 263.

130. See, for example, Barak, *On Time*, 61. The phrase appears in Lord Cromer's foundational (though tendentious) *Modern Egypt,* in the context of a speech in 1878 by the Khedive addressed to Sir River Wilson, member of the Commission of Inquiry sent to regulate the payment of Egyptian debt. Cromer attributes authorship of the speech to Nubar Paşa. See Evelyn Baring Cromer, *Modern Egypt* (New York: Macmillan, 1908), 1:62.

5. THALASSOMANIA

1. Lewis, "Dividing the Ocean Sea," 188.

2. Ibid.

3. Ibid.

4. Ian Hacking, *The Social Construction of What?* (Cambridge, MA: Harvard University Press, 1999), 21–22. Subsequent page citations to this work are given parenthetically in the text.

5. Michael Herzfeld, "Practical Mediterraneanism: Excuses for Everything, from Epistemology to Eating," in *Rethinking the Mediterranean*, ed. W. V. Harris (Oxford: Oxford University Press, 2005), 62. The problem of "Mediterraneanism," which he coined in conscious echo to Edward Said's Orientalism, has been a

long-standing theme of Herzfeld's work. See, notably, his *Anthropology through the Looking-Glass: Critical Ethnographies in the Margins of Europe* (Cambridge: Cambridge University Press, 1987).

6. Herzfeld, "Practical Mediterraneanism," 47.

7. Ibid., 50. The reference is to J. L. Austin's *How To Do Things with Words.*

8. Herzfeld, "Practical Mediterraneanism."

9. Michel Foucault, *The Order of Things: An Archaeology of the Human Sciences* (New York: Vintage Books, 1994).

10. Richard Tuck, "Grotius and Selden," in *The Cambridge History of Political Thought, 1450–1700*, ed. J.H. Burns (Cambridge: Cambridge University Press, 1991), 509.

11. Hugo Grotius, *Commentary on the Law of Prize and Booty* (Indianapolis, IN: Liberty Fund, 2006), 23.

12. Ibid.

13. Hugo Grotius, *The Free Sea* (Indianapolis, IN: Liberty Fund, 2004), 24.

14. Ibid., 25.

15. Ibid., 30.

16. Ibid.

17. Ibid., 32.

18. John Locke, *Second Treatise of Government* (Indianapolis, IN: Hackett, 1980), 22, 20.

19. "Homme libre, toujours tu chériras la mer! / La mer est ton miroir; tu contemples ton âme / Dans le déroulement infini de sa lame, / Et ton esprit n'est pas un gouffre moins amer." In *Les fleurs du mal*, trans. Richard Howard (Boston: David Godine, 1982), 22–23 (English), 200 (French). The sonnet, entitled "Man and sea," then goes crescendo in lyrical tension, reaching a climax with the final line: "Oh implacable brothers and eternal foes!" ("Ô lutteurs éternels, ô frères implacables").

20. Adam Smith, *An Inquiry into the Nature and Causes of the Wealth of Nations,* vol. 1 (Indianapolis, IN: Liberty Classics, 1981), 32. Subsequent page citations to this work are given parenthetically in the text.

21. Richard Cantillon, *Essai sur la nature du commerce* (London: Macmillan, 1931). Seemingly written around 1730, it quickly became famous but was not published until 1755.

22. Adam Smith, *Lectures on Jurisprudence* (Indianapolis, IN: Liberty Fund, 1982), 408.

23. Ibid.

24. Ibid., 409.

25. Jean-Marc Drouin, "Bory de Saint-Vincent et la géographie botanique," in *L'invention scientifique de la Méditerranée—Égypte, Morée, Algérie*, ed. Marie-Noëlle Bourguet et al. (Paris: École des hautes études en sciences sociales, 1998), 153.

26. Cited in ibid., 152.

27. Bory de Saint-Vincent, entry "Mer," in *Dictionnaire classique d'histoire naturelle,* vol. 10 (Paris: Rey et Gravier, 1826), 380. Subsequent page citations to this work are given parenthetically in the text.

28. Bory de Saint-Vincent, *Relation du voyage de la commission scientifique de Morée dans le Péloponnèse, les Cyclades et l'Attique* (Paris: F.-G. Levrault, 1836), 1:42. The term *Mediterranean* reappears abundantly throughout the text as the primary unit to define the flora of Morea.

29. Drouin, "Bory de Saint-Vincent," 156.

30. See the quotes by Nicolas Desmarest and Alexander von Humboldt cited by Marie-Noëlle Bourguet in "De la Méditerranée," in Bourguet et al., *L'invention scientifique*, 8 n. 3.

31. *LPH*, 92. Subsequent page citations to this work are given parenthetically in the text.

32. *LPWH*, 190–91.

33. Hegel, *Philosophy of Mind*, 41.

34. Ibid., 46.

35. Robert F. Brown and Peter C. Hodgson, "Editorial Introduction" to *Lectures on the Philosophy of World History*, vol. 1, *Manuscripts of the Introduction and the Lectures of 1822–3*, by G. W. F. Hegel, ed. and trans. Robert F. Brown and Peter C. Hodgson with the assistance of William G. Geuss (Oxford: Oxford University Press, 2011), 191 n. 55. The actual reference to Ritter appears on 195 n. 62.

36. William Gage, *Life of Carl Ritter* (New York: Charles Scribner, 1858), 238.

37. Cited in John Leighly, "Methodologic Controversy in Nineteenth Century German Geography," *Annals of the Association of American Geographers* 28, no. 4 (1938): 242–43.

38. Cited in ibid., 245–46.

39. Gage, *Life of Carl Ritter*, 208.

40. Leighly, "Methodologic Controversy," 241.

41. Carl Ritter, "The Historical Element in Geography as a Science," in *Geographical Studies*, trans. William L. Gage (Boston: Gould and Lincoln, 1863), 241–77.

42. Ibid.

43. Carl Ritter, "Introductory Essay to General Comparative Geography," in *Geographical Studies*, 77.

44. Ibid., 71.

45. Carl Ritter, "The Geographical Position and Horizontal Extension of the Continents," in *Geographical Studies*, 201–2.

46. Ibid.

47. Ibid.

48. Ibid., 203.

49. Strictly speaking, this unit only took on that title in 1844. Before then, it had been called the Navy's Depot of Charts and Instruments; after 1854, it became known as the Naval Observatory and Hydrographical Office; in 1866, the Hydrographical Office gained independence and was separated from the Naval Observatory. See John Leighly, introduction to *The Physical Geography of the Sea, and Its Meteorology*, by Matthew Fontaine Maury (Cambridge, MA: Harvard University Press, 1963), xi.

50. The use of the term *oceanography* here is anachronistic, as it emerged only in the last decades of the century. Maury's book was such a bestseller that scholars have difficulty tracing the avalanche of its re-editions and translations. See Leighly, introduction to Maury, *Physical Geography*, xiii–xv.

51. Maury, *Physical Geography*, 6. Humboldt then returned the nod of appreciation by lauding Maury's book as the founding statement of a new science.

52. S.A. Mitchell, "Obituary: Matthew Fontaine Maury," *Science* 73, no. 1902 (1931): 633.

53. Leighly, introduction to Maury, *Physical Geography*, xxviii.

54. Leighly, "Methodologic Controversy."

55. See Leighly, introduction to Maury, *Physical Geography*, xxvi.

56. Ibid., xi.

57. Charles Vevier, "American Continentalism: An Idea of Expansion, 1845–1910," *American Historical Review* 65, no. 2 (January 1960): 328.

58. First published in 1890 by Little, Brown in Boston, it was immensely popular and influential and has been through many re-editions since.

59. Captain A.T. Mahan, *The Influence of Sea Power upon History, 1660–1783* (London: Sampson Low, Marston, Searle, and Rivington, 1890), 25.

60. Ibid., 33.

61. Ibid., 34–35. Emphasis added.

62. Christopher L. Connery, "Ideologies of Land and Sea: Alfred Thayer Mahan, Carl Schmitt, and the Shaping of Global Myth Elements," *boundary 2* 28, no. 2 (2001): 185.

63. Ibid., 186.

64. Jules Michelet, *La mer* (Paris: Michel Lévy Frères, 1875). The French version consulted here is the fifth edition, published a mere fourteen years after the original one.

65. Quoted in Darby, "On the Relations," 2.

66. For insightful discussion of *La mer* and its style, see Linda Orr, *Jules Michelet: Nature, History, Language* (Ithaca, NY: Cornell University Press, 1976), 156.

67. Jules Michelet, *The Sea,* trans. W.H.D. Adams (London: T. Nelson and Sons, 1875), 39. Subsequent page citations to this work are given parenthetically in the text.

68. Cf. Michelet, *Mer,* 19.

69. Cf. ibid., 35.

70. The sublime lyricism and raw power of Michelet's style are untranslatable (ibid., 129–30).

71. Michelet had in fact used the first-person singular, making the phrase even more personal, individual, soulful: "L'Océan respire comme moi, il concorde à mon mouvement intérieur, à celui d'en haut" (ibid., 21).

72. J.H. Hexter, "Fernand Braudel and the *Monde Braudellien,*" *Journal of Modern History* 44, no. 4 (December 1972): 480–539; Paul Ricoeur, *Time and Narrative,* 3 vols., trans. Kathleen McLaughlin and David Pellauer (Chicago: University of Chicago Press, 1990), 1:216.

73. Fernand Braudel, ed., *La Méditerranée: L'espace et l'histoire* (1977; repr., Paris: Flammarion, 1985).

74. Matvejevic, *Mediterranean*. For example, he often speaks of the "Mediterranean flavor" of a town.

75. Fernand Braudel, "Méditerranée," in Braudel, *Méditerranée*, 10.

76. Fernand Braudel, "L'aube," in Braudel, *Méditerranée*, 83.

77. Fernand Braudel, "L'histoire," in Braudel, *Méditerranée*, 157–58.

78. Fernand Braudel, "Méditerranée," in Braudel, *Méditerranée*, 29–30. The use of ethnographic data is also very present in Braudel, *Mediterranean*, with, notably, references to Carlo Levi, Lawrence Durrell, Gabriele Audisio, and Jean Giono.

79. Braudel, "L'histoire," 157–58.

80. Ibid.

81. Ibid., 160. His empirical examples ("Where they were at the time of Caesar or Augustus, there they remain at the time of Mustapha Kemal or Colonel Nasser") are sometimes truly astounding.

82. Ibid., 158–59.

83. Fernand Braudel, "La terre," in Braudel, *Méditerranée*, 41.

84. Braudel, "L'histoire," 159–60.

85. From the translator's preface to Carl Ritter, "De la configuration des continents sur la surface du globe et de leurs fonctions dans l'histoire," *Revue Germanique* (1859): 241–67.

86. Abā al-Ḥasan ʿAlī al-Masʿūdī, *Murūj al-dhahab wa maʿādin al-jawhar*, ed. K. Ḥ. Murʿī (Beirut: Al-Maktaba al-ʿaṣriyya, 2005), 98. The available English translation, *El-Masudi's Historical Encylopaedia Entitled "Meadows of Gold and Mines of Gems,"* trans. Aloys Sprenger (London: Oriental Translation Fund, 1841), 297, is incorrect on this passage.

87. C. Edmund Bosworth, "The Nomenclature of the Persian Gulf," *Iranian Studies* 30, nos. 1–2 (Winter–Spring 1997): 86.

88. Fernand Braudel, *La Méditerranée et le monde méditerranéen à l'époque de Philippe II*, vol. 1, *La part du milieu* (1966; repr., Paris: Armand Colin, 1990), 202.

89. Braudel, *Mediterranean*, 1:169.

CONCLUSION

Section epigraphs: Derek Walcott, *Collected Poems, 1948–1984* (London: Faber and Faber, 1992): 364; Raymond Queneau, *Le voyage en Grèce* (Paris: Gallimard, 1973), quoted in Oulipo, *Atlas de littérature potentielle* (Paris: Gallimard, 1981), 57; and Braudel, *Mediterranean*, 1:13.

1. Pierre Hadot, *Philosophy as a Way of Life* (Malden, MA: Blackwell, 1995).

2. Erlend Rogne, "The Aim of Interpretation Is to Create Perplexity in the Face of the Real: Hayden White in Conversation with Erlend Rogne," *History and Theory* 48 (February 2009): 63–75.

3. See Bernhard Klein and Gesa Mackenthum, "Introduction: The Sea Is History," in *Sea Changes: Historicizing the Ocean*, ed. Bernhard Klein and Gesa Mackenthum (New York: Routledge, 2004); and Baucom, *Specters of the Atlantic.*

4. Derek Walcott, "The Sea Is History," in *Frontiers of Caribbean Literature in English*, ed. Frank Birbalsingh (New York: St. Martin's Press, 1996), 22.

5. Fernand Braudel, *Identity of France,* trans. Siân Reynolds (London: Fontana Press, 1989–90).

6. Peregrine Horden and Nicholas Purcell, *The Corrupting Sea: A Study of Mediterranean History* (Malden, MA: Blackwell, 2000), 2. Emphasis in original.

7. Ibid., 3.

8. Ibid.

9. Faruk Tabak, *The Waning of the Mediterranean, 1550–1870: A Geohistorical Approach* (Baltimore: Johns Hopkins University Press, 2008).

10. Ibid., 1.

11. Edney, *Mapping an Empire*, 21.

12. Jorge Luis Borges, "On Exactitude in Science," in *Collected Fictions* (New York: Penguin Books, 1998), 325.

13. Umberto Eco, *How to Travel with a Salmon and Other Essays* (Orlando, FL: Harcourt Brace, 1994), 101.

14. Barthes, "Reality Effect."

15. Nancy Partner, "The Form of the Content," *History and Theory* 37, no. 2 (May 1998): 171.

16. Both the 1949 and the 1966 editions were published in French by Armand Colin in Paris. The book has since been republished numerous times, in various formats. A celebrated English translation by Siân Reynolds appeared in two volumes in 1972 with Harper and Row in New York.

17. Horden and Purcell, "Mediterranean," 724. Braudel was already conscious of the life of its own that his book had taken by the time of the second edition: "This book has been in circulation now for almost twenty years: it has been quoted, challenged, criticized (too seldom) and praised (too often)." Braudel, *Mediterranean,* 2:1238.

18. Braudel, *Mediterranean,* 1:19.

19. Ibid., 2:1265.

20. Ibid., 1:14.

21. Hans Kellner, "Disorderly Conduct: Braudel's Mediterranean Satire," *History and Theory* 18, no. 2 (May 1979): 217.

BIBLIOGRAPHY

Agatharchides of Cnidus. *On the Erythraean Sea*. Edited and translated by Stanley Burnstein. London: Haklyut Society, 1989.

Agius, Dionisius A. *Classic Ships of Islam: From Mesopotamia to the Indian Ocean*. Leiden: Brill, 2008.

Aksan, Virginia. "Theoretical Ottomans." *History and Theory* 47 (February 2008): 109–22.

Althusser, Louis, and Etienne Balibar. *Reading "Capital."* London: NLB, 1970.

Anscombe, Frederick. *The Ottoman Gulf: The Creation of Kuwait, Saudi Arabia and Qatar*. New York: Columbia University Press, 1997.

Arrian. *The Anabasis of Alexander, or, The History of the Wars and Conquests of Alexander the Great*. Translated by E.J. Chinnock. London: Hodder and Stroughton, 1883.

Asad, Talal. "The Concept of Cultural Translation in British Social Anthropology." In *Writing Culture: The Poetics and Politics of Ethnography*, edited by James Clifford and George Marcus, 141–64. Berkeley: University of California Press, 1986.

Austin, J. L. *How to Do Things with Words*. Oxford: Clarendon Press, 1962.

Bachelard, Gaston. *The Poetics of Space*. Translated by Maria Jolas. Boston: Beacon Press, 1994.

Bacqué-Grammont, Jean-Louis. "Autour des premières mentions du café dans les sources ottomanes." In *Le commerce du café avant l'ère des plantations coloniales*, edited by Michel Tuchscherer, 17–21. Cairo: Institut français d'archéologie orientale, 2001.

Bacqué-Grammont, Jean-Louis, and Anne Kroell. *Mamlouks, Ottomans et Portugais en mer Rouge: L'affaire de Djedda en 1517*. Cairo: Institut français d'archéologie orientale, 1988.

Bailyn, Bernard. *The Idea of Atlantic History*. Cambridge, MA: Harvard University Press, 2005.

Baldwin, George. *Political Recollections Relative to Egypt*. London: W. Bulmer, 1802.

Barak, On. *On Time: Technology and Temporality in Modern Egypt*. Berkeley: University of California Press, 2013.

Barros, João de. *Da Asía de João de Barros—Dos feitos, que os Portuguezes fizeram no descubrimento, e conquista dos mares, e terras do Oriente. Decada Secunda. Parte Secunda.* 1553. Reprint, Lisbon: Regia Oficina Typografica, 1777.

Barthes, Roland. "The Reality Effect." In *The Rustle of Language,* translated by Richard Howard, 141–48. Berkeley: University of California Press, 1989.

Başbakanlık Devlet Arşivleri Genel Müdürlüğu. *Başbakanlık Osmanlı Arşivi Rehberi.* Istanbul, 2010.

Bāshā, Ḥasan al-. *Al-Alqāb al-Islāmiyya fi al-tārīkh wa al-wathā᾽iq wa al-āthār.* Cairo: Maktabat al-nahḍa al-miṣriyya, 1957.

Baucom, Ian. *Specters of the Atlantic: Finance Capital, Slavery and the Philosophy of History.* Durham, NC: Duke University Press, 2005.

Baudelaire, Charles. *Les fleurs du mal.* French and English text. Translated by Richard Howard. Boston: David Godine, 1982.

Bayyūmī, Muḥammad ʿAlī Fahīm. *Mukhaṣṣaṣāt al-ḥaramayn al-sharīfayn fi Miṣr ibān al-ʿaṣr al-ʿuthmānī fī al-fatra min 923–1220h/1517–1805m.* Cairo: Dār al-Qāhira li-l-kitāb, 2001.

Bayyūmī, Ṭariq ʿAbd al-ʿĀṭī Ghunaym. *Siyāsat Miṣr fī al-Baḥr al-ʾAḥmar fī al-niṣf al-awwal min al-qarn al-tāsiʿ ʿashar.* Cairo: Al-haiʾa al-miṣriyya al-ʿāmma lil-kitāb, 1999.

Benjamin, Walter. "Theses on the Philosophy of History." In *Illuminations,* edited by Hannah Arendt, translated by Harry Zohn, 253–67. New York: Schocken Books, 1968.

Blue, Lucy. "The Red Sea." In *The Oxford Handbook of Maritime Archaeology,* edited by Alexis Catsambia, Ben Ford, and Donny L. Hamilton, 495–512. Oxford: Oxford University Press, 2011.

Blumi, Isa. *Foundations of Modernity: Human Agency and the Imperial State.* New York: Routledge, 2012.

Borges, Jorge Luis. "On Exactitude in Science." In *Collected Fictions*, 325. New York: Penguin Books, 1998.

Bory de Saint-Vincent. "Mer." In *Dictionnaire classique d'histoire naturelle,* vol. 10. Paris: Rey et Gravier, 1826.

———. *Relation du voyage de la commission scientifique de Morée dans le Péloponnèse, les Cyclades et l'Attique.* Paris: F.-G. Levrault, 1836.

Bosworth, C. Edmund. "The Nomenclature of the Persian Gulf." *Iranian Studies* 30, nos. 1–2 (Winter-Spring 1997): 77–94.

Bourguet, Marie-Noëlle. "De la Méditerranée." In *L'invention scientifique de la Méditerranée—Égypte, Morée, Algérie,* edited by Marie-Noëlle Bourguet, Bernard Lepetit, Daniel Nordman, and Maroula Sinarellis, 7–28. Paris: École des hautes études en sciences sociales, 1998.

Bourguet, Marie-Noëlle, Bernard Lepetit, Daniel Nordman, and Maroula Sinarellis, eds. *L'invention scientifique de la Méditerranée—Égypte, Morée, Algérie.* Paris: École des hautes études en sciences sociales, 1998.

Braithwaite, Colin. "Geology and Paleogeography of the Red Sea Region." In *Red Sea*, edited by Alasdair Edwards and Stephen Head, 22–44. Oxford: Pergamon Press, 1987.
Braudel, Fernand. "L'aube." In *La Méditerranée: L'espace et l'histoire*, edited by Fernand Braudel. 1977. Reprint, Paris: Flammarion, 1985.
———. *Civilisation matérielle, économie et capitalisme, XVe-XVIIIe siècle.* Vol. 2. *Les jeux de l'échange*. Paris: Armand Colin, 1979.
———. *Civilization and Capitalism, 15th-18th Century: The Wheels of Commerce.* London: William Collins Sons, 1982.
———. "Les Espagnols en Algérie (1492–1792)." In *Histoire et historiens de l'Algérie*, 231–66. Paris: Félix Alcan, 1931.
———. "L'histoire." In *La Méditerranée: L'espace et l'histoire*, edited by Fernand Braudel. 1977. Reprint, Paris: Flammarion, 1985.
———. *Identity of France.* Translated by Siân Reynolds. London: Fontana Press, 1989–90.
———. *The Mediterranean and the Mediterranean World in the Age of Philip II.* Translated by Siân Reynolds. Berkeley: University of California Press, 1996.
———. "La Méditerranée." In *La Méditerranée: L'espace et l'histoire*, edited by Fernand Braudel. 1977. Reprint, Paris: Flammarion, 1985.
———. *La Méditerranée et le monde méditerranéen à l'époque de Philippe II.* 1966. Reprint, Paris: Armand Colin, 1990.
———, ed. *La Méditerranée: L'espace et l'histoire.* 1977. Reprint, Paris: Flammarion, 1985.
———. *Les mémoires de la Méditerranée.* Paris: Éditions de Fallois, 1998.
———. "Personal Testimony." *Journal of Modern History* 44 (December 1972): 448–67.
———. "La terre." In *La Méditerranée: L'espace et l'histoire*, edited by Fernand Braudel. 1977. Reprint, Paris: Flammarion, 1985.
———. "Toward a Serial History: Seville and the Atlantic, 1504–1650." In *On History*, 91–104. Chicago: University of Chicago Press, 1980. Originally published in *Annales: Économies, Sociétés, Civilisations* 18, no. 3 (1963): 541–53.
Brown, Robert F., and Peter C. Hodgson. "Editorial Introduction" to *Lectures on the Philosophy of World History,* vol. 1, *Manuscripts of the Introduction and the Lectures of 1822–3*, by G. W. F. Hegel, edited and translated by Robert F. Brown and Peter C. Hodgson with the assistance of William G. Geuss. Oxford: Oxford University Press, 2011.
Brownlie, Alexander. "Varieties of Tides: The Red Sea Variety." *Bulletin of the American Geographical Society* 35, no. 1 (1903): 17–23.
Brummett, Palmira. "The Ottomans as a World Power: What We Don't Know about Ottoman Sea-Power." *Oriente Moderno* 20, no. 1 (2001): 1–21.
———. *Ottoman Seapower and Levantine Diplomacy in the Age of Discovery.* Albany: SUNY Press, 1993.
Buheiry, Marwan. "Colonial Scholarship and Muslim Revivalism in 1900." *Arab Studies Quarterly* 4, nos. 1–2 (1982): 1–16.

Buist, George. "On the Physical Geography of the Red Sea." *Journal of the Royal Geographical Society of London* 24 (1854): 227–38.
Bulliet, Richard. *The Camel and the Wheel*. New York: Columbia University Press, 1990.
Burckhardt, John Lewis. *Travels in Nubia*. 2nd ed. London: John Murray, 1822.
Buti, Gilbert. "Marseille entre Moka et café des îles: Espaces, flux, réseaux, XVIIe-XVIIIe siècles." In *Le commerce du café avant l'ère des plantations coloniales*, edited by Michel Tuchscherer, 214–44. Cairo: Institut français d'archéologie orientale, 2001.
Cantillon, Richard. *Essai sur la nature du commerce*. London: Macmillan, 1931.
Cappers, René. "Trade and Subsistence at the Roman Port of Berenike, Red Sea Coast, Egypt." In *The Exploitation of Plant Resources in Ancient Africa*, edited by Marijke van der Veen, 81–88. New York: Kluwer Academic/Plenum, 1999.
Casale, Giancarlo. "The Ethnic Composition of Ottoman Ship Crews and the 'Rumi Challenge' to Portuguese Identity." *Medieval Encounters* 13 (2007): 122–44.
———. *The Ottoman Age of Exploration*. Oxford: Oxford University Press, 2011.
Casey, Edward. *The Fate of Place: A Philosophical History*. Berkeley: University of California Press, 1997.
Casson, Lionel. *The Ancient Mariners: Seafarers and Sea Fighters of the Mediterranean in Ancient Times*. New York: Macmillan, 1959.
———, ed. *The Periplus Maris Erythraei: Text with Introduction, Translation, and Commentary*. Princeton, NJ: Princeton University Press, 1989.
———. *Ships and Seamanship in the Ancient World*. Baltimore: Johns Hopkins University Press, 1995.
Chakrabarty, Dipesh. *Provincializing Europe*. Princeton, NJ: Princeton University Press, 2000.
Chaudhuri, K. N. *Asia before Europe: Economic and Civilisation of the Indian Ocean from the Rise of Islam to 1750*. Cambridge: Cambridge University Press, 1990.
———. *Trade and Civilization in the Indian Ocean: An Economic History from the Rise of Islam to 1750*. Cambridge: Cambridge University Press, 1985.
Clowes, Wm. Laird. *The Royal Navy: A History, From the Earliest Times to the Present*. London: Sampson Low, Martons and Cie, 1899.
Connery, Christopher L. "Ideologies of Land and Sea: Alfred Thayer Mahan, Carl Schmitt, and the Shaping of Global Myth Elements." *Boundary 2* 28, no. 2 (2001): 173–201.
Cook, Andrew. "Establishing the Sea Route to India and China: Stages in the Development of Hydrographical Knowledge." In *The Worlds of the East India Company*, edited by H. V. Bowen, Margarette Lincoln, and Nigel Rigby, 119–36. Woodbridge: Boydell Press, 2002.
Copisarow, Maurice. "Ancient Egyptian, Greek and Hebrew Concept of the Red Sea." *Vetus Testamentum* 12, no. 1 (1962): 1–13.
Crabitès, Pierre. *Ismail, the Maligned Khedive*. London: George Routledge and Sons, 1933.

Creswell, K. A. C. "The Ka'ba in A.D. 608." *Archaeologia* 94 (1951): 97–102.
Cromer, Evelyn Baring. *Modern Egypt*. New York: Macmillan, 1908.
Dağlı, Murat. "The Limits of Ottoman Pragmatism." *History and Theory* 52 (May 2013): 194–213.
Daguenet, Roger Joint. *Histoire de la mer Rouge*. Vol. 1. *De Moïse à Bonaparte*. Paris: Perrin, 1995.
———. *Histoire de la mer Rouge*. Vol. 2. *De Bonaparte à nos jours*. Paris: Perrin, 1995.
d'Anville, Jean Baptiste Bourguinon. *Compendium of Ancient Geography*. 3 vols. New York: R. M'Dermut and D. D. Arden, 1814.
Darby, H. C. "On the Relations of Geography and History." *Transactions and Papers (Institute of British Geographers)* 19 (1953): 1–11.
D'Arcy, Paul. *The People of the Sea: Environment, Identity, and History in Oceania*. Honolulu: University of Hawai'i Press, 2006.
Daston, Lorraine. "The Coming into Being of Scientific Objects." In *Biographies of Scientific Objects*, edited by Lorraine Daston, 1–14. Chicago: University of Chicago Press, 2000.
Davis, Colin. *Critical Excess: Overreading in Derrida, Deleuze, Levinas, Zizek and Cavell*. Stanford, CA: Stanford University Press, 2010.
Davison, Roderic. *Essays in Ottoman and Turkish History, 1774–1923*. Austin: University of Texas Press, 1990.
Dawson, Llewellyn Styles. *Memoirs of Hydrography Including Brief Biographies of the Principal Officers Who Have Served in H.M. Naval Surveying Service, Part I—1750–1850*. Eastbourne: Henry W. Keay, 1885.
de Planhol, Xavier. *Les fondements géographiques de l'Islam*. Paris: Flammarion, 1968.
———. "The Geographical Setting." In *The Cambridge History of Islam*, edited by P. M. Holt, Ann K. S. Lambton, and Bernard Lewis, 2B:443–68. Cambridge: Cambridge University Press, 1970.
———. *L'Islam et la mer: La mosquée et le matelot, VIIe-XXe siècles*. Paris: Perrin, 2000.
de Sacy, Silvestre. *Chrestomathie arabe*. Paris: Imprimerie impériale, 1806.
de Testa, Le Baron I. *Recueil des traités de la Porte ottomane*. Vol. 1. Paris: Amyot, 1864.
Diaz, Vicente M., and J. Kehaulani Kauanui, eds. "Native Pacific Cultural Studies on the Edge." Special issue, *Contemporary Pacific* 22, no. 1 (Spring 2010).
Diderot, Denis, and Jean d'Alembert. *Encyclopédie, ou Dictionnaire raisonné des sciences, des arts et des métiers*. Vol. 11. Lausanne: Société Typographique, 1782. http://encyclopedie.uchicago.edu (accessed December 13, 2012).
d'Ohsson, Mouradgea. *Tableau général de l'empire othoman*. Paris: Imprimerie de Monsieur, 1791.
Drouin, Jean-Marc. "Bory de Saint-Vincent et la géographie botanique." In *L'invention scientifique de la Méditerranée—Égypte, Morée, Algérie*, edited by Marie-Noëlle Bourguet, Bernard Lepetit, Daniel Nordman, and Maroula Sinarellis, 139–57. Paris: École des hautes études en sciences sociales, 1998.

Duckett, M. W. *Dictionnaire de la conversation et de la lecture, Inventaire raisonné des notions générales les plus indispensables à tous, Par une société de savants et de gens de lettres, Sous la direction de M. W. Duckett, Seconde édition, entièrement refondue, corrigée et augmenté de plusieurs milliers d'articles tout d'actualité.* Vol. 15. Paris: Comptoirs de la Direction, 1857.

Eco, Umberto. *How to Travel with a Salmon and Other Essays.* Orlando, FL: Harcourt Brace, 1994.

Edney, Matthew. *Mapping an Empire: The Geographical Construction of British India, 1769–1843.* Chicago: University of Chicago Press, 1997.

Edwards, Alasdair, and Stephen Head, eds. *Red Sea.* Oxford: Pergamon Press, 1987.

Edwards, Frederick. "Climate and Oceanography." In *Red Sea,* edited by Alasdair Edwards and Stephen Head, 45–69. Oxford: Pergamon Press, 1987.

Ehrenberg, C. G. "New Observations on the Blood-like Phenomena observed in Egypt, Arabia, and Siberia; with a View and Critique of the Early Accounts of Similar Appearances." In *The Edinburgh New Philosophical Journal, Exhibiting a View of the Progressive Discoveries and Improvements in the Sciences and the Arts . . . October 1830 . . . April 1831,* edited by Robert Jameson, 122–36, 341–52. Edinburgh: Adam Black, 1831.

Ergin, Osman. *Muallim M. Cevdetin Hayatı, Eserleri, ve Kütüphanesi.* Istanbul: Bozkurt Basımevi, 1937.

Evliyā Çelebī. *Evliya Çelebi Seyahatnamesi: Anadolu, Suriye, Hicaz (1672–1672).* Edited by Ahmed Refik Altnay. Istanbul: Devlet Matbaasi, 1935.

———. *Seyāhatnāmesi.* Edited by Ahmed Cevdet. Istanbul: Iḳdām matbaʿasī, 1896–1938.

Fabian, Johannes. *Time and the Other: How Anthropology Makes Its Object.* New York: Columbia University Press, 1983.

Facey, William. "The Red Sea: The Wind Regime and Location of Ports." In *Trade and Travel in the Red Sea Region,* edited by Paul Lunde and Alexandra Porter. Oxford: Archaeopress, 2004.

Fahmy, Khaled. *All the Pasha's Men: Mehmed Ali, His Army and the Making of Modern Egypt.* Cairo: American University in Cairo Press, 1997.

Faroqhi, Suraiya, ed. *The Cambridge History of Turkey.* Vol. 3. *The Late Ottoman Empire, 1603–1839.* Cambridge: Cambridge University Press, 2006.

———. "Coffee and Spices: Official Ottoman Reactions to Egyptian Trade in the Later Sixteenth Century." *Wiener Zeitschrift für die Kunde des Morgenlandes* 76 (1986): 87–93.

———. Introduction to *The Cambridge History of Turkey,* vol. 3, *The Later Ottoman Empire, 1603–1839,* edited by Suraiya Faroqhi, 3–17. Cambridge: Cambridge University Press, 2006.

———. *Pilgrims and Sultans: The Hajj under the Ottomans.* London: I. B. Tauris, 1994.

———. "Red Sea Trade and Communications as Observed by Evliya Çelebi (1671–72)." In *Making a Living in the Ottoman Lands, 1480 to 1820,* edited by Suraiya Faroqhi, 87–106. Istanbul: Isis Press, 1995.

———. "Trade Controls, Provisioning Policies and Donations: The Egypt-Hijaz Connection during the Second Half of the Sixteenth Century." In *Süleymân the Second and His Time*, edited by Halil İnalcık and Cemal Kafadar, 131–44. Istanbul: Isis Press, 1993.

Fleischer, Cornell. "Royal Authority, Dynastic Cyclism, and 'Ibn Khaldunism' in Sixteenth Century Ottoman Letters." *Journal of Asian and African Studies* 18, nos. 3–4 (1983): 198–220.

Foucault, Michel. *The Order of Things: An Archaeology of the Human Sciences*. 1970. Reprint, New York: Vintage Books, 1994.

———. "La vie: L'expérience et la science." In *Dits et écrits*, vol. 4, *1980–1988*, 263–76. Paris: Gallimard, 1994.

Freeman, Donald. *The Pacific*. New York: Routledge, 2009.

Gage, William. *Life of Carl Ritter*. New York: Charles Scribner, 1858.

Games, Alison. "Atlantic History: Definitions, Challenges, and Opportunities." *American Historical Review* 111, no. 3 (June 2006): 741–57.

Gavin, R. J. *Aden under British Rule, 1839–1967*. London: C. Hurst, 1975.

Gekas, Sakis. "Colonial Migrants and the Making of a British Mediterranean." *European Review of History* 19, no. 1 (February 2012): 75–92.

Genç, Mehmet. "Contrôle et taxation du commerce du café dans l'Empire ottoman fin XVIIe–première moitié du XVIIIe siècle." In *Le commerce du café avant l'ère des plantations coloniales*, edited by Michel Tuchscherer, 161–80. Cairo: Institut français d'archéologie orientale, 2001.

———. *Osmanlı İmparatorluğu'nda Devlet ve Ekonomi*. Istanbul: Ötüken Neşriyat, 2000.

———. "Ottoman Industry in the Eighteenth Century: General Framework, Characteristics and Main Trends." In *Manufacturing in the Ottoman Empire and Turkey, 1500–1950*, edited by Donald Quataert, 59–86. Albany: SUNY Press, 1994.

———. "State and the Economy in the Age of Reforms: Continuity and Change." In *Ottoman Past and Today's Turkey*, edited by Kemal Karpat, 188–211. Leiden: Brill, 2000.

Gibbons, Herbert. *The Foundation of the Ottoman Empire*. New York: Century, 1916.

Gilroy, Paul. *The Black Atlantic: Modernity and Double Consciousness*. Cambridge, MA: Harvard University Press, 1993.

Ginzburg, Carlo. *History, Rhetoric, and Proof*. Hanover, NH: University Press of New England, 1999.

Greenlaw, Jean-Pierre. *The Coral Buildings of Suakin*. London: Oriel Press, 1976.

Gregory, Derek. "Scripting Egypt: Orientalism and the Cultures of Travel." In *Writes of Passage: Reading Travel Writing*, edited by James Duncan and Derek Gregory, 114–50. London: Routledge, 1999.

Grotius, Hugo. *Commentary on the Law of Prize and Booty*. Indianapolis, IN: Liberty Fund, 2006.

———. *The Free Sea*. Indianapolis, IN: Liberty Fund, 2004.

Guo, Li. *Commerce, Culture and Community in a Red Sea Port in the Thirteenth Century: The Arabic Documents from Quseir*. Leiden: Brill, 2004.
Hacking, Ian. *Representing and Intervening*. Cambridge: Cambridge University Press, 1983.
———. *The Social Construction of What?* Cambridge, MA: Harvard University Press, 1999.
Hadot, Pierre. *Philosophy as a Way of Life*. Malden, MA: Blackwell, 1995.
Hagen, Gottfried. "Ottoman Understandings of the World in the Seventeenth Century." Afterword to *Evliya Çelebi: An Ottoman Mentality*, by Robert Dankoff, 215–56. Leiden: Brill, 2006.
Hallaq, Wael. "What Is Shari'a?" In *Yearbook of Islamic and Middle Eastern Law*, vol. 12, *2005–2006*, edited by Eugene Cotran and Martin Lau, 151–80. Leiden: Brill, 2007.
Ḥamawī, Yāqūt al-. *Muʿjam al-buldān*. Beirut: Dār Ṣādir, 1977.
Hanley, Will. "When Did Egyptians Stop Being Ottomans? An Imperial Citizenship Case Study." In *Multilevel Citizenship*, edited by Willem Maas, 89–109. Philadelphia: University of Pennsylvania Press, 2013.
Harris, W.V., ed. *Rethinking the Mediterranean*. New York: Oxford University Press, 2005.
Ḥasan, Yūsuf Faḍl, ed. *Tārīkh al-dawla al-ʿuthmānīya—Malāmiḥ min al-ʿilāqāt al-Sūdānīya al-Turkīya*. Khartoum: Khartoum University Press, 2004.
Hattox, Ralph. *Coffee and Coffeehouses: The Origins of a Social Beverage in the Medieval Near East*. Seattle: University of Washington Press, 1985.
Hau'ofa, Epeli. "Our Sea of Islands." In *We Are the Ocean: Selected Works*, 27–40. Honolulu: University of Hawai'i Press, 2008. Originally published in *A New Oceania: Rediscovering Our Sea of Islands*, edited by Eric Waddell, Vijay Naidu, and Epeli Hau'ofa (Suva: University of the South Pacific, 1993), 2–16.
Head, Stephen. Introduction to *Red Sea*, edited by Alasdair Edwards and Stephen Head, 1–21. Oxford: Pergamon Press, 1987.
Headrick, Daniel. *The Tentacles of Progress: Technology Transfer in the Age of Imperialism, 1850–1940*. New York: Oxford University Press, 1988.
Hegel, G.W.F. *Lectures on the Philosophy of History*. Translated by John Sibree. London: Henry Bone, 1857.
———. *Lectures on the Philosophy of World History. Introduction: Reason in History*. Translated by H.B. Nisbet. London: Cambridge University Press, 1975.
———. *Lectures on the Philosophy of World History*. Vol. 1. *Manuscripts of the Introduction and the Lectures of 1822–3*. Edited and translated by R.F. Brown and P.C. Hodgson, with the assistance of W.G. Geuss. Oxford: Clarendon Press, 2011.
———. *Philosophy of Mind—Being Part Three of the Encyclopaedia of the Philosophical Sciences, Together with the Zusätze*. Translated by William Wallace and A.V. Miller. Oxford: Oxford University Press, 1971.
———. *Philosophy of Right*. Translated with notes by T.M. Knox. Oxford: Oxford University Press, 1970.

———. *Vorlesungen über die Philosophie der Weltgeschichte, Berlin 1822/1823*. Edited by Karl Heinz Ilting, Karl Brehmer, and Hoo Nam Seelmann. Vorlesungen: Ausgewählte Nachschriften und Manuskripte 12. Hamburg: Felix Meiner, 1996.
Heidegger, Martin. "The Age of the World Picture." In *The Question Concerning Technology and Other Essays,* edited by William Lovitt, 115–54. New York: Harper, 1977.
Herzfeld, Michael. *Anthropology through the Looking-Glass: Critical Ethnographies in the Margins of Europe*. Cambridge: Cambridge University Press, 1987.
———. "Practical Mediterraneanism: Excuses for Everything, from Epistemology to Eating." In *Rethinking the Mediterranean*, edited by W. V. Harris, 45–63. New York: Oxford University Press, 2005.
Hess, Andrew. "The Ottoman Conquest of Egypt (1517) and the Beginning of the Sixteenth-Century World War." *International Journal of Middle East Studies* 4, no. 1 (January 1973): 55–76.
Hexter, J. H. "Fernand Braudel and the *Monde Braudellien*." *Journal of Modern History* 44, no. 4 (December 1972): 480–539.
Heyd, Uriel. *Ottoman Documents on Palestine, 1552–1615: A Study of the Firman According to the Mühimme Defteri*. Oxford: Clarendon Press, 1960.
Heywood, Colin. Review of *The Ottoman Empire, 1300–1650: The Structure of Power,* by Colin Imber. Reviews in History, review no. 431, November 2004. www.history.ac.uk/reviews/review/431.
Hinkkanen, Merja-Liisa, and David Kirby. *The Baltic and the North Seas*. New York: Routledge, 2000.
Ho, Engseng. *The Graves of Tarim: Genealogy and Mobility across the Indian Ocean*. Berkeley: University of California Press, 2006.
Hodgson, Marshall. *The Venture of Islam: Conscience and History in a World Civilization*. Chicago: University of Chicago Press, 1974.
Holt, P. M. Review of *Le livre du Soudan,* by Cheykh Muḥammad ibn 'Alī ibn Zayn al-'Abidīn. *Bulletin of the School of Oriental and African Studies* 45, no. 3 (1982): 582–83.
Horden, Peregrine, and Nicholas Purcell. *The Corrupting Sea: A Study in Mediterranean History*. Malden, MA: Blackwell, 2000.
———. "The Mediterranean and 'the New Thalassology.'" *American Historical Review* 111, no. 3 (June 2006): 722–40.
Horsburgh, James, ed. *The India Directory, or, Directions for Sailing to and from the East Indies, China, Australia, and the Interjacent Ports of Africa and South America*. 6th ed. Vol. 1. London: W. M. H. Allen, 1852.
Horton, Mark. "The Human Settlement of the Red Sea." In *Red Sea*, edited by Alasdair Edwards and Stephen Head, 339–62. Oxford: Pergamon Press, 1987.
Hoskins, Halford Lancaster. *British Routes to India*. London: Cass, 1966.
Hourani, George. *Arab Seafaring in the Indian Ocean in Ancient and Early Medieval Times*. Princeton, NJ: Princeton University Press, 1995.
Houtsma, M. Th., T. W. Arnold, R. Basset, and R. Hartmann, eds. *Encyclopedia of Islam, First Edition (1913–1936)*. Brill Online, accessed March 12, 2015.

Hoyland, Robert. *Arabia and the Arabs: From the Bronze Age to the Coming of Islam*. London: Routledge, 2001.
Hoyt, Sarah. "The Name of the Red Sea." *Journal of the American Oriental Society* 32, no. 2 (1912): 115–19.
Huber, Valeska. *Channelling Mobilities: Migration and Globalisation in the Suez Canal Region and Beyond, 1869–1914*. Cambridge: Cambridge University Press, 2013.
Huntingford, G. W. B. ed. *The Periplus of the Erythraean Sea, by an Unknown Author, with Some Extracts from Agatharkhides "On the Erythraean Sea."* Farnham: Ashgate, 2010.
Hussein, Taha. *The Future of Culture in Egypt*. Washington, DC: American Council of Learmed Societies, 1954.
Ibn Iyās, Muḥammad. *Badāʾiʿ al-zuhūr fī waqāʾiʿ al-duhūr,* edited by Muḥammad Muṣṭafā. Cairo: al-Haiyʾa al-misriyya al-ʿāmma li'l-kitāb, 1984.
Ibn Jubayr, Muḥammad. *Riḥlat Ibn Jubayr*. Beirut: Dār Ṣāder, 1980.
Ibn Khaldūn, ʿAbd al-Raḥmān. *The Muqaddimah: An Introduction to History*. Translated by Franz Rosenthal. New York: Pantheon Books, 1958.
———. *Muqaddimat Ibn Khaldūn*. Edited by Khalīl Sheḥāda. Beirut: Dār al-fikr, 2001.
Ibn Manẓūr, Muḥammad. *Lisān al-ʿArab*. Vol. 5. Beirut: Dār Ṣādir, n.d.
İnalcık, Halil. "The Ottoman Economic Mind and Aspects of the Ottoman Economy." In *Studies in the Economic History of the Middle East,* edited by Michael Cook, 207–18. Oxford: Oxford University Press, 1970.
Irwin, Eyles. *A Series of Adventures in the Course of a Voyage up the Red-Sea, on the Coasts of Arabia and Egypt, and of a Route through the Desarts of Thebais hitherto unknown to the European Traveller in the year M.DCC.LXXVII. in Letters to a Lady*. London: J. Dodsley, 1780.
Jabartī, ʿAbd al-Raḥmān al-. *ʿAbd al-Rahman al-Jabartī's History of Egypt: ʿAjāʾib al-āthār fi'l-tarājim wa'l-akhbār*. Edited by Thomas Philipp and Moshe Pearlmann. 4 vols. in 2. Stuttgart: Franz Steiner, 1994.
Jacob, Heinrich Eduard. *The Saga of Coffee: The Biography of an Economic Product*. London: George Allen and Unwin, 1935.
Jamieson, Ross. "The Essence of Commodification: Caffeine Dependencies in the Early Modern World." *Journal of Social History* 35, no. 2 (Winter 2001): 269–94.
Jolly, Margaret. "Imagining Oceania: Indigenous and Foreign Representations of a Sea of Islands." *Contemporary Pacific* 19, no. 2 (2007): 508–45.
Jomier, Jacques. *Le Maḥmal et la caravane égyptienne des pèlerins de La Mecque (XIIIe-XXe siècles)*. Cairo: Institut français d'archéologie orientale, 1953.
Kafadar, Cemal. *Between Two Worlds: The Construction of the Ottoman State*. Berkeley: University of California Press, 1995.
———. "How Dark Is the History of the Night, How Black the Story of Coffee, How Bitter the Tale of Love: The Changing Measure of Leisure and Pleasure in Early Modern Istanbul." Kamal Salibi Memorial Lecture, May 17, 2013, American University of Beirut.

Kammerer, Albert. *La mer Rouge, l'Abyssinie, et l'Arabie depuis l'antiquité: Essai d'histoire et de géographie historique*. Cairo: Société royale de géographie d'Égypte, 1929–35.

Karbe, Ludwig. "Hot Brines and the Deep Sea Environment." In *Red Sea*, edited by Alasdair Edwards and Stephen Head, 70–89. Oxford: Pergamon Press, 1987.

Kâtib Çelebi. *The Gift of the Great Ones on Naval Campaigns*. Edited by Idris Bostan. Ankara: Prime Ministry Undersecretariat for Maritime Affairs, 2008.

———. *Kitāb-ı Cihānnūma*. Istanbul: Dār al-ṭibā'a al-'āmira, 1732.

———. *Tuḥfat al-kibār fī asfār al-biḥār*. Istanbul: Dār al-ṭibā'a al-ma'mūra, 1728.

Kawatoko, Mutsua. "Coffee Trade in the al-Tur Port, South Sinai." In *Commerce du café avant l'ère des plantations coloniales*, edited by Michel Tuchscherer, 51–66. Cairo: Institut français d'archéologie orientale, 2001.

Kellner, Hans. "Disorderly Conduct: Braudel's Mediterranean Satire." *History and Theory* 18, no. 2 (May 1979): 197–222.

King, Charles. *The Black Sea: A History*. New York: Oxford University Press, 2005.

King, J. S. "The Red Sea: Why So Called." *Journal of the Royal Asiatic Society of Great Britain and Ireland* 30, no. 3 (July 1898): 617–18.

Kirch, Patrick. *On the Road of the Winds: An Archaeological History of the Pacific Islands before European Contact*. Berkeley: University of California Press, 2002.

Kirli, Cengiz. "Coffeehouses: Public Opinion in the Nineteenth-Century Ottoman Empire." In *Public Islam and the Common Good*, edited by Armando Salvatore and Dale F. Eickelman, 75–97. Leiden: Brill, 2004.

Klein, Bernhard, and Gesa Mackenthum. "Introduction: The Sea Is History." In *Sea Changes: Historicizing the Ocean*, edited by Bernhard Klein and Gesa Mackenthum. New York: Routledge, 2004.

LaCapra, Dominick. "Rethinking Intellectual History and Reading Texts." *History and Theory* 19, no. 3 (October 1980): 245–76.

Lane, Frederic. "The Mediterranean Spice Trade: Further Evidence of Its Revival in the 16th Century." *American Historical Review* 45, no. 3 (1940): 571–90.

Latour, Bruno, and Steve Woolgar. *Laboratory Life: The Construction of Scientific Facts*. 2nd ed. Princeton, NJ: Princeton University Press, 1986. Originally published as *Laboratory Life: The Social Construction of Scientific Facts* (Beverly Hills, CA: Sage Publications, 1979).

Lawson, Fred. *The Social Origins of Egyptian Expansionism during the Muhammad 'Ali Period*. New York: Columbia University Press, 1992.

Leighly, John. Introduction to *The Physical Geography of the Sea, and Its Meteorology*, by Matthew Fontaine Maury. Cambridge, MA: Harvard University Press, 1963.

———. "Methodologic Controversy in Nineteenth Century German Geography." *Annals of the Association of American Geographers* 28, no. 4 (1938): 238–58.

Leiser, Gary. "The Crusader Raid in the Red Sea in 578, 1182/83." *Journal of the American Research Center in Egypt* 14 (1977): 87–100.

Lesure, Michel. "Un document ottoman de 1525 sur l'Inde portugaise et les pays de la mer Rouge." *Mare Luso-Indicum* 3 (1976): 137–60.

Lewis, Martin. "Dividing the Ocean Sea." *Geographic Review* 89, no. 2 (April 1999): 188–214.

Lewis, Martin, and Kären Wigen. "A Maritime Response to the Crisis in Area Studies." *Geographical Review* 89, no. 2 (April 1999): 161–68.

———. *The Myth of Continents: A Critique of Metageography*. Berkeley: University of California Press, 1997.

Livingstone, David. "Race, Space and Moral Climatology: Notes toward a Genealogy." *Journal of Historical Geography* 28, no. 2 (2002): 159–80.

Locke, John. *Second Treatise of Government*. Indianapolis, IN: Hackett, 1980.

Low, Charles R. *History of the Indian Navy, 1613–1863*. 2 vols. London: R. Bentley and Son, 1877.

Lucas, C. P. *A Historical Geography of the British Colonies*. Vol. 1. *The Mediterranean and Eastern Colonies*. 2nd ed. Revised by R. E. Stubbs. Oxford: Clarendon Press, 1906.

Luksch, J. "The Austro-Hungarian Expedition to the Red Sea." *Geographical Journal* 12, no. 6 (December 1898): 571–72.

Mackenzie, James. "Egypt and Arabia." *Literary Gazette; and Journal of Belles Lettres, Arts, Sciences, &c.* (London), no. 1072, August 5, 1837, 489–92.

Magris, Claudio. Foreword to *Mediterranean: A Cultural Landscape*, by Pedrag Matvejevic, 1–6. Berkeley: University of California Press, 1999.

Mahan, Alfred Thayer. *The Influence of Sea Power upon History, 1660–1783*. London: Sampson Low, Marston, Searle, and Rivington, 1890.

Maqrīzī, Taqī al-Dīn al-. *Al-Mawāʿiẓ wa al-ʾiʿtibār bi-dhikr al-khiṭaṭ wa al-āthār*. Cairo: Maktabat al-thaqafa al-dīniyya, 1987.

Margariti, Roxani. *Aden and the Indian Ocean Trade*. Chapel Hill: University of North Carolina Press, 2007.

Marini, Ludovico. "On the Method of Studying Thalassology." *Geographical Journal* 25, no. 2 (1905): 191–97.

Markham, Clements Robert. *A Memoir on the Indian Surveys*. London: W. H. Allen, 1871.

Marston, Thomas. *Britain's Imperial Role in the Red Sea, 1800–1878*. Hamden, CT: Shoe String Press, 1961.

Masʿūdī, Abā al-Ḥasan ʿAlī al-. *El-Masudi's Historical Encylopaedia Entitled "Meadows of Gold and Mines of Gems."* Translated by Aloys Sprenger. London: Oriental Translation Fund, 1841.

———. *Murūj al-dhahab wa maʿādin al-jawhar*. Edited by K. Ḥ. Murʿī. Beirut: Al-Maktaba al-ʿaṣriyya, 2005.

Matsuda, Matt. "The Pacific." *American Historical Review* 111, no. 3 (June 2006): 758–80.

———. *Pacific Worlds: A History of Seas, Peoples, and Cultures*. Cambridge: Cambridge University Press, 2012.

Matthews, Derek. "The Red Sea Style." *Kush* 1 (1953): 60–86.

Matvejević, Predrag. *Mediterranean: A Cultural Landscape*. Translated by Michael Henry Heim. 1987. Reprint, Berkeley: University of California Press, 1999.

Mauro, Frédéric. *Histoire du café*. Paris: Desjonquères, 2002.
Maury, Matthew Fontaine. *The Physical Geography of the Sea, and Its Meteorology*. Cambridge, MA: Harvard University Press, 1963.
Meloy, John. *Imperial Power and Maritime Trade: Mecca and Cairo in the Later Middle Ages*. Chicago: University of Chicago Press, 2010.
———. "Imperial Strategy and Political Exigency: The Red Sea Spice Trade and the Mamluk Sultanate in the Fifteenth Century." *Journal of the American Oriental Society* 123, no. 1 (2003): 1–19.
Michelet, Jules. *La mer*. 5th ed. Paris: Michel Lévy Frères, 1875.
———. *The Sea*. Translated by W. H. D. Adams. London: T. Nelson and Sons, 1875.
Mikhail, Alan. *Nature and Empire in Ottoman Egypt: An Environmental History*. Cambridge: Cambridge University Press, 2011.
Mitchell, S. A. "Obituary: Matthew Fontaine Maury." *Science* 73, no. 1902 (1931): 632–33.
Mitchell, Timothy. *Colonising Egypt*. 1988. Reprint, Berkeley: University of California Press, 1991.
———. "Fixing the Economy." *Cultural Studies* 12, no. 1 (1998): 82–101.
———. *Rule of Experts: Egypt, Techno-Politics, Modernity*. Berkeley: University of California Press, 2002.
———. "The Stage of Modernity." In *Questions of Modernity*, edited by Timothy Mitchell, 1–34. Minneapolis: University of Minnesota Press, 2000.
Mitchell, W. J. T. Introduction to *Landscape and Power*, edited by W. J. T. Mitchell, 1–4. Chicago: University of Chicago Press, 2002.
Mohamed, A. F. "The Egyptian Exploration of the Red Sea." *Proceedings of the Royal Society of London, Series B, Biological Sciences* 128, no. 852 (February 1940): 306–16.
Mollat du Jourdin, Michel. *Europe and the Sea*. London: Blackwell, 1993. Originally published as *L'Europe et la mer* (Paris: Seuil, 1993).
Morcos, S. A. "Physical and Chemical Oceanography of the Red Sea." *Oceanography and Marine Biology: An Annual Review* 8 (1970): 73–202.
Moresby, Robert, and Thomas Elwon. *Sailing Instructions for the Red Sea*. In *The India Directory*, edited by James Horsburgh, 6th ed., 1:279–356. London: W. M. H. Allen, 1852.
Nadel, George. "Philosophy of History before Historicism." *History and Theory* 3, no. 3 (1964): 291–315.
Nahrawālī, Qutb al-dīn al-. *Al-Barq al-yamānī fi al-fatḥ al-ʿuthmānī*. Edited by Ḥamad al-Jāsir. Riyadh: Manshūrāt dār al-yamāma li-l-baḥth, 1967.
Niebuhr, Carsten. *Beschreibung von Arabien aus eigenen Beobachtungen und im Lande selbst gesammleten Nachrichten*. Copenhagen: Möller, 1772.
———. *Travels through Arabia and other Countries in the East*. Translated by Robert Heron. Edinburgh: Morison and Son, 1792.
Nubarian, Nubar. *Mémoires de Nubar Pacha*. Beirut: Libraire du Liban, 1983.
Nunn, Patrick. *Vanished Islands and Hidden Continents of the Pacific*. Honolulu: University of Hawai'i Press, 2008.

Orhonlu, Cengiz. *Osmanlı İmparatorluğu'nun Güney Siyaseti: Habeş Eyaleti*. 1974. Reprint, Ankara: Türk Tarih Kurumu Basımevi, 1996.

Orr, Linda. *Jules Michelet: Nature, History, Language*. Ithaca, NY: Cornell University Press, 1976.

Oulipo. *Atlas de littérature potentielle*. Paris: Gallimard, 1981.

Özcan, Azmi. *Pan-Islamism: Indian Muslims, the Ottomans and Britain, 1877–1924*. Leiden: Brill, 1997.

Özkoçak, Selma Akyazici. "Coffeehouses: Rethinking the Public and Private in Early Modern Istanbul." *Journal of Urban History* 33, no. 6 (2007): 965–86.

Palmer, Alan. *The Baltic: A History of the Region and Its People*. Woodstock, NY: Overlook Press, 2006.

Pamuk, Şevket. *A Monetary History of the Ottoman Empire*. Cambridge: Cambridge University Press, 2000.

Partner, Nancy. "The Form of the Content." *History and Theory* 37, no. 2 (May 1998): 162–72.

Pascual, Jean-Paul. "Café et cafés à Damas: Contribution à la chronologie de leur diffusion au XVIème siècle." *Berytus* 42 (1995–96): 141–55.

Pedersen, Ralph. "Under the Erythraean Sea: An Ancient Shipwreck in Eritrea." *INA Quarterly* 27, nos. 2/3 (Summer/Fall 2000): 3–12.

Peters, Edward. "*Quid nobis cum pelago?* The New Thalassology and the Economic History of Europe." *Journal of Interdisciplinary History* 34, no. 1 (2003): 49–61.

Picaudou, Nadine. "'Les Arabes' comme catégorie du discours mandataire britannique en Palestine." In *Temps et espaces en Palestine: Flux et resistances identitaires*, edited by Roger Heacock, 235–45. Beirut: Institut français du Proche-Orient, 2008.

Pîrî Reis. *Kitab-ı Bahriye*. Edited by E. Z. Ökte. Istanbul: Historical Research Foundation, 1988.

Piterberg, Gabriel. *An Ottoman Tragedy: History and Historiography at Play*. Berkeley: University of California Press, 2003.

Pocock, J. G. A. "Adam Smith and History." In *The Cambridge Companion to Adam Smith*, edited by Knud Haakonssen, 270–87. Cambridge: Cambridge University Press, 2006.

Popham, Henry. *Concise Statement of Facts*. London: John Stockdale, 1805.

Power, Timothy. *The Red Sea from Byzantium to the Caliphate, AD 500–1000*. Cairo: American University in Cairo Press, 2012.

Prakash, Gyan. "Science 'Gone Native' in Colonial India." *Representations* 40 (1992): 153–78.

Qalqashandī, Shihāb al-Dīn al-. *Subḥ al-aʿshā fī kitābat al-ʾinshā*. Cairo: al-Maṭbaʿa al-ʾamīriyya, 1914.

Ranke, Leopold von. *History of the Latin and Teutonic Nations, 1494–1514*. New York: AMS Press, 1976.

———. *The Ottoman and the Spanish Empires, in the Sixteenth and Seventeenth Centuries*. Philadelphia: Lea and Blanchard, 1845.

———. "Preface: Histories of Romance and Germanic Peoples." In *The Varieties of History: From Voltaire to the Present,* edited by Fritz Stern. New York: Vintage Books, 1973.

———. *The Theory and Practice of History.* Edited by Georg G. Iggers and Konrad von Moltke. Indianapolis, IN: Bobbs-Merrill, 1973.

———. *Universal History: The Oldest Group of Nations and the Greeks.* Edited by G. W. Prothero. Translated by D. C. Tovey. New York: Charles Scribner's Sons, 1884.

Raymond, André. *Artisans et commerçants au Caire au XVIIIe siècle.* 2nd ed. Cairo: Institut français d'archéologie orientale, 1999.

———. "Le commerce des épices au Caire, du XVIe au XVIIIe siècle." In *Herbes, drogues et épices en Méditerranée,* edited by Georges J. Aillaud et al., 115–24. Marseille: CNRS, 1988.

Redhouse, James. *A Turkish and English Lexicon.* 3rd ed. 1890. Reprint, Istanbul: Çağrı Yayınları, 2006.

The Red Sea and Gulf of Aden Pilot. 5th ed. London: Hydrographic Office, 1900.

The Red Sea and Gulf of Aden Pilot. 16th ed. London: Hydrographic Office, 2009.

Reese, Scott, ed. *The Transmission of Learning in Islamic Africa.* Leiden: Brill, 2004.

Renan, Ernest. "The Religions of Antiquity." In *Studies of Religious History and Criticism,* translated by O. B. Frothingham, 61–106. New York: Carleton, 1864.

Ricoeur, Paul. *Time and Narrative.* Chicago: University of Chicago Press, 1990.

Ritter, Carl. "De la configuration des continents sur la surface du globe et de leurs fonctions dans l'histoire." Translated by Élisée Reclus. *Revue Germanique* 8 (1859): 241–67.

———. "The Geographical Position and Horizontal Extension of the Continents." In *Geographical Studies,* translated by William L. Gage, 177–211. Boston: Gould and Lincoln, 1863.

———. "The Historical Element in Geography as a Science." In *Geographical Studies,* translated by William L. Gage, 241–77. Boston: Gould and Lincoln, 1863.

———. "Introductory Essay to General Comparative Geography." In *Geographical Studies,* translated by William L. Gage, 55–132. Boston: Gould and Lincoln, 1863.

Rogne, Erlend. "The Aim of Interpretation Is to Create Perplexity in the Face of the Real: Hayden White in Conversation with Erlend Rogne." *History and Theory* 48 (February 2009): 63–75.

Ruel, Anne. "L'invention de la Méditerranée." *Vingtième Siècle* 32 (October-December 1991): 7–14.

Rycaut, Paul. *The Present State of the Ottoman Empire. Containing the Maxims of the Turkish Politie, The most material Points of the Mahometan Religion, Their Sect and Heresies, their Convents and Religious Votaries. Their Military Discipline, With an exact Computation of their Forces both by Land and Sea.* London: J. Starkey and H. Brome, 1668.

Said, Edward. *Culture and Imperialism.* New York: Vintage Books, 1994.

———. *Orientalism.* 1978. Reprint, New York: Vintage, 1994.

Sailing Directions for the Red Sea and the Gulf of Aden. Washington, DC: Government Printing Office, 1943.
Sami, Şemseddin. *Ḳāmūs-i Turkī*. 1900. Reprint, Çağrı Yayınları, 2007.
Sarhank, Ismāʿīl. *Ḥaqāʾiq al-akhbār ʿan duwal al-biḥār*. Vol. 1. Cairo: Bulāq, 1894.
Sarıyıldız, Gülden. "Misirda Kurulan Mecidiye Vapur Kumpanyasi ve Faaliyetleri." *Türk Kültürü Incelemeler Dergisi* 9 (2003): 17–36.
Saussure, Léopold de. "L'origine des noms de mer Rouge, mer Blanche et mer Noire." *Le Globe* 63 (1924): 23–36.
Schaefer, Charles. "Coffee Unobserved: Consumption and Commoditization of Coffee in Ethiopia before the Eighteenth Century." In *Le commerce du café avant l'ère des plantations coloniales*, edited by Michel Tuchscherer, 23–34. Cairo: Institut français d'archéologie orientale, 2001.
Schmitt, Carl. *The* Nomos *of the Earth in the International Law of the* Jus Publicum Europaeum. New York: Telos Press, 2003.
Sells, Michael. "The *Muʿallaqa* of Ṭarafa." *Journal of Arabic Literature* 17 (1986): 21–33.
Servier, André. *L'Islam et la psychologie du Musulman*. Paris: Augustin Challamel, 1923.
Shaw, Stanford. *The Financial and Administrative Organisation and Development of Ottoman Egypt, 1517–1798*. Princeton, NJ: Princeton University Press, 1962.
Shinnawī, ʿAbd al-ʿAzīz Muḥammad al-. *Al-Sukhra fi ḥafr qanāt al-Suez*. Cairo: al-Haiʾa al-misriyya al-ʿāmma lil-kitāb, 2002.
Sidebotham, Steven. *Berenike and the Ancient Maritime Spice Route*. Berkeley: University of California Press, 2011.
Smith, Adam. *An Inquiry into the Nature and Causes of the Wealth of Nations*. Indianapolis, IN: Liberty Classics, 1981.
———. *Lectures on Jurisprudence*. Indianapolis, IN: Liberty Fund, 1982.
Smith, Bonnie. *The Gender of History: Men, Women, and Historical Practice*. Cambridge, MA: Harvard University Press, 1998.
Smith, Stephen, ed. *The Red Sea Region: Sovereignty, Boundaries and Conflict: 1839–1967*. Cambridge: Archive Editions, 2008.
Stern, Fritz, ed. *The Varieties of History: From Voltaire to the Present*. New York: Vintage Books, 1973.
Stoler, Ann Laura. *Along the Archival Grain: Epistemic Anxieties and Colonial Common Sense*. Princeton, NJ: Princeton University Press, 2009.
Strabo. *The Geography of Strabo*. Translated by H. L. Jones. London: William Heinemann, 1930.
Tabak, Faruk. *The Waning of the Mediterranean, 1550–1870: A Geohistorical Approach*. Baltimore: Johns Hopkins University Press, 2008.
Ṭahṭāwī, Rifāʿa Rāfiʿ, al-. *Al-Aʿmāl al-kāmila li Rifāʿa Rāfiʿ al-Ṭahṭāwī*. Edited by Muḥammad ʿImāra. Beirut: Al-Muʾassasa al-ʿarabiyya li'l-dirāsāt wa'l-nashr, 1973.
———. *An Imam in Paris: Account of a Stay in France by an Egyptian Cleric (1826–1831)*. Edited and translated by Daniel Newman. London: Saqi, 2004.
———. *Kitāb al-taʿrībāt al-shāfiya li-murīd al-jughrāfiya*. Cairo: Bulaq, 1835.

Takamatsu, Yoichi. "Formation and Custody of the Ottoman Archives during the Pre-Tanzimat Period." *Memoirs of the Toyo Bunku* 64 (2006): 125–48.
Tibbetts, G.R. "Arabia in the Fifteenth-Century Navigational Texts." *Arabian Studies* 1 (1974): 86–102.
———. *Arab Navigation in the Indian Ocean before the Coming of the Portuguese, Being a Translation of Kitāb al-Fawāʾid fī uṣūl al-baḥr waʾl-qawaʾid of Aḥmad b. Mājid al-Najdī.* London: Royal Asiatic Society of Great Britain and Ireland, 1981.
———. "Arab Navigation in the Red Sea." *Geographical Journal* 127, no. 3 (1961): 322–34.
Towers, John. "The Red Sea." *Journal of Near Eastern Studies* 18, no. 2 (1959): 150–53.
Tuchscherer, Michel. "Coffee in the Red Sea Area from the Sixteenth to the Nineteenth Century." In *The Global Coffee Economy in Africa, Asia and Latin America, 1500–1989*, edited by William Gervase Clarence Smith and Steven Topik, 50–66. Cambridge: Cambridge University Press, 2003.
———, ed. *Le commerce du café avant l'ère des plantations coloniales.* Cairo: Institut français d'archéologie orientale, 2001.
———. "Le commerce en mer Rouge aux alentours de 1700: Flux, espaces et temps." *Res Orientales* 5 (1993): 159–78.
———. "Les échanges commerciaux entre les rives africaine et arabe de l'espace mer Rouge-golfe d'Aden aux XVIe et XVIIe siècles." In *Trade and Travel in the Red Sea Region*, edited by Paul Lunde and Alexandra Porter, 157–63. Oxford: Archaeopress, 2004.
———. "Trade and Port Cities in the Red Sea–Gulf of Aden Region in the Sixteenth and Seventeenth Century." In *Modernity and Culture from the Mediterranean to the Indian Ocean*, edited by Leila Fawaz and C.A. Bayly, 28–45. New York: Columbia University Press, 2002.
Tuck, Richard. "Grotius and Selden." In *The Cambridge History of Political Thought, 1450–1700*, edited by J.H. Burns, 509. Cambridge: Cambridge University Press, 1991.
Udovitch, Abraham. "An Eleventh Century Islamic Treatise on the Law of the Sea." *Annales Islamologiques* 27 (1993): 37–54.
Ukers, William H. *All about Coffee.* 2nd ed. New York: Tea and Coffee Trade Journal, 1935.
Um, Nancy. *The Merchant Houses of Mocha: Trade and Architecture in an Indian Ocean Port.* Seattle: University of Washington Press, 2009.
Uzunçarşılı, İsmail Hakkı. *Osmanlı Devleti'nin Merkez ve Bahriye Teşkilatı.* Ankara: Türk Tarih Kurumu Basımevi, 1948.
Valentia, George Annesley. *Voyages and Travels to India, Ceylon, the Red Sea, Abyssinia and Egypt, in the Years 1802, 1803, 1804, 1805, and 1806.* London: F., C., and J. Rivington, 1881.
Vallet, Eric. *L'Arabie marchande: État et commerce sous les sultants rasūlides du Yémen, 626–858/1229–1454.* Paris: Publications de la Sorbonne, 2010.

Vermeeren, Caroline. "The Use of Imported and Local Wood Species at the Roman Port of Berenike, Red Sea Coast, Egypt." In *The Exploitation of Plant Resources in Ancient Africa*, edited by Marijke van der Veen, 199–204. New York: Kluwer Academic/Plenum, 1999.

Vevier, Charles. "American Continentalism: An Idea of Expansion, 1845–1910." *American Historical Review* 65, no. 2 (1960): 323–35.

Villiers, Alan. *Sons of Sindbad*. 1940. Reprint, New York: Charles Scribner's Sons, 1969.

Vink, Markus. "Indian Ocean Studies and the 'New Thalassology.'" *Journal of Global History* 2 (2007): 41–62.

Walcott, Derek. "The Sea Is History." In *Frontiers of Caribbean Literature in English*, edited by Frank Birbalsingh, 22–28. New York: St. Martin's Press, 1996.

Webster, Anthony. "The Political Economy of Trade Liberalization." *Economic History Review* 43, no. 3 (1990): 404–19.

Wellsted, James. *Travels in Arabia*. London: John Murray, 1838.

White, Hayden. *The Content of the Form: Narrative Discourse and Historical Representation*. Baltimore: Johns Hopkins University Press, 1987.

———. *Metahistory: The Historical Imagination in Nineteenth-Century Europe*. Baltimore: Johns Hopkins University Press, 1975.

———. *Tropics of Discourse: Essays in Cultural Criticism*. Baltimore: Johns Hopkins University Press, 1986.

Wick, Alexis. "Narcissus: Woman, Water and the West." *Feminist Review* 103 (2013): 42–57.

Wigen, Kären. "Oceans of History: Introduction." AHR Forum. *American Historical Review* 111, no. 3 (June 2006): 717–21.

Young, Robert. *Colonial Desire: Hybridity in Theory, Culture and Race*. London: Routledge, 1995.

Zahlan, Rosemarie Said. "George Baldwin: Soldier of Fortune?" In *Travellers in Egypt*, edited b Paul and Janet Starkey, 24–38. New York: I. B. Tauris, 2001.

Zakī, Aḥmad. *Dictionary of Ancient Geography/Qāmūs al-jughrāfiya al-qadīma*. Cairo: Bulaq, 1899.

INDEX

ʿAbdulḥamīd I, 60–1, 103
Abraham, Prophet, 28, 39
Abū al-Dhahab, Muḥammad, 129
Abyssinia, 29, 30, 38, 43, 50, 75, 77, 92, 106, 133. *See also* Ethiopia
Abyssinian Sea, 92, 201n3
Acre, 131, 149
Aden, 30, 34, 36, 39–40, 42, 45, 77, 133, 147–148, 216n8, 224n60; Gulf of, 24, 27, 41, 43; Ridge, 22
Aelius Gallus, 24, 142, 203n23
Africa, 12, 18, 22, 32, 37, 44, 49, 52, 57–8, 65, 73–8, 87, 94, 148–49, 154, 162, 164–7, 174, 185, 224–25n60; Hegel on, 58, 167–71; Ritter on, 174
Africans, 4, 65, 73–8, 170–71
Agatharchides of Cnidus, 19, 23, 31, 202n6
Aḥmad ibn Mājid, 30, 85, 91, 109–10, 227n117
Ainslie, Robert, 70–1, 130, 223n39
Aksan, Virginia, 55, 55n52
Alexander the Macedonian, 34
Alexandretta, 114, 119
Alexandria, 69, 105, 131–2, 153, 214n78, 224n60
Ali Raja of Kannur, 105
Althusser, Louis, 13
Americas, continent, 32, 42, 45, 47, 94, 156, 169
ʿAmr ibn al-ʿĀṣ, 38
Annales school, 56, 174, 194
Antarctica, 156
anthropomorphism (of historical subject), 10, 21, 90, 138, 178–85, 188–89, 199n28
applied metaphysics, 122–25
Aqaba, 18; Gulf of, 22
Arabia, 20, 24, 28, 30, 34, 37, 43–4, 78, 139, 143, 224n60; Hegel on, 169; Smith on, 163; Renan on, 64
Arabian Gulf, 19–20, 84–6
Arabian Peninsula, 18, 22, 63, 91, 93, 184, 203n23
Arabs, 4, 56, 56–9, 73–8, 84, 91, 135, 144, 149, 201n2; Hegel on, 59; Planhol on, 64–5
archives, 4; and modern history, 80, 199n30; Ottoman, 5, 54, 68, 71, 76, 79, 80–2, 90–1, 106–7, 147–8, 228n122; British, 82, 128, 215n99, 224n60, 227n112
Arrian, 34
Asad, Talal, 54
Asia, 2, 12, 32, 36–7, 64, 74, 94, 131, 165, 174; Hegel on, 57–8, 167–69; Mollat on, 62–3; Smith on, 162
Asiatic, 54
Atlantic Ocean, 5, 9, 13, 22, 25, 37, 47, 64, 187, 201n3; Bory de Saint-Vincent on, 166
Austin, J. L., 125, 159, 222n18, 229n7
Australasia, 165
Aydhab, 30, 36
Ayyubids, 36, 39, 61, 149
al-Azhar, 49

Bab al-Mandab, 18, 22, 27, 143
Bachelard, Gaston, 4, 124, 201n1
Baḥr-ı Aḥmer, 6, 83–5, 148. 150–51*fig.*, 226n111, 227n113
Baḥr-ı Süveys, 6, 83–6, 92, 94, 106, 110, 125–26, 132, 149, 214n90
Bailyn, Bernard, 5
Baldwin, George, 74–5, 129–33, 223n35
Balta-Liman, treaty of (1838), 134
Barak, On, 153
Barsbāy, 39–40
Barthes, Roland, 123, 191
Baucom, Ian, 116–17
Baudelaire, Charles, 161, 229n19
Beirut, 149
Benjamin, Walter, 117
Berenike, 25, 29
Berlin, university of, 167, 173
Bible, 1, 20, 25, 34, 138
Black Sea, 2, 5, 20, 92–4, 103, 114
Blumi, Isa, 45, 55, 122
Bombay, 37, 45, 134, 141–2
Borges, Jorge Luis, 191
Bory de Saint-Vincent, 13, 164, 177, 179
Bosporus, 2, 16, 105
Braudel, Fernand, 5, 8, 13, 15, 21, 32, 43–4, 46–7, 59, 66, 80, 113, 167, 173, 180–85, 189–90, 193–95, 207nn92,97,100, 210n18, 232nn78,81, 233n17
Bruce, James, 107, 129
Buheiry, Marwan, 153
Buist, George, 139–40
bullion, 36
Burckhardt, John, 107, 111

Cairo, 33–4, 39–41, 44, 49–52, 61, 67–9, 71, 75, 79, 81–2, 85, 96, 98, 101, 105, 108, 113–14, 119, 130–33, 148–49, 208n113, 208n119, 209n128, 216n8, 227n116
Campo Formio, treaty of (1797), 131
canal, Red Sea-Nile, 22, 38–9
Candolle, Augustin Pyramus de, 163–4
Cantillon, Richard, 162, 229n21
Cape of Good Hope, 42, 129
captain, 110–13, 118–19, 142–43, 145
Captain Court, 127–28, 132
cartography, 6, 95, 127, 191, 196
Casale, Giancarlo, 42, 60, 206nn81,82
Casey, Edward, 215n1
Caspian Sea, 2, 157, 162, 165
Casson, Lionel, 29
Chaudhuri, K. N., 5
China, 32, 37, 58, 162
Christian, 37, 59–60, 64–5, 70–1, 74, 103, 149, 171–2, 175, 185, 216n18
Cicero, 160
Claudel, Paul, 211n39
coffee, 15, 29, 32, 35, 44–52, 68–72, 77–8, 207n97, 208nn106,110,119, 209nn122,128,129, 210n130, 212n58
coffeehouse, 51, 208n119, 209n123
common sense, 1, 62, 64, 181, 181, 195
Congress of Vienna (1815), 133
Connery, Christopher, 178
Constantinople. *See* Istanbul
continentality, 63
continents, 12, 47, 57, 63, 73–4, 93, 155–6, 165–75, 184; Bory de Saint-Vincent on, 165; Hegel on, 168; Ritter on, 171–75
corals, 20, 22, 25–7, 94, 107, 110, 137–8, 140, 144–6, 225n77
Coral Sea, 26, 94, 203n27
Corrupting Sea (The), 7, 189

Dağlı, Murat, 55
Dahlak, 30
Dalrymple, Alexander, 134
Danube, 2
Daston, Lorraine, 124–5, 136
Davis, Colin, 89
Denmark, 20
Dietrich, Albert, 33
d'Ohsson, Mouradgea, 51, 209n129
Drouin, Jean-Marc, 164
Dundas, Henry, 132, 223n41
Dutch, 44, 51, 149, 159

East India Company, 45, 82, 106, 129, 132, 134, 136, 141
Eco, Umberto, 191
Edney, Matthew, 127, 190
Edom, 20, 34
Egypt, 20, 24, 29, 31, 33–36, 38–46, 49, 52, 58, 61, 69–71, 73–5, 77, 81–3, 85, 94, 97–8, 100–1, 105–6, 109, 111–2, 115, 118–9, 128–131, 133, 144, 147–9, 153–4,

203n23, 205n76, 209nn122,128, 224nn57,60, 227nn113,119; Smith on, 162
Egyptian delta, 28
Ehrenberg, C. G., 140, 226n88
Elwon, Thomas, 135–8, 141, 146, 148
Eritrea, 22, 24, 31, 110, 141
Erythraean Sea, 19–20, 29, 36–7, 165, 202n6
Ethiopia, 24–5, 31, 37–8, 46–9, 94, 205n73. *See also* Abyssinia
Euphrates, 2
Eurocentrism, 6, 15, 46, 82, 141, 162, 185, 200n37
Evliyā Çelebī, 68, 94, 110, 228n122
exemplar history, 11, 199n35
Exodus, 20
eyesight (necessary for navigation), 143–6
Ezion-geber, 25, 34, 138

Fabian, Johannes, 4, 80
Facey, William, 21, 45
Fahmy, Khaled, 44, 218n41
Faroqhi, Suraiya, 67, 95, 100, 212n47
Foucault, Michel, 4, 124, 167, 195
freedom, 4, 57–8, 61, 73, 161, 163, 193
free trade, 153–4, 159, 161
French Invasion of Egypt, 83, 130
Fresnel, Fulgence, 76
Freud, Sigmund, 161

Gage, William, 171–2
Gary, Roman, 24
Genç, Mehmet, 66, 72–3
genealogy, 3, 5, 15, 17, 61, 75, 91, 122, 176, 184, 192
General Treaty (1820), 45
Genesis, 1
geohistoricism, 6–7, 167
Ghālib ibn Musā'id, 131
al-Ghūrī, Qānsūh, 41–2
Gibbons, Herbert, 54
Ginzburg, Carlo, 54, 96, 217n28
Glissant, Édouard, 117
Golden Horn, 2
Gospel of St. John, 185
Green Sea, 18, 92, 201n3
Grotius, Hugo, 159–61

Hacking, Ian, 125, 157–8
Hallaq, Wael, 108
al-ḥamawī, Yāqūt, 84, 214n91
Hammer-Purgstall, Joseph von, 53–4
Hanley, Will, 108
Hastings, Warren, 129
Hatshepsut, 34
Hau'ofa, Epeli, 14, 95, 200n51
Headrick, Daniel, 147, 228n121
Hegel, G. W. F., 10–13, 53, 57–61, 64–6, 80–81, 90, 92, 122, 161, 166–171, 174, 177–78, 180, 183, 188, 199n35, 200n36
Heidegger, Martin, 9
Herodotus, 19–20, 62
Herzfeld, Michael, 158–59, 228n5
Hijaz, 24, 28–9, 31, 38–40, 49–50, 62, 68, 71, 75, 83–4, 91, 93–4, 100, 106–7, 113, 115, 131, 142, 184, 205n76
history writing, 7, 14, 78, 81, 95, 186–7, 192
Hodgson, Marshall, 33
Horden, Peregrine and Nicholas Purcell, 7–9, 189, 194, 199n21
Horsburgh, James, 134, 136
Hoyt, Sarah, 140
Huber, Valeska, 153
Hudayda, 25, 29–30
human sciences, 7, 15, 167, 174, 196
Humboldt, Alexander von, 175, 231n51

Ibn Iyās, Muḥammad, 206n79
Ibn Jubayr, Muḥammad, 36, 109
Ibn Khaldūn, 'Abd al-Raḥmān, 18, 91–3, 201n3, 215n5
ideas, 12, 15, 58, 62, 68, 73, 124, 157, 171, 188
imperialism, 126, 140, 148, 196, 228n121
İnalcık, Halil, 66, 72
incense, 32–5, 48
India, 21, 33, 35–7, 45, 57–8, 82–3, 106, 127–32, 133–7, 141–2, 147–9, 159; Smith on, 162; Hegel on, 57–8
Indian Navy, 122, 134, 136, 144
Indian Ocean, 2, 5, 8, 18–9, 21–2, 25, 27, 32–3, 35–7, 40–45, 47, 51, 71, 91–2, 105, 121, 127–8, 134, 141, 143, 147, 149, 201n2, 210n18
Inner Sea, 21, 190, 194
interactivity, 158
Ionian islands, 122, 133

Irwin, Eyles, 29, 109, 143
Islam, 4, 32, 38, 40, 57–65, 70, 73–4, 76, 91, 205n72, 208n119, 209n123, 210n13n18, 216n8; and the sea, 57–65; Braudel on, 59, 182; Hegel on, 58–9; Planhol on, 59, 63–5
Ismāʿīl, Khedive, 148, 154, 227n119
Istanbul, 2, 5, 43, 51, 52, 61, 68–71, 84, 96, 103, 105, 108, 111–13, 119, 148, 153, 212n58, 214n90, 227n113, 228n122

Al-Jabartī, ʿAbd al-Raḥmān, 45–6, 208n119, 209nn120,121,128, 210n130, 217n36
al-Jazīrī, ʿAbd al-Qādir, 48–50, 77–8, 208nn113,115
Jerusalem, 149
Jiddah, 25, 27–8, 30, 39–43, 50, 52, 70–2, 76, 79, 83–4, 99, 104–8, 132, 135, 138, 141–3, 145, 149, 227n113
Joint-Daguenet, Roger, 82
Jordan, 24

Kaʿba, 38
Kafadar, Cemal, 51, 55
Kammerer, Albert, 41
Karīm Khān Zand, 103
kārimi merchants, 33
Kātib Çelebī, 2, 49, 60, 94, 208n110
Kavala, 114, 119
Kellner, Hans, 195
Küçük Kaynarca, treaty of (1774), 102

LaCapra, Dominick, 125
land, 1–3, 8, 13–15, 21, 23–4, 34, 36, 38, 40–2, 57, 59–61, 67, 88, 91, 100, 138, 141, 155–6, 160, 161–75, 177, 182, 200n51, 203n23
Latour, Bruno and Steve Woolgar, 122, 222n8
Lawson, Fred, 44
Leighly, John, 173, 176
Lesseps, Ferdinand de, 153
Lewis, Martin, 155, 214n94
Locke, John, 160
longue durée, 15, 28, 36, 95, 101–2, 111, 116–8, 182, 185, 189, 195
Ludwig, Emil, 194
Luhayya, 25, 29–30
Luxor, 34

MacIntyre, Alasdair, 116
Magris, Claudio, 7
Mahan, Alfred Thayer, 177–8, 180
Malabar, 37, 105, 108, 119, 149
Malta, 133
Mamluk, 32, 39–42, 50, 61, 83, 113, 129–31, 149, 205n75–76
al-Maqrīzī, Taqī al-Dīn, 38–9
Margariti, Roxani, 36, 216n8
Marini, Ludovico, 7
maritimity, 3, 13, 15, 57–9, 61, 63, 65, 162–3, 170, 174
Markham, Clements, 128, 135–7, 223n30
al-Masʿūdī, Abā al-ḥasan, 33, 183
Matthews, Derek, 138
Matvejević, Pedrag, 7, 181, 201n2
Maury, Matthew Fontaine, 175–9, 183, 231n50–51
Mecca, 3, 28, 33, 38, 40, 50, 70–2, 86, 94, 100, 104, 112, 131–2, 206n76
Mecidiye company for steamboats, 148
Medina, 28, 40, 72, 94, 100, 112, 206n76, 217n36
Mediterranean, 1–2, 5, 7, 15, 21–2, 25–6, 32–3, 35–7, 39, 42, 47, 61, 82, 91–3, 113–14, 120–22, 131, 133, 147, 152–4, 158; American, 177; and Europe, 69, 79–80; Bory de Saint-Vincent on, 164–67; Braudel on, 181–90, 193–96; Candolle on, 163–64; Hegel on, 11–13, 169; Herzfeld on, 158–59; Mahan on, 178; Ranke on, 11–12; Smith on, 162
Mediterranean and the Mediterranean World in the Age of Philip II (The), 5–9, 15, 181, 184–85, 189–90, 193–96, 206n87, 232n78
Mediterraneanism, 163, 194, 228n5
Méditerranée: L'espace et l'histoire (La), 181–183
Meḥmed ʿAlī, 21, 42, 44–5, 79, 133–4, 148, 154, 209n128, 218n41, 224n60
Meloy, John, xii, 30–1, 33, 39
Menou, Jacques-François, 132
Merleau-Ponty, Maurice, 4, 124
Metageography, 155
Michelet, Jules, 123, 178–80, 231nn70,71
Mitchell, Timothy, 67, 144, 215n97, 226n99
Mitchell, W. J. T., 222n20

Mocha, 29–30, 48–9, 51, 142–43, 208n110, 224n60
modernity, 3–4, 15–17, 46, 55, 61, 72–3, 79, 81, 117, 155, 157, 159, 182, 189–90, 215n97; modern disciplines, 17, 167, 183, 185, 191; modern geography, 7, 155; modern historical discourse, 4, 9, 53, 191, 199n30
Mollat, Michel, 61–3
monsoon, 25–7, 35, 37
Moresby, Robert, 134–8, 141–2, 146, 227n112
Moses, 20
Mount Lebanon, 29
mountain, 19–20, 23–5, 31, 48, 62, 100, 110, 114, 164–5, 170, 173, 182, 189, 211n39
Muḥammad ibn ʿAbd Allah, Prophet, 38, 65, 91, 94
Mühimme-i Mısır, 81, 96, 97*fig.*, 213n58, 217n29
al-Muqaddasī, Muḥammad, 184
Mussawa, 30

al-Nahrawālī, Qutb al-dīn, 41, 227n117
Napoleon Bonaparte, 83, 131, 133
Napoleonic wars, 173
narrative form, 93
nation-state, 8, 11, 21, 42, 79–80, 87, 172
New Testament, 34
Niebuhr, Carsten, 20, 84, 107
Nile, 2, 22, 28, 31, 38, 41, 94, 168–9, 228n122

objects, 57, 62, 122, 124–5, 136, 141, 157–8, 222n20
ocean, 2, 5, 7–9, 13–4, 17–9, 25, 32, 35–7, 40–5, 47, 51, 58, 71, 86, 91–2, 94–5, 105, 121, 127–8, 134, 141, 143, 147, 149, 155–6, 161–2, 164–6, 174, 178–80, 184, 188, 194, 198n13, 201n2n53, 206n76n82, 211n18
Oceania, 14, 200n51
oceanic turn, 5, 8, 198n13
oceanography, 7, 17, 175, 183, 202n15, 231n50
Orhonlu, Cengiz, 107
Orient, 21, 54, 57, 66, 73–4, 80, 83, 103, 128, 153
orientalism, 48, 54, 58, 64, 73–4, 87, 152, 196, 205n72
Ottoman, 2–6, 11–2, 14–7, 25–6, 29, 32, 35–6, 40–6, 48–57, 60–1, 63, 65–73, 75–83, 85–97, 99–103, 105–110, 115–7, 118–21, 125–6, 130, 132–4, 147–8, 152–3, 206n79n82, 207n97, 208n119, 213n67, 213n72, 214n81, 214n85, 214n90, 215n4, 215n5, 216n18n21, 217n26, 218n41, 223n39, 224n49, 227n112n16n117, 228n122; economy, 66–70; geography, 2–4; studies, 53–55
overreading, 88–9
Özcan, Azmi, 105

Pacific, 5, 14, 37, 95, 177–8, 200n51
Pamuk, Şevket, 67, 212n47
Panama Canal, 177–8
Paris, treaty of (1814), 133
performativity, 68, 90, 113, 125, 154, 159
Periplus of the Erythraean Sea, 29, 36–7
Persian Gulf, 2–3, 18, 20, 35, 42, 45, 92, 122, 129, 185, 211n18
Peters, Edward, 7
pilot, 25, 109, 111, 142–6
Pīrī Reʾīs, 93
Piterberg, Gabriel, 55
place, 10, 13–15, 18–21, 26, 28, 31, 33, 45–6, 52–3, 55–7, 59, 61, 63, 72–3, 77, 80, 82–3, 88–9, 91, 95, 101, 111, 115–6, 119, 129, 132, 138, 142, 163, 167, 169–72, 181, 184, 201, 214
Planhol, Xavier de, 59, 61, 63–5
Popham, Home, 128, 132–3
Portuguese, 36, 41–4, 86, 94, 149, 159, 227n117
Poseidon, 188
progress, 4, 10–12, 59, 144–5, 152, 157, 161–3, 171, 173, 185
Proust, Marcel, 18, 20, 201n1
provisioning, 30, 40, 66, 70, 99–100, 112, 115, 118–20, 205n76;
provisionism, 65–70, 72
Ptolemy, 18, 201n3
Punt, 32, 34

Qulzum, 30, 38, 84, 92, 201n3, 214n91, 216n21
Quran, 1, 38, 184, 205n72
Quraysh, 91

Qusayr, 30, 33, 131–2

race, 31, 54, 75, 139, 167
Ranke, Leopold von, 10–12, 53, 80, 117, 167, 194, 199n33n35, 200n37
Rathlef, Carl, 194
Raymond, André, 35, 44, 70–1
realism, 10, 17, 123–4, 156, 190–1
Reclus, Élisée, 183
Red Sea Hills, 24
reef, 22, 25–6, 94, 110, 135, 137–39, 143, 145, 225n76
Reginald of Châtillon, 142–3
Rhodes, 114, 119
Ritter, Carl, 57, 92, 166–7, 171–8, 183–4, 230n35, 232n85
Rolland, Romain, 161
Roman Empire, 79
Rome, 2–3, 181–2, 211n18
Ross, Daniel, 128, 135
Ruel, Anne, 121
Russia, 63, 102–3
Rycaut, Paul, 60–1, 66

Sacy, Silvestre de, 48
Safad, 149
Sahara, 73–5, 164–5, 169, 181, 184–5
Said, Edward, 4, 54, 126, 196, 228n5
Sailing Directions for the Red Sea, 121, 135–47, 190, 221n2
Saint-Simonians, 153
Ṣalāh al-Dīn, 149
Salt, Henry, 132, 224
Sana'a, 42
Sarawat, 24
Sawakin, 3, 25, 30, 49, 107, 208n110, 225n77
science, 1, 86, 90, 93, 110, 122–3, 125–6, 128–9, 137, 147, 149, 153, 156, 158, 164, 166–7, 171–3, 179, 183, 190–1, 231n51
scientific object, 6, 16, 74, 88, 121–2, 125, 136, 138, 140–41, 146, 178, 195
scientific theology, 183, 185
Sea of Marmara, 2,
Selmān Re'īs, 42–3, 206n76
shoal, 25–6, 137, 143–5
social construction, 156–9
social sciences, 158–9, 184
sovereign sea, 6, 15, 159, 195–6
Selīm I, 21, 40–2, 61
Servier, André, 59
Shādhiliyya, 48
ships, 5, 26–7, 29–30, 34, 36–7, 39–41, 45, 70–1, 98–9, 101–5, 107, 109, 111–12, 114–16, 118–19, 126, 130, 137–39, 142–43, 147, 149, 177, 205n65, 213n67, 223n39; ship building, 162; shipyards, 36, 205n65
Sidebotham, Steven, 35–6
Sinai, 24, 48, 86, 208n113
slavery, 75, 77, 170
Smith, Adam, 57, 66, 161–3, 199n35
space, 2, 4–5, 9–11, 13–18, 20–22, 26, 35, 44–5, 51, 54, 61, 67, 72–3, 76, 78, 83–8, 91–2, 94–7, 104, 106, 110, 113, 115–17, 125–27, 134–35, 137–38, 140, 142, 145, 148, 152, 160–61, 171, 173, 177–78, 181–84, 188, 191, 193–95, 198n14, 201n53, 202n15, 209n119, 216n8
spice trade, 32–5, 39, 42–4, 51, 204n52
steam navigation, 128–9, 147–8, 224n60
Strabo, 19, 110, 140, 203n23
Sudan, 24, 29, 94, 107, 152, 211n18
Suez, 6, 18, 27, 30, 38, 42, 45, 52, 71–2, 74–5, 82, 84, 86, 98, 101–6, 109–10, 112, 114–15, 118–19, 125, 129–32, 134–35, 137, 143, 148, 201n3, 214n90, 216n21, 224n49, 227n113
Suez Canal, 45, 82, 147, 152–54, 228n121
sufis, 48–50
Suleymān the Magnificent, 40, 60, 100
Surūr ibn Musā'id, Sharif, 21, 71
Swahili coast, 2
Syria, 20, 35, 44, 71, 91–2, 149, 164, 218n41

Tabak, Faruk, 190
Ṭarafa ibn al-'Abd, 91
teak, 36
teleology, 9, 17, 72, 78, 88
thalassology, 7–8, 10, 13, 16, 53, 56–8, 61, 159, 161, 166, 174–5, 177–78, 180, 184–5, 190, 192, 195
Tigris, 2
Tihama, 24, 29, 48
timber, 29, 36, 38, 114, 218n41
time, 4–13, 15, 17–21, 26, 30, 32, 37, 45, 51, 54–6, 58, 62, 67, 72, 76–7, 81, 83, 88, 92, 95, 97, 99, 101, 104, 113–20, 131, 145,

147, 152, 162, 165, 173, 182–85, 188–92, 198n14, 201n1, 204n50, 228n130, 232n81
T-O (orbis terrarum) maps, 21
Topkapı, 2, 43
Tor, 30, 48–9, 208n113
Toulon, 131
trade, 25, 29–30, 32–36, 39–40, 42–45, 47, 49–50, 52, 67, 69–71, 74–5, 83, 105, 107, 129–30, 133–4, 152, 159, 161–2, 178, 186, 204n56, 205n76, 206n87, 210n130, 227n116
triangulation, 95, 127–8, 135, 190–1
Trigonometrical Survey of India, 142
Trucial Coast, 45
Truguet, Chevalier de, 130
Tuchscherer, Michel, 32, 47, 50, 203n37, 204n50
Ṭūmān Bāy, 41–2
Two Noble Sanctuaries, 99, 101, 102, 114, 116, 118

Utrecht, treaty of (1713), 133

Valentia, George Annesley (Lord), 128, 132–3, 137, 223n30
Villiers, Alan, 227n120
Vink, Marcus, 8

Walcott, Derek, 187–8
waqf (Turkish vakıf), 40, 98, 101, 103, 109, 114, 205n76
water, 1–4, 7–9, 12–13, 18–20, 22–27, 34, 39, 48, 56–7, 63, 70, 84, 86, 91–2, 94–5, 100, 103, 110, 128–9, 131, 134–41, 145–6, 152, 154–6, 161–8, 173–4, 177–80, 184, 194, 198, 203n23, 226n88
Wellsted, James, 137, 139, 145–7, 225n74
West, 21, 47, 59–60, 67, 74, 94, 153, 163, 168, 182, 198n15, 211n39, 214n83; Western, 10, 29, 54, 58–9, 61, 63, 65–6, 70, 75, 82, 148, 152–3, 159–61, 174, 177, 216n18, 227n117
White, Hayden, 9–10, 54, 187, 191
Wigen, Kären, 8, 155
Wittek, Paul, 54

Yemen, 22, 24, 29–32, 40–9, 52, 71–2, 77, 84, 86, 93, 106–7, 149, 184, 205n57, 206n76, 209n128–9, 227n117

Zakī, Aḥmad, 84